Southern Selves

WITHDRAWN

Southern Selves

From Mark Twain and Eudora Welty to
Maya Angelou and Kaye Gibbons

A Collection of Autobiographical Writing

Edited and with an introduction by
JAMES H. WATKINS

Vintage Books
A Division of Random House, Inc.
New York

A VINTAGE ORIGINAL, AUGUST 1998
FIRST EDITION

Copyright © 1998 by James H. Watkins

Library of Congress Cataloging-in-Publication Data
Southern selves : from Mark Twain and Eudora Welty
to Maya Angelou and Kaye Gibbons :
a collection of autobiographical writing /
edited and with an introduction by James H. Watkins.
p.   cm.
"A Vintage original"—T.p. verso.
ISBN 0-679-78103-X
1. Authors, American—Southern States—Biography.
2. Autobiographies—Southern States.
3. Southern States—Biography.
I. Watkins, James H.
PS551.S575   1998
810.9'975—dc21
[B]   97-50206
CIP

randomhouse.com

Designed by Cassandra J. Pappas

Manufactured in the United States of America
10 9 8 7 6 5 4 3 2 1

For Susan, Will, and Sam

Acknowledgments

I WOULD LIKE to express my appreciation to the following individuals who helped make this book a reality: First of all, Kaye Gibbons encouraged me to write the prospectus for *Southern Selves* and put me in contact with the right people after hearing my idea for the anthology. Anne Goodwyn Jones introduced me to a number of the works included in this collection in her graduate course on southern literature at the University of Florida, then enthusiastically agreed to direct my dissertation on southern autobiography. Four student research assistants at Berry College—Tereasa Lowry, Crys O'Neal, Nathan Hilkert, and especially Alicia Clavell—provided invaluable secretarial support as I waded through the copyright permission acquisition process and other potentially engulfing frustrations. Finally, this book would not have been possible without the generous guidance and support I received from LuAnn Walther and Diana Secker at Random House.

Contents

Introduction

FOR MORE THAN a century, the American South has been recognized as a region blessed with a wealth of literary talent and subject matter. While that reputation has been based primarily on its many fine novelists and short story writers (and, to a lesser extent, its poets), southern soil has also proven fertile ground for the flowering of a rich autobiographical tradition that is stronger today than it has ever been. The same deep-rooted "sense of place" that allowed William Faulkner to create his microcosm of the South, the fictional Yoknapatawpha County, has also provided the impulse and materials for southern autobiographers and memoirists to present their lives, and to do so in ways that call attention to their intimate knowledge of place. As Eudora Welty has written, "Place absorbs our earliest notice and attention, it bestows on us our original awareness; and our critical powers spring up from the study of it and the growth of experience inside it."[1] With few exceptions, autobiographical writing in the South gives

---

[1] Eudora Welty. "Place in Fiction." In *The Eye of the Story: Selected Essays and Reviews.* New York: Random House, 1978, pp. 116–33.

proof to Welty's claim, providing an occasion for the author to reflect upon the ways in which his or her identity has been shaped by its attachment to a specific southern locale.

But "place" signifies much more than mere geographical location. When William Alexander Percy begins *Lanterns on the Levee: Recollections of a Planter's Son* with the words, "My country is the Mississippi Delta, the river country," he implies that his sense of personal identity is intimately intertwined with both the physical and cultural landscape of the Delta, with its rhythms of speech, its patterns of social interaction, its history—even its cuisine. Thus, in order to fully appreciate the degree to which the selections in this anthology present located lives, we must pay attention to the subtle links that are drawn between the lay of the land and the manners of the people who inhabit that land. Nevertheless, not all of the writers represented in *Southern Selves* identify so easily as Percy seems to with the communities into which they were born. Strict and often violent enforcement of the racial status quo and (to a lesser though no less pervasive extent) rigid expectations concerning gender roles and class position remind us that "place" can also connote a fixed position in a racial or social hierarchy. Therefore, many of the selections in *Southern Selves* represent the author's effort to reject the place he or she had been assigned. Paradoxically, such an effort requires the author to describe in a convincingly detailed manner the ways in which individuals are kept in their "places," and in order to accomplish this he or she must speak as an insider, one who is intimately familiar with the full range of his or her home community's methods of social control.

No group has had more at stake in resisting its "place" in the South than African Americans, whose literature has its primary sources in the slave narrative. The basic plot pattern of oppression, acquisition of literacy, then flight to the North that can be found in the writings of Frederick Douglass and Harriet Jacobs has been mirrored in the lives of so many other southern-born blacks that its narrative structure can be traced in most of the classic writings—fiction as well as non-fiction—by African

Americans. Although most autobiographies by African Americans conclude with the narrator's escape from a benighted South, resistance to white racism takes other forms as well, one of which is the strong bonds formed within the African-American community. From Zora Neale Hurston's Eatonville, Florida (according to Hurston, the first incorporated all-black township in the U.S.), to Maya Angelou's Stamps, Arkansas, to Clifton Taulbert's Glen Allan, Mississippi, we find close-knit communities held together in times of joy and adversity by storytelling, feasting, and, most importantly, religious worship.

Though their situation was vastly preferable to that of most African Americans, many white female autobiographers and memoirists have used life-writing as an opportunity to articulate their frustrations with the rigid expectations concerning gender roles in the traditional South. In fact, the assumption that southern ladies did not engage in public discourse stifled the development of an autobiographical tradition among this group of southerners until the beginning of the twentieth century, long after women in other parts of the country had found public voices. From turn-of-the-century suffragist Belle Kearney to literary iconoclast Evelyn Scott to antisegregationists Lillian Smith and Katherine Du Pre Lumpkin, we find privileged women who struggle against patriarchy by deconstructing the image of the southern belle and exposing the paternalistic logic that had positioned them as desexualized icons of white southern culture. Nowhere is the task of toppling the image of the southern belle handled with such biting humor as in Florence King's aptly titled *Confessions of a Failed Southern Lady,* where we observe a grandmother who polishes silver daily, worshiping at the altar of southern shintoism and obsessing about the family tendency to "fallen wombs."

If many of the white female writers in this collection have an axe to grind about the restrictions placed on women in southern society, quite a few of the white autobiographers, male and female, focus their attention on the negative effects of racism in the South. Perhaps the most noticeable pattern to be found in the autobiographies of white southern liberals is the confessional motif, in which painful memories of past racist sins are recounted as acts of expiation. Lillian Smith describes a long-repressed traumatic event from her childhood in which she was forced to recognize the hypocrisy of her parents' profession of Christian values, while Willie Morris writes with unflinching honesty about the race-baiting he and his friends would engage in between baseball games and other forms of amusement. For Tim McLaurin, the recollection of a childhood interracial friendship becomes the medium in which he explores his own complicity in southern racism.

Many of the more recent examples of southern memoir can be classified as writer's reminiscences. These works use the act of remembrance as a means of tracing the sources of the author's art. For Eudora Welty, Zora Neale Hurston, Harry Crews, and Reynolds Price, it is the sounds they grew up with, the voices of loved ones and neighbors, that provide the inspiration to write, and it is to those voices—and the stories they told—that they have turned as professional writers. Hurston writes that "the store porch was the most interesting place I could think of," for that was the hub of verbal activity in the community: "Men sat around on boxes and benches and passed this world and the next one through their mouths. The right and the wrong, the who, when and why was passed on, and nobody doubted their conclusions." For others like Richard Wright and Kaye Gibbons, voices play a significant role, but it is also their formative experiences with books that these authors reflect upon, as (in a scene from *Black Boy* not excerpted in *Southern Selves*) when Wright discovers at the public library H. L. Mencken's scathing denunciations of southern bigotry, or when Gibbons's writerly sensibilities are awakened by the incongruities she finds in her first grade reader.

The writers presented in this collection come from a wide variety of subregions within the South, from the dirt hills of Arkansas to the coastal plains of the Carolinas, from the southern banks of the Chesapeake Bay to the marshlands of south-central Florida. Collectively, they look at two centuries of life in the South from both sides of the color line, from feminine and masculine perspectives, and from various class positions. Yet, despite their diversity, all of the writers featured here either directly state or clearly imply that their sense of selfhood is shaped in important ways by the verbal and nonverbal language of the South. These are "southern" selves, then, not in the sense that there is some essential southern identity that makes the speakers of these accounts inherently different from narrators of memoirs and autobiographies written outside of the region, but because the authors have taken pains to trace their responses to social practices and cultural assumptions they associate with the South. Through the agency of the autobiographical "I," each of the writers asserts the uniqueness of her or his own voice and experience, however representative of race, class, gender, or region that voice may be. In doing so they remind us that we are much more than assemblages of sociological data. The example of autobiography teaches us that through the power of words we have the capacity to imagine ourselves and, thus, our world in new ways.

Southern Selves

James Agee

1909–1955

The journalist, novelist, poet, and film and literature critic James Agee was born in Knoxville, Tennessee, just a few blocks from the campus of the University of Tennessee. Not long after the death of his father in an auto accident in 1916, an event that would haunt Agee for the rest of his short life and provide the backdrop for his novel A Death in the Family *(1957), Agee's mother moved the family to the campus of St. Andrew's School, an Episcopalian academy atop Monteagle Mountain in Sewanee, Tennessee. There Agee had the good fortune to fall under the influence of his mentor and lifelong friend Father Flye, who helped the boy cultivate his appreciation and mastery of the written word. After completing his high school education at Phillips Academy in Exeter, New Hampshire, Agee attended Harvard, receiving his degree in 1932. In 1936, while working at* Fortune *magazine, he convinced his superiors to let him write an article about the plight of southern tenant farmers. With the photographer Walker Evans, he traveled to Alabama and lived briefly with a family of sharecroppers. But when Agee became absorbed in his research and kept expanding the scope and length of the "article,"* Fortune *dropped the project, which ultimately became* Let Us Now Praise Famous Men *(1941). Had he timed the book to appear sooner, he might have avoided the lackluster response that greeted this experimental blend of documentary history, social commentary, and autobiography; at the onset of World War II, however, many readers had lost interest in the subject of class struggle in the U.S. A victim of chronic depression, Agee struggled with the manuscript of* A Death in the Family *while earning his living as a screenwriter and as a feature writer and film and book reviewer for prestigious na-*

tional publications like Nation, Life, *and* Time. *Two years after his death, Agee was posthumously awarded the Pulitzer Prize for* A Death in the Family, *which his editors pulled together from the nearly completed manuscript he left behind.*

"Knoxville: Summer, 1915" was originally published in the Partisan Review *in 1938, but it also appears as a prologue to* A Death in the Family. *An unusual piece that resists generic classification, its autobiographical dimensions are unmistakable. In 1948, American composer Samuel Barber premiered "Knoxville: Summer of 1915," a musical piece for strings and voice inspired by Agee's reminiscence.*

FROM *A Death in the Family*

KNOXVILLE: SUMMER 1915

WE ARE TALKING now of summer evenings in Knoxville, Tennessee, in the time that I lived there so successfully disguised to myself as a child. It was a little bit mixed sort of block, fairly solidly lower middle class, with one or two juts apiece on either side of that. The houses corresponded: middle-sized gracefully fretted wood houses built in the late nineties and early nineteen hundreds, with small front and side and more spacious back yards, and trees in the yards, and porches. These were softwooded trees, poplars, tulip trees, cottonwoods. There were fences around one or two of the houses, but mainly the yards ran into each other with only now and then a low hedge that wasn't doing very well. There were few good friends among the grown people, and they were not poor enough for the other sort of intimate acquaintance, but everyone nodded and spoke, and even might talk short times, trivially, and at the two extremes of the general or the particular, and ordinarily nextdoor neighbors talked quite a bit when they happened to run into each other, and never paid calls. The men

were mostly small businessmen, one or two very modestly exec-
utives, one or two worked with their hands, most of them cleri-
cal, and most of them between thirty and forty-five.

But it is of these evenings, I speak.

Supper was at six and was over by half past. There was still
daylight, shining softly and with a tarnish, like the lining of a
shell; and the carbon lamps lifted at the corners were on in the
light, and the locusts were started, and the fire flies were out,
and a few frogs were flopping in the dewy grass, by the time the
fathers and the children came out. The children ran out first hell
bent and yelling those names by which they were known; then
the fathers sank out leisurely in crossed suspenders, their collars
removed and their necks looking tall and shy. The mothers
stayed back in the kitchen washing and drying, putting things
away, recrossing their traceless footsteps like the lifetime jour-
neys of bees, measuring out the dry cocoa for breakfast. When
they came out they had taken off their aprons and their skirts
were dampened and they sat in rockers on their porches quietly.

It is not of the games children play in the evening that I want
to speak now, it is of a contemporaneous atmosphere that has
little to do with them: that of the fathers of families, each in his
space of lawn, his shirt fishlike pale in the unnatural light and his
face nearly anonymous, hosing their lawns. The hoses were
attached at spigots that stood out of the brick foundations of the
houses. The nozzles were variously set but usually so there was a
long sweet stream of spray, the nozzle wet in the hand, the water
trickling the right forearm and the peeled-back cuff, and the
water whishing out a long loose and low-curved cone, and so
gentle a sound. First an insane noise of violence in the nozzle,
then the still irregular sound of adjustment, then the smoothing
into steadiness and a pitch as accurately tuned to the size and
style of stream as any violin. So many qualities of sound out of
one hose: so many choral differences out of those several hoses
that were in earshot. Out of any one hose, the almost dead
silence of the release, and the short still arch of the separate big
drops, silent as a held breath, and the only noise the flattering

noise on leaves and the slapped grass at the fall of each big drop. That, and the intense hiss with the intense stream; that, and that same intensity not growing less but growing more quiet and delicate with the turn of the nozzle, up to that extreme tender whisper when the water was just a wide bell of film. Chiefly, though, the hoses were set much alike, in a compromise between distance and tenderness of spray (and quite surely a sense of art behind this compromise, and a quiet deep joy, too real to recognize itself), and the sounds therefore were pitched much alike; pointed by the snorting start of a new hose; decorated by some man playful with the nozzle; left empty, like God by the sparrow's fall, when any single one of them desists: and all, though near alike, of various pitch; and in this unison. These sweet pale streamings in the light lift out their pallors and their voices all together, mothers hushing their children, the hushing unnaturally prolonged, the men gentle and silent and each snail-like withdrawn into the quietude of what he singly is doing, the urination of huge children stood loosely military against an invisible wall, and gentle happy and peaceful, tasting the mean goodness of their living like the last of their suppers in their mouths; while the locusts carry on this noise of hoses on their much higher and sharper key. The noise of the locust is dry, and it seems not to be rasped or vibrated but urged from him as if through a small orifice by a breath that can never give out. Also there is never one locust but an illusion of at least a thousand. The noise of each locust is pitched in some classic locust range out of which none of them varies more than two full tones: and yet you seem to hear each locust discrete from all the rest, and there is a long, slow, pulse in their noise, like the scarcely defined arch of a long and high set bridge. They are all around in every tree, so that the noise seems to come from nowhere and everywhere at once, from the whole shell heaven, shivering in your flesh and teasing your eardrums, the boldest of all the sounds of night. And yet it is habitual to summer nights, and is of the great order of noises, like the noises of the sea and of the blood her precocious grandchild, which you realize you are hearing only when you catch yourself listening. Meantime from low in the dark, just outside the swaying horizons of the hoses, conveying always grass in the damp of dew and its strong green-black smear of smell, the regular yet spaced noises of the crickets, each a sweet cold silver noise threenoted, like the slipping each time of three matched links of a small chain.

But the men by now, one by one, have silenced their hoses and drained and coiled them. Now only two, and now only one, is left, and you see only ghostlike shirt with the sleeve garters, and sober mystery of his mild face like the lifted face of large cattle enquiring of your presence in a pitchdark pool of meadow; and now he too is gone; and it has become that time of evening when people sit on their porches, rocking gently and talking gently and watching the street and the standing up into their sphere of possession of the trees, of birds hung havens, hangars. People go by; things go by. A horse, drawing a buggy, breaking his hollow iron music on the asphalt; a loud auto; a quiet auto; people in pairs, not in a hurry, scuffling, switching their weight of aestival body, talking casually, the taste hovering over them of vanilla, strawberry, pasteboard and starched milk, the image upon them of lovers and horsemen, squared with clowns in hueless amber. A street car raising its iron moan; stopping, belling and starting; stertorous; rousing and raising again its iron increasing moan and swimming its gold windows and straw seats on past and past and past, the bleak spark crackling and cursing above it like a small malignant spirit set to dog its tracks; the iron whine rises on rising speed; still risen, faints; halts; the faint stinging bell; rises again, still fainter; fainting, lifting, lifts, faints forgone: forgotten. Now is the night one blue dew.

Now is the night one blue dew, my father has drained, he has
    coiled the hose.
Low on the length of lawns, a frailing of fire who breathes.
Content, silver, like peeps of light, each cricket makes his
    comment over and over in the drowned grass.
A cold toad thumpily flounders.

Within the edges of damp shadows of side yards are hovering
   children nearly sick with joy of fear, who watch the
   unguarding of a telephone pole.
Around white carbon corner lamps bugs of all sizes are lifted
   elliptic, solar systems. Big hardshells bruise themselves,
   assailant: he is fallen on his back, legs squiggling.
Parents on porches: rock and rock: From damp strings morning
   glories: hang their ancient faces.
The dry and exalted noise of the locusts from all the air at once
   enchants my eardrums.

On the rough wet grass of the back yard my father and
mother have spread quilts. We all lie there, my mother, my
father, my uncle, my aunt, and I too am lying there. First we
were sitting up, then one of us lay down, and then we all lay
down, on our stomachs, or on our sides, or on our backs, and
they have kept on talking. They are not talking much, and the
talk is quiet, of nothing in particular, of nothing at all in particular, of nothing at all. The stars are wide and alive, they seem
each like a smile of great sweetness, and they seem very near. All
my people are larger bodies than mine, quiet, with voices gentle
and meaningless like the voices of sleeping birds. One is an
artist, he is living at home. One is a musician, she is living at
home. One is my mother who is good to me. One is my father
who is good to me. By some chance, here they are, all on this
earth; and who shall ever tell the sorrow of being on this earth,
lying, on quilts, on the grass, in a summer evening, among the
sounds of the night. May God bless my people, my uncle, my
aunt, my mother, my good father, oh, remember them kindly in
their time of trouble; and in the hour of their taking away.

   After a little I am taken in and put to bed. Sleep, soft smiling,
draws me unto her: and those receive me, who quietly treat me,
as one familiar and well-beloved in that home: but will not, oh,
will not, not now, not ever; but will not ever tell me who I am.

Dorothy Allison

(1949–)

A native of Greenville, South Carolina, Dorothy Allison has emerged as
an important and iconoclastic voice in contemporary southern writing.
Whether cofounding a feminist bookstore in Tallahassee, Florida, directing
a feminist credit union in Washington, D.C., or editing the journal
Quest, A Feminist Quarterly, Allison has been an activist in the
women's and lesbian movements since early adulthood. She earned a master's degree from the New School for Social Research in New York City
before turning her attention to literary pursuits. Known primarily for her
first novel, Bastard Out of Carolina (1992), which was nominated for
the National Book Award and has recently been made into a film directed
by Angelica Huston, Allison is an accomplished poet, essayist, and memoirist, as well as a fiction writer. Her other works include a collection of
poems, The Women Who Hate Me (1983); a collection of short fiction,
Trash (1985); a collection of personal essays, Skin: Talking About Sex,
Class, & Literature (1994); and a memoir adapted from a spoken-word
performance, Two or Three Things I Know for Sure (1995). Her most
recent work is Cavedweller (1998), a novel about a single mother's return
to a spiteful and closed-minded small town in Georgia, where she struggles
to reclaim and raise the daughters she abandoned over a decade earlier.

   In part because the term "redneck" has always had a masculine
emphasis, most writers who identify openly with lower- and working-
class southern white identity have been men. Yet in her autobiographical
writing and fiction alike, Dorothy Allison has added her voice to the growing number of authors who write from the perspective of the southern
"poor white." In the following selection, the essay "Gun Crazy" from
Skin, she recalls her early fascination with firearms and her attraction to
the masculine world of power they represent.

GUN CRAZY

WHEN WE WERE LITTLE, my sister and I would ride with the cousins in the back of my uncle Bo's pickup truck when he drove us up into the foothills where we could picnic and the men could go shooting. I remember standing up behind the cab, watching the tree branches filter the bright Carolina sunshine, letting the wind push my hair behind me, and then wrestling with my cousin, Butch, until my aunt yelled at us to stop.

"Ya'll are gonna fall out," she was always screaming, but we never did.

Every stop sign we passed was pocked with bullet holes.

"Fast flying bees," Uncle Jack told us with a perfectly serious expression.

"Hornets with lead in their tails," Bo laughed.

MY MAMA'S YOUNGEST BROTHER, Bo, kept his guns, an ought-seven rifle and a lovingly restored old Parker shotgun, wrapped in a worn green army blanket. A fold of the blanket was loosely stitched down a third of its length to make a cloth bag, the only sewing Bo ever did in his life. He kept his cleaning kit—a little bag of patches and a plastic bottle of gun oil—in the blanket pouch with the guns. Some evenings he would spread the blanket out in front of the couch and sit there happily cleaning his guns slowly and thoroughly. All the while he would sip cold beer and talk about what a fine time a man could have with his weapons out in the great outdoors. "You got to sit still, perfectly still," he'd say, nod, and sip again, then dab a little more gun oil on the patch he was running through the rifle barrel.

"Oh, you're good at that," someone would always joke.

"The man an't never shot an animal once in his life," Bo's wife, Nessa, told us. "Shot lots of bottles, whiskey bottles, beer bottles, coke-cola bottles. The man's one of the great all-time bottle destroyers."

I grinned. Stop signs and bottles, paper targets and wooden fences. My uncles loved to shoot, it was true, but the only deer they ever brought home was one found drowned in a creek and another that Uncle Jack hit head-on one night when he was driving his Pontiac convertible with the busted headlights.

"LET ME help you," I begged my uncle Bo one night when he had pulled out his blanket kit and started the ritual of cleaning his gun. I was eleven, shy but fearless. Bo just looked at me over the angle of the cigarette jutting out of the corner of his mouth. He shook his head.

"I'd be careful," I blurted.

"Nessa, you hear this child?" Bo yelled in the direction of the kitchen and then turned back to me. "An't no such thing as careful where girls and guns are concerned." He took the cigarette out of his mouth and gave me another of those cool, distant looks. "You an't got no business thinking about guns."

"But I want to learn to shoot."

He laughed a deep throaty laugh, coughed a little, then laughed again. "Girls don't shoot," he told me with a smile. "You can do lots of things, girl, but not shooting. That just an't gonna happen."

I glared at him and said, "I bet Uncle Jack will teach me. He knows how careful I can be."

Bo shook his head and tucked the cigarette back in the corner of his mouth. "It an't about careful, it's about you're a girl. You can whine and wiggle all you wont. An't nobody in this family gonna teach you to shoot." His face was stern, his smile completely gone. "That just an't gonna happen."

WHEN I WAS in high school my best girlfriend was Anne, whose mama worked in the records division at the local children's hospital. One Sunday Anne invited me to go over to the woods out behind the mental hospital, to a hollow there where we could do some plinking.

"Plinking?"

"You know, plinking. Shooting bottles and cans." She pushed her hair back off her face and smiled at me. "If there's any water we'll fill the bottles up and watch it shoot up when the glass breaks. That's my favorite thing."

"You got a gun?" My mouth was hanging open.

"Sure. Mama gave me a rifle for my birthday. Didn't I tell you?"

"I don't think so." I looked away, so she wouldn't see how envious I felt. Her mama had given her a gun for her sixteenth birthday! I had always thought Anne's mama was something special, but that idea was simply amazing.

Anne's mama refused to cook, smoked Marlboros continuously, left the room any time any of her three children mentioned their dead father, and drank cocktails every evening while leaning back in her Lazy-Boy lounge chair and wearing dark eyeshades. "Don't talk to me," she'd hiss between yellow stained teeth. "I got crazy people and drunken orderlies talking at me all day long. I come home, I want some peace and quiet."

"My mama thinks a woman should be able to take care of herself," Anne told me.

"Right," I agreed. "She's right." Inside, I was seething with envy and excitement. Outside, I kept my face smooth and noncommittal. I wanted to shoot, wanted to shoot a shotgun like all my uncles, pepper stop signs and scare dogs. But I'd settle for a rifle, the kind of a rifle a woman like Anne's mama would give her sixteen-year-old daughter.

THAT SUNDAY I watched closely as Anne slid a bullet into the chamber of her rifle and sighted down the gully to the paper target we had set up thirty feet away. Anne looked like Jane Fonda in *Cat Ballou* after she lost her temper—fierce, blonde, and competent. I swallowed convulsively and wiped sweaty palms on my jeans. I would have given both my big toes to have been able to stand like that, legs apart, feet planted, arms up, and the big rifle perfectly steady as the center circle target was fissured with little bullet holes.

Anne was myopic, skinny, completely obsessed with T.E. Lawrence, and neurotically self-conscious with boys, but holding that rifle tight to her shoulder and peppering the target, she looked different—older and far more interesting. She looked sexy, or maybe the gun looked sexy, I wasn't sure. But I wanted that look. Not Anne, but the power. I wanted to hold a rifle steady, the stock butting my shoulder tightly while I hit the target dead center. My mouth went dry. Anne showed me how to aim the gun a little lower than the center of the target.

"It shoots a little high," she said. "You got to be careful not to let it jump up when it fires." She stood behind me and steadied the gun in my hands. I put the little notch at the peak of the barrel just under the target, tightened my muscles, and pulled the trigger. The rifle still jerked up a little, but a small hole appeared at the outer edge of the second ring of the target.

"Goddamn!" Anne crowed. "You got it, girl." I let the barrel of the rifle drop down, the metal of the trigger guard smooth and warm under my hand.

You got to hold still, I thought. Perfectly still. I sighted along the barrel again, shifting the target notch to the right of the jars Anne had set up earlier. I concentrated, focused, felt my arm become rigid, stern and strong. I pulled back on the trigger slowly, squeezing steadily, the way in the movies they always said it was supposed to be done. The bottle exploded, water shooting out in a wide fine spray.

"Goddamn!" Anne shouted again. I looked over at her. Her glasses had slipped down on her nose and her hair had fallen forward over one eye. Sun shone on her sweaty nose and the polished whites of her teeth. She was staring at me like I had stared at her earlier, her whole face open with pride and delight.

Sexy, yeah. I pointed the barrel at the sky and let my mouth widen into a smile.

"Goddamn," I said, and meant it with all my heart.

Maya Angelou

(1928–   )

Born Marguerite Johnson in St. Louis, Missouri, Maya Angelou and her brother spent most of their youth in Stamps, Arkansas, where they were raised by their paternal grandmother. Despite the painful lessons she learned in Stamps about racial prejudice in the South, she also learned through the example of her grandmother to take pride in herself and to appreciate the strong bonds that held together the African-American community in the small-town, segregated South. During the fifties, Angelou pursued a career in dance and theater, eventually touring twenty-two countries in the cast of Porgy and Bess before moving to Harlem in 1959, where she immersed herself in the burgeoning Black Arts movement. After living abroad for several years she returned to the States and continued to write and act for the stage and film. Her creative interests expanded into autobiography and poetry in the late sixties, and with the publication of I Know Why the Caged Bird Sings in 1970, she received resounding critical acclaim as a major new voice in American literature. The author of six volumes of poetry, she has been the Reynolds Professor of American Studies at Wake Forest University in North Carolina since 1981.

No other major writer in America today has engaged in the autobiographical act in such a sustained manner as Angelou, who has written, to date, five volumes of autobiography. I Know Why the Caged Bird Sings spans her early childhood to age sixteen, ending with the out-of-wedlock birth of her first son. Her life story is continued sequentially in Gather Together in My Name (1974), covering the period from age sixteen to nineteen, and Singin' and Swingin' and Gettin' Merry Like Christmas (1976), which traces her life up to the mid-1950s. The Heart of a Woman (1981) recounts her personal and artistic growth *against the backdrop of the larger struggle for racial justice in the United States during the fifties and early sixties. And in* All God's Children Need Traveling Shoes *(1986) she describes her years in Africa and the spiritual rebirth that occurs as a result of her connection to her ancestral roots. Each of the five volumes emphasizes a different aspect of her personal growth, but through them all runs the constant process of self-discovery and self-affirmation. In the following excerpt from* I Know Why the Caged Bird Sings, *Angelou describes a joyous gathering of the immediate community while subtly evoking the lurking fear of whites that made African-American racial solidarity in the Jim Crow South an imperative rather than a luxury.*

FROM *I Know Why the Caged Bird Sings*

*T*HE LAST INCH of space was filled, yet people continued to wedge themselves along the walls of the Store. Uncle Willie had turned the radio up to its last notch so that youngsters on the porch wouldn't miss a word. Women sat on kitchen chairs, dining-room chairs, stools and upturned wooden boxes. Small children and babies perched on every lap available and men leaned on the shelves or on each other.

The apprehensive mood was shot through with shafts of gaiety, as a black sky is streaked with lightning.

"I ain't worried 'bout this fight. Joe's gonna whip that cracker like it's open season."

"He gone whip him till that white boy call him Momma."

At last all the talking was finished and the string-along songs about razor blades were over and the fight began.

"A quick jab to the head." In the Store the crowd grunted. "A left to the head and a right and another left." One of the listeners cackled like a hen and was quieted.

"They're in a clench, Louis is trying to fight his way out."

Some bitter comedian on the porch said, "That white man don't mind hugging that niggah now, I betcha."

"The referee is moving in to break them up, but Louis finally pushed the contender away and it's an uppercut to the chin. The contender is hanging on, now he's backing away. Louis catches him with a short left to the jaw."

A tide of murmuring assent poured out the doors and into the yard.

"Another left and another left. Louis is saving that mighty right . . ." The mutter in the Store had grown into a baby roar and it was pierced by the clang of a bell and the announcer's "That's the bell for round three, ladies and gentlemen."

As I pushed my way into the Store I wondered if the announcer gave any thought to the fact that he was addressing as "ladies and gentlemen" all the Negroes around the world who sat sweating and praying, glued to their "master's voice."

There were only a few calls for the R. C. Colas, Dr. Peppers, and Hire's root beer. The real festivities would begin after the fight. Then even the old Christian ladies who taught their children and tried themselves to practice turning the other cheek would buy soft drinks, and if the Brown Bomber's victory was a particularly bloody one they would order peanut patties and Baby Ruths also.

Bailey and I lay the coins on top of the cash register. Uncle Willie didn't allow us to ring up sales during a fight. It was too noisy and might shake up the atmosphere. When the gong rang for the next round we pushed through the near-sacred quiet to the herd of children outside.

"He's got Louis against the ropes and now it's a left to the body and a right to the ribs. Another right to the body, it looks like it was low . . . Yes, ladies and gentlemen, the referee is signaling but the contender keeps raining the blows on Louis. It's another to the body, and it looks like Louis is going down."

My race groaned. It was our people falling. It was another lynching, yet another Black man hanging on a tree. One more woman ambushed and raped. A Black boy whipped and maimed. It was hounds on the trail of a man running through slimy swamps. It was a white woman slapping her maid for being forgetful.

The men in the Store stood away from the walls and at attention. Women greedily clutched the babes on their laps while on the porch the shufflings and smiles, flirtings and pinching of a few minutes before were gone. This might be the end of the world. If Joe lost we were back in slavery and beyond help. It would all be true, the accusations that we were lower types of human beings. Only a little higher than the apes. True that we were stupid and ugly and lazy and dirty and, unlucky and worst of all, that God Himself hated us and ordained us to be hewers of wood and drawers of water, forever and ever, world without end.

We didn't breathe. We didn't hope. We waited.

"He's off the ropes, ladies and gentlemen. He's moving towards the center of the ring." There was no time to be relieved. The worst might still happen.

"And now it looks like Joe is mad. He's caught Carnera with a left hook to the head and a right to the head. It's a left jab to the body and another left to the head. There's a left cross and a right to the head. The contender's right eye is bleeding and he can't seem to keep his block up. Louis is penetrating every block. The referee is moving in, but Louis sends a left to the body and it's the uppercut to the chin and the contender is dropping. He's on the canvas, ladies and gentlemen."

Babies slid to the floor as women stood up and men leaned toward the radio.

"Here's the referee. He's counting. One, two, three, four, five, six, seven . . . Is the contender trying to get up again?"

All the men in the store shouted, "NO."

"—eight, nine, ten." There were a few sounds from the audience, but they seemed to be holding themselves in against tremendous pressure.

"The fight is all over, ladies and gentlemen. Let's get the

microphone over to the referee . . . Here he is. He's got the Brown Bomber's hand, he's holding it up . . . Here he is . . ."

Then the voice, husky and familiar, came to wash over us— "The winnah, and still heavyweight champeen of the world . . . Joe Louis."

Champion of the world. A Black boy. Some Black mother's son. He was the strongest man in the world. People drank Coca-Colas like ambrosia and ate candy bars like Christmas. Some of the men went behind the Store and poured white lightning in their soft-drink bottles, and a few of the bigger boys followed them. Those who were not chased away came back blowing their breath in front of themselves like proud smokers.

It would take an hour or more before the people would leave the Store and head for home. Those who lived too far had made arrangements to stay in town. It wouldn't do for a Black man and his family to be caught on a lonely country road on a night when Joe Louis had proved that we were the strongest people in the world.

Larry Brown

(1951–)

Content to be the second most famous novelist to hail from Oxford, Mississippi, Larry Brown currently lives and writes in Yocona, a hamlet just a few miles away from Rowan Oak, William Faulkner's former home, and the University of Mississippi. After graduating from Oxford High School in 1969, Brown served a stint in the U.S. Marine Corps before returning to his home county in Mississippi and joining the Oxford Fire Department. Primarily a self-taught writer with little formal literary training, Brown painstakingly honed his craft as a writer for years during his days off from the fire department. The publication of his story "Facing the Music" in the Mississippi Review *in 1986 delivered him from obscurity and earned him many admirers, but it would be another four years before he would place enough trust in his talents to let go of the financial security of his regular job. Upon the critical and financial success of his first novel,* Dirty Work *(1990), Brown left his job as a firefighter to embark on a full-time career in writing. He is the author of two additional novels,* Joe *(1991) and* Father and Son *(1996), and two collections of short fiction,* Facing the Music *(1989) and* Big Bad Love *(1991). The son of a sharecropper, Brown writes mainly of working-class southerners who have reached the end of their ropes; yet critics have praised his ability to render his often desperate characters with sympathy and compassion.*

In his gripping memoir On Fire *(1994), from which the following selection is taken, he discusses his dual career as a fireman and author of serious fiction, and reflects upon his decision to make writing his full-time vocation.*

FROM *On Fire*

I**T GRIEVES ME** deep in my heart now to have to write about the death of Sam. He died while I was staying overnight at the University of Notre Dame, where I had gone to give a reading. He was involved in two fights with a black chow over a bitch that was in heat. He was hurt badly in the first fight, and did not survive the second one.

Only a few days before I left for South Bend, I had noticed that he was running with a little cocker spaniel one of my neighbors owned. I figured she was in heat and this turned out to be the case. I was driving by one day and Sam was there, and he trotted out into the road to meet me. I told him to stay out of the road, and to get his little ass home after a while. I knew he was happy, because he looked happy, and I knew he was probably finally at long last getting himself a little from the cocker spaniel, so I was happy for him.

But on Saturday afternoon, the kids brought him home pretty chewed up. His throat was wet from where the chow had mauled him, and he was all hunched up, and he stank. He just kind of stood there in the carport in a little miserable drawn-up ball, shivering. He looked really bad, but I never thought of taking him to the vet. He'd been in fights before and had healed up okay. I told the kids to put him in the pen and not let him out. He smelled too bad to stay in the house.

I had an early flight out of Memphis the next morning, and Mary Annie took me up there like she always does. She couldn't go to the gate with me because of the terrorist threat and tighter security while the Gulf War was being fought, so we had to say goodbye in the terminal. I got to South Bend late in the afternoon, and had just forty-five minutes to take a shower and be ready to go to dinner with some people and then give my reading. There was a party afterward, like there always is, and it was nearly midnight when I got back to my hotel on the campus. A couple of kids from the university walked up just as I was about to go in, and wanted to talk some more, so I invited them up to my room for a drink.

My thoughts were more on home than anything else as I talked to these kids. The place I was in held no importance to me other than the money it brought me. I felt sometimes that I was just a whore with a high price. I could be had, I'd do my gig and jump through my hoops, but you had to come up with a check and some plane tickets. Otherwise I'd stay home.

I never went to college, and I felt alien on college campuses. All I had done was stay in a room for ten years and write. I felt that I was ill-equipped to spout any advice to fledgling writers, and I liked critiquing their manuscripts even less. There was always something so terrible, so bad, written by somebody who had no idea what a story was supposed to be about, that it would be nearly impossible to find anything good to say about it. I didn't like that part of it. What I liked was standing before a couple of hundred people and reading one of my stories and watching what happened to them. That night I had a new one, a long one, one that I had worked on for nearly a year, one that had taken nearly an hour to read, and I was about talked out.

The students finally left. I probably hastened their departure by starting to pour them Cokes instead of whiskey and Cokes, by giving the gentle hint that the hour was late and I was tired. I had probably given them more of my time than they had hoped for. I wished them good luck with their work.

Next morning I went down to the dining room and had a huge breakfast by myself, then lingered over my coffee and cigarettes. I love my coffee and cigarettes, although I'm certainly aware of how bad smoking is for you. My body is getting older and I can feel the ravages of time much sharper now than I could twenty years ago. I wouldn't be happy if I couldn't smoke, because I would always want something I couldn't have. It's the same way with drinking. I've seen many people damaged by drinking and I still see them, and I know the evils of it, having tasted them myself many times.

Most all the trouble I was ever in was caused by drinking, whether it was trouble with the law or fights or whatever, because whiskey twists my head and I need to stay away from it unless there's somebody around who can take care of me, but there's nothing more enjoyable to me than to get into my truck late on a summer evening and ride down the road for an hour or so, drinking a beer, looking out at the fields and the warm horizon where the sun has just gone down, listening to Otis Redding or ZZ Top or Leonard Cohen, and watching the road go by. I love the land I was born to and I never tire of seeing the seasons and the weather change over it, or the hawks that sit high in the trees, or the rabbits that bound across the road, or the coons that band together in spring when they're rutting, or later at night, the owls that swoop low across the ditches or fly down to light in the road in front of you with mice caught in their talons, owls that glare at you with a hateful look before gathering their prey and swooping back up into a black and rainy night on their huge beating wings.

I finished my coffee, went back to my room and called MA's office, and found out that she and Shane had been in a wreck and had been taken to the hospital. Everything fell apart in that minute. I tried to hold myself together, but all I could find out was that they had been in a wreck and had been taken to the hospital by ambulance. My mind blanked out and I couldn't think of any of the phone numbers I needed. I tried to call my mother and she was gone. I tried to call MA's mother and she was gone. Both of them gone to the hospital, I knew. I couldn't even remember the fire station numbers. The only number I could think of was Square Books in Oxford, so I called Richard Howorth, told him where I was and what had happened and gave him my number, and asked him to find out what he could and then call me back. Then I sat down beside the phone to wait.

It was a terrible time, that waiting. I couldn't drive it out of my mind that one of them or maybe both of them were dead. All those dead in the highways I'd seen, the bodies I'd pulled from cars. I knew that was the wrong thing to think, and I sat there and willed the phone to ring. It did. It was Richard, saying he had talked to a nurse at the hospital who was reluctant to give him any information, always a bad sign. He gave me the number of the hospital, and I called, and was eventually connected to my brother who was there waiting, and he told me that MA and Shane were bruised up some, but not seriously hurt.

It was nearly time to meet with my class, but I had other plans. I took my bags downstairs and told the group waiting for me about what had happened, and asked them to get me to the airport as soon as they could. I had a ticket for a flight at three o'clock, and I wanted to exchange it for an earlier flight if I could.

I missed a United flight by five minutes and couldn't buy a ticket for a Northwest flight that was already overbooked. What I had to do was hold onto the ticket I had and wait for the three o'clock flight. I spent most of the time in a bar drinking whiskey and making phone calls. I finally got ahold of MA and talked to her for a while. Her chest was badly bruised, and Shane had come out of his seatbelt and hit the windshield and had a big knot on his head, but they had no cuts, no broken bones. She promised that they were all right, and then she said there was something she had to tell me. That's when she told me that Sam was dead. He had gotten out of the pen and gone down and fought the chow again.

She had taken him to Dr. Harlan, our vet, and he had put Sam on a table and shaved his neck to expose the dozen big cuts in his throat, and had done all he could do for him. She said the whole time she moved around the room as the vet did his work, Sam kept his eyes on her, and she said he seemed to pleading with his eyes, seemed to be trying to say, Please help me. Then he died.

Maybe the whiskey made me cry in a public place, in an airport in South Bend, Indiana, with people watching, with snow falling. Maybe I was so overcome with relief that they were all right that I couldn't take the extra load of losing him. I knew that I was still over six hours away from home, and those six hours had to be gone through and lived through and there wasn't any way to shorten them.

They went somewhere. I went through them. Richard picked me up at the airport in Memphis and at eight-thirty that night I walked into my house. I even missed the funeral. Billy Ray had already buried him under a good tree in the pasture. He wouldn't speak of him then, and he won't speak of him now.

Will D. Campbell

(1924–)

A self-proclaimed "redneck" and "renegade Baptist preacher," Will Campbell has followed his ministerial calling wherever it has led him, whether it be as an adviser to Martin Luther King during the early battles of the war for civil rights in the South, or as a goodwill ambassador and guidance counselor to members of hate organizations. Born on a small farm near Como, Mississippi, Campbell was immersed from infancy in the evangelical religious culture of the Deep South and was ordained a minister in the Southern Baptist Church at age seventeen. After earning a doctoral degree at the Yale Divinity School, Campbell served for a short while as a chaplain at the University of Mississippi before leaving in 1956 to work for the National Council of Churches, on whose behalf he served as a liaison to the Southern Christian Leadership Conference. Campbell stepped into one of the most memorable tableaus of the civil rights era when he helped escort a group of African-American students through a jeering mob in Little Rock, Arkansas, only to be turned away at the entrance to the school. Campbell lives with his wife, Brenda, on the small farm outside of Nashville, Tennessee, that has been their home for over thirty years.

The author of more than ten books, Campbell has written on various aspects of southern religion, history, and culture. His books include The Glad River *(1982), a novel about a combat veteran's spiritual recovery;* Forty Acres and a Goat *(1986), a memoir reflecting on the lessons of the civil rights movement; and* Providence *(1992), a mixture of memoir and documentary history in which he traces the history of one square mile of land from its days as a hunting ground for the Chickasaws, to its use as a cotton plantation, to an interracial Christian cooperative, to its present use. His best known work is his autobiography,* Brother to a

Dragonfly, *which was nominated for a National Book Award in 1978. Moving gracefully between his relationship with his older brother Joe, who died of a drug overdose, and his involvement in, then disaffection from, the civil rights movement, Campbell uses the two parallel stories to affirm the dignity and humanity of the poor white. In the following selection, Campbell recounts his initial meetings with Ku Klux Klansmen, which initially met with considerable resistance from his brother Joe. When Campbell reminds his brother of the "long conversation in Fairhope," he refers to an earlier scene in which they learned of the murder of Jonathan Daniels, a close friend of Campbell's who was registering African-American voters in Alabama. In that scene, the grieving (and somewhat inebriated) Campbell was forced by his agnostic friend P. D. to admit that, as a Christian, he must find it in his heart to forgive his enemies, even if that means the men who killed his friend.*

FROM *Brother to a Dragonfly*

SEVERAL STATES of the South had seen a rapid resurgence of the Ku Klux Klan. That organization had intrigued and frightened me since the group of robed and hooded men had presented the pulpit Bible to the church and Uncle Jessie had walked out on them. I had been faintly aware of the paradoxical symbolism the day I had preached my first sermon, holding that huge book with my nervous hand, my fingers trembling on the large embossed letters, K.K.K., raised on the outside back cover.

Since 1956 when I began my work with the National Council of Churches, a large part of my time had been spent in combating the brush fires of violence for which the Klan was said to be responsible. Even prior to that, Joe and I were more than vaguely aware of their activities. I was still the chaplain at Ole Miss when Autherine Lucy had been admitted to the University of Alabama by Court order. There had been student demonstrations and there had been riots. Since Robert Shelton, Imperial

Wizard of the United Klans of America, lived in Tuscaloosa it was assumed that his organization was involved. Meridian is not far from the Alabama line and Joe had followed the incident with great interest. During the upheaval he called one night and said that he had overheard a conversation in the drug store to the effect that several carloads of Ole Miss students were on their way to Tuscaloosa to join the demonstration which was then a full blown riot and completely out of control. He gave me the name of a particular fraternity which had been mentioned and I recognized it as the one to which two sons of the most prominent segregationist in Mississippi belonged. I walked across the campus to the fraternity house, had some coffee with some students and asked if I could use the telephone. There was a notebook by the phone where long distance calls were logged. Casually thumbing through it I saw that there had been several calls made to Tuscaloosa that day and one of the boys had made three calls to his home town. I assumed that what Joe had heard had been accurate when I discovered the next day that several students known to be involved in segregationist activities were not on campus. But neither of us ever knew for sure. Three days later Miss Lucy was suspended for "safety," and that university remained all-white until 1963. (Today every member of the starting basketball team is black, as is the president of the student body.)

It was assumed that the Klan was responsible for many of the acts of violence directed at the Freedom Riders in the spring of 1961. Beginning in Washington with New Orleans as their goal, a group organized by the Congress of Racial Equality had boarded a Greyhound bus with the stated purpose of riding as an integrated group. In Anniston, Alabama, the bus was stoned and burned and in Birmingham the group was so harassed with violence and arrests that they gave up. But in Nashville a tough and determined little group headed by John Lewis and C. T. Vivian vowed that the ride would be completed. After days of negotiation between Federal and State officials and the bus company, the trip resumed. With air cover and a military convoy ahead and behind the trip was safe enough. But when the bus reached Montgomery it was the job of city police to protect them. As they left the bus there were no police in sight and for fifteen minutes the riders were beaten and terrorized by the waiting mob. Most of them were friends and acquaintances of mine. Few of them escaped injury. John Seigenthaler, then administrative assistant to Robert Kennedy, and now publisher of the Nashville *Tennessean,* was on the scene as the personal representative of the President. When he saw two young women being attacked he stepped between them and their attackers, announcing that he represented the President of the United States. And that was the last thing he remembered for a long time. A blow to the head left him unconscious where he lay in the sun for more than an hour before being taken to a hospital. Because the National Council of Churches was so unpopular in the South at the time, Seigenthaler had often kidded me about my role. "How does it feel to represent forty million Protestants?" When I walked into his hospital room the next morning, just as the priest who had come to give him communion was leaving, I said, "John, I'm here representing forty million Protestants." "Well, by god, come on in. I'm pretty sure one of your forty million Protestants hit me on the head yesterday. But I have never been so glad to see an old Baptist reprobate in my life. I hope representing forty million Protestants is safer than representing the President of two hundred and thirty million people."

The following year, 1962, James Meredith enrolled at the University of Mississippi, after being blocked physically in the school doorway by Governor Ross Barnett and Lieutenant Governor Paul B. Johnson, Jr. The resulting riot left two men dead and scores injured and the campus was occupied by army troops. When I visited Meredith six weeks later I had to pass through three military check points to reach him and found as his roommate Ramsey Clark.

William Moore, a white Baltimore postman, was slain as he walked along a lonely road in northeastern Alabama carrying a sign urging "Equal Rights for All."

In Birmingham that same year, Dr. Martin Luther King, Jr. and several other ministers were arrested, fire hoses were turned on demonstrators with such force that their only defense was to lie flat on the streets, letting the velocity of the water roll them along like seashells at high tide. Police dogs were used on marchers, including school children. It was the year four little girls were murdered at their prayers when a bomb exploded in the Sixteenth Street Baptist Church. President Kennedy expressed Americans' "deep sense of outrage and grief," but the crime was never solved. There was little doubt in the minds of most people that the Klan was involved.

The following June three young civil rights workers, Michael Schwerner, Andrew Goodman and James Chaney, were killed while working in a voter registration drive in Mississippi. Six weeks later their bodies were unearthed from a recently constructed pond levee. All of those charged, including the sheriff of the county and his chief deputy, were said to be Klan members.

IT WAS the same year Joe had wept on the telephone when he, knowing that I was on my way home to visit our parents, called to say that Daddy had asked him to relate to me that it would be best if I not come. It was not because he did not want to see me, not because he disapproved of anything I was doing, not because he did not love me. He had learned from a neighbor that a local racist group had said if I came home that summer I would leave in a box. Joe said it was the hardest thing our Daddy ever had to do—ask one of his own sons not to come home— and that it was one of the few times he ever remembered seeing him cry.

It was of such things that Joe talked when I told him that I was going to North Carolina to visit with a Klan leader, said by the FBI to be potentially the most dangerous man in the state.

A young television journalist, Peter Young, then living in North Carolina, had read an article I had written concerning the death of Jonathan Daniel in which I had expressed compassion for his killer. Despite the fact that his own racial views were opposed to theirs, he had become so involved in covering Klan activities in the state, had so related to their condition and tragedy that he had suffered serious physical and emotional exhaustion. He wanted to introduce me to some of his Klan friends. Joe wasn't interested in their tragedy, insisting that we had enough of our own without taking on more.

"Will, these people are killers. You don't know what you're getting into. They know who you are. The whole thing is a trap and you're walking straight into it with your hand on the trigger. I really thought you had better sense."

He begged, pleaded, argued and cajoled.

"If you do it it means you don't love me. It means you don't love Mamma and Daddy. You don't love Brenda and the children. Now I'm asking you. Just don't do it. Getting mixed up with the Negroes was one thing. Getting mixed up with the damn Ku Klux Klan is sheer lunacy."

I reminded him of our long conversation in Fairhope.

"Well, hell. That was drunk talk. I didn't agree with all that crap anyway. P. D. is crazy, Brother. He's a nut. Don't be influenced by something he told you. He was just kidding anyway. You know how he is. He just likes to argue. And anyway, he sure as hell has no love for the Ku Klux Klan. You remember what he said about that guy . . . what's his name? Coleman, who killed your buddy Jonathan."

His words were in a fashion reminiscent of the time he had tried to keep me out of the Army.

He tried another tack. "Let's come at it this way then. You're not a nut. You're a respected and responsible Christian clergyman. Right?"

I said I hoped that was the case.

"Okay. You know it's the case. So what you're going to do is simply give a bunch of hoodlums respectability. Is that what you want to do? Give respectability to the Ku Klux Klan?"

It was my time to score. "Sure. Why not? What better way to neutralize an organization than to give it respectability? Look what respectability did to the Christian Church."

"I don't know, Brother. Maybe you are a nut!"

But he knew my head was made up. That I was going to do it. He went and unlocked a gun cabinet and removed a small, single-shot twenty-two-caliber derringer.

"Here. Keep this in your pocket at all times. It only fires once. But one is all it takes."

"Come on, Joe. I don't want that thing. Nobody is going to bother me and if they did what chance would I have against the experts? Keep it."

But he wouldn't have it, insisting that if I wouldn't listen to reason I could at least be prepared for what he was certain would occur.

I HAD RECENTLY watched a documentary film which the Columbia Broadcasting System had done called "The Ku Klux Klan: An Invisible Empire." It showed such horrors as the murder of the three civil rights workers, the castration of Judge Aaron in Alabama, the death of the four Sunday School children in Birmingham. It took the viewer inside a Georgia Klan Klavern hall where an initiation ceremony was in progress. At one point the candidates were lined up in military formation and the command, "Left face," was shouted. One scared and pathetic figure turned right, bringing confusion to the formation and bringing cheers, jeers, catcalls and guffaws from the audience viewing the film.

I felt a sickening in my stomach. Those viewing the film were a conference convened by the U. S. National Student Association and consisted of representatives of the young New Left radicals of the sixties. They were alleged to be the mad militants. Students for a Democratic Society, the Port Huron group, black and white, men and women who had in recent months taken over campus after campus, burned down buildings, coined and used such words as "establishment" when referring to the social order and "pigs" when speaking of the police. Who were they beyond that? Most of them were from middle to upper class families. They were of Westchester, Ann Arbor and Cambridge. Fortunes awaited them as soon as their daddies deemed them to be sufficiently family facsimiles, which I knew would be soon for most of them. They were students in or recent graduates of rich and leading colleges and universities. They were mean and tough but somehow I sensed that there wasn't a radical in the bunch. For if they were radical how could they laugh at a poor ignorant farmer who didn't know his left hand from his right. If they had been radical they would have been weeping, asking what had produced him. And if they had been radical they would not have been sitting, soaking up a film produced for their edification and enjoyment by the Establishment of the establishment—C.B.S.

I was there to make a speech and lead a discussion following the film. As soon as it was over I stood before them and said, "My name is Will Campbell. I'm a Baptist preacher. I'm a native of Mississippi. And I'm pro-Klansman because I'm pro-human being. Now, that's my speech. If anyone has any questions I will be glad to try to answer them."

Even before my last sentence a huge black man was on the floor, slapping his hands and screaming loudly, "Out! Out! All blacks out of the hall! Out of the hall! Out! Out! Everybody out of the hall!" He started for the door with more than half the audience following him. The half hour that followed was sheer pandemonium. Bedlam. All of the blacks except two or three departed. Many of the whites went with them, feeling, I suppose, that they would be thought non-radical if they remained. It was one of the few times I have ever been genuinely fearful of bodily harm. And it was the first time I had realized the power of words. I had intended to begin a dialogue, maybe even a heated dialogue, with my statement. But I had not intended to start a riot.

Of those who remained, a hundred or so, most were speaking

at once. I could only filter and sift out an occasional thing that was said.

"Pro-human. You think they're human!"

"How can you say you're a preacher and think like that?"

"Fascist pig."

"Insulting to our intelligence."

"No. Don't tell him he's not a Christian. That's what Christians are!"

"Mississippi redneck!"

"I guess you would have helped Hitler. Guess you thought he was human."

As a matter of fact, I did think Hitler was human. Only a human could have been responsible for killing seven million other humans. That was what I wanted to talk about. What does it mean to be human and how do we humans get to be the sort of humans we are.

But it took time to get my little band of radicals settled down enough to point out to them that just four words uttered—"pro-Klansman Mississippi Baptist preacher," coupled with one visual image, white, had turned them into everything they thought the Ku Klux Klan to be—hostile, frustrated, angry, violent and irrational. And I was never able to explain to them that pro-Klansman is not the same as pro-Klan. That the former has to do with person, the other with an ideology. I tried to stand patiently, even in the face of fear and danger, because I had so recently learned that lesson myself. . . .

JOE LISTENED as I related to him the events of that evening and what it was that I was trying to say. The film had been skillfully done and it told them a lot. But there was a lot it did not tell them. It did not, for example, tell them the story of the man I was on my way to visit. It did not tell them that his father left him when he was six years old and his mother went to work in a textile sweat shop where for thirty-seven years, she would tell me later when I came in one day wearing a pair of bib overalls, her job was to sew the seam down the right leg of those overalls. The outside right leg, for thirty-seven years. Never the inside of the right leg, never the left leg. The boy was sent to reform school, ran away and joined the Army when he was fourteen, was jumping out of airplanes as a paratrooper when he was sixteen, was leading a platoon in the jungles when he was eighteen. For seventeen years he was taught the fine arts of torture, interrogation and guerrilla warfare.

Shortly before the conference of radicals was held, President Johnson had gone on national television and in a plea for the cessation of racial violence had pointed his finger at the viewing audience and said, "Get out of the Klan, and back into decent society while there is still time."

The closing five words certainly must have been heard by those in the Klan as a threat from an impending police state. And the President did not tell them just how they could get into the decent society of which he spoke, how they could break out of the cycle of milltown squalor, generations of poverty, a racist society presided over, not by a pitiful and powerless few people marching around a burning cross in a Carolina cow pasture, not by a Georgia farmer who didn't know his left hand from his right, but by those in the "decent society" to which the President referred, the mammas and daddies of the young radicals who would soon go home to run the mills, the factories, the courthouses and legislative halls, the universities and churches and prisons they were then threatening to burn to the ground.

The film had said that only the Ku Klux Klan had a record of violence as an organization. It neglected to mention the Ford Motor Company, the textile industry and their own system of violence, the American State Department, the war in Vietnam which was then raging out of all sense and control, the American churches with their vast holdings and investments and power, the University which teaches, fosters and carries out more violence in one semester than the Klan has committed in its history, for it is they who produce the owners, the managers, the governors and presidents, the rulers and the warriors.

The film could have added, but didn't, what my journalist friend had pointed out, that the same social forces which produced the Klan's violence had also produced the violence of Watts, Rochester and Harlem, Cleveland, Chicago, Houston, Nashville, Atlanta and Dayton, because they are all pieces of the same garment—social isolation, deprivation, economic conditions, rejections, working mothers, poor schools, bad diets, and all the rest.

Eventually Joe had heard enough. He said that he understood what I was saying. But he insisted that I keep the gun.

There was, of course, another reason for my wanting to develop a relationship with those who were alleged to be the heart and center of Southern racism. The romance of "black and white together, we shall overcome" was wearing thin and more and more blacks were telling us that if we wanted to do something in race relations maybe we should go and work with our own people. Stokely Carmichael had recently stood on the bed of a farm truck in Mississippi and used the term "Black Power," and the separatist movement was gaining momentum in many quarters. By then I was suspicious of all "movements" but what they were saying did make sense to me. If that is where the problem lies, if one is interested in a solution, that is certainly where he should be investing his energies.

With all these things running through my head I made the trip to what was being referred to by Peter Young as "Klan Country." And I would again be learner more than I was teacher.

As my acquaintances and friendships with various individuals actively involved in the Klan widened, Joe would insist upon an almost weekly report. "You had any crosses burned on your lawn, Brother?" "Nope. No crosses." "Well, you must be lying to them. They must not know what you believe."

But I didn't lie to them. And they didn't lie to me. Neither of us had any reason to distrust the other. I never asked any of them to get out of the Klan and I never asked any of them to get out of any of the respectable and fashionable organizations or institutions of which they were a part and party, all of which, I was learning, were more truly racist than their Klan.

On one occasion I was spending several days with a man who headed up what my journalist friend called the Maoist wing of the Ku Klux Klan—Maoist because he had split with the larger United Klans of America and because it was revisionist and too moderate. His wife had had a serious operation and because I had been in the Army Medics I knew how to do such things as change a simple surgical dressing or empty a bedpan. The man was a fairly large tobacco farmer and one of the jobs he had asked me to do was to drive the workers to the huge barn where they were "sheeting" tobacco. He had shown me the houses the workers lived in the evening before. Also the evening before he had exploded during the television news when it was reported that there were demonstrations in one of the North Carolina cities for open occupancy housing. I noted with more than passing interest the color of each worker as they got in my car that morning. The first one was an elderly black man. Not more than a hundred yards down the road a young white woman joined us. The next one was a middle-aged white woman. The last was a young black man who looked to be not more than twenty years old. When we reached the tobacco barn it soon became obvious that the elderly black man was in charge of the labor. He decided when the tobacco was in case, when there was enough in each sheet, when it was time to move on to the next barn. That night when my friend returned from town where he had attended the sale of some of his crop we talked about various and sundry things. At one point I asked him if he paid all the workers the same amount.

"Well, yes. I say, yes but I pay that old man a little more, because, well, he's been here a long time, knows more than the others what to do and all, you know." He couldn't bring himself to refer to him as the foreman but I knew. And he knew.

"We have to pay them minimum wage, you know."

"Well, okay. The truth is you operate a Fair Employment Opportunity agency here. And I noticed that you have open occupancy housing. The houses aren't very big but they all look pretty much the same to me. The truth is you have more integration right here on this farm than those demonstrators you wanted to get your thirty-caliber, air-cooled machine gun and mow down."

He took more than a modest exception to the term "integration" so I did not press him.

We talked of other things some more. I had come to feel comfortable in his presence and secure in our friendship. So I got around to asking him a question I had wanted to ask for a long time. He spoke often of the Klan and its activities.

"How about telling me what the Ku Klux Klan stands for?"

It was as if he had been waiting for me to ask.

"The Ku Klux Klan stands for peace, for harmony, and for freedom."

I suppose I was not as ready for his answer as he was in giving it. I was an educated man and he had not even finished high school. But he was extremely bright and read a lot. I thought I would play a little Socratic game with him so I asked, "And what do you mean by peace, harmony and freedom?"

"I just mean peace, harmony and freedom. Those three words. If you don't know what they mean go look them up. There's a dictionary if you want one."

The dialogue was proceeding to my satisfaction. "In other words, *you* define the words. You don't ask others you may not like to define them."

"Of course I define the words. Who defines the words you use? When you use them they're your words and you know what they mean." He meant, I suppose, what I should have known already—that words are symbols and nothing more. Ever.

But I still felt we were moving where I wanted to go. "Okay. Your organization stands for peace, harmony and freedom. You define the words. Now one more question. What means are you willing to use to accomplish those glorious ends?"

"Oh. Now I see what you're getting at. The means we are

willing to use are as follows: murder, torture, threats, blackmail, intimidation, burning, guerrilla warfare. Whatever it takes."

And then he stopped. And I stopped. I knew that I had set a little trap for him and had cleverly let him snap the trigger.

But then he started again. "Now, Preacher. Let me ask you a question. You tell me what we stand for in Vietnam."

Suddenly I knew a lot of things I had not known before. I knew that I had been caught in my own trap. Suddenly I knew that we are a nation of Klansmen. I knew that as a nation we stood for peace, harmony and freedom in that war, that we defined the words, and that the means we were employing to accomplish those ends were identical with the ones he had listed.

I REMEMBERED an Ivy League Divinity School dean who had invited me to talk about the racial happenings of the South. In our conversation before my scheduled address I had asked him about the recent demonstration at his university intended by the students to stop Dow Chemical from recruiting on their campus. He told me that he was very much in sympathy with what the students felt and believed, that he had stayed up all night in a negotiating session with them. "But," he added, "we can't tolerate that kind of tactics. You can't run a university in the midst of chaos."

They were the identical words I had heard from mayors, governors, and merchants in the South during the sit-ins. "We have nothing against integration but you can't operate a business in the midst of chaos." Each spoke the truth. And each revealed his idol. And ultimately one has to question and doubt if the Almighty holds the University to be any more sacred than F. W. Woolworth or the Mississippi plantation system.

Later in the evening my friend was showing me his new Klan robe. It looked very much like those seen in any academic procession or Sunday morning church parade. It was made of crimson satin and he was very proud of it—like everyone who wears a robe for any purpose is proud. He strolled and strutted about the room for my inspection.

"Whatda I look like, Preacher?"

I said, "You look like a Harvard professor." This he denied with considerable embellishment for he was almost violently anti-intellectual. He had once told me, "You show me a Ph.D. and I'll show you a communist. Show me a Master's degree and I'll show you a socialist. And show me a college graduate and I'll show you a damn liberal."

But I bet him fifty dollars that the next time there was an academic procession at any one of the nearby universities, preferably one with a divinity school, he could go and join it and not be challenged. He thought about that for a long time. Then he said some words which I would never forget. He said, "No, Preacher. You're wrong. They would know the difference."

"How? How would they know the difference?"

"Because," he said, "my robe has a cross on it." He pointed to a golden felt cross sewed just over his heart.

"They'd know the difference because their robe ain't got a cross on it."

I had discovered a strange kind of school. I was learning things I had only suspected before. Or had not known at all. Important things. Things from and about people some of my colleagues referred to as "the Enemy." Things from and about people who were our people—mine and Joe's. Whatever they stood for. Whatever they did. In a strange sequence of crosscurrents we were of them and they were of us. Blood of our blood. Our people. And God's people.

I shared the things I was learning with my brother in Meridian, Mississippi.

AND HE UNDERSTOOD. As he would understand them now to be part of the chronicles of his day and time.

Harry Crews

(1935–)

The leading practitioner of the neo-Gothic style of hard-boiled fiction known in some circles as "Grit Lit," Harry Crews is finally beginning to receive the serious critical attention he has long deserved as he reaches the thirtieth anniversary of the publication of his first novel, The Gospel Singer *(1968). Born in Bacon County, Georgia, in the southeastern corner of the state, Crews lived a life marked by hardship after the death of his father in 1937. Fleeing her abusive second husband, Crews's mother brought her two sons to the Springfield section of Jacksonville, Florida, where she worked as a tobacco roller. It was there that the young Crews learned that his alcoholic stepfather was not his biological parent but his paternal uncle, who had divorced his wife and married his brother's widow only weeks after the death of Crews's real father. Crews's family eventually returned to Bacon County, where his mother eked out a living as a tenant farmer. After graduating from high school, Crews served four years in the U.S. Marines before attending the University of Florida, where he received a B.A. in 1960 and a M.S.Ed. in 1962, and where he has taught creative writing since 1968. In the twelve novels he has written, Crews draws upon his working-class rural background to create characters who often respond with violence to the world of modernity they find themselves inhabiting. His essays, some of which are collected in* Blood and Grits *(1979) and* Florida Frenzy *(1982), have appeared in* Esquire, Playboy, Harper's, *and* Oxford American. *The year 1993 witnessed the publication of* Classic Crews: A Harry Crews Reader, *containing two early novels,* Car *(1972) and* The Gypsy's Curse *(1974), and his autobiography,* A Childhood: The Biography of a Place *(1978).*

For all of the fiction he has produced over the last thirty years,

Crews's most lasting contribution to southern literature may well be A Childhood, *in which he describes the often violent and grotesque, yet paradoxically beautiful world of rural Bacon County. Although the figure of the poor white has been a prominent feature in representations of the South since the antebellum period, it was not until public education made inroads into the region that members of this class began to write from their own perspectives and bring some balance to the subject. Although Crews does not shy away from the violence and ignorance that is part of that world, his portraits of family and neighbors allow us to see their strength and humanity, as in the following selection.*

FROM *A Childhood:*
The Biography of a Place

A S WINTER GREW deeper and we waited for hog-killing time, at home the center was not holding. Whether it was because the crops were in and not much work was to be done or whether it was because of my having just spent so long a time crippled in the bed, daddy had grown progressively crazier, more violent. He was gone from home for longer and longer periods of time, and during those brief intervals when he was home, the crashing noise of breaking things was everywhere about us. Daddy had also taken to picking up the shotgun and screaming threats while he waved it about, but at that time he had not as yet fired it.

While that was going on, it occurred to me for the first time that being alive was like being awake in a nightmare.

I remember saying aloud to myself: "Scary as a nightmare. Jest like being awake in a nightmare."

Never once did I ever think that my life was not just like everybody else's, that my fears and uncertainties were not universal. For which I can only thank God. Thinking so could only have made it more bearable.

My sleepwalking had become worse now that I could get out

of bed on my unsure legs. I woke up sometimes in the middle of the night in the dirt lane by the house or sometimes sitting in my room in a corner chewing on something. It didn't matter much what: the sleeve of my gown or the side of my hand or even one time the laces of a shoe. And when I would wake up, it was always in terror, habitually remembering now what Auntie had said about the birds spitting in my mouth. No, more than *remembering* what she had said. Rather, seeing what she had said, the image of a bird burned clearly on the backs of my eyelids, its beak hooked like the nose of a Byzantine Christ, shooting spit thick as phlegm on a solid line into my open and willing mouth. With such dreams turning in my head it came time for us to all help kill and butcher hogs. Daddy was laid up somewhere drunk; we had not seen him in four days. So he did not go with us to Uncle Alton's to help with the slaughter. Farm families swapped labor at hog-killing time just as they swapped labor to put in tobacco or pick cotton. Early one morning our tenant farmers, mama, my brother, and I walked the half mile to Uncle Alton's place to help put a year's worth of meat in the smokehouse. Later his family would come and help us do the same thing.

Before it was over, everything on the hog would have been used. The lights (lungs) and liver—together called haslet— would be made into a fresh stew by first pouring and pouring again fresh water through the slit throat—the exposed throat called a goozle—to clean the lights out good. Then the fat would be trimmed off and put with the fat trimmed from the guts to cook crisp into cracklins to mix with cornbread or else put in a wash pot to make soap.

The guts would be washed and then turned and washed again. Many times. After the guts had been covered with salt overnight, they were used as casings for sausage made from shoulder meat, tenderloin, and—if times were hard—any kind of scrap that was not entirely fat.

The eyes would be removed from the head, then the end of the snout cut off, and the whole thing boiled until the teeth could be picked out. Whatever meat was left, cheeks, ears, and so on, would be picked off, crushed with herbs and spices and packed tightly into muslin cloth for hog's headcheese.

The fat from the liver, lungs, guts, or wherever was cooked until it was as crisp as it would get and then packed into tin syrup buckets to be ground up later for cracklin cornbread. Even the feet were removed, and after the outer layer of split hooves was taken off, the whole thing was boiled and pickled in vinegar and peppers. If later in the year the cracklins started to get rank, they would be thrown into a cast-iron wash pot with fried meat's grease, any meat for that matter that might have gone bad in the smokehouse, and some potash and lye and cooked into soap, always made on the full of the moon so it wouldn't shrink. I remember one time mama out in the backyard making soap when a chicken for some reason tried to fly over the wash pot but didn't make it. The chicken dropped flapping and squawking into the boiling fat and lye. Mama, who was stirring the mixture with an old ax handle, never missed a beat. She just stirred the chicken right on down to the bottom. Any kind of meat was good for making soap.

By the time we got to Uncle Alton's the dirt floor of the smokehouse had been covered with green pine tops. After the pork stayed overnight in tubs of salt, it would be laid on the green pine straw all night, sometimes for two nights, to get all the water out of it. Then it was taken up and packed again in salt for three or four days. When it was taken out of the salt for the last time, it was dipped in plain hot water or else in a solution of crushed hot peppers and syrup or wild honey. Then it was hung over a deep pile of smoldering hickory spread across the entire floor of the smokehouse. The hickory was watched very carefully to keep any sort of blaze from flaring up. Day and night until it was over, light gray smoke boiled continuously from under the eaves and around the door where the meat was being cured. It was the sweetest smoke a man was ever to smell.

It was a bright cold day in February 1941, so cold the ground was still frozen at ten o'clock in the morning. The air was full of the steaming smell of excrement and the oily, flatulent odor of intestines and the heavy sweetness of blood—in every way a perfect day to slaughter animals. I watched the hogs called to the feeding trough just as they were every morning except this morning it was to receive the ax instead of slop.

A little slop *was* poured into their long communal trough, enough to make them stand still while Uncle Alton or his boy Theron went quietly among them with the ax, using the flat end like a sledgehammer (shells were expensive enough to make a gun out of the question). He would approach the hog from the rear while it slopped at the trough, and then he would straddle it, one leg on each side, patiently waiting for the hog to raise its snout from the slop to take a breath, showing as it did the wide bristled bone between its ears to the ax.

It never took but one blow, delivered expertly and with consummate skill, and the hog was dead. He then moved with his hammer to the next hog and straddled it. None of the hogs ever seemed to mind that their companions were dropping dead all around them but continued in a single-minded passion to eat. They didn't even mind when another of my cousins (this could be a boy of only eight or nine because it took neither strength nor skill) came right behind the hammer and drew a long razor-boned butcher knife across the throat of the fallen hog. Blood spurted with the still-beating heart, and a live hog would sometimes turn to one that was lying beside it at the trough and stick its snout into the spurting blood and drink a bit just seconds before it had its own head crushed.

It was a time of great joy and celebration for the children. We played games and ran (I gimping along pretty well by then) and screamed and brought wood to the boiler and thought of that night, when we would have fresh fried pork and stew made from lungs and liver and heart in an enormous pot that covered half the stove.

The air was charged with the smell of fat being rendered in tubs in the backyard and the sharp squeals of the pigs at the troughs, squeals from pure piggishness at the slop, never from pain. Animals were killed but seldom hurt. Farmers took tremendous precautions about pain at slaughter. It is, whether or not they ever admit it when they talk, a ritual. As brutal as they sometimes are with farm animals and with themselves, no farmer would ever eat an animal he had willingly made suffer.

The heel strings were cut on each of the hog's hind legs, and a stick, called a gambreling stick, or a gallus, was inserted into the cut behind the tendon and the hog dragged to the huge cast-iron boiler, which sat in a depression dug into the ground so the hog could be slipped in and pulled out easily. The fire snapped and roared in the depression under the boiler. The fire had to be tended carefully because the water could never quite come to a boil. If the hog was dipped in boiling water, the hair would set and become impossible to take off. The ideal temperature was water you could rapidly draw your finger through three times in succession without being blistered.

Unlike cows, which are skinned, a hog is scraped. After the hog is pulled from the water, a blunt knife is drawn over the animal, and if the water has not been too hot, the hair slips off smooth as butter, leaving a white, naked, utterly beautiful pig.

To the great glee of the watching children, when the hog is slipped into the water, it defecates. The children squeal and clap their hands and make their delightfully obscene children's jokes as they watch it all.

On that morning, mama was around in the back by the smokehouse where some hogs, already scalded and scraped, were hanging in the air from their heel strings being disemboweled. Along with the other ladies she was washing out the guts, turning them inside out, cleaning them good so they could later be stuffed with ground and seasoned sausage meat.

Out in front of the house where the boiler was, I was playing pop-the-whip as best I could with my brother and several of my cousins. Pop-the-whip is a game in which everyone holds hands and runs fast and then the leader of the line turns sharply. Because he is turning through a tighter arc than the other children, the line acts as a whip with each child farther down the line having to travel through a greater space and consequently having to go faster in order to keep up. The last child in the line literally gets *popped* loose and sent flying from his playmates.

I was popped loose and sent flying into the steaming boiler of water beside a scalded, floating hog.

I remember everything about it as clearly as I remember anything that ever happened to me, except the screaming. Curiously, I cannot remember the screaming. They say I screamed all the way to town, but I cannot remember it.

What I remember is John C. Pace, a black man whose daddy was also named John C. Pace, reached right into the scalding water and pulled me out and set me on my feet and stood back to look at me. I did not fall but stood looking at John and seeing in his face that I was dead.

The children's faces, including my brother's, showed I was dead, too. And I knew it must be so because I knew where I had fallen and I felt no pain—not in that moment—and I knew with the bone-chilling certainty most people are spared that, yes, death does come and mine had just touched me.

John C. Pace ran screaming and the other children ran screaming and left me standing there by the boiler, my hair and skin and clothes steaming in the bright cold February air.

In memory I stand there alone with the knowledge of death upon me, watching steam rising from my hands and clothes while everybody runs and, after everybody was gone, standing there for minutes while nobody comes.

That is only memory. It may have been but seconds before my mama and Uncle Alton came to me. Mama tells me she heard me scream and started running toward the boiler, knowing already what had happened. She has also told me that she could not bring herself to try to do anything with that smoking ghostlike thing standing by the boiler. But she did. They all did. They did what they could.

But in that interminable time between John pulling me out and my mother arriving in front of me, I remember first the pain. It didn't begin as bad pain, but rather like maybe sandspurs under my clothes.

I reached over and touched my right hand with my left, and the whole thing came off like a wet glove. I mean, the skin on the top of the wrist and the back of my hand, along with the fingernails, all just turned loose and slid on down to the ground. I could see my fingernails lying in a little puddle my flesh made on the ground in front of me.

Then hands were on me, taking off my clothes, and the pain turned into something words cannot touch, or at least my words cannot touch. There is no way for me to talk about it because when my shirt was taken off, my back came off with it. When my overalls were pulled down, my cooked and glowing skin came down.

I still had not fallen, and I stood there participating in my own butchering. When they got the clothes off me, they did the worst thing they could have done; they wrapped me in a sheet. They did it out of panic and terror and ignorance and love.

That day there happened to be a car at the farm. I can't remember who it belonged to, but I was taken into the backseat into my mama's lap—God love the lady, out of her head, pressing her boiled son to her breast—and we started for Alma, a distance of about sixteen miles. The only thing that I can remember about the trip was that I started telling mama that I did not want to die. I started saying it and never stopped.

The car we piled into was incredibly slow. An old car and very, very slow, and every once in a while Uncle Alton, who was like a daddy to me, would jump out of the car and run alongside it and helplessly scream for it to go faster and then he would jump on the running board until he couldn't stand it any longer and then he would jump off again.

But like bad beginnings everywhere, they sometimes end well. When I got to Dr. Sharp's office in Alma and he finally managed to get me out of the sticking sheet, he found that I was scalded over two-thirds of my body but that my head had not gone under the water (he said that would have killed me), and for some strange reason I have never understood, the burns were not deep. He said I would probably even outgrow the scars, which I have. Until I was about fifteen years old, the scars were puckered and discolored on my back and right arm and legs. But now their outlines are barely visible.

The only hospital at the time was thirty miles away, and Dr. Sharp said I'd do just as well at home if they built a frame over the bed to keep the covers off me and also kept a light burning over me twenty-four hours a day. (He knew as well as we did that I couldn't go to a hospital anyway, since the only thing Dr. Sharp ever got for taking care of me was satisfaction for a job well done, if he got that. Over the years, I was his most demanding and persistent charity, which he never mentioned to me or mama. Perhaps that is why in an age when it is fashionable to distrust and hate doctors, I love them.)

So they took me back home and put a buggy frame over my bed to make it resemble, when the sheet was on it, a covered wagon, and ran a line in from the Rural Electrification Administration so I could have the drying light hanging just over me. The pain was not nearly so bad now that I had for the first time in my life the miracle of electricity close enough to touch. The pain was bad enough, though, but relieved to some extent by some medicine Dr. Sharp gave us to spray out of a bottle onto the burns by pumping a black rubber ball. When it dried, it raised to form a protective, cooling scab. But it was bad to crack. The bed was always full of black crumbs, which Auntie worked continually at. When they brought me home, Auntie, without anybody saying a word to her, came back up the road to take care of me.

The same day Hollis Toomey came, too. He walked into the house without knocking or speaking to anyone. Nobody had sent for him. But whenever anybody in the county was burned, he showed up as if by magic, because he could talk the fire out of you. He did not call himself a faith healer, never spoke of God, didn't even go to church, although his family did. His was a gift that was real, and everybody in the county knew it was real. For reasons which he never gave, because he was the most reticent of men and never took money or anything else for what he did, he was drawn to a bad burn the way iron filings are drawn to a magnet, never even saying, "You're welcome," to those who thanked him. He was as sure of his powers and as implacable as God.

When he arrived, the light had not yet been brought into the house, and the buggy frame was not yet over my bed and I was lying in unsayable pain. His farm was not far from ours, and it was unlike any other in the county. Birds' nests made from gourds, shaped like crooked-necked squash with a hole cut in one side with the seeds taken out, hung everywhere from the forest of old and arching oak trees about his house. Undulating flocks of white pigeons flew in and out of his hayloft. He had a blacksmith shed, black as smut and always hot from the open hearth where he made among other things iron rims for wagon wheels. He could handcraft a true-shooting gun, including the barrel which was not smooth-bore but had calibrated riflings. He owned two oxen, heavier than mules, whose harness, including the double yoke, he had made himself. His boys were never allowed to take care of them. He watered them and fed them and pulled them now and again to stumps or trees. But he also had the only Belgian draft horse in the county. The horse was so monstrously heavy that you could hitch him to two spans of good mules—four of them—and he would walk off with them as though they were goats. So the oxen were really useless. It just pleased him to keep them.

He favored very clean women and very dirty men. He thought it was the natural order of things. One of the few things I ever heard him say, and he said it looking off toward the far horizon, speaking to nobody: "A man's got the *right* to stink."

His wife always wore her hair tightly bunned at the back of her head under a stiffly starched white bonnet. Her dresses were nearly to her ankles, and they always looked and smelled as if they had just come off the clothesline after a long day in the sun.

Hollis always smelled like his pockets were full of ripe

chicken guts, and his overalls were as stiff as metal. He didn't wear a beard; he wore a stubble. The stubble was coal black despite the fact he was over sixty, and it always seemed to be the same length, the length where you've got to shave or start telling everybody you're growing a beard. Hollis Toomey did neither.

When I saw him in the door, it was as though a soothing balm had touched me. This was Hollis Toomey, who was from my county, whose boys I knew, who didn't talk to God about your hurt. He didn't even talk to *you;* he talked to the *fire.* A mosquito couldn't fly through a door he was standing in he was so wide and high, and more, he was obviously indestructible. He ran on his own time, went where he needed to go. Nobody ever thought of doing anything for him, helping him. If he wanted something, he made it. If he couldn't make it, he took it. Hollis Toomey was not a kind man.

My daddy had finally come home, red-eyed and full of puke. He was at the foot of the bed, but he didn't say a word while Hollis sat beside me.

Hollis Toomey's voice was low like the quiet rasping of a file on metal. I couldn't hear most of what he had to say, but that was all right because I stopped burning before he ever started talking. He talked to the fire like an old and respected adversary, but one he had beaten consistently and had come to beat again. I don't remember him once looking at my face while he explained: "Fire, this boy is mine. This bed is mine. This room is mine. It ain't nothing here that's yours. It's a lot that is, but it ain't nothing here that is."

At some point while he talked he put his hands on me, one of them spread out big as a frying pan, and I was already as cool as spring water. But I had known I would be from the moment I had seen him standing in the door. Before it was over, he cursed the fire, calling it all kinds of sonofabitch, but the words neither surprised nor shocked me. The tone of his voice made me know that he was locked in a real and terrible conflict with the fire. His hands flexed and hurt my stomach, but it was nothing compared to the pain that had been on me before he came.

I had almost dozed off when he suddenly got up and walked out of the room. My daddy called, "Thank you," in a weak, alcohol-spattered voice. Hollis Toomey did not answer.

When they finally got the buggy frame up, it was not as terrible as I at first thought it was going to be. I was, of course, by then used to the bed and that was no problem and the buggy frame gave a new dimension, a new feeling to the sickbed. With the frame arching over me it was a time for fantasy and magic because I lived in a sort of playhouse, a kingdom that was all mine.

At least I pretended it was a kingdom, pretended it in self-defense. I did not want to be there, but there was no help for it, so I might as well pretend it was a kingdom as anything else. And like every child who owns anything, I ruled it like a tyrant. There was something very special and beautiful about being the youngest member of a family and being badly hurt.

Since it pleased me to do so, I spent a lot of time with the Sears, Roebuck catalogue, started writing and nearly finished a detective novel, although at that time I had never seen a novel, detective or otherwise. I printed it out with a soft-lead pencil on lined paper, and it was about a boy who, for his protection, carried not a pistol but firecrackers. He solved crimes and gave things to poor people and doctors. The boy was also absolutely fearless.

I was given a great deal of ginger ale to drink because the doctor or mama or somebody thought that where burns were concerned, it had miraculous therapeutic value. This ginger ale was the store-bought kind, too, not some homemade concoction but wonderfully fizzy and capped in real bottles. Since Hoyet and I almost never saw anything from the store, I drank as much of it as they brought me, and they brought me a lot. I never learned to like it but could never get over my fascination with the bubbles that rose in the bottle under the yellow light hanging from the buggy frame.

But I was tired of being alone in bed, and since I was going into my second major hurt back to back, I decided I might as well assert myself.

Old Black Bill had sired several kids the previous spring, and one of them was himself black and a male, so I named him Old Black Bill, too, and he grew up with me under the buggy frame. No animal is allowed in a farmhouse in Bacon County, at least to my knowledge. Dogs stay in the yard. Cats usually live in the barn catching rats, and goats, well, goats only get in the house if they have first been butchered for the table.

But I had been scalded and I was special. And I knew even then that an advantage unused becomes no advantage at all. So I insisted Old Black Bill's kid be brought to my bed. I was only about three weeks into my recovery, and I thought that a goat would be good company.

They brought him in, and I fed him bits of hay and shelled corn under the buggy frame. We had long conversations. Or rather, I had long monologues and he, patiently chewing, listened.

The two tall windows at the foot of my bed opened onto a forty-acre field. Through the long winter days Old Black Bill and I watched it being prepared to grow another crop. First the cornstalks were cut by a machine with revolving blades, pulled by a single mule. Then two mules were hitched to a big rake, so big a man could ride on it. When all the stalks were piled and burned, the land had to be broken, completely turned under, the single hardest job on a farm for the farmer and his mules.

Every morning, when the light came up enough for me to see into the field, Willalee's daddy, Will, would already be out there behind a span of mules walking at remarkable speed, breaking the hard, clayish earth more than a foot deep. Sometimes daddy was out there plowing, too. Most of the time he was not.

Willalee's daddy would mark off an enormous square, fifteen acres or better, then follow that square around and around, always taking about a fourteen-inch bite with the turnplow so that when he went once around on each of the four sides of the square, the land still to be broken would have been reduced by fourteen inches on a side.

A man breaking land would easily walk thirty miles or more every day, day in and day out, until the entire farm was turned under. Even though the mules were given more corn and more hay than they were used to, they still lost weight. Every night when they were brought to the barn, they had high stiff ridges of salt outlining where their collars and backbands and trace chains and even their bridles had been.

With only my head out from under the buggy frame, continually dried and scabbed by the burning light, I watched the plows drag on through the long blowing days, Willalee's daddy moving dim as a ghost in the sickly half-light of the winter sun. Then after the longest, hardest time, the turnplow was taken out of the field, and the row marker brought in to lay off the lines in the soft earth where the corn would finally begin to show in the springtime. The row marker was made out of a trunk of a tree, sometimes a young oak, more often a pine, made by boring holes thirty-six inches apart, and inserting a straight section of limb into each of the holes. Two holes were bored into the top of the log for handles and two holes in the front of the log for the shaves, between which the mule was hitched to drag the whole rig across the turned-under field, marking off four rows at a time.

Some farmers always had crops that grew in rows straight as a plumb line. Others didn't seem to care about it much, one way or the other. It was not unusual for a farmer bumping along in a wagon behind a steaming mule in the heat of summer to comment on how the rows were marked off on each farm he passed.

"Sumbitch, he musta been drunk when he laid them off."

"I bet he has to git drunk again ever time he plows that mess."

"I guess he figgers as much'll grow in a crooked row as a straight one."

For reasons I never knew, perhaps it was nothing more complicated than pride of workmanship, farmers always associated crooked rows with sorry people. So much of farming was beyond a man's control, but at least he could have whatever nature allowed to grow laid off in straight rows. And the feeling was that a man who didn't care enough to keep his rows from being crooked couldn't be much of a man.

In all the years in Bacon County, I never saw any rows straighter than the ones Willalee's daddy put down. He would take some point of reference at the other end of the field, say, a tree or a post, and then keep his eye on it as the mule dragged the row marker over the freshly broken ground, laying down those first critical rows. If the first four rows were straight, the rest of the field would be laid off straight, because the outside marker would always run in the last row laid down.

It didn't hurt to have a good mule. As was true of so many other things done on the farm, it was much easier if the abiding genius of a good mule was brought to bear on the job. There were mules in Bacon County that a blind man could have laid off straight rows behind. Such mules knew only one way to work: the right way. To whatever work they were asked to do, they brought a lovely exactitude, whether it was walking off rows, snaking logs, sledding tobacco without a driver, or any of the other unaccountable jobs that came their way during a crop year.

After the field was marked in a pattern of rows, Willalee's daddy came in with the middlebuster, a plow with a wing on both sides that opens up the row to receive first the fertilizer and then the seed. When all the rows had been plowed into shallow trenches, Will appeared in the field early one morning with a two-horse wagon full of guano, universally called *gyou-anner*. It was a commercial fertilizer sold in 200-pound bags, and Will had loaded the wagon before daylight by himself and brought it at sunup into the field where he unloaded one bag every three rows across the middle of the field.

Shortly after he left with the wagon, he came back with the guano strower and Willalee Bookatee. Willalee had a tin bucket with him. He plodded sleepily behind his daddy, the bucket banging at his knees. The guano strower was a kind of square wooden box that got smaller at the bottom, where there was a metal shaft shaped like a corkscrew and over which the guano had to fall as it poured into the trench opened by the middle-buster. The corkscrew shaft broke up any lumps in the fertilizer and made sure it kept flowing. Two little tongue-shaped metal plows at the back of the guano strower were set so that one ran on each side of the furrow. They covered up the thin stream of fertilizer the instant after it was laid down.

Willalee was out there to fill up the guano strower for his daddy, a bad, boring job and one reserved exclusively for small boys. Willalee would open one of the bags, fill the strower, and his daddy would head for the end of the row. As soon as he was gone, Willalee would go back to the sack, and since he could not pick up anything that heavy, he would have to dip the bucket full with his hands. Then he had nothing to do but shift from foot to foot, the fertilizer burning his arms and hands and before long his eyes, and wait for his daddy to come back down the row. When he did, Willalee would fill up the strower and the whole thing would be to do over again.

Frederick Douglass

(1818–1895)

Frederick Douglass was the most prominent African-American orator of his day and one of the most widely read American authors of the nineteenth century, regardless of color. In addition to his work as an autobiographer and his public speaking activities for the abolitionist movement, he was an advocate of women's rights and worked as a journalist, editor, U.S. marshal, diplomat, and unofficial presidential adviser. Born Frederick Augustus Washington Bailey, Douglass later assumed a new identity in order to elude fugitive slave agents. When he was eight years old, Douglass was placed in the service of a family in Baltimore, where he learned through various forms of subterfuge to read and write, a skill that ultimately enabled him to effect his escape in 1838.

Narrative of the Life of Frederick Douglass, an American Slave, Written by Himself, *published in 1845, combines the kind of rags-to-riches story of American self-reliance found in Benjamin Franklin's* Autobiography *with the basic form of the spiritual autobiography to describe the author's growing awareness of his own humanity and subsequent desire for unfettered freedom. Realizing that even sympathetic abolitionist readers would be inclined to regard the authorship of his account with suspicion, he takes pains in the narrative to recount in detail his acquisition of literacy and to provide testimonials by prominent white abolitionists attesting to the veracity of the account and the literary abilities of the author. Like other former slaves who wrote accounts of their bondage, Douglass reveals a keen understanding of the mechanisms of oppression within the institution of slavery, explaining in meticulous detail the methods used by owners to keep their human chattel "adjusted" to their circumstances. The 1845* Narrative *is the* *first of three book-length autobiographical accounts by Douglass. The other narratives—*My Bondage and My Freedom *(1855) and* Life and Times of Frederick Douglass: Written by Himself *(1892)— each revisit the time period covered in* Narrative of the Life *before picking up where the previous book leaves off, but critics prefer the first account for its economy and moral force. The following selection recounts some of the stratagems Douglass used in order to learn to write and describes the initial devastating emotional consequences of his newly acquired literacy. Recognizing that his primarily white audience might have difficulty empathizing with African Americans, he also takes care to show the "disastrous" effects of slavery on his new master and mistress.*

FROM *Narrative of the Life of*
Frederick Douglass, an American Slave,
Written by Himself

CHAPTER VII

I LIVED IN Master Hugh's family about seven years. During this time, I succeeded in learning to read and write. In accomplishing this, I was compelled to resort to various stratagems. I had no regular teacher. My mistress, who had kindly commenced to instruct me, had, in compliance with the advice and direction of her husband, not only ceased to instruct, but had set her face against my being instructed by any one else. It is due, however, to my mistress to say of her, that she did not adopt this course of treatment immediately. She at first lacked the depravity indispensable to shutting me up in mental darkness. It was at least necessary for her to have some training in the exercise of irresponsible power, to make her equal to the task of treating me as though I were a brute.

My mistress was, as I have said, a kind and tender-hearted woman; and in the simplicity of her soul she commenced, when I first went to live with her, to treat me as she supposed one human being ought to treat another. In entering upon the duties of a slaveholder, she did not seem to perceive that I sustained to her the relation of a mere chattel, and that for her to treat me as a human being was not only wrong, but dangerously so. Slavery proved as injurious to her as it did to me. When I went there, she was a pious, warm, and tender-hearted woman. There was no sorrow or suffering for which she had not a tear. She had bread for the hungry, clothes for the naked, and comfort for every mourner that came within her reach. Slavery soon proved its ability to divest her of these heavenly qualities. Under its influence, the tender heart became stone, and the lamblike disposition gave way to one of tiger-like fierceness. The first step in her downward course was in her ceasing to instruct me. She now commenced to practise her husband's precepts. She finally became even more violent in her opposition than her husband himself. She was not satisfied with simply doing as well as he had commanded; she seemed anxious to do better. Nothing seemed to make her more angry than to see me with a newspaper. She seemed to think that here lay the danger. I have had her rush at me with a face made all up of fury, and snatch from me a newspaper, in a manner that fully revealed her apprehension. She was an apt woman; and a little experience soon demonstrated, to her satisfaction, that education and slavery were incompatible with each other.

From this time I was most narrowly watched. If I was in a separate room any considerable length of time, I was sure to be suspected of having a book, and was at once called to give an account of myself. All this, however, was too late. The first step had been taken. Mistress, in teaching me the alphabet, had given me the *inch,* and no precaution could prevent me from taking the *ell*.

The plan which I adopted, and the one by which I was most successful, was that of making friends of all the little white boys whom I met in the street. As many of these as I could, I converted into teachers. With their kindly aid, obtained at different times and in different places, I finally succeeded in learning to read. When I was sent on errands, I always took my book with me, and by doing one part of my errand quickly, I found time to get a lesson before my return. I used also to carry bread with me, enough of which was always in the house, and to which I was always welcome; for I was much better off in this regard than many of the poor white children in our neighborhood. This bread I used to bestow upon the hungry little urchins, who, in return, would give me that more valuable bread of knowledge. I am strongly tempted to give the names of two or three of those little boys, as a testimonial to the gratitude and affection I bear them; but prudence forbids;—not that it would injure me, but it might embarrass them; for it is almost an unpardonable offence to teach slaves to read in this Christian country. It is enough to say of the dear little fellows, that they lived on Philpot Street, very near Durgin and Bailey's ship-yard. I used to talk this matter of slavery over with them. I would sometimes say to them, I wished I could be as free as they would be when they got to be men. "You will be free as soon as you are twenty-one, *but I am a slave for life!* Have not I as good a right to be free as you have?" These words used to trouble them; they would express for me the liveliest sympathy, and console me with the hope that something would occur by which I might be free.

I was now about twelve years old, and the thought of being *a slave for life* began to bear heavily upon my heart. Just about this time, I got hold of a book entitled "The Columbian Orator." Every opportunity I got, I used to read this book. Among much of other interesting matter, I found in it a dialogue between a master and his slave. The slave was represented as having run away from his master three times. The dialogue represented the conversation which took place between them, when the slave was retaken the third time. In this dialogue, the whole argument in behalf of slavery was brought forward by the master, all of which was disposed of by the slave. The slave was made to say some very smart as well as impressive things in reply to his master—things which had the desired though unexpected effect; for the conversation resulted in the voluntary emancipation of the slave on the part of the master.

In the same book, I met with one of Sheridan's mighty speeches on and in behalf of Catholic emancipation. These were choice documents to me. I read them over and over again with unabated interest. They gave tongue to interesting thoughts of my own soul, which had frequently flashed through my mind, and died away for want of utterance. The moral which I gained from the dialogue was the power of truth over the conscience of even a slaveholder. What I got from Sheridan was a bold denunciation of slavery, and a powerful vindication of human rights. The reading of these documents enabled me to utter my thoughts, and to meet the arguments brought forward to sustain slavery; but while they relieved me of one difficulty, they brought on another even more painful than the one of which I was relieved. The more I read, the more I was led to abhor and detest my enslavers. I could regard them in no other light than a band of successful robbers, who had left their homes, and gone to Africa, and stolen us from our homes, and in a strange land reduced us to slavery. I loathed them as being the meanest as well as the most wicked of men. As I read and contemplated the subject, behold! that very discontentment which Master Hugh had predicted would follow my learning to read had already come, to torment and sting my soul to unutterable anguish. As I writhed under it, I would at times feel that learning to read had been a curse rather than a blessing. It had given me a view of my wretched condition, without the remedy. It opened my eyes to the horrible pit, but to no ladder upon which to get out. In moments of agony, I envied my fellow-slaves for their stupidity. I have often wished myself a beast. I preferred the condition of the meanest reptile to my own. Any thing, no matter what, to get rid of thinking! It was this everlasting thinking of my condition that tormented me. There was no getting rid of it. It was pressed upon me by every object within sight or hearing, animate or inanimate. The silver trump of freedom had roused my soul to eternal wakefulness. Freedom now appeared, to disappear no more forever. It was heard in every sound, and seen in every thing. It was ever present to torment me with a sense of my wretched condition. I saw nothing without seeing it, I heard nothing without hearing it, and felt nothing without feeling it. It looked from every star, it smiled in every calm, breathed in every wind, and moved in every storm.

I often found myself regretting my own existence, and wishing myself dead; and but for the hope of being free, I have no doubt but that I should have killed myself, or done something for which I should have been killed. While in this state of mind, I was eager to hear any one speak of slavery. I was a ready listener. Every little while, I could hear something about the abolitionists. It was some time before I found what the word meant. It was always used in such connections as to make it an interesting word to me. If a slave ran away and succeeded in getting clear, or if a slave killed his master, set fire to a barn, or did any thing very wrong in the mind of a slaveholder, it was spoken of as the fruit of *abolition*. Hearing the word in this connection very often, I set about learning what it meant. The dictionary afforded me little or no help. I found it was "the act of abolishing"; but then I did not know what was to be abolished. Here I was perplexed. I did not dare to ask any one about its meaning, for I was satisfied that it was something they wanted me to know very little about. After a patient waiting, I got one of our city papers, containing an account of the number of petitions from the north, praying for the abolition of slavery in the District of Columbia, and of the slave trade between the States. From this time I understood the words *abolition* and *abolitionist,* and always drew near when that word was spoken, expecting to hear something of importance to myself and fellow-slaves. The light broke in upon me by degrees. I went one day down on the wharf of Mr. Waters; and seeing two Irishmen unloading a scow of stone, I went, unasked, and helped them. When we had finished, one of them came to me and asked me if I were a slave. I told him I was. He asked, "Are ye a slave for life?" I told him that I was. The good Irishman seemed to be deeply affected by the statement. He said to the other that it was a pity so fine a little fellow as myself should be a slave for life. He said it was a shame to hold me. They both advised me to run away to the north; that I should find friends there, and that I should be free. I pretended not to be interested in what they said, and treated them as if I did not understand them; for I feared they might be treacherous. White men have been known to encourage slaves to escape, and then, to get the reward, catch them and return them to their masters. I was afraid that these seemingly good men might use me so; but I nevertheless remembered their advice, and from that time I resolved to run away. I looked forward to a time at which it would be safe for me to escape. I was too young to think of doing so immediately; besides, I wished to learn how to write, as I might have occasion to write my own pass. I consoled myself with the hope that I should one day find a good chance. Meanwhile, I would learn to write.

The idea as to how I might learn to write was suggested to me by being in Durgin and Bailey's ship-yard, and frequently seeing the ship carpenters, after hewing, and getting a piece of timber ready for use, write on the timber the name of that part of the ship for which it was intended. When a piece of timber was intended for the larboard side, it would be marked thus— "L." When a piece was for the starboard side, it would marked thus—"S." A piece for the larboard side forward would be marked thus—"L. F." When a piece was for starboard side forward, it would be marked thus—"S. F." For larboard aft, it would be marked thus—"L. A." For starboard aft, it would be marked thus—"S. A." I soon learned the names of these letters, and for what they were intended when placed upon a piece of timber in the ship-yard. I immediately commenced copying them, and in a short time was able to make the four letters named. After that, when I met with any boy who I knew could write, I would tell him I could write as well as he. The next word would be, "I don't believe you. Let me see you try it." I would then make the letters which I had been so fortunate as to learn, and ask him to beat that. In this way I got a good many lessons in writing, which it is quite possible I should never have gotten in any other way. During this time, my copy-book was the board fence, brick wall, and pavement; my pen and ink was a lump of chalk. With these, I learned mainly how to write. I then commenced and continued copying the Italics in Webster's Spelling Book, until I could make them all without looking on the book. By this time, my little Master Thomas had gone to school, and learned how to write, and had written over a number of copy-books. These had been brought home, and shown to some of our near neighbors, and then laid aside. My mistress used to go to class meeting at the Wilk Street meetinghouse every Monday afternoon, and leave me to take care of the house. When left thus, I used to spend the time in writing in the spaces left in Master Thomas's copy-book, copying what he had written. I continued to do this until I could write a hand very similar to that of Master Thomas. Thus, after a long, tedious effort for years, I finally succeeded in learning how to write.

CHAPTER VIII

In a very short time after I went to live at Baltimore, my old master's youngest son Richard died; and in about three years and six months after his death, my old master, Captain Anthony, died, leaving only his son, Andrew, and daughter, Lucretia, to share his estate. He died while on a visit to see his daughter at Hillsborough. Cut off thus unexpectedly, he left no will as to the disposal of his property. It was therefore necessary to have a valuation of the property, that it might be equally divided between Mrs. Lucretia and Master Andrew. I was immediately sent for, to be valued with the other property. Here again my feelings rose up in detestation of slavery. I had now a new conception of my degraded condition. Prior to this, I had become, if not insensible to my lot, at least partly so. I left Baltimore with a young heart overborne with sadness, and a soul full of apprehension. I took passage with Captain Rowe, in the schooner Wild Cat, and, after a sail of about twenty-four hours, I found myself near the place of my birth. I had now been absent from it almost, if not quite, five years. I, however, remembered the place very well. I was only about five years old when I left it to go and live with my old master on Colonel Lloyd's plantation; so that I was now between ten and eleven years old.

We were all ranked together at the valuation. Men and women, old and young, married and single, were ranked with horses, sheep, and swine. There were horses and men, cattle and women, pigs and children, all holding the same rank in the scale of being, and were all subjected to the same narrow examination. Silvery-headed age and sprightly youth, maids and matrons, had to undergo the same indelicate inspection. At this moment, I saw more clearly than ever the brutalizing effects of slavery upon both slave and slaveholder.

After the valuation, then came the division. I have no language to express the high excitement and deep anxiety which were felt among us poor slaves during this time. Our fate for life was now to be decided. We had no more voice in that decision than the brutes among whom we were ranked. A single word from the white men was enough—against all our wishes, prayers, and entreaties—to sunder forever the dearest friends, dearest kindred, and strongest ties known to human beings. In addition to the pain of separation, there was the horrid dread of falling into the hands of Master Andrew. He was known to us all as being a most cruel wretch,—a common drunkard, who had, by his reckless mismanagement and profligate dissipation, already wasted a large portion of his father's property. We all felt that we might as well be sold at once to the Georgia traders, as to pass into his hands; for we knew that that would be our inevitable condition,—a condition held by us all in the utmost horror and dread.

I suffered more anxiety than most of my fellow-slaves. I had known what it was to be kindly treated; they had known nothing of the kind. They had seen little or nothing of the world. They were in very deed men and women of sorrow, and acquainted with grief. Their backs had been made familiar with the bloody lash, so that they had become callous; mine was yet tender; for while at Baltimore I got few whippings, and few

slaves could boast of a kinder master and mistress than myself;
and the thought of passing out of their hands into those of Master Andrew—a man who, but a few days before, to give me a
sample of his bloody disposition, took my little brother by the
throat, threw him on the ground, and with the heel of his boot
stamped upon his head till the blood gushed from his nose and
ears—was well calculated to make me anxious as to my fate.
After he had committed this savage outrage upon my brother, he
turned to me, and said that was the way he meant to serve me
one of these days,—meaning, I suppose, when I came into his
possession.

Thanks to a kind Providence, I fell to the portion of Mrs.
Lucretia, and was sent immediately back to Baltimore, to live
again in the family of Master Hugh. Their joy at my return
equalled their sorrow at my departure. It was a glad day to me. I
had escaped a fate worse than lion's jaws. I was absent from Baltimore, for the purpose of valuation and division, just about one
month, and it seemed to have been six.

Very soon after my return to Baltimore, my mistress, Lucretia,
died, leaving her husband and one child, Amanda; and in a very
short time after her death, Master Andrew died. Now all the
property of my old master, slaves included, was in the hands of
strangers,—strangers who had had nothing to do with accumulating it. Not a slave was left free. All remained slaves, from the
youngest to the oldest. If any one thing in my experience, more
than another, served to deepen my conviction of the infernal
character of slavery, and to fill me with unutterable loathing of
slaveholders, it was their base ingratitude to my poor old grandmother. She had served my old master faithfully from youth to
old age. She had been the source of all his wealth; she had
peopled his plantation with slaves; she had become a great
grandmother in his service. She had rocked him in infancy,
attended him in childhood, served him through life, and at his
death wiped from his icy brow the cold death-sweat, and closed
his eyes forever. She was nevertheless left a slave—a slave for
life—a slave in the hands of strangers; and in their hands she saw

her children, her grandchildren, and her great-grandchildren, divided, like so many sheep, without being gratified with the small privilege of a single word, as to their or her own destiny. And, to cap the climax of their base ingratitude and fiendish barbarity, my grandmother, who was now very old, having outlived my old master and all his children, having seen the beginning and end of all of them, and her present owners finding she was of but little value, her frame already racked with the pains of old age, and complete helplessness fast stealing over her once active limbs, they took her to the woods, built her a little hut, put up a little mud-chimney, and then made her welcome to the privilege of supporting herself there in perfect loneliness; thus virtually turning her out to die! If my poor old grandmother now lives, she lives to suffer in utter loneliness; she lives to remember and mourn over the loss of children, the loss of grandchildren, and the loss of great-grandchildren. They are, in the language of the slave's poet, Whittier,—

"Gone, gone, sold and gone
To the rice swamp dank and lone,
Where the slave-whip ceaseless swings,
Where the noisome insect stings,
Where the fever-demon strews
Poison with the falling dews,
Where the sickly sunbeams glare
Through the hot and misty air:—
Gone, gone, sold and gone
To the rice swamp dank and lone,
From Virginia hills and waters—
Woe is me, my stolen daughters!"

The hearth is desolate. The children, the unconscious children, who once sang and danced in her presence, are gone. She gropes her way, in the darkness of age, for a drink of water. Instead of the voices of her children, she hears by day the moans of the dove, and by night the screams of the hideous owl. All is gloom. The grave is at the door. And now, when weighed down by the pains and aches of old age, when the head inclines to the feet, when the beginning and ending of human existence meet, and helpless infancy and painful old age combine together—at this time, this most needful time, the time for the exercise of that tenderness and affection which children only can exercise towards a declining parent—my poor old grandmother, the devoted mother of twelve children, is left all alone, in yonder little hut, before a few dim embers. She stands—she sits—she staggers—she falls—she groans—she dies—and there are none of her children or grandchildren present, to wipe from her wrinkled brow the cold sweat of death, or to place beneath the sod her fallen remains. Will not a righteous God visit for these things?

In about two years after the death of Mrs. Lucretia, Master Thomas married his second wife. Her name was Rowena Hamilton. She was the eldest daughter of Mr. William Hamilton. Master now lived in St. Michael's. Not long after his marriage, a misunderstanding took place between himself and Master Hugh; and as a means of punishing his brother, he took me from him to live with himself at St. Michael's. Here I underwent another most painful separation. It, however, was not so severe as the one I dreaded at the division of property; for, during this interval, a great change had taken place in Master Hugh and his once kind and affectionate wife. The influence of brandy upon him, and of slavery upon her, had effected a disastrous change in the characters of both; so that, as far as they were concerned, I thought I had little to lose by the change. But it was not to them that I was attached. It was to those little Baltimore boys that I felt the strongest attachment. I had received many good lessons from them, and was still receiving them, and the thought of leaving them was painful indeed. I was leaving, too, without the hope of ever being allowed to return. Master Thomas had said he would never let me return again. The barrier betwixt himself and brother he considered impassable.

I then had to regret that I did not at least make the attempt to carry out my resolution to run away; for the chances of success are tenfold greater from the city than from the country.

I sailed from Baltimore for St. Michael's in the sloop Amanda, Captain Edward Dodson. On my passage, I paid particular attention to the direction which the steamboats took to go to Philadelphia. I found, instead of going down, on reaching North Point they went up the bay, in a north-easterly direction. I deemed this knowledge of the utmost importance. My determination to run away was again revived. I resolved to wait only so long as the offering of a favorable opportunity. When that came, I was determined to be off.

Kaye Gibbons

(1960–   )

The author of five highly successful novels before her thirty-fifth birthday, Kaye Gibbons stands today as one of the most respected writers in the South and promises to be one of the leading practitioners of southern fiction in the next century. She was born Kaye Batts in Rocky Mount, North Carolina, and spent her early years in the nearby community of Bend of the River. After her mother committed suicide in 1970, she remained for a short while with her father, then lived with different relatives until she moved into a foster home much like the one depicted in her first novel, Ellen Foster (1987). When she moved into the home of her older brother and his new wife in 1973, she entered a period of relative stability in her life, remaining with them for five years, until she graduated from Rocky Mount High School and entered North Carolina State University in Raleigh. Shortly afterward she transferred to the University of North Carolina in Chapel Hill, but her college education came to a temporary halt when she had to be hospitalized for manic-depression. It was during her recovery that she met and married Michael Gibbons, with whom she had three daughters. By 1985 she was taking classes again at UNC. There she showed her southern literature professor, the renowned scholar Louis D. Rubin, a thirty-page partial draft of a novel about a young girl whose mother had killed herself and left her with an alcoholic father. Upon Rubin's encouragement, Gibbons quickly completed Ellen Foster and made a name for herself as a new force to be reckoned with in southern literature. She has since written A Virtuous Woman (1989), A Cure for Dreams (1991), Charms for the Good Life (1993), and Sights Unseen (1995).

In 1996, Gibbons gained more than a million new readers in a matter of weeks when Ellen Foster and A Virtuous Woman were the *featured book club selections on* The Oprah Winfrey Show. *December of 1996 also witnessed the airing of the Hallmark Hall of Fame television movie adaptation of* Ellen Foster. *Gibbons currently lives with her children and second husband in Raleigh, where she has recently completed* On the Occasion of My Last Afternoon, *a historical novel spanning the years before the Civil War to the end of the nineteenth century.*

The following selection, "The First Grade, Jesus, and the Hollyberry Family," is published in its entirety here for the first time. Ms. Gibbons read this writer's reminiscence in April of 1996, when she was the Conson Wilson Lecturer at the second Southern Women Writers Conference at Berry College in Rome, Georgia.

"The First Grade, Jesus, and the Hollyberry Family"

THE DAY I STARTED school I wore a plaid dress with English smocking across the chest and a white, round collar; black patent leather shoes; lacy panties (bought new for the occasion); a crinoline; white, ribbed cotton anklets; and white cotton gloves with a line of three tiny pearls across the top of my hands. My usual dress wasn't so ornate, or expensive. I usually went about from one mudhole to the other in a striped dress made of a ticking fabric. It had a red scarecrow appliquéd on the front. My mother would never have let me wear the scarecrow dress on the first or any other day of school. This was 1966, the outer edge of the age when children were still sent to school looking like Dick and Jane. Mothers had the time and desire and peace of mind to pet and groom us. My hair was bobbed, making me resemble the little boy who lived, with his dog Tige, inside Buster Brown shoes. I had a barrel-shaped body, the kind that boxy, cap-sleeved undershirts ride up on. On that first day I wasn't wearing an undershirt, as it was one month too early. Undershirts were worn by all decent southern children from October to April. Common children of the ringwormy, runny-nosed, scab-picking variety who lived in the trailer park next to Chicken Stew's house, which was next to the pony pasture next to our house, were not held to this rule. Their mothers never seemed organized enough to remember the undershirt rule. They were too busy remembering other rules of trailer park life: (1) Slap your children in public. (2) Throw your husband's belongings in the yard on Saturday night. (3) Sell Avon cosmetics to your neighbors in an uninterested manner.

The dress probably came from Bib 'N Tucker, a children's shop on Main Street that catered to my hometown's version of the carriage trade, that is, people whose family vehicle was not necessarily a truck. I think my grandmother bought the dress for me. One of my chief memories of this store is of the counter display of birthstone rings. I wanted one desperately. On Saturdays my mother and I would wander in "just to look," and I would check to see if the May emerald was in stock. The shoes came from Roscoe Griffin Company, also on Main Street. They sold Stride Rite, Buster Brown, and Hush Puppy brands, and at the end of each transaction children were allowed to pick a cheap plastic surprise out of a treasure chest. I remember selecting a sheriff's badge. I liked telling other children what to do.

The socks and underwear came from Belk Tyler, a department store to which I felt a special inside connection because my second cousin worked in the shoe department. If you wanted to make extra money at Christmastime, "Call Gene!" a relative would exclaim. "I bet he can get you on at Belk's." One could ask why my mother didn't buy my shoes from Gene, especially if a little something might've been shaved off the price. It was said that Roscoe Griffin "carries a better shoe." I always felt a little shy around Gene, knowing my mother was marching me past his store, on down Main Street to be fitted with a better shoe.

The second the country store down the road from us displayed its sorry selection of school supplies, I hounded my mother into buying me several items I did not need. I did, however, need the red school bag. It was made of a sturdy, tarplike fabric, fastened by two metal hooks of the sort I believed secured Pilgrim shoes. She also bought a Fat Boy writing tablet and a blue, cloth-covered three-ring notebook upon which I immediately drew a picture of my true ideal of a schoolhouse and also misspelled my name, in indelible ink. Although I cannot remember my mother openly chastising me, I do remember something in her manner that said, "There. You have gone and ruined your nice notebook. You will have to live with it." I also remember that as soon as I learned how my name was really spelled, I felt like an idiot and hid the notebook in the dark bottom of a tall cedar chifforobe, where I was later to hide several gnarled Slinkys.

The store in which we bought the supplies is the store I use whenever one is called for in my writing. In fiction, I put the store under different management because I didn't like the people who owned the store in real life. In *A Cure for Dreams* a man named Porter runs the place. I named him Porter because this sounded, to me, like a fine, solid name for a small businessman. I caused his cash register to be repossessed during the Depression. He counted change out of his wife's muffin tin. I liked him tremendously, and when I needed another small businessman, a pharmacist in *Charms for the Easy Life,* I called on Porter again. I saw his face again, and his gentle ways. I know now that my problem with the real store owners was one of envy. They seemed to have a lot of the best of everything, and I wanted some of it. I believed them to be, in Kurt Vonnegut's words, "fabulously well-to-do." Other people's houses, including ours, seemed lifeless and forlorn by comparison. Their roof was not made of corrugated tin. It was shingled. Real grass, not wiregrass, grew in their yard, the kind that died in the winter and came back soft and lovely in the spring. Their house did not smell perpetually of boiled cabbage, and their furniture was not solely utilitarian. They seemed to have more household stuff than they needed, more dishes than they could use at one meal, more chairs than they could sit on, all signs of great wealth.

Here is a list of other things that as a child I associated with

great wealth: regular dental check-ups; a subscription to a magazine other than *The Progressive Farmer;* basement rec rooms; wool
coats of the sort worn by John-John and Caroline at their
father's funeral; croquet sets; framed art from Heileg-Myers Furniture Company; a crate of Coca-Colas in the pantry; a steady
flow of Twinkies, Ho-Ho's, and other store-bought treats; piano
lessons from someone other than the preacher's wife; Buicks and
Sunday afternoon drives to town to top off the tank of your
Buick with gasoline. Also, being Episcopalian or Jewish; taking
family vacations to Florida; living in a brick house; having a
bathtub and Mr. Bubble; having French Provincial bedroom furniture; going to the beach; owning a beach umbrella or staying
at a hotel that supplies huge, striped ones for you at no charge.
And having Mrs. Butterworth's Pancake Syrup. Not Karo.

Off I went to Coopers School, which was, as I later described
it in *Ellen Foster,* shaped like a shoe box. My mother led me to a
covered walkway, where my class was lined up to go to the
lunchroom. I have no idea why we were late. She introduced me
to my teacher, and although my mother rarely left the farm
except for Saturday trips to town and Sunday trips to her
mother's house in Elm City, expressed herself with clarity and
ease. She was forty-three then, tall and slender, with wavy
brown hair. During the week, she wore cotton shirtwaist dresses
belted with a narrow strip of matching fabric, usually a tiny flo-
ral print, and on weekends she wore nicer models of the same.
She didn't wear hats, although in the picture of her taken in
California in 1943 that appears on the cover of *A Cure for
Dreams,* she's wearing a turban. I imagine she was wearing this
not out of any sense of style, but because, perhaps, my father
snapped the picture of her as she was cleaning their apartment. It
would've been like her not to get dust in her hair.

How fortuitous that my teacher put me at the front of the
line marching to the lunchroom. There is, I'm sure, a direct cor-
relation between my position in line that day and my success in
elementary school. My classmates seemed to grow dumber on
toward the end of lunch, assembly, and recess lines, usually end-

ing with a girl as gormless as Eudora Welty's Edna Earle Ponder, who could chew up so much of her time trying to figure out how the loop on the "C" got through the "L" on the Coca-Cola sign.

Now, in memory I go from the front of the lunch line to the front of a line moving toward the auditorium, sometime later in the year, where we will receive religious instruction from a New Life Ministries preacher. This man came to school and raised, as it were, Holy Hell, three or four times a year until I graduated from the sixth grade. My imagination has realigned his features so that he looks exactly like Jim Jones of Guyana. The first-graders sat in the front rows. What a treat! He was a grandly sebaceous sort of southern preacher, stereotypical in every magnificent way. His text was a Bible he held open in one hand, and when he turned from Scripture to improvisation, he could not help but cry.

It was during my first encounter with him that I learned how God gives all children under twelve a certain amount of slack for being ignorant. If we died before our twelfth birthday, "the age of accountability," we would not burn in Hell. God was also lenient on pygmies, cannibals, and Africans in general. Coma victims, as long as they had gone into this state before they were twelve, also made the list. And finally, the minister said something like: "It boils down to this. It doesn't matter who you are or where you live, if you haven't heard The Word of God not one time in your life, you can slip through on the children–African pygmy–coma victim ticket." Then, he would move on to What Hell Looks Like. He spoke with the conviction of one who had, quite literally, been there and back. This was a true waste of his time because everybody in the auditorium was Baptist. We had a very clear understanding of Hell. The children who attended the crazed, renegade Baptist churches that had splintered off from similarly outrageous evangelical congregations could've gone to the bathroom in Hell in the dark. No wonder so many of these children turned out to be so worthless and mean, hardened as they were over the years by such relentless descriptions of doom. I like to think I turned out neither worthless nor mean. In fact, I may be a better person and a better writer because I paid attention every time I was told What Hell Looks Like. It is still hard for me to believe that I will not spend eternity in blazing agony. The preacher stocked me with a load of vivid and frightful images to be used in fiction. He spoke almost entirely in metaphor and simile, making an imaginary place seem more real than the life I was living at that moment. This is one of the attributes that separates a good story of dramatic realism from a bad one. *Did it seem real to you? Could you believe it happened?* Even writers of magical realism, like Gabriel García Marquez, are able, like the preacher, to make me believe that what does not appear possible is not only possible but inevitable. Carpets will fly. I will dangle over a fiery furnace.

The preacher would also explain that the world was going to end any minute now because of World Communism. The advent of this evil was the main indicator that God was perturbed with humanity. He said that when the world ended trumpets would sound and clouds would part and Jesus would step out and wow us all. Sort of the way Jackie Gleason did at the beginning of his show. But there would be no June Taylor dancers. Oh, Hell no. The saved would be sucked up into Heaven, where there would no doubt be much gloating and back slapping, and the sinners would maul each other during the Battle of Armageddon. Living and dead sinners. Gravestones would slide back, coffins would rise and open and release sinners who were now doubly evil by virtue of having been exposed to all the other unsaved souls. Like prisoners we hear about who come out of the Big House twice as hateful as before they went in. After this great war, God would destroy the planet. This was awfully bad news, as I didn't want 1966 to end. Not with my mother so healthy and my father so sober. Pop-Tarts, Barbie, and Hawaiian Punch, for Jesus' sake, had just been *invented*.

Although the preacher couldn't name an exact date, he said what all preachers said about the time of our great appointment: "Jesus will come when you least expect him. He will come in the twinkling of an eye." That is a direct quote, and what a fine one it is. *The twinkling of an eye.* This is an indirect quote: "If you, for one minute, take your mind off God, THAT is when he'll come. He will surprise you." A sneak attack. The only thing I could do to avoid this messy, unscheduled end of the world was to think about Him all the time, like the Salinger character with her incessant Jesus prayer.

I vowed to think about God all the time as soon as the preacher offered the invitation, that is, as soon as he asked all evil youngsters in the audience to come forward and confess their sins before God and man. I was always embarrassed for people who actually did this with apparent sincerity. Once, at a Billy Graham Crusade, I saw maybe a thousand evil sinners come down out of the football stands and flock onto the field. This sort of wholesale salvation has always, at least in the South, had the reputation of not being quite as effective as proclamations of faith made in tiny churches where everybody knows you and can call you a backslider the next time you curse, drink, philander, and smoke, dip, or chew tobacco. The elementary school call never yielded any converts.

Am I saved? Yes. I was to be saved in 1968, the year much of America was in dire need of salvation. My cousin answered the call at church one Sunday morning, and not to be outdone, I went forward as well. Had she been marching to the altar to take part in blood sacrifice, I would've followed her. The point was not to let this girl, whom I considered an intellectual cripple, get one up on me. The following Sunday the preacher led us down into an outsize aquarium that was housed in a niche high above the pulpit, squeezed our nostrils shut, said something biblical, leaned us back, submerged us, and then yanked us back up. He had on waders. I had somehow forgotten to take off the bloomers that went with my shorty pajamas when I dressed that morning, and thus they filled like balloons and had to be squeezed before I could get back out of the aquarium. To my highly saved little cousin, this suggested a damning cynicism that would make me grow up and do something perverse, like writing novels. The floating bloomers may have negated my salvation.

What became of the pledge to keep Jesus on the brain at all times? I remember remembering it standing in line to leave the auditorium, and I remember forgetting it somewhere on the way to my classroom, which, like all elementary school rooms, smelled of crayons. My youngest daughter, a second-grader, comes into my office each day after school and nudges her head underneath my arm, like a cat. Her hair always smells, I tell her, like school. She smells as if she spent her day inside the supply cabinet with all the construction paper and Elmer's glue and fat, indestructible crayons. I was in love with the rigid order in which all the paints and books and learning toys were kept. A place for everything. The books were kept on a small bookshelf between the girls' and boys' bathrooms. I see my teacher standing in front of me, saying something to the effect that I had to find something that would hold my attention. She showed me a Dr. Seuss book. I read a page or two and handed it back to her, saying whatever a child would've said in 1966 to convey the message, "Get real."

We went to the school library, where I was shown the tall bookcases full of Easy Readers. There I found a book about a boy named Caleb, one about a New England boy who tapped maple trees with his father and wore a hat with earflaps, and best of all, a *Ginn Basic Reader* with a "New Words in this Book" section in the back. It was called *Around the Corner*. A few years ago I found a copy of this book at a yard sale and have told my daughters, perhaps one too many times, what it meant to me as a young reader. The first story, "Here Comes the Parade," is about three children named Ben, Joe, and Mary Ann. They're standing at the window of their high-rise apartment watching a balloon parade. "The three children laughed at the funny big balloons." They move away from the window and watch the parade on television with Mother.

Another swell story was "The Hollyberrys at the Shore." The Hollyberrys' dog, named Puppy, barks at the water and helps

Jerry and Jean dig for treasure, which turns out to be a box lunch packed by their clever and attentive parents, who, for some reason, are dressed in long-sleeve shirts and slacks. "There was cold turkey and bread and butter. There were apples and ginger cakes and nuts." I started at this stage in my life of reading to ask questions about stories. Why, for instance, didn't the parents wear bathing suits? Didn't the food get grit in it, buried as it was in the sand? Did they have any mustard and mayonnaise? What did they drink? There wasn't a thermos pictured on the green picnic blanket. The father is shown wearing brown pants and loafers and sky-blue socks. Why couldn't he match his socks?

I think I was the only reader of *Around the Corner* who was concerned about certain inconsistencies in "The Hollyberrys at the Shore." Students with similar concerns about my novels write and ask me to explain myself. Their teachers encourage them to do this. I wish they would stop. The fact that I did not know why the Hollyberrys had nothing to drink on their picnic was my problem. Part of understanding literature is, simply put, figuring things out. Part of growing up is leaving things alone and forgetting about them if the answers promise to be stupid or inconsequential. As for the Hollyberrys, maybe Odille Osley and David H. Russell, the men responsible for the 1964 edition of the *Ginn Basic Reader,* put blue socks on the father because they liked that shade of blue. Or maybe they had a lot of blue paint they wanted to use up because it was time to quit and it would dry up overnight. Maybe they were nerds. Maybe they thought Mr. Hollyberry would fade into the sand unless he had a color on his person to set him off. Maybe they were trying to pick up the color of their summer sky. Maybe it doesn't matter. And, maybe it doesn't matter that the Hollyberrys didn't have anything to wash their mayonnaise-free turkey sandwiches down with. Maybe they didn't own a thermos. Maybe they brought Kool-Aid in a glass jar and then they saw a sign on the beach that said NO GLASS ALLOWED, and so Mr. Hollyberry, like a good father, put the jar back in the station wagon. Maybe this doesn't matter either. All that matters is that the story taught me an early literary lesson about the value of a little surprise in one's fiction. Family secrets, like picnic boxes, can be dug out of the sand by a dog named Puppy or a Faulkner character named Quentin Compson and exposed to the light of day.

Before my family life blew completely apart and nice children couldn't come play with me anymore, I had plenty of friends, all my first-grade pals who would've never thought to feel sorry for little Jean Hollyberry choking down her dry turkey sandwich. My best friend, Martha, appeared at a book signing a couple of years ago. She brought her mother with her, and as they stood in B. Dalton in front of a card table full of books and more Bic pens than I would ever, unless I were Rush Limbaugh, need, all I could think was, "I'm sorry you lived in that house." I didn't say this, of course. She was a very poor girl, that grinding, gray, hopeless poor of Walker Evans photographs. Even though my family didn't have much stuff, we weren't poor. We never had any money, but we weren't poor. Our house was painted. That was one of the ways I knew we weren't that bad off. My friend's house was black. It sat way back from the road and had a little crooked chimney pipe sticking out of the roof. If I had asked Martha, in 1966, if she thought the Hollyberrys had a jug of Kool-Aid in the station wagon, she would've looked at me with her sweet, blank face and said, "Huh?"

Harvey, another friend, lived down the road from her, also in an unpainted house. Harvey, with his many large teeth and his unctuous demeanor, messed in his pants throughout elementary school and carried about him an abhorrent odor like that of an unwashed thermos. He wouldn't have given a damn whether the Hollyberrys had mustard or mayonnaise, and in fact, if he read the story at all, he would've stopped as soon as he realized that it didn't have any cows or hogs in it.

Stuart, another first-grade pal, thought he was smarter than I was because he lived in a brick house. His parents worked in town. That's why they could afford a house that made me so severely envious that I once lied outright and told Stuart that I too had a brick house, a silly, futile lie as he knew exactly where I lived. His grades were always second to mine, but then, some-time in the third or fourth grade he won the school spelling bee with the word "boulevard." I was convinced that the principal, who was calling out the words, heard me wrong. In my memory I'm trying to tell Mr. Thorp B. Smith that a major, major injus-tice is taking place, but the thunderous applause for Stuart is too loud. Like some adults who specialize in attributing any and all deficiencies to childhood trauma, rather than laziness and inat-tention and refusal to get to work on time, I'm a lousy speller because Stuart lived in a brick house and had, therefore, all the advantages that would enable a child to spell boulevard. I have no idea what he's doing now. My instincts say he blew his early lead on me and is taking apart a lawn mower engine somewhere.

I rode the school bus home every afternoon along paved sec-ondary roads that, to me, now, seem too winding, thin and worn to have borne the jangling, swaying weight of children. My bus, Number 72, was driven by a high school boy named Ernie, who, on one very hot day, let me ride past my house, all the way to the end of the line, which was his backyard. I was afraid to get off the bus at home because a ridiculous chocolate-flavored kiddie-food product for which I had begged had escaped from its Tupperware container and soaked my clothing. I wanted to spend the night on his bus, live on it if possible. Ernie betrayed me and called my father, who came to collect me right away. He stepped up onto the bus and called to me. I was hiding underneath one of the seats. I remember thinking that mothers and fathers do not belong on school buses. The sight of people pulled out of their natural habitats and stuck else-where has always discomforted me. I was slightly alarmed, for instance, a few months ago to see my doctor in a restaurant. Here is where memory offers me two outcomes. I have no earthly idea which memory is the imposter. Did my father chuckle over having a baby daughter with so much gumption, or did he yank me up by the collar and drag me off the bus?

He took me home to my mother. I know this because I know

it was late in the day, near suppertime, and there was nowhere else we would've gone. She would've been cooking. She would've been there, because this was 1966. Not 1967 or 1968 or 1969 or 1970, the year she died. During those years, she wasn't always around. I would get off the school bus and see one of my aunts' cars in the yard and know that my mother had been taken to the hospital again. She would come home in a few days or weeks, looking older and older with each return. But in 1966 she still looked girlish. Her life wasn't ruined yet. Events in her household were not yet so bizarre as to be surreal. Like the family in *Cat on a Hot Tin Roof,* we were to become the converse of what southern families have always believed they, by virtue of manifest destiny and good manners, are supposed to be, only we lacked the money necessary to smooth our slide downhill. The vision of my mother holding my hand on the walkway, introducing me to my teacher, is the last one I have of the two of us together that is whole and round and complete. We look so incredibly, so indelibly normal.

William J. Grayson

(1788–1863)

The South Carolina planter, educator, statesman, and poet William J. Grayson is best known today for his pro-slavery poem The Hireling and the Slave *(1855), in which he sought to defend the South's "peculiar institution" of slavery by comparing it to the North's factory labor system. For all his professed belief in the southern practice of human bondage, though, Grayson was no advocate of secession. He broke from the ranks of South Carolina's "fire breathers" to advocate publicly the unionist position, which in turn made him something of a pariah after the shelling of Fort Sumter. As the country descended into war, Grayson mourned what he called in his autobiography "the demise of the great American Republic," even as he gave his reluctant support to the newly formed Confederacy.*

Written in 1862, Witness to Sorrow: The Antebellum Autobiography of William J. Grayson *was given its current title by historian and editor Richard J. Calhoun. It provides a relatively intimate glimpse into the mind of the privileged antebellum southern male at a time when members of that group were seeking to distinguish the region's newly emerging cultural identity from that of the larger nation in general, and of the North in particular. Part political memoir, part personal autobiography, the narrative ranges in subject matter from the moral character of the South and literary criticism of the day to modern methods of agriculture and their negative effects on social patterns in the region. The following selection is taken from the opening of the autobiography. Grayson's expression of reluctance to reveal his private feelings and thoughts reflects the general pattern of personal reticence in white southerners' autobiographical writings before the twentieth century.*

Witness to Sorrow:
The Antebellum Autobiography
of William J. Grayson

*T*HERE ARE few lives, Dr. Johnson remarks, of which the narrative could fail to amuse and instruct if faithfully and judiciously written. It may well be so, since every life has its lesson and romance. All that is necessary for the writer is to tell the story in a fitting manner—with just regard to truth on the one hand and a decent reserve on the other.

In every such narrative truth should be carefully respected. The story professes to be a true story not a fictitious one. But although the witness should be exact in saying what he knows, he must not say all that he knows. He should tell the truth only, but not the whole truth. To tell the whole truth is hardly possible and if it were possible it would not be advisable. The exposure of human infirmity that must follow such unreserved revelations could neither satisfy the reader's taste nor commend itself to his judgment. It would disgust not gratify. Even truth in its disclosures must be guarded by a modest reserve.

The occasional violaters of this sober rule have few imitators. The example of J. J. Rousseau warns not invites. Not many men are willing to be the heralds of their own infirmity or infirmities. If not able to abstain from doing a bad act most men are modest enough to be ashamed of it. They are not so base as to proclaim their infamy to the world. Boswell in his "Life of Johnson" reveals much of his own. He is always presenting himself in the most pitiable plight while he glorifies the wit or wisdom of his illustrious friend. He crawls in the dust to elevate his hero. He is glad to be contemptible if it elicits an oracle from his idol. His book, Macaulay says, is the best of biographies, "It has no second." Yet Macaulay would not have imitated the biographer's self abasement to surpass his work. Rousseau and Boswell are moral suicides. For Boswell we feel some kindness notwithstanding his meanness; he honoured virtue and venerated genius after his fashion. Rousseau is detestable—an impersonation of selfishness and sensuality with no one redeeming quality; without the natural affection that brutes themselves entertain for their young. Yet even these men Boswell and Rousseau have, no doubt, kept back from public view some secret places in their hearts which they had not hardihood enough to expose. As far as they have gone their example is not alluring. It warns, not invites.

A life then to be fully written should be written with some reserve. The frankness of the narrative must be kept within the bounds of a reasonable decorum. The human heart will not bear to be shown to the proper world divested of all drapery. It must be veiled like the body in decent clothing. In some such way it occurred to me in an idle hour to test the truth of the saying that any one's life may be so told as to impart instruction or amusement. I may confirm the adage or disprove it by relating mine.

I was born in November 1788, in the town of Beaufort, South Carolina. The town is situated in the Southern Corner of the State, on Port Royal, in a parish of islands. It was on one of these islands that Ribaut attempted in 1562 to establish the French Colony whose story is so disastrous. To Port Royal the Lords Proprietors ordered the expedition under Sayle in 1670. The colonists arrived in safety but afraid of Spanish hostility they abandoned the noble bay and its islands in a few weeks for the safer banks of Ashley river. Again in 1682 Lord Cardross began a settlement of Scotch adventurers in this beautiful portion of the State. They were assailed and dispersed by the Spaniards from Augustine in 1686. The country was nevertheless too inviting to be neglected and emigrants from the South Western counties of England soon found their way to its shores. They began the town of Beaufort in 1712 and once more, in

1716, Port Royal was desolated with the country around it. In the Spring of that year the Yamassee war broke out. The Savages killed many of the whites and drove the rest to seek shelter in Charleston. During the revolution of 1776, British troops occupied the luckless place and now in 1862 Northern invaders have seized the town, plundered the islands, demoralized the slaves and are occupied in drilling them for servile war. The marauders come as friends to restore peaceful relations by fire and Sword. They have union on their lips and confiscation in their hearts. They are missionaries of union and the constitutory of confiscation and blood shed.

The little town has not increased as American towns are accustomed to do. It is remarkable for the conservative property of standing still. Its population is no greater than it was fifty years ago and its condition as to all material advantages is very much the same. It has always been on good terms with itself nevertheless and for better reasons than usually accompany self complacency. It is quiet, healthy, religious, dresses well, is of good manners and morals and not a little addicted to mental cultivation. It has been eulogized moreover in the geographical works of Jedediah [sic] Morse. In the early editions of his book he praises Beaufort for its intelligence, hospitality and refinement. The account of Mr. Morse was written before the days of the modern Apostles that now flourish in New York and Boston and while Paul and his contemporaries were still authorities in all Christian churches amicable relations too existed in Morse's time among the States. The friendship of the Revolution had not yet been superseded by the hatred that now prevails between North and South. Subscriptions for various purposes were received and praise duly administered by New England travellers in the Southern States. It was a pleasant traffic for the Northern visitor and he was never weary of pursuing it. There was always something craved for a book, or a church, or a college, and money was never refused to those who asked it. Contributions are now lured in a different manner, by armed bands and ships of war. Courteous solicitation is changed into robbery and the eulogy of old into libel. And yet the virtues of the ancient town have gone on steadily increasing. It has become more and more remarkable for intelligence, piety and good works while those who praised it formerly now occupy it as enemies.

My father, John Grayson, was an officer of artillery in the continental army during the Revolutionary War. My father's father was an Englishman, a native of Yorkshire. He had carried on commercial business in the West Indies and afterwards in Carolina and Georgia. An old field near Satilla river in the last state still bears his name. He married the daughter of Col. Thomas Wigg whose father had been among the earliest emigrants from England to Port Royal. Col. Wigg dying in 1760 left five children, three daughters—Mrs. Hazzard, Mrs. Heyward and Mrs. Grayson—and two sons. One of the sons left a daughter, the mother of Captain John Rivers of James Island, the other had a son who died in early manhood without issue. The name so common at one time as to comprise a majority of the vestry in St. Helena parish is now confined to Mr. William Wigg and his family, lately residents of St. Lukes parish.

★   ★   ★

THE CHIEF PLEASURES I remember of my early boyhood are those I enjoyed in the house of my father's mother. I spent my holidays of Easter and Christmas at her plantation on Parris Island. I was a favourite child, the son of a favourite son and was petted accordingly. How well I remember the eagerness with which I looked forward to the months of April and December; how I regretted the rapidity with which the days passed by; how much I enjoyed them; how reluctantly at their close, I returned home to school and its troubles! My grandmother was an admirable specimen of loveable old age. I still see the dear old lady, at seventy, actively ordering her household. The white muslin cap with the broad black ribbon around it, the ample folds of the same material covering her neck and bosom, the clear blue eye undimmed by age, the grave and gentle expression of countenance, the fair and delicate features, all rise up before me as of yesterday. I never had from her a harsh word or angry look at my boyish mischief. All my memories of respecting her are of unmixed reverence and love.

She had a neighbour Mrs. Ann Rippon of her own age whose plantation lay on the opposite side of the island, on the Broad river shore, about three miles off. The brother of one of the friends had married the sister of the other and a son, the only offspring of the marriage, bound the two old aunts together in a closer intimacy. I was a frequent and willing guest at Mrs. Rippon's. Never was hostess more devoted to the comfort and enjoyment of her friends or better pleased at having a house full. She was wonderfully managing, always bustling, scolding and unwearily devoted to the callers. The finest hams of her own curing, the fattest turkies of her own raising, the choicest fish and oysters and puddings and pies and dainties without number were marshalled on her dinner table in suitable order. How she insisted on one's eating! There was no escaping. No knife and fork were ever active enough or sufficiently persevering at her table. If you eat never so much, she earnestly pressed you to eat more, not for form sake or imaginary politeness, but with an air of absolute distress to see you, as she would say, so delicate in your appetite or so little satisfied with her fare of her table. Should there be a dozen guests at her table her eye appeared to be on every one. If she saw the smallest falling off in the enjoyment of her dishes, she became at once restless, fidgety and unhappy at having nothing that could please you. Her plantation abounded in all good things. Her garden was excellent, producing every fruit and vegetable. Oranges were plentiful, figs without number, peaches and pomegranates in profusion. At that time and before people lived on their plantations and all useful and pleasant things flourished accordingly. Now plantations are cotton fields rearing a crop for foreign markets and little more. The fruits have almost disappeared. Oranges are rare, pomegranates formerly seen everywhere are seldom met with, figs are scarce and small. Few planters have a good peach or strawberry; worms destroy one and weeds choak the other. Formerly they were cultivated under the owner's eye and flourished accordingly. Even the fish and oysters of the coast and inlets were better of old or better looked after. They have become less abundant like the deer of the woods and the small game of the fields, or the people are less diligent in seeking them. The planter's whole attention now is absorbed by his cotton crop.

The cultivation of a great staple like cotton or tobacco starves everything else. The farmer curtails and neglects all crops. He buys from distant places not only the simplest manufactured article his brooms and buckets, but farm productions, grain, meat, hay, butter, all of which he could make at home. What is obtained in this way is sparingly consumed. If grain and hay are bought, horses, mules, cattle suffer from short supplies. Success or failure in the crop for market makes little difference in the supply of food. If the crop is short everything is put on half rations; if it succeeds, the planter seeks an additional enjoyment, a jaunt to the North, or a voyage to Europe, and mules, pigs, and cattle, fare little better than before. This is true in a greater or less degree of the whole cotton growing region. It is especially true of the low country planters in Georgia and Carolina. They devote themselves to their cotton fields. They buy their corn from North Carolina, their meat from Kentucky, their hay from New York, their butter from farmers a thousand miles away in a climate that makes it necessary to house and feed everything six months in the year. Under this system the country that might be the most abundant in the world is the least plentiful. The beef is lean, the poultry poor, the hogs a peculiar breed with long snouts and gaunt bodies, toiling all summer to keep themselves alive with partial success, and in the winter making a slender and uncertain return for the damage they have wrought to fields and fences. The planter buys salt butter from the North when he might enjoy homemade fresh butter all the year round. It is said he has no grasses. He may have green pastures of rye or oats through the winter and in summer make ample supplies of roots and hay. He neglects them all. With a hundred head of cattle he is without milk for his coffee. The practice is to turn the cattle out in November that they may take care of themselves among the woods and swamps. They are driven up in May, the calves marked, the cows milked, and butter made for a few months of summer. Twenty cows will then produce what a good dairy cow yields in England. It never occurs to the planter to keep up a few cows and feed them. He goes on year after year buying salt butter and drinking coffee without milk. A friend of mine, in a sudden emergency, fell on a singular device to obtain milk which may illustrate the system that produced it. My friend and cousin, Mick O'Brien, was an Island planter, on a large plantation, with a fine stock of cattle. He did with them as his neighbours were accustomed to do; he turned them out in the winter to feed as they might around the woods and marshes. He had no milk, but he was alone and liked his coffee as well without it. One day however a family in a boat overtaken by bad weather stopt at his landing and claimed shelter and entertainment. Mick was the son of an Irishman and as generous as the day. He received them with warm hospitality. But in the family was a young child needing milk. What was our host to do? His cattle had been for months in the woods and were wild as deer. To hunt them up, pen them, milk them in the usual way would require a long time. The occasion was pressing. A brilliant idea suggested itself. He ordered his cattle minder to mount a horse and drive the cattle through the woods, posted his hunter at a convenient place and instructed him to shoot the best cow with a young calf that should pass in the herd. The order was obeyed, the cow knocked over, and speedily milked as she lay disabled on the ground; the child received its food and the calls of hospitality were answered by an improvement in dairy management not discreditable to the genius of the old Country and suggested by the customs prevailing in our own.

During the holiday times that I spent in the Country I learned the arts of fishing and shooting at an early age, as all boys do in Carolina. At first my fishing was confined to catching minnows with a pack thread line and pin hooks. Attended by a retinue of little negroes, I caught in the shallow creeks of the marshes, mud fish and sometimes an eel which we ran away from, thinking it a snake. Next I attempted yellow tail and whiting. In due time I became initiated in the noble sport of drum fishing. Port Royal, or Broad river as it is locally called, is the favourite haunt of the drum. It is a large heavy fish, weighing fifty or sixty pounds and sometimes more. It makes a singular noise, in Spring of the year like the tap of a drum, which explains its name. The sound is heard distinctly from the bottom of the river at a depth of five or six fathoms. The fish afford excellent sport to the fisherman and no bad dish for the table. Among sea or river delicacies the roe of the drum is an unsurpassed dainty. The fish bite only in the Spring of the year but seem never to leave the rivers in the vicinity of Port Royal. It is supposed that like many other productions of the Country they are not so numerous as formerly. The largest number ever caught, as far as I have heard, was caught a half century ago. In this great success it was my fortune to have a share. With ten lines, from half ebb to low water, we took ninety six great fish and when the sport was at an end the fish were biting as rapidly as before. Our bait gave out and we rowed away from the ground, in our loaded boat, unsated with the day's sport and eager to continue it. It was a beautiful day, a bright sky, a gentle South wind just sufficient to ripple the green sea water of the bay and moderate the warmth of an April sun and the landscape around us with Hilton Head and Parris Island and Saint Helena and the single palm tree on Dawes' Island looked out through the pure atmosphere, in all its beauty, clearly and distinctly defined. In the eagerness of competition through the day we lost a great number of fish after hooking them. The hook tore out, or the line broke, or the hook, or strap gave way and the mortified and impatient fisherman was obliged to stop and repair his tackle while his companions were catching more fish by his side. Since the great achievement of ninety six, I have never known more than forty drum caught in a day's fishing and that but seldom. It has become common to coil a whole tide and take only two or three. The drum is not confined to Port Royal. They are found as far North as New York and they are common on the coast of Florida, but no where except in Port Royal sound is drum fishing an institution and a jubilee cultivated and enjoyed by old and young, white and black, master and slave.

Zora Neale Hurston

(1891–1960)

Zora Neale Hurston was one of the luminaries of the Harlem Renaissance and is considered today to be among the most accomplished of African-American authors. Born and raised in Eatonville, Florida, the nation's first all-black incorporated township, she was exposed to a rich cultural heritage that, because of the virtual absence of whites in Eatonville, could be expressed without inhibition and circumspection. Later, she would draw upon that heritage as a folklorist, novelist, short story writer, dramatist, and autobiographer. In 1925, after intermittent studies at Howard University, Hurston came to Harlem and immediately introduced herself to the key literary figures of the Harlem Renaissance. There she proved equally adept at winning prestigious literary prizes for her fiction and securing the good graces of wealthy white patrons who wished to provide financial assistance to promising new writers. One of those patrons, Annie Nathan Meyer, arranged for her to continue her education at Barnard College, where she earned her degree in 1928. While at Barnard, Hurston's work in African-American folklore gained the attention of the renowned anthropologist Franz Boaz, who urged her to conduct fieldwork in the South that eventually resulted in the publication of Mules and Men *in 1935, considered to be the first study of its kind written by an African American. In addition to* Mules and Men *and another collection of folklore,* Tell My Horse *(1938), Hurston penned four novels (including the masterpiece* Their Eyes Were Watching God, *written in 1937), several plays, numerous short stories and essays, and an autobiography,* Dust Tracks on a Road *(1942). She collaborated with Langston Hughes on* Mule Bone, *a play celebrating African-American vernacular humor, but the project led to an acrimonious dispute between the two authors and was never pro-*

duced during Hurston's lifetime. After a series of personal and profes-
sional setbacks, Hurston returned to South Florida where she faded into
obscurity and poverty. Destitute at the time of her death, she was buried
in an unmarked pauper's grave in Fort Pierce, Florida.

Dust Tracks on a Road has begun to receive renewed scholarly
attention, but its critical reception has been mixed since its publication,
when some African-American reviewers objected to what they saw as
unrealistically positive depictions of race relations in the South. Not sur-
prisingly, whites responded more favorably to her treatment of race. (It
should be noted that her publishers "convinced" her to delete sections of
the autobiography that they deemed "objectionable" to white readers.)
More recently, Dust Tracks *has been faulted for the liberties the author*
takes with the facts of her life story. Nevertheless, it remains an impor-
tant work by one of the South's most gifted and enigmatic authors. The
following selection explores the effects of Eatonville's colorful oral culture
on the impressionable imagination of the young Hurston.

FROM *Dust Tracks on a Road*

NOTHING THAT God ever made is the same thing to
more than one person. That is natural. There is no
single face in nature, because every eye that looks
upon it, sees it from its own angle. So every man's spice-box seasons his own food.

Naturally, I picked up the reflections of life around me with
my own instruments, and absorbed what I gathered according to
my inside juices.

There were the two churches, Methodist and Baptist, and the
school. Most people would say that such institutions are always
the great influences in any town. They would say that because it
sounds like the thing that ought to be said. But I know that Joe
Clarke's store was the heart and spring of the town.

Men sat around the store on boxes and benches and passed
this world and the next one through their mouths. The right

and the wrong, the who, when and why was passed on, and nobody doubted the conclusions. Women stood around there on Saturday nights and had it proven to the community that their husbands were good providers, put all of their money in their wives' hands and generally glorified them. Or right there before everybody it was revealed that one man was keeping some other woman by the things the other woman was allowed to buy on his account. No doubt a few men found that their wives had a brand new pair of shoes oftener than he could afford it, and wondered what she did with her time while he was off at work. Sometimes he didn't have to wonder. There were no discreet nuances of life on Joe Clarke's porch. There was open kindnesses, anger, hate, love, envy and its kinfolks, but all emotions were naked, and nakedly arrived at. It was a case of "make it and take it." You got what your strengths would bring you. This was not just true of Eatonville. This was the spirit of that whole new part of the state at the time, as it always is where men settle new lands.

For me, the store porch was the most interesting place that I could think of. I was not allowed to sit around there, naturally. But, I could and did drag my feet going in and out, whenever I was sent there for something, to allow whatever was being said to hang in my ear. I would hear an occasional scrap of gossip in what to me was adult double talk, but which I understood at times. There would be, for instance, sly references to the physical condition of women, irregular love affairs, brags on male potency by the parties of the first part, and the like. It did not take me long to know what was meant when a girl was spoken of as "ruint" or "bigged."

For instance, somebody would remark, "Ada Dell is ruint, you know." "Yep, somebody was telling me. A pitcher can go to the well a long time, but its bound to get broke sooner or later." Or some woman or girl would come switching past the store porch and some man would call to her, "Hey, Sugar! What's on de rail for de lizard?" Then again I would hear some man say, "I got to have my ground-rations. If one woman can't take care of it, I gits me another one." One man told a woman to hold her ear close, because he had a bug to put in her ear. He was sitting on a box. She stooped over to hear whatever it was he had to whisper to her. Then she straightened up sharply and pulled away from him. "Why, you!" she exclaimed. "The idea of such a thing! Talking like dat to me, when you know I'm a good church-worker, and you a deacon!" He didn't seem ashamed at all. "Dat's just de point I'm coming out on, sister. Two clean sheets can't dirty one 'nother, you know." There was general laughter, as the deacon moved his foot so that I could get in the store door. I happened to hear a man talking to another in a chiding manner and say, "To save my soul, I can't see what you fooled with her for. I'd just as soon pick up a old tin can out of the trash pile."

But what I really loved to hear was the menfolks holding a "lying" session. That is, straining against each other in telling folks tales. God, Devil, Brer Rabbit, Brer Fox, Sis Cat, Brer Bear, Lion, Tiger, Buzzard, and all the wood folk walked and talked like natural men. The wives of the story-tellers might yell from backyards for them to come and tote some water, or chop wood for the cook-stove and never get a move out of the men. The usual rejoinder was, "Oh, she's got enough to go on. No matter how much wood you chop, a woman will burn it all up to get a meal. If she got a couple of pieces, she will make it do. If you chop up a whole boxful, she will burn every stick of it. Pay her no mind." So the story-telling would go right on.

I often hung around and listened while Mama waited on me for the sugar or coffee to finish off dinner, until she lifted her voice over the tree tops in a way to let me know that her patience was gone: "You Zora-a-a! If you don't come here, you better!" That had a promise of peach hickories in it, and I would have to leave. But I would have found out from such story-tellers as Elijah Moseley, better known as "Lige," how and why Sis Snail quit her husband, for instance. You may or nay not excuse my lagging feet, if you know the circumstances of the case:

One morning soon, Lige met Sis Snail on the far side of the road. He had passed there several times in the last few years and seen Sis Snail headed towards the road. For the last three years he had stepped over her several times as she crossed the road, always forging straight ahead. But this morning he found her clean across, and she seemed mighty pleased with herself, so he stopped and asked her where she was headed for.

"Going off to travel over the world," she told him. "I done left my husband for good."

"How come, Sis Snail? He didn't ill-treat you in no ways, did he?"

"Can't exactly say he did, Brother Lige, but you take and take just so much and then you can't take no more. Your craw gits full up to de neck. De man gits around too slow to suit me, and look like I just can't break him of it. So I done left him for good. I'm out and gone. I gits around right fast, my ownself, and I just can't put up with nobody dat gits around as slow as he do."

"Oh, don't leave de man too sudden, Sis Snail. Maybe he might come to move round fast like you do. Why don't you sort of reason wid de poor soul and let him know how you feel?"

"I done tried dat until my patience is all wore out. And this last thing he done run my cup over. You know I took sick in de bed—had de misery in my side so bad till I couldn't rest in de bed. He heard me groaning and asked me what was de matter. I told him how sick I was. Told him, 'Lawd, I'm so sick!' So he said 'If you's sick like dat, I'll go git de doctor for you.' I says, 'I sho would be mighty much obliged if you would.' So he took and told me, 'I don't want you laying there and suffering like that. I'll go git de doctor right away. Just lemme go git my hat.'

"So I laid there in de bed and waited for him to go git de doctor. Lawd! I was so sick! I rolled from pillar to post. After seven I heard a noise at de door, and I said, 'Lawd, I'm so glad! I knows dats my husband done come back wid de doctor.' So I hollered out and asked, 'Honey, is dat you done come back wid de doctor?' And he come growling at me and giving me a short answer wid, 'Don't try to rush me. I ain't gone yet.' It had done took him seven years to get his hat and git to de door. So I just up and left him."

Then one late afternoon, a woman called Gold, who had come to town from somewhere else, told the why and how of races that pleased me more than what I learned about race derivations later on in Ethnology. This was her explanation:

God did not make folks all at once. He made folks sort of in His spare time. For instance one day He had a little time on his hands, so He got the clay, seasoned it the way He wanted it, then He laid it by and went on to doing something more important. Another day He had some spare moments, so He rolled it all out, and cut out the human shapes, and stood them all up against His long gold fence to dry while He did some important creating. The human shapes all got dry, and when He found time, He blowed the breath of life in them. After that, from time to time, He would call everybody up, and give them spare parts. For instance, one day He called everybody and gave out feet and eyes. Another time He give out toe-nails that Old Maker figured they could use. Anyhow, they had all that they got up to now. So then one day He said, "Tomorrow morning, at seven o'clock *sharp,* I aim to give out color. Everybody be here on time. I got plenty of creating to do tomorrow, and I want to give out this color and get it over wid. *Everybody* be 'round de throne at seven o'clock tomorrow morning!"

So next morning at seven o'clock, God was sitting on His throne with His big crown on His head and seven suns circling around His head. Great multitudes was standing around the throne waiting to get their color. God sat up there and looked east, and He looked west, and He looked north and He looked Australia, and blazing worlds were falling off His teeth. So He looked over to His left and moved His hands over a crowd and said, "You's yellow people!" They all bowed low and said, "Thank you, God," and they went on off. He looked at another crowd, moved His hands over them and said, "You's red folks!" They made their manners and said, "Thank you, Old Maker," and they went on off. He looked towards the center and moved

His hand over another crowd and said, "You's white folks!" They bowed low and said, "Much obliged, Jesus," and they went on off. Then God looked way over to the right and said, "Look here, Gabriel, I miss a lot of multitudes from around the throne this morning." Gabriel looked too, and said, "Yessir, there's a heap of multitudes missing from round de throne this morning." So God sat there an hour and a half and waited. Then He called Gabriel and said, "Looka here, Gabriel, I'm sick and tired of this waiting. I got plenty of creating to do this morning. You go find them folks and tell 'em they better hurry on up here and they expect to get any color. Fool with me, and I won't give out no more."

So Gabriel run on off and started to hunting around. Way after while, he found the missing multitudes lying around on the grass by the Sea of Life, fast asleep. So Gabriel woke them up and told them, "You better get up from there and come on up to the throne and get your color. Old Maker is might wore out from waiting. Fool with Him and He won't give out no more color."

So as the multitudes heard that, they all jumped up and went running towards the throne hollering, "Give us our color! We want our color! We got just as much right to color as anybody else." So when the first ones got to the throne, they tried to stop and be polite. But the ones coming on behind got to pushing and shoving so till the first ones got shoved all up against the throne so till the throne was careening all over to one side. So God said, "Here! Here! Git back! Git back!" But they was keeping up such a racket that they misunderstood Him, and thought He said, "Git black!" So they just got black, and kept the thing a-going.

In one way or another, I heard dozens more of these tales. My father and his preacher associates told the best stories on the church. Papa, being moderator of the South Florida Baptist Association, had numerous preacher visitors just before the Association met, to get the politics of the thing all cut and dried before the meetings came off. After it was decided who would

put such and such a motion before the house, who would second it, and whom my father would recognize first and things
like that, a big story-telling session would get under way on our
front porch, and very funny stories at the expense of preachers
and congregations would be told.

No doubt, these tales of God, the Devil, animals and natural
elements seemed ordinary enough to most people in the village.
But many of them stirred up fancies in me. It did not surprise
me at all to hear that the animals talked. I had suspected it all
along. Or let us say, that I wanted to suspect it. Life took on a
bigger perimeter by expanding on these things. I picked up
glints and gleams out of what I heard and stored it away to turn
it to my own uses. The wind would sough through the tops of
the tall, long-leaf pines and say things to me. I put in the words
that the sounds put into me. Like "Woo woo, you wooo!" The
tree was talking to me, even when I did not catch the words. It
was talking and telling me things. I have mentioned the tree near
our house that got so friendly I named it "the loving pine."
Finally all of my playmates called it that too. I used to take a seat
at the foot of that tree and play for hours without any toys. We
talked about everything in my world. Sometimes we just took it
out in singing songs. That tree had a mighty fine bass voice
when it really took a notion to let it out.

There was another tree that used to creep up close to the
house around sundown and threaten me. It used to put on a
skull-head with a crown on it every day at sundown and make
motions at me when I had to go out on the back porch to wash
my feet after supper before going to bed. It never bothered
around during the day. It was just another pine tree about a hundred feet tall then, standing head and shoulders above a grove.
But let the dusk begin to fall, and it would put that crown on its
skull and creep in close. Nobody else ever seemed to notice
what it was up to but me. I used to wish it would go off somewhere and get lost. But every evening I would have to look to
see, and every time, it would be right there, sort of shaking and

shivering and bowing its head at me. I used to wonder if some-times it was not going to come in the house.

When I began to make up stories I cannot say. Just from one fancy to another, adding more and more detail until they seemed real. People seldom see themselves changing.

So I was making little stories to myself, and have no memory of how I began. But I do remember some of the earliest ones.

I came in from play one day and told my mother how a bird had talked to me with a tail so long that while he sat up in the top of the pine tree his tail was dragging the ground. It was a soft beautiful bird tail, all blue and pink and red and green. In fact I climbed up the bird's tail and sat up the tree and had a long talk with the bird. He knew my name, but I didn't know how he knew it. In fact, the bird had come a long way just to sit and talk with me.

Another time, I dashed into the kitchen and told Mama how the lake had talked with me, and invited me to walk all over it. I told the lake I was afraid of getting drowned, but the lake assured me it wouldn't think of doing *me* like that. No, indeed! Come right on and have a walk. Well, I stepped out on the lake and walked all over it. It didn't even wet my feet. I could see all the fish and things swimming around under me, and they all said hello, but none of them bothered me. Wasn't that nice?

My mother said that it was. My grandmother glared at me like open-faced hell and snorted.

"Luthee!" (She lisped.) "You hear dat young 'un stand up here and lie like that? And you ain't doing nothing to break her of it? Grab her! Wring her coat tails over her head and wear out a handful of peach hickories on her back-side! Stomp her guts out! Ruin her!"

"Oh, she's just playing," Mama said indulgently.

"Playing! Why dat lil' heifer is lying just as fast as a horse can trot. Stop her! Wear her back-side out. I bet if I lay my hands on her she'll stop it. I vominates a lying tongue."

Mama never tried to break me. She's listen sometimes, and

sometimes she wouldn't. But she never seemed displeased. But her mother used to foam at the mouth. I was just as sure to be hung before I got grown as gun was iron! The least thing Mama could do to straighten me out was to smack my jaws for me. She outraged my grandmother scandalously by not doing it. Mama was going to be responsible for my downfall when she stood up in judgment. It was a sin before the living justice, that's what it was. God knows, grandmother would break me or kill me, if she had her way. Killing me looked like the best one, anyway. All I was good for was to lay up and wet the bed half of the time and tell lies, besides being the spitting image of dat good-for-nothing yaller bastard. I was the punishment God put on Mama for marrying Papa. I ought to be thrown in the hogslops, that's what. She could beat me as long as I last.

I knew that I did not have to pay too much attention to the old lady and so I didn't. Furthermore, how was she going to tell what I was doing inside? I could keep my inventions to myself, which was what I did most of the time.

One day, we were going to have roasting-ears for dinner and I was around while Mama was shucking the corn. I picked up an inside chunk and carried it off to look at. It was such a delicate, blushy green. I crawled under the side of the house to love it all by myself.

In a few minutes, it had become Miss Corn-Shuck, and of course needed some hair. So I went back and picked up some cornsilk and tied it to the pointed end. We had a lovely time together for a day or two, and then Miss Corn-Shuck got lonesome for some company.

I do not think that her lonesomeness would have come down on her as it did, if I had not found a cake of sweet soap in Mama's dresser drawer. It was a cake of Pears' scented soap. It was clear like amber glass. I could see straight through it. It delighted my senses just as much as the tender green cornshuck. So Miss Corn-Shuck fell in love with Mr. Sweet Smell then and there. But she said she could not have a thing to do with him unless he went and put on some clothes. I found a piece of red and white string that had come around some groceries and made him a suit of clothes. Being bigger in the middle than he was on either end, his pants kept falling off—sometimes over his head and sometimes the other way. So I cut little notches in his sides around the middle and tied his suit on. To other people it might have looked like a cake of soap with a bit of twine tied around it, but Miss Corn-Shuck and I knew he had on the finest clothes in the world. Every day it would be different, because Mr. Sweet Smell was very particular about what he wore. Besides he wanted Miss Corn-Shuck to admire him.

There was a great mystery about where Mr. Sweet Smell came from. I suppose if Mama had been asked, she would have said that it was the company soap, since the family used nothing but plain, yellow Octagon laundry soap for bathing. But I had not known it was there until I happened to find it. It might have been there for years. Whenever Miss Corn-Shuck asked him where his home was, he always said it was a secret which he would tell her about when they were married. It was not very important anyway. We knew he was some very high-class man from way off—the farther off the better.

But sad to say, Miss Corn-Shuck and Mr. Sweet Smell never got married. They always meant to, but before very long, Miss Corn-Cob began to make trouble. We found her around the kitchen door one day, and she followed us back under the house and right away started her meanness. She was jealous of Miss Corn-Shuck because she was so pretty and green, with long silky hair, and so Miss Corn-Cob would make up all kinds of mean stories about her. One day there was going to be a big party and that was the first time that the Spool People came to visit. They used to hop off of Mama's sewing machine one by one until they were a great congregation—at least fifteen or so. They didn't do anything much besides second the motion on what somebody else did and said, so they must have been the common people.

Reverend Door-Knob was there, too. He used to live on the

inside of the kitchen door, but one day he rolled off and came under the house to be with us. Unconsciously he behaved a lot like Mayor Joe Clarke. He was roundish and reddish brown, and used to laugh louder than anything when something funny happened. The Spool People always laughed whenever he laughed. They used to cry too, whenever Mr. Sweet Smell or Miss Corn-Shuck cried. They were always doing whatever they saw other people do. That was the way the Spool People were.

When Mr. Sweet Smell left his fine house in the dresser drawer that day, he came through the kitchen and brought a half can of condensed milk for the refreshments. Everybody liked condensed milk for refreshment. Well, Miss Corn-Cob sneaked around and ate up all the refreshments and then she told everybody that Miss Corn-Shuck ate it. That hurt Mr. Sweet Smell's feelings so bad till he went home and so he didn't marry Miss Corn-Shuck that day. Reverend Door-Knob was so mad with Miss Corn-Cob that he threw her clear over the house and she landed in the horse trough, which everybody said served her just right.

But not getting married that day sort of threw Mr. Sweet Smell in a kind of fever. He was sick in the bed for several days. Miss Corn-Shuck went to see him every day, and that was very nice. He rubbed off some of his smell on her because she was so nice to come to see him.

Some people might have thought that Miss Corn-Shuck's green dress had faded and her silky hair all dried up. But that was because they didn't know any better. She just put on a brownish cloak over it, so it wouldn't get dirty. She would let me see it any time I wanted to. That was because she liked me better than anyone else except Mr. Sweet Smell. She lay under the mattress of my bed every night. Mr. Sweet Smell always went home to the dresser drawer. The Spool People slept on the sill under the house because Reverend Door-Knob used to sleep there. They couldn't do a thing unless they saw somebody else doing it. They wore a string around their waist, trying to dress up like Mr. Sweet Smell.

Miss Corn-Cob played a very mean trick once. Miss Corn-Shuck and Mr. Sweet Smell were going to get married down by the lake. The lake had kindly moved into the washbasin for the occasion. A piece of cold cornbread had turned into a magnificent cake. Plenty of egg-nogg had come out of a cake of shaving soap. The bride and groom were standing side by side and ready. When what did Miss Corn-Cob do? She shoved Reverend Door-Knob into the lake, because she knew he couldn't swim. Here everybody was waiting and nobody would have known where the preacher was if one of the Spool People had not seen him kicking down at the bottom of the lake and rescued him.

While he was getting dry and putting on a fresh suit of clothes, Miss Corn-Cob sent our old dominecker rooster to steal the wedding cake. So the wedding had to be put off until Christmas because then there would be plenty of cake for everybody. The Spool People said they were glad of it, because there ought to be enough cake to go around if you wanted a really nice wedding. The lake told everybody good-bye, jumped out in the yard and went on home. It could not stay off too long, because it would be missed and people would not know what to think.

Miss Corn-Cob went and hid down a gopher hole for a whole week. Every night she used to cry so loud that we could hear her at the house. You see she was scared of the dark. Her mama gave her a good whipping when she got back home and everybody stood around and said, "Goody! Goody! Goody! Goody! Goody!" Because that makes everybody feel bad. That is, no child likes to hear another one gloating "Goody!" when he is in trouble.

They all stayed around the house for years, holding funerals and almost weddings and taking trips with me to where the sky met the ground. I do not know exactly when they left me. They kept me company for so long. Then one day they were gone. Where? I do not know. But there is an age when children are fit company for spirits. Before they have absorbed too much of earthly things to be able to fly with the unseen things that soar. There came a time when I could look back on the fields where we had picked flowers together but they, my friends, were nowhere to be seen. The sunlight where I had lost them was still of Midas gold, but that which touched me where I stood had somehow turned to gilt. Nor could I return to the shining meadow where they had vanished. I could not ask of others if they had seen which way my company went. My friends had been too shy to show themselves to others. Now and then when the sky is the right shade of blue, the air soft, and the clouds are sculptured into heroic shapes, I glimpse them for a moment, and believe again that the halcyon days have been.

When inanimate things ceased to commune with me like natural men, other dreams came to live with me. Animals took on lives and characteristics which nobody knew anything about except myself. Little things that people did or said grew into fantastic stories.

There was a man who turned into an alligator for my amusement. All he did was live in a one-room house by himself down near Lake Belle. I did the rest myself. He came into the village one evening near dusk and stopped at the store. Somebody teased him about living out there by himself, and said that if he did not hurry up and get married, he was liable to go wild.

I saw him tending his little garden all day, and otherwise just being a natural man. But I made an image of him for after dark that was different. In my imagination, his work-a-day hands and feet became the reptilian claws of an alligator. A tough, knotty hide crept over him, and his mouth became a huge snout with prong-toothed, powerful jaws. In the dark of the night, when the alligators began their nightly mysteries behind the cloaking curtain of cypress tress that all but hid Lake Belle, I could see him crawling from his door, turning his ugly head from left to right to see who was looking, then gliding down into the dark waters to become a 'gator among 'gators. He would mingle his bellow with other bull 'gator bellows and be strong and terrible. He was the king of 'gators and the others minded him. When I heard the thunder of bull 'gator voices from the lake on dark nights, I used to whisper to myself, "That's Mr. Pendir! Just listen at him!"

I kept adding detail. For instance, late one afternoon, my mother had taken me for a walk down around Lake Belle. On our way home, the sun had set. It was good and dark when we came to the turning-off place that would take us straight home. At that spot, the trees stood apart, and the surface of the lake was plain. I saw the early moon laying a shiny track across the water. After that, I could picture the full moon laying a flaming red sword of light across the water. It was a road of yellow-red light made for Mr. Pendir to tread. I could see him crossing the lake down this flaming road wrapped in his awful majesty, with thousands on thousands of his subject-'gators moving silently along beside him and behind him in an awesome and mighty convoy.

I added another chapter to the Pendir story when a curious accident happened in the village. One old woman, Mrs. Bronson, went fishing in Blue Sink late one afternoon and did not return. The family, who had opposed the idea of a woman of Mrs. Bronson's age going off to Blue Sink to fish so late in the day, finally became worried and went out to hunt for her. They went around the edge of the lake with lanterns and torches and called and called, but they could not see her, and neither did she answer. Finally, they found her, though people were beginning to be doubtful about it. Blue Sink drops down abruptly from its shores, and is supposed to be bottomless. She was in the lake, at the very edge, still alive, but unable to crawl out. She did not even cry out when she heard herself being called and could discern the moving lanterns. When she was safely home in bed, she said that she had sat there till sundown because she knew the fish would begin to bite. She did catch a few. But just as black dark came on, a terrible fear came on her somehow, and something like a great wind struck her and hurled her into the water. She had fallen on the narrow inside rim of the lake, otherwise she would have sunk into the hidden deeps. She said that she screamed a few times for help, but something rushed across Blue

Sink like a body-fied wind and commanded her to hush-up. If she so much as made another sound, she would never get out of that lake alive. That was why she had not answered when she was called, but she was praying inside to be found.

The doctor came and said that she had suffered a stroke. One whole side of her body was paralyzed, so when she tumbled over into the lake, she could not get out. Her terror and fear had done the rest. She must have had two or three horrible hours lying there in the edge of the water, hard put to it to keep her face above water, and expecting the attack of an alligator, water moccasin, gar fish, and numerous other creatures which existed only in her terrified mind. It is a wonder that she did not die of fright.

Right away, I could see the mighty tail of Mr. Pendir slapping Old Lady Bronson into the lake. Then he had stalked away across the lake like the Devil walking up and down in the earth. But when she had screamed, I pictured him recrossing to her, treading the red-gold of his moon-carpet, with his mighty minions swimming along beside him, his feet walking the surface like a pavement. The soles of his feet never even being damp, he drew up his hosts around her and commanded her to hush.

The old woman was said to dabble in hoodoo, and some said that Pendir did too. I had heard often enough that it was the pride of one hoodoo doctor to "throw it back on the one that done it." What could be more natural then than for my 'gator-man to get peeved because the old lady had tried to throw something he did back on him? Naturally, he slapped her in to the lake. No matter what the doctor said, I knew the real truth of the matter.

I told my playmates about it and they believed it right away. I got bold and told them how I had seen Mr. Pendir turning into a 'gator at night and going down into the lake and walking the water. My chums even believed part of it in a way. That is, they liked the idea and joined in the game. They became timid in the presence of the harmless little man and on the sly would be looking for 'gator signs on him. We pretended a great fear of him. Lest we meet him in 'gator form some night and get carried off into the lake, and die on that terrible road of light.

I told them how he couldn't die anyway. That is, he couldn't die anymore. He was not a living man. He had died a long time ago, and his soul had gone to the 'gators. He had told me that he had no fear of death because he had come back from where other folks were going.

The truth of the matter was, that poor Mr. Pendir was the one man in the village who could not swim a lick. He died a very ordinary death. He worked too long in the hot sun one day, and some said on an empty stomach, and took down sick. Two days later he just died and was buried and stayed where he was put. His life had not agreed with my phantasy at any point. He had no female relatives around to mourn loud and make his funeral entertaining, even, and his name soon ceased to be called. The grown folks of the village never dreamed what an exciting man he had been to me. Even after he was dead and buried, I would go down to the edge of Lake Belle to see if I could run across some of his 'gator hides that he had sloughed off at daybreak when he became a man again. My phantasies were still fighting against the facts.

Harriet Jacobs

(1813–1897)

Author of the most well-known female slave's narrative, Incidents in the Life of a Slave Girl *(1861), Harriet Jacobs was born around 1813 in Edenton, North Carolina. Although she was orphaned while still very young, her maternal grandmother, a free black who owned her own home in town, played a defining role in her upbringing, providing young Harriet with a sense of belonging and stability that was something of an anomaly among slave families. After years of sexual harassment at the hands of her master, Jacobs went into hiding for an extended period, finally escaping to New England, where she was reunited with her son and daughter, whose freedom had already been purchased by their father, a wealthy white neighbor of her master's family. Jacobs wrote* Incidents in the Life of a Slave Girl *in her off hours during a period when she was employed as a domestic servant and nanny in the Massachusetts home of her sponsors, Mr. and Mrs. Nathaniel Willis. Whether from distrust or timidity, she hid her literary activities from her employers and assumed the pseudonym of Linda Brent to protect her identity when she published the narrative. In 1852, Mrs. Willis purchased Jacobs's freedom. During the Reconstruction period, Jacobs returned to the South where she worked with the Society of Quakers and other groups to bring relief to the freed slaves.*

A truly revolutionary book, Incidents in the Life of a Slave Girl *dared to address the then-taboo subject of slave women's sexual exploitation (it even alludes at one point to a male slave's sexual mistreatment at the hands of his master). By explaining to her predominantly female audience how the institution of slavery created the conditions in which any slaveholding home could become contaminated by sexual impurity, she lodged a critique of slavery that appealed to* some of the most basic beliefs of northern middle-class white women, who saw the home as a "separate sphere" in which women were the dominant moral force. Because of the sexual double standards of the day and the corresponding conventions of the genteel literary tradition, Jacobs was compromised in her agenda by her admission that she had an affair with her master's white neighbor. Though she attempts to explain her motivations (taking a wealthy and influential white lover gave her some degree of protection from her licentious owner), she must also resort to the melodramatic rhetoric of the sentimental novel's "fallen woman," begging "Pity me, and pardon me, O virtuous reader!" In the first of two excerpted chapters, Jacobs calls the reader's attention to the relationship between gender and race as she seeks to convince her master's wife that she has repulsed her master's advances. The second chapter recounts the violence that followed the news of Nat Turner's unsuccessful rebellion in nearby Southampton County, Virginia, and reveals the author's sharp wit as well as her sophisticated understanding of the relationship between class exploitation and racial privilege in the South.

FROM *Incidents in the Life of a Slave Girl*

THE JEALOUS MISTRESS

I WOULD ten thousand times rather that my children should be the half-starved paupers of Ireland than to be the most pampered among the slaves of America. I would rather drudge out my life on a cotton plantation, till the grave opened to give me rest, than to live with an unprincipled master and a jealous mistress. The felon's home in a penitentiary is preferable. He may repent, and turn from the error of his ways, and so find peace; but it is not so with a favorite slave. She is not allowed to have any pride of character. It is deemed a crime in her to wish to be virtuous.

Mrs. Flint possessed the key to her husband's character before I was born. She might have used this knowledge to counsel and to screen the young and the innocent among her slaves; but for them she had no sympathy. They were the objects of her constant suspicion and malevolence. She watched her husband with unceasing vigilance; but he was well practised in means to evade it. What he could not find opportunity to say in words he manifested in signs. He invented more than were ever thought of in a deaf and dumb asylum. I let them pass, as if I did not understand what he meant; and many were the curses and threats bestowed on me for my stupidity. One day he caught me teaching myself to write. He frowned, as if he was not well pleased; but I suppose he came to the conclusion that such an accomplishment might help to advance his favorite scheme. Before long, notes were often slipped into my hand. I would return them, saying, "I can't read them, sir." "Can't you?" he replied; "then I must read them to you." He always finished the reading by asking, "Do you understand?" Sometimes he would complain of the heat of the tea room, and order his supper to be placed on a small table in the piazza. He would seat himself there with a well-satisfied smile, and tell me to stand by and brush away the flies. He would eat very slowly, pausing between the mouthfuls. These intervals were employed in describing the happiness I was so foolishly throwing away, and in threatening me with the penalty that finally awaited my stubborn disobedience. He boasted much of the forbearance he had exercised towards me, and reminded me that there was a limit to his patience. When I succeeded in avoiding opportunities for him to talk to me at home, I was ordered to come to his office, to do some errand. When there, I was obliged to stand and listen to such language as he saw fit to address to me. Sometimes I so openly expressed my contempt for him that he would become violently enraged, and I wondered why he did not strike me. Circumstanced as he was, he probably thought it was better policy to be forbearing. But the state of things grew worse and worse daily. In desperation I told him that I must and would apply to my grandmother for protection. He threatened me with death, and worse than death, if I made any complaint to her. Strange to say, I did not despair. I was naturally of a buoyant disposition, and always I had a hope of somehow getting out of his clutches. Like many a poor, simple slave before me, I trusted that some threads of joy would yet be woven into my dark destiny.

I had entered my sixteenth year, and every day it became more apparent that my presence was intolerable to Mrs. Flint. Angry words frequently passed between her and her husband. He had never punished me himself, and he would not allow any body else to punish me. In that respect, she was never satisfied; but, in her angry moods, no terms were too vile for her to bestow upon me. Yet I, whom she detested so bitterly, had far more pity for her than he had, whose duty it was to make her life happy. I never wronged her, or wished to wrong her, and one word of kindness from her would have brought me to her feet.

After repeated quarrels between the doctor and his wife, he announced his intention to take his youngest daughter, then four years old, to sleep in his apartment. It was necessary that a servant should sleep in the same room, to be on hand if the child stirred. I was selected for that office, and informed for what purpose that arrangement had been made. By managing to keep within sight of people, as much as possible, during the day time, I had hitherto succeeded in eluding my master, though a razor was often held to my throat to force me to change this line of policy. At night I slept by the side of my great aunt, where I felt safe. He was too prudent to come into her room. She was an old woman, and had been in the family many years. Moreover, as a married man, and a professional man, he deemed it necessary to save appearances in some degree. But he resolved to remove the obstacle in the way of his scheme; and he thought he had planned it so that he should evade suspicion. He was well aware how much I prized my refuge by the side of my old aunt, and he determined to dispossess me of it. The first night the doctor had the little child in his room alone. The next morning, I was ordered to take my station as nurse the following night. A kind Providence interposed in my favor. During the day Mrs. Flint heard of this new arrangement, and a storm followed. I rejoiced to hear it rage.

After a while my mistress sent for me to come to her room. Her first question was, "Did you know you were to sleep in the doctor's room?"

"Yes, ma'am."

"Who told you?"

"My master."

"Will you answer truly all the questions I ask?"

"Yes, ma'am."

"Tell me, then, as you hope to be forgiven, are you innocent of what I have accused you?"

"I am."

She handed me a Bible, and said, "Lay your hand on your heart, kiss this holy book, and swear before God that you tell me the truth."

I took the oath she required, and I did it with a clear conscience.

"You have taken God's holy word to testify your innocence," said she. "If you have deceived me, beware! Now take this stool, sit down, look me directly in the face, and tell me all that has passed between your master and you."

I did as she ordered. As I went on with my account her color changed frequently, she wept, and sometimes groaned. She spoke in tones so sad, that I was touched by her grief. The tears came to my eyes; but I was soon convinced that her emotions arose from anger and wounded pride. She felt that her marriage vows were desecrated, her dignity insulted; but she had no compassion for the poor victim of her husband's perfidy. She pitied herself as a martyr; but she was incapable of feeling for the condition of shame and misery in which her unfortunate, helpless slave was placed.

Yet perhaps she had some touch of feeling for me; for when the conference was ended, she spoke kindly, and promised to protect me. I should have been much comforted by this assurance if I could have had confidence in it; but my experiences in slavery had filled me with distrust. She was not a very refined woman, and had not much control over her passions. I was an object of her jealousy, and, consequently, of her hatred; and I knew I could not expect kindness or confidence from her under the circumstances in which I was placed. I could not blame her. Slaveholders' wives feel as other women would under similar circumstances. The fire of her temper kindled from small sparks, and now the flame became so intense that the doctor was obliged to give up his intended arrangement.

I knew I had ignited the torch, and I expected to suffer for it afterwards; but I felt too thankful to my mistress for the timely aid she rendered me to care much about that. She now took me to sleep in a room adjoining her own. There I was an object of her especial care, though not of her especial comfort, for she spent many a sleepless night to watch over me. Sometimes I woke up, and found her bending over me. At other times she whispered in my ear, as though it was her husband who was speaking to me, and listened to hear what I would answer. If she startled me, on such occasions, she would glide stealthily away; and the next morning she would tell me I had been talking in my sleep, and ask who I was talking to. At last, I began to be fearful for my life. It had been often threatened; and you can imagine, better than I can describe, what an unpleasant sensation it must produce to wake up in the dead of night and find a jealous woman bending over you. Terrible as this experience was, I had fears that it would give place to one more terrible.

My mistress grew weary of her vigils; they did not prove satisfactory. She changed her tactics. She now tried the trick of accusing my master of crime, in my presence, and gave my name as the author of the accusation. To my utter astonishment, he replied, "I don't believe it: but if she did acknowledge it, you tortured her into exposing me." Tortured into exposing him! Truly, Satan had no difficulty in distinguishing the color of his soul! I understood his object in making this false representation.

It was to show me that I gained nothing by seeking the protection of my mistress; that the power was still all in his own hands. I pitied Mrs. Flint. She was a second wife, many years the junior of her husband; and the hoary-headed miscreant was enough to try the patience of a wiser and better woman. She was completely foiled, and knew not how to proceed. She would gladly have had me flogged for my supposed false oath; but, as I have already stated, the doctor never allowed any one to whip me. The old sinner was politic. The application of the lash might have led to remarks that would have exposed him in the eyes of his children and grandchildren. How often did I rejoice that I lived in a town where all the inhabitants knew each other! If I had been on a remote plantation, or lost among the multitude of a crowded city, I should not be a living woman at this day.

The secrets of slavery are concealed like those of the Inquisition. My master was, to my knowledge, the father of eleven slaves. But did the mothers dare to tell who was the father of their children? Did the other slaves dare to allude to it, except in whispers among themselves? No, indeed! They knew too well the terrible consequences.

My grandmother could not avoid seeing things which excited her suspicions. She was uneasy about me, and tried various ways to buy me; but the neverchanging answer was always repeated: "Linda does not belong to *me*. She is my daughter's property, and I have no legal right to sell her." The conscientious man! He was too scrupulous to *sell* me; but he had no scruples whatever about committing a much greater wrong against the helpless young girl placed under his guardianship, as his daughter's property. Sometimes my persecutor would ask me whether I would like to be sold. I told him I would rather be sold to any body than to lead such a life as I did. On such occasions he would assume the air of a very injured individual, and reproach me for my ingratitude. "Did I not take you into the house, and make you the companion of my own children?" he would say. "Have I ever treated you like a negro? I have never allowed you to be punished, not even to please your mistress. And this is the recompense I get, you ungrateful girl!" I answered that he had reasons of his own for screening me from punishment, and that the course he pursued made my mistress hate me and persecute me. If I wept, he would say, "Poor child! Don't cry! don't cry! I will make peace for you with your mistress. Only let me arrange matters in my own way. Poor, foolish girl! you don't know what is for your own good. I would cherish you. I would make a lady of you. Now go, and think of all I have promised you."

I did think of it.

Reader, I draw no imaginary pictures of southern homes. I am telling you the plain truth. Yet when victims make their escape from this wild beast of Slavery, northerners consent to act the part of bloodhounds, and hunt the poor fugitive back into his den, "full of dead men's bones, and all uncleanness." Nay, more, they are not only willing, but proud, to give their daughters in marriage to slaveholders. The poor girls have romantic notions of a sunny clime, and of the flowering vines that all the year round shade a happy home. To what disappointments are they destined! The young wife soon learns that the husband in whose hands she has placed her happiness pays no regard to his marriage vows. Children of every shade of complexion play with her own fair babies, and too well she knows that they are born unto him of his own household. Jealousy and hatred enter the flowery home, and it is ravaged of its loveliness.

Southern women often marry a man knowing that he is the father of many little slaves. They do not trouble themselves about it. They regard such children as property, as marketable as the pigs on the plantation; and it is seldom that they do not make them aware of this by passing them into the slavetrader's hands as soon as possible, and thus getting them out of their sight. I am glad to say there are some honorable exceptions.

I have myself known two southern wives who exhorted their husbands to free those slaves towards whom they stood in a "parental relation"; and their request was granted. These husbands blushed before the superior nobleness of their wives' natures. Though they had only counselled them to do that which it was their duty to do, it commanded their respect, and rendered their conduct more exemplary. Concealment was at an end, and confidence took the place of distrust.

Though this bad institution deadens the moral sense, even in white women, to a fearful extent, it is not altogether extinct. I have heard southern ladies say of Mr. Such a one, "He not only thinks it no disgrace to be the father of those little niggers, but he is not ashamed to call himself their master. I declare, such things ought not to be tolerated in any decent society!"

FEAR OF INSURRECTION

Not far from this time Nat Turner's insurrection broke out; and the news threw our town into great commotion. Strange that they should be alarmed, when their slaves were so "contented and happy"! But so it was.

It was always the custom to have a muster every year. On that occasion every white man shouldered his musket. The citizens and the so-called country gentlemen wore military uniforms. The poor whites took their places in the ranks in every-day dress, some without shoes, some without hats. This grand occasion had already passed; and when the slaves were told there was to be another muster, they were surprised and rejoiced. Poor creatures! They thought it was going to be a holiday. I was informed of the true state of affairs, and imparted it to the few I could trust. Most gladly would I have proclaimed it to every slave; but I dared not. All could not be relied on. Mighty is the power of the torturing lash.

By sunrise, people were pouring in from every quarter within twenty miles of the town. I knew the houses were to be searched; and I expected it would be done by country bullies and the poor whites. I knew nothing annoyed them so much as to see colored people living in comfort and respectability; so I made arrangements for them with especial care. I arranged every thing in my grandmother's house as neatly as possible. I put white quilts on the beds, and decorated some of the rooms with flowers. When all was arranged, I sat down at the window to watch. Far as my eye could reach, it rested on a motley crowd of soldiers. Drums and fifes were discoursing martial music. The men were divided into companies of sixteen, each headed by a captain. Orders were given, and the wild scouts rushed in every direction, wherever a colored face was to be found.

It was a grand opportunity for the low whites, who had no negroes of their own to scourge. They exulted in such a chance to exercise a little brief authority, and show their subserviency to the slaveholders; not reflecting that the power which trampled on the colored people also kept themselves in poverty, ignorance, and moral degradation. Those who never witnessed such scenes can hardly believe what I know was inflicted at this time on innocent men, women, and children, against whom there was not the slightest ground for suspicion. Colored people and slaves who lived in remote parts of the town suffered in an especial manner. In some cases the searchers scattered powder and shot among their clothes, and then sent other parties to find them, and bring them forward as proof that they were plotting insurrection. Every where men, women, and children were whipped till the blood stood in puddles at their feet. Some received five hundred lashes, others were tied hands and feet, and tortured with a bucking paddle, which blisters the skin terribly. The dwellings of the colored people, unless they happened to be protected by some influential white person, who was nigh at hand, were robbed of clothing and every thing else the marauders thought worth carrying away. All day long these unfeeling wretches went round, like a troop of demons, terrifying and tormenting the helpless. At night, they formed themselves into patrol bands, and went wherever they chose among the colored people, acting out their brutal will. Many women hid themselves in woods and swamps, to keep out of their way. If any of the husbands or fathers told of these outrages, they were tied up to the public whipping post, and cruelly scourged for telling lies about white men. The consternation was universal. No two people that had the slightest tinge of color in their faces dared to be seen talking together.

I entertained no positive fears about our household, because we were in the midst of white families who would protect us. We were ready to receive the soldiers whenever they came. It was not long before we heard the tramp of feet and the sound of voices. The door was rudely pushed open; and in they tumbled, like a pack of hungry wolves. They snatched at every thing within their reach. Every box, trunk, closet, and corner underwent a thorough examination. A box in one of the drawers containing some silver change was eagerly pounced upon. When I stepped forward to take it from them, one of the soldiers turned and said angrily, "What d'ye foller us fur? D'ye s'pose white folks is come to steal?"

I replied, "You have come to search; but you have searched that box, and I will take it, if you please."

At that moment I saw a white gentleman who was friendly to us; and I called to him, and asked him to have the goodness to come in and stay till the search was over. He readily complied. His entrance into the house brought in the captain of the company, whose business it was to guard the outside of the house, and see that none of the inmates left it. This officer was Mr. Litch, the wealthy slaveholder whom I mentioned, in the account of neighboring planters, as being notorious for his cruelty. He felt above soiling his hands with the search. He merely gave orders; and, if a bit of writing was discovered, it was carried to him by his ignorant followers, who were unable to read.

My grandmother had a large trunk of bedding and table cloths. When that was opened, there was a great shout of surprise; and one exclaimed, "Where'd the damned niggers git all dis sheet an' table clarf?"

My grandmother, emboldened by the presence of our white protector, said, "You may be sure we didn't pilfer 'em from *your* houses."

"Look here, mammy," said a grim-looking fellow without

any coat, "you seem to feel mighty gran' 'cause you got all them 'ere fixens. White folks oughter have 'em all."

His remarks were interrupted by a chorus of voices shouting, "We's got 'em! We's got 'em! Dis 'ere yaller gal's got letters!"

There was a general rush for the supposed letter, which, upon examination, proved to be some verses written to me by a friend. In packing away my things, I had overlooked them. When their captain informed them of their contents, they seemed much disappointed. He inquired of me who wrote them. I told him it was one of my friends. "Can you read them?" he asked. When I told him I could, he swore, and raved, and tore the paper into bits. "Bring me all your letters!" said he, in a commanding voice. I told him I had none. "Don't be afraid," he continued, in an insinuating way. "Bring them all to me. Nobody shall do you any harm." Seeing I did not move to obey him, his pleasant tone changed to oaths and threats. "Who writes to you? half free niggers?" inquired he. I replied, "O, no; most of my letters are from white people. Some request me to burn them after they are read, and some I destroy without reading."

An exclamation of surprise from some of the company put a stop to our conversation. Some silver spoons which ornamented an old-fashioned buffet had just been discovered. My grand-mother was in the habit of preserving fruit for many ladies in the town, and of preparing suppers for parties; consequently she had many jars of preserves. The closet that contained these was next invaded, and the contents tasted. One of them, who was helping himself freely, tapped his neighbor on the shoulder, and said, "Wal done! Don't wonder de niggers want to kill all de white folks, when dey live on 'sarves" [meaning preserves]. I stretched out my hand to take the jar, saying, "You were not sent here to search for sweetmeats."

"And what *were* we sent for?" said the captain, bristling up to me. I evaded the question.

The search of the house was completed, and nothing found to condemn us. They next proceeded to the garden, and knocked about every bush and vine, with no better success. The captain called his men together, and, after a short consultation, the order to march was given. As they passed out of the gate, the captain turned back, and pronounced a malediction on the house. He said it ought to be burned to the ground, and each of its inmates receive thirty-nine lashes. We came out of this affair very fortunately; not losing any thing except some wearing apparel.

Towards evening the turbulence increased. The soldiers, stimulated by drink, committed still greater cruelties. Shrieks and shouts continually rent the air. Not daring to go to the door, I peeped under the window curtain. I saw a mob dragging along a number of colored people, each white man, with his musket upraised, threatening instant death if they did not stop their shrieks. Among the prisoners was a respectable old colored minister. They had found a few parcels of shot in his house, which his wife had for years used to balance her scales. For this they were going to shoot him on Court House Green. What a spectacle was that for a civilized country! A rabble, staggering under intoxication, assuming to be the administrators of justice!

The better class of the community exerted their influence to save the innocent, persecuted people; and in several instances they succeeded, by keeping them shut up in jail till the excitement abated. At last the white citizens found that their own property was not safe from the lawless rabble they had summoned to protect them. They rallied the drunken swarm, drove them back into the country, and set a guard over the town.

The next day, the town patrols were commissioned to search colored people that lived out of the city; and the most shocking outrages were committed with perfect impunity. Every day for a fortnight, if I looked out, I saw horsemen with some poor panting negro tied to their saddles, and compelled by the lash to keep up with their speed, till they arrived at the jail yard. Those who had been whipped too unmercifully to walk were washed with brine, tossed into a cart, and carried to jail. One black man, who had not fortitude to endure scourging, promised to give information about the conspiracy. But it turned out that he knew nothing at all. He had not even heard the name of Nat Turner. The poor fellow had, however, made up a story, which augmented his own sufferings and those of the colored people.

The day patrol continued for some weeks, and at sundown a night guard was substituted. Nothing at all was proved against the colored people, bond or free. The wrath of the slaveholders was somewhat appeased by the capture of Nat Turner. The imprisoned were released. The slaves were sent to their masters, and the free were permitted to return to their ravaged homes. Visiting was strictly forbidden on the plantations. The slaves begged the privilege of again meeting at their little church in the woods, with their burying ground around it. It was built by the colored people, and they had no higher happiness than to meet there and sing hymns together, and pour out their hearts in spontaneous prayer. Their request was denied, and the church was demolished. They were permitted to attend the white churches, a certain portion of the galleries being appropriated to their use. There, when every body else had partaken of the communion, and the benediction had been pronounced, the minister said, "Come down, now, my colored friends." They obeyed the summons, and partook of the bread and wine, in commemoration of the meek and lowly Jesus, who said, "God is your Father, and all ye are brethren."

Belle Kearney

(1863–1939)

Social reformer Belle Kearney belonged to a prominent Mississippi family that, like most families in the South of the late nineteenth century, discouraged its women from seeking an active role in the public sphere. While New England women had participated in numerous organizations and public campaigns since the 1848 Seneca Falls convention, their southern counterparts had restricted their work to localized, mostly church-sponsored activities, generally avoiding reform issues. Kearney became involved in the Women's Christian Temperance Union, one of the first major national reform groups to gain wide support from southern women. When the WCTU allied itself with the women's suffrage movement, she became active in that cause as well, eventually rising to the presidency of the Mississippi Woman Suffrage Association and state chapter of the WCTU by the early part of the century. Kearney earned a place in history when she became the first woman to be elected to the Mississippi state senate and in 1921 she made a failed bid for the U.S. Senate. In addition to her autobiography, A Slaveholder's Daughter *(1900), she is the author of a work of fiction,* Conqueror or Conquered *(1921).*

Although A Slaveholder's Daughter *has virtually been ignored by scholars, it represents the beginnings of a southern white women's autobiographical tradition in the sense that it was, unlike Mary Chesnut's* A Civil War Diary *(1884) and others of its kind, written expressly for publication. Taking as its central subject her activities in the WCTU, it documents the general break from traditional constraints that some women in the South were able to effect in the last decades of the nineteenth century. Kearney expresses a moderate feminism in her autobiography, but her egalitarianism is severely compromised by her pater-*

nalistic racism. *In fact, Kearney's views were not an anomaly among her peers; women suffragists in the South argued that adoption of woman suffrage could help usher in a new era of political white supremacy, so long as property and educational qualifications were attached that would exclude African Americans from participating in the electoral process. Nevertheless, Kearney's racial views by no means make her a southern traditionalist. In her autobiography she links the emergence of the women's movement in the South to "the evolution of events set in motion by the bombardment of Fort Sumter" (i.e., the defeat of the Confederacy and the gradual disintegration of the Old South). In the following excerpt, Kearney recounts her father's refusal to let her study law under him and describes her growing impatience with the white southern patriarchy.*

FROM *A Slaveholder's Daughter*

We are haunted by an ideal life, and it is because we have within us the beginning and the possibility of it.

— PHILLIPS BROOKS

My early and invincible love of reading, I would not exchange for the treasures of India.

— GIBBON

SINCE THE CLOSE of the civil war as complete a change had taken place in the South as followed the revolution in France of the latter part of the eighteenth century. Under the new régime which began with the liberation of over 4,000,000 slaves the upper and the middle classes have become amalgamated by the action of the elements of circumstance.

Many of the old families, boasting a long line of descent from blue-blooded and distinguished ancestors, soon were the most sorely pressed financially. Thousands of middle-aged—and younger—men had come home from the last battle-field maimed by wounds or weakened in health by privations. When they entered the gloom of lost fortunes, added to the sorrows of a lost cause, they quickly sank under the triple weight. Hundreds of them were followed to the grave by communities that sorely felt the need of their ripe judgment, their accustomed leadership. The stress of poverty, the paralysis of indolence and the want of purpose benumbed the energies and stultified the pride of other descendants of the old slaveholders, many of whom bore the pitiless stamp of incapacity to wrest success out of new conditions.

The middle classes were equal to the emergency. Adjustment is easier than readjustment. Trained to activities they sprang rapidly to the front, becoming possessors of wealth and leaders in church and state. The inevitable in social life has developed. Marriage into the higher class followed as a matter of course with the middle, for the one wanted prestige and the other money. The distinctions of half a century ago have gradually lost their outlines. The "strenuous life" of the day now engrosses the mind of the Southerner more than the ancient "family tree."

Next to the destruction of caste, the most radical change that has followed in the wake of the surrender of the Confederate armies is that young Southern men and women have learned that work is honorable. Idleness has grown to be a shame. No boy and girl can now hope to realize their highest destiny except through hard, earnest toil of hands or brain. The unsafe and unnatural code of the manorial leisure of other days vanished with slavery. This transition of sentiment, however, has been the slow growth of years. The blossoming "of the tree" whose "leaves" are "for the healing of the Nations" had scarcely begun when my feet stood on the threshold of eager life,—wrestling in strong agony with hopeless but unconquerable purposes.

One of the most unfortunate conditions in all the world is a state of aimlessness. It saps the springs of power and dulls the finest soul. It drags down and destroys. I was only fifteen. What *was* my future to be? Never to go to the Academy again? Never to attend a Northern college? Never to cross the sea? What *was* there for me to do? How *could* the days be filled so as to keep down the heart-break? Those were the questions that were never stilled. If my life had to be spent on the plantation, and if living meant no more for me than it meant for the women about me, what was the use of reading, of trying to cultivate my mind when it would have the effect of making me more miserable and of widening the intellectual gulf that already stretched between most of the neighbors and myself? What a terrible thing life seemed! And how every impulse of my being hated it with an immeasurable hatred! In those days I died ten thousand deaths. I died to God and to humanity.

From the hour of leaving school in Canton a deadness settled upon my soul. "The door was shut." The night closed in. That was the beginning of an unbelief that haunted me for ten dreary agonizing years. My natural tendency to *questioning* had been intensified by the environments of my childhood; but the spirit of inquiry had not led me further than the human side. The orthodox version of Creator and creation was accepted as credulously as the air that was breathed or the perfume of flowers. It was only the grindings of poverty, the raspings of the jagged edges of every-day existence and the perpetual witnessing of misery in the world about me that caused me first to ask: What is life? Up to the age of fifteen my soul had hoped and prayed and *listened* for the voice of God. I *believed* in Him, and *waited*— not patiently but imperatively,—but—I *believed* and *waited*. In the great storm that engulfed me at that time my faith let go its moorings, and I found myself drifting, without a gleam of light, out upon the waste of midnight waters known as skepticism. As the darkness deepened and thoughts heavy with increasing doubts surged through my brain like a lava-tide, my soul demanded verification for my convictions.

There was no one in the home with whom conversation on such a subject would have been particularly satisfying, so, in desperation a search was made through the library for some book that would answer my queries; but nothing was found touching infidelity except the materialism of certain philosophers. These works were devoured until my mind became saturated with their ideas. I grew to despise Christianity and sneered at every profession of trust in a Supreme Being. Church members were observed critically and every sin and inconsistency which was discovered in them brought out that degree of derision and contempt to which only youth, ignorance and prejudice are equal. Mother had a habit of devoting several hours each morning to study of the Bible. On seeing her surrounded by rows of commentaries and bending over the Scriptures, comparing passages or memorizing texts, I felt my heart hardening, and was conscious of an increased aversion to religion. Our home was headquarters for all Methodist ministers who passed that way, to mother's intense delight and my intense disgust. It was a rule of mine to avoid them whenever possible. My voluntary entrance into the church dated from my twelfth year, during a great revival. Now, when the scene occurred to me I laughed at myself for having yielded to so much emotion, and requested that my name be removed from the church books.

Our home was headquarters not only for Methodist preachers but as well for Democratic politicians. Every candidate for office in the county found his way there, to mother's infinite chagrin and the unbounded delight of father and me. Mother often declined to appear at the table, so I would preside and afterward go into the parlor and talk with the visitors for hours on the situation of public affairs. The aspirants were of all descriptions—from the sleek, town-bred lawyer, "out" for the Senate, to the thin, country granger, who yearned to be a constable. They afforded me ample opportunity to learn the methods of political campaigns and to study the motives and natures of men. Often requests were made by the different candidates for my support in a canvass; but there were others who had little regard for a woman's assistance.

One summer when the roads were kept dusty by the continuous goings to and fro of the anxious office-seekers, one of these interesting subjects dined at our house. He was a most forlorn specimen, with heavy, drooping eyes, straggling moustache and languid movements. His clothes, from the disconsolate set of his collar down to his edge-frayed trousers, draggling over his well-worn boots, gave evidence of a long, hard race on the war path. My sympathies were so aroused that as soon as dinner was over I followed him to the front gallery and, in a burst of condolence, said impulsively: "Mr. F., it is my intention to throw the whole weight of my influence to have you elected!" Looking at me in a sleepily-quizzical fashion, he replied in a droning tone: "It had never occurred to me to ask the assistance of ladies in a political campaign. I supposed they were too busy in other matters to be interested in anything so weighty."

Then he proceeded to tell this joke: There was a great convention of women held somewhere, and a certain local society sent its delegate. When the representative returned a meeting was called that the ladies might hear her report. When this was finished she remarked that questions were "in order." A slim little woman, with a weazen face peering out from a flaring poke-bonnet, arose in the rear of the room, and in a thin, high key called out: "Sister, what sort of hats did the women wear?" Then my hopeful candidate, turning towards me more fully, with a glimmer of something in his eyes which *he* would have called humor, said: "It was my impression that *all* ladies thought more about hats and such things than politics."

It is needless to say the facetious gentleman, with the well-worn apparel and Don Quixote air, lost my support suddenly and completely.

As the days went by they found me more and more deeply immersed in reading. Father bought me translations of the Greek, Latin and Italian poets. An old physician, quite a literateur, who had recently come into the neighborhood, loaned me valuable books that we did not own. He put me under special obligations by sending Allison's "Essays" and Montesquieu's "Spirit of Laws." From other sources some of the works of Ruskin, Carlyle and Herbert Spencer came to me and found an honored place among my treasures. Although applying myself sedulously to books, I was being consumed with a feverish restlessness. My wretchedness went beyond the power of words to express. A deep-rooted desire to do something definite was always present; but every undertaking that suggested itself seemed walled off by insurmountable barriers.

Finally I concluded to study law under father, but when my intention was announced to him he discouraged it utterly, arguing that if there were in my possession the legal lore of Blackstone and the ability of a Portia it would not guarantee me the opportunity of practising in the South. No woman had ever attempted such an absurdity, and any effort on my part, in that line, would subject me to ridicule and ostracism. After this fatal ending to my aspirations, I again sought refuge in books. With no definite object ahead and with not the faintest rim of a crescent of hope above my dull horizon.

IT WAS the summer of 1878. That terrible scourge, known as yellow-fever, crept relentlessly over the South. For the period of time that it lasted its deadly ravages exceeded the destruction of the civil war. Thousands stood shuddering in "The Valley of the Shadow." Death, grim and awful, stalked through the land knowing no surfeit. It was the blackness of despair. The acme of desolation. Pitiless quarantines were instituted; families were separated by a short dividing line never to be reunited. Others fled in terror from their homes in towns, seeking refuge in tents and cabins; while those who could, went to distant states. Food supplies failed. Hunger, gaunt and hollow-eyed, stole in at the open doors. Men, women and little children moved about listlessly, abandoning all work, looking hopelessly into each other's eyes, wondering, with a speechless fear, who would go out first from among them to return no more. Friends did not visit nor church bells ring. All was silent as the tomb—waiting, waiting, waiting. In the cities, the roll of the death-cart broke the stillness of the streets as it passed swiftly from house to house, collecting the bodies and carrying them to the cemeteries. There was the thud of spades in the earth, driven by men digging grave after grave, but all else was silent—waiting, waiting, waiting. A white woman and her two little children died near us and were buried by a negro man. He dug the graves and, unaided, lowered the bodies into the earth. The husband dared not leave the bedside of the other sufferers in the afflicted family. A physician stopped one morning at the gate to give father a list of fresh victims. In four days the young doctor was dead. A family of ten persons, friends of ours, living near Vicksburg, were all stricken at one time. Nobody dared go near the house but the Italian nurses who had been sent out from the city. As death followed death the plantation bell would be tolled to notify those who acted as undertakers that another grave must be dug. For the sake of those still living the dead were lowered in sheets from the windows, to avoid the slow, ominous tramp of feet through the hall. All were gone but two—the father and a young widowed daughter. A swarthy Dago sat watching the latter, while the blood settled in her hands and neck. The bell began to toll. "What is that for?" she asked. "To have your grave made ready, lady," was the answer.

Late in the autumn the pall lifted. The quarantines were raised. The refugees returned to their deserted homes. The voice of traffic was heard. Life waked up with startled, saddened eyes from her long, deep sleep. It was the middle of November. Some said that Mrs. Woodman, our Northern friend, was very ill. Mother and I walked over the fields to see her. The dying sun streamed across the faded grass and lay in long, glinting lines upon the distant woods that had many days since laid aside their summer vesture. The tall rows of golden-rod and yellow coreopsis that fringed the winding path swayed noiselessly in the passing breeze. The houses of the little village, scattered here and there in a lonely way, had a pathetic mournfulness. Away to the east a glimpse could be caught of the headstones that marked the quiet resting place of our dead. The surrounding country, with its gentle undulations, was wrapped in unbroken solitude. A peculiar sadness brooded over all. There is an inexplicable heart-break in those early days of a Southern winter;—changing sunshine, shifting shadows and still air full of a mystic haze.

Florence King

(1936–   )

Born and raised in Washington, D.C. (a segregated, thus arguably "southern" city at that time), Florence King grew up in an unconventional home environment that included her unflappable British father (whom she refers to as Herb in the following section), her highly temperamental and decidedly unladylike Virginian mother, and her maternal grandmother, who was determined to turn young Florence into the southern belle her mother had refused to become. In 1957, after studying French at American University, King entered the graduate program in history at the University of Mississippi, where she supplemented her stipend by writing outlandish stories for True Confessions *magazine. After a three-year stint as a reporter for the Raleigh* News and Courier, *King worked as an assistant editor at* Uncensored Confessions *and authored over thirty pornographic novels before settling into more mainstream journalistic pursuits. An astute observer of various aspects of southern culture, King, a self-proclaimed misanthrope, deploys a savage wit in all of her writings, whether the subject happens to be ancestor worship, sexuality, or anti-intellectualism. Her articles have appeared in* Harper's, Cosmopolitan, Ms., *the* New York Times Book Review, *and* Oxford American. *She is the author of ten books (excluding her work outside the mainstream press), including* Southern Ladies and Gentlemen *(1975),* Reflections in a Jaundiced Eye *(1989), and* With Charity Toward None: A Fond Look at Misanthropy *(1992).*

Although the dominant tone in King's autobiography, Confessions of a Failed Southern Lady *(1985), is comic, its funniest sections are in the first half of the book, with the grandmother becoming the most frequent target of King's wicked sense of humor. In the second half, which includes her account of the confusion she feels over a disastrous love affair with a female graduate student at Ole Miss, King is less flippant, more willing to expose her own vulnerabilities. The following selection is taken from the first half of the book and describes the bizarre clash of contradictory cultural influences in her parents' tiny apartment.*

FROM *Confessions of a Failed Southern Lady*

OUR APARTMENT GAVE every evidence of having been decorated by Jekyll and Hyde. "Herb's alcove," as it was known, was a model of spartan order, while Mama's bedroom looked at all times as if the Gestapo had just searched it. Granny saw nothing unladylike about this and in fact encouraged slovenliness as a mark of aristocracy. She looked down on good housekeepers, dismissing them as "scrubbers." A scrubber, I learned early on, is a Northern woman who substitutes good housekeeping for good blood; knowing that she can never be a lady, she develops a bee in her bonnet (i.e., unfeminine insanity) about being able to "eat off the floor."

It was virtually impossible to eat off our table, hidden as it was under skeins of crochet yarn and clippings from the sports page that Mama was saving for her baseball scrapbook. Slut's wool like gone-to-seed dandelions lay undisturbed under our furniture, dishes were piled up to the spigot in the sink, the refrigerator handle stuck to our hands, little pieces of singed food clung to the stove burners, and the oven door had a permanent gummy border of gravy and long rivulets of greasy scum. In *Reflections in a Golden Eye,* describing the stove of the Captain's wife, who was half-Yankee, Carson McCullers wrote: "Their gas stove was not crusted with generations of dirt as her grandmother's had been, but then it was by no means clean."

Ours was a pureblooded stove.

Jensy still came once a week, but except for washing the dishes she did little to alleviate the mess. She and Granny spent most of the day sitting at the cluttered table drinking coffee and talking about how wonderful the world would be if only they could run it. When they finished their encyclicals, they polished the silver.

Their silver ritual was supposed to teach me the ladylike art of taking care of my "things." Silver is the Southern woman's proudest possession and highest priority as well as the subject of much of her conversation. The night before her daughter's wedding, a Southern mother will sit on the bed and talk intimately about silver. Every decent woman goes to her husband with twelve "covers," and if the knives have hollow handles he'll be running with other women before the year is out, you wait and see. No man respects a woman with hollow handles.

A marriage can fall apart if a bride does not choose her silver pattern carefully. A good pattern is known as "They've been making that one forever." A bad pattern is known as "They don't make silver the way they used to." Bad patterns are the stark modern designs that are easy to keep clean; a good pattern is as busy as a Grecian frieze and manifests what silver company brochures call "the elegant and highly prized glow of deep patina," i.e., those black lines made by ground-in dirt that you can't get at no matter how many gauze-wrapped toothpicks you use.

My first household chore was wrapping gauze around toothpicks so Granny and Jensy could sit in the midst of wall-to-wall patina and polish silver. They polished it while it was still shining from their last polishing; they polished it while a mouse gnawed happily through a soggy bag of garbage; they polished it while a flapping window shade gave off a duststorm under their noses. Our silver was the only thing in our home that was ever really clean, which is a sure sign of a Southern home.

Granny's pattern was the goodest of the good, as furrowed as a damaged brain and so full of acorns and rosebuds that our palms ached after every meal. Thanks to its Laocoön intricacies, it frequently served as a salvaging conversation piece for appalled visitors who were trying not to look at the filth, like Mr. Van Vrees, the insurance man, who was from Poughkeepsie. Granny always offered him coffee and asked for news of his ailing mother.

"She's having trouble with her knees," he said. "They're so sore and swollen she can't stand up."

"Oh, what a shame," Granny commiserated. "Whatever caused it?"

"I . . . er . . . I really don't know. . . . The doctor can't—Say! This is beautiful silver. What's it called?"

"Williamsburg Carbuncle," said Herb.

*   *   *

WE WERE EVICTED from Park Road early in January of 1941 after a building inspector saw the plumbing pipes that the distraught owner had installed all by himself. The structure was condemned and we were given a month to move.

Mama and Herb responded with alarm. Their marriage depended upon old houses that had been cut up into apartments by people who did not know what they were doing. As long as there was an extra piece or an accidental cul-de-sac, Herb could play St. Jerome in the Desert and Mama could litter in peace, but a logical floor plan would lead to divorce or worse.

It was the only time I ever saw Herb bestir himself. He hurried out with the newspaper and returned an hour later wearing his old serene look. He had signed a lease on a two-bedroom apartment around the corner at 1020 Monroe. We already knew the building. It lay overtop a block of small stores. Some were convenient, like the Chinese laundry and the Greek deli, but the Monroe Bar & Grill was not. Worse, the windows of our new home faced the streetcar tracks, there was no cross-ventilation, and the rent was an exorbitant sixty-five dollars. Never has an apartment boasted so many unwinning features, but Herb insisted that it was a find.

He meant that it had an alcove. Actually it was a dressing room off the master bedroom and thus more connubial in spirit than his former kitchen hideaway, but even so it was *haut* Herb.

Mama took one look at it and started singing "There'll Always Be an Alcove."

Since we were moving only around the corner, we did not hire a van. Jensy produced three strong nephews named Booker, Kincaid, and Donald to take the furniture, and the rest of us followed with linens, pictures, and clocks. It looked like an integrated looting.

Granny and the nephews hit it off superbly. Each time they returned from a sprint across the street with a table or a bed, she promised to dance at their weddings. Soon the ambience reached such dizzy heights that they were inspired to make her a bet: they could carry her seated in our heaviest armchair all the way over to Monroe Street without stopping to rest.

They took our huge leather Morris chair out to the sidewalk and Granny sat down. Hefting her aloft, the nephews got a running start and careened down to the corner just as a streetcar was approaching. Unable to stop their momentum, they dashed across the tracks in front of it as the astonished motorman and all the passengers stared. Seeing their interest, Granny smiled graciously and, remembering to keep her wrist stiff like Queen Mary in the newsreels, gave them a perfect imitation of the royal wave.

"The last of the great white goddesses," Herb said.

She made friends in the new building at once. To her great joy, our immediate neighbors were all women in their forties or fifties whose menopauses were either in progress or fresh in their minds. She was thrilled to learn that 12B contained a bizarre vibratory condition known at quilting bees as a "singing ovary." It was the well-nurtured property of Miss Inez Shields, a fluttery, domestically inclined spinster who stayed home and kept house for her capable, efficient sister, Miss Rose Shields, who supported them both with her job at the Bureau of Engraving. Miss Rose made money and Miss Inez made a buzzing sound. Peeking into their kitchen, I saw Granny holding a rolled-up magazine to Miss Inez's stomach and listening at the other end.

"I'll tell you what's wrong with her ovary," said Mama. "Those goddamn streetcars did it. We're all going to have singing brains. They'll have to carry us out of here in rubber bags and take us to St. Elizabeth's."

The streetcars were the old-fashioned kind with wicker seats and motors front and back. Eleventh and Monroe being the end of the line, the tracks simply stopped at the corner. There was no way to turn the cars around for the trip back downtown, so the motormen made the juice flow in the opposite direction by driving over the switch, which lay directly under our windows. They had to approach it at a certain speed to keep from getting stuck on it; to make sure the tracks were clear of traffic and pedestrians, they rang the bell from Park Road to Monroe Street. When the wheels hit the switch, they exploded with a metallic roar and gave off cascades of sparks, bringing cheers from the drunks leaning up against the Monroe Bar & Grill. The motorman then reversed the seats manually—twenty separate crunching slams—and manned the opposite set of controls. Sometimes, of course, a car got stuck on the switch. When this happened, the motorman had to grind back and forth like someone trying to saw through a knight in full armor, until the car came free.

Anything for an alcove.

Having moved to 1020 in the winter, we did not receive the full impact of this procedure until it was time to sleep with the windows open. By August we were as scrambled as Quasimodo, so we took off for a vacation at Colonial Beach.

Granny always enjoyed the drive down because of all the historical road markers around Fredericksburg. HERE WAS FOUGHT . . . ONCE STOOD THE HOME OF . . . BURIED NEARBY . . . GRANTED BY KING CHARLES II TO . . . and Herb's favorite, ON THIS SPOT, all filled her with immense pride.

"Think of it," she said to no one in particular.

When we arrived at the cabin site we found Uncle Botetourt and Aunt Charlotte, Dora Madison with a group of her girl-friends, and the usual assortment of Uptons. These were the people we had expected to find. Also present that year was someone who was destined to make the summer of 1941 a season that would live in imbecility. Charlotte was in the middle of saying "There's something you should know . . ." when suddenly a cabin door opened and there stood Evelyn Cunningham in a pink seersucker sunsuit.

Seeing us, she sprinted down the cabin steps and threw herself into Granny's arms.

"Oh, Aunt Lura! Aunt Nana made me go to a new doctor and he's going to hook my head up to a machine and read my brain!"

"If he can find it," Mama muttered under her breath.

Soap operas at this time were modest radio offerings concerned solely with love affairs, so none of us knew what brain waves and electroencephalograms were, but Evelyn was eager to enlighten us. She followed us into our cabin and recited a year's worth of medical history as we unpacked, talking faster and faster, higher and higher, gasping for breath, widening her eyes, licking her lips, until at last she crossed wires and had a choking fit.

"Now you stop this foolishness," Granny ordered. "There's nothing wrong with your mind, Aunt Nana's just talking through her hat. It's female trouble that's causing those spells. You've got a descending womb. It runs in the family—I had the same trouble myself and I can see all the signs in you."

"You think so, Aunt Lura?" Evelyn asked hopefully.

"I don't think it, I *know* it. You're delicate down below, that's all. All of us Upton women are." She sighed. "I've told you this over and over, Evelyn. Why do you let Aunt Nana fill your head with nonsense?"

The answer was easy. Evelyn and Billy had rented Granny's old house, putting Evelyn in dire propinquity to Aunt Nana, who had jumped at the chance to plump for insanity again. If God was on the side of the strongest battalion, Evelyn was on the side of the nearest.

Now Granny was the nearest. As she launched into her lecture on the descending womb (known to medical science by the cold name of prolapsed uterus), Evelyn's strained face relaxed and she returned to the female trouble fold.

"Oh, Aunt Lura, you're smarter than that old doctor any day!" she shrieked, rushing over to give Granny a big hug.

When she scampered out of our cabin, Herb opened a bottle of beer and sank wearily into a chair.

"That woman has a voice like a castrated Irish tenor."

"She's nuts," Mama proclaimed flatly.

"Oh, Louise! You sound just like Aunt Nana with her talk of the Cunningham taint. Evelyn has *female trouble.*"

"Mrs. Ruding," Herb sighed, "Evelyn's problem has nothing to do with either the Upton womb or the Cunningham taint. She's suffering from historical displacement brought on by her unsuccessful struggle to be a Southern belle."

"Why, she was a belle," Granny said indignantly. "Men flocked around her."

"That's only one small part of being a belle," Herb replied. "Many women throughout the world are admired by the opposite sex, but they aren't Southern belles."

"Then what is a Southern belle?" Granny demanded.

"A state of mind," Herb said. "One which Evelyn is geographically incapable of achieving. The belle is a product of the Deep South, which is a product of the nineteenth century and the Age of Romanticism. Virginia is a product of the eighteenth century. It's impossible to extract a belle from the Age of Reason."

"Do you mean to say that Virginia has no belles?" Granny asked incredulously.

"That is correct."

"Herb's right," Charlotte said pensively. "Look at all those plantation novels and movies about Southern belles. They're never set in Virginia, it's always somewhere 'way down South. Scarlett was from Georgia and Jezebel was from New Orleans."

Granny scowled at her traitorous daughter-in-law.

"What about Sally Fairfax?" she huffed.

"Her fame rests solely on the fact that George Washington fell in love with her," Herb replied. "But she was a married woman when it happened, so she can hardly be considered a belle, especially since she discouraged him firmly and consistently without indulging in coy games."

"No wonder they never made a movie about it," Dora Madison said, giggling.

Mama was enjoying Granny's defeat.

"Name another Virginia belle, Mother," she challenged.

Silence fell. Mama threw Herb a grin and punched him in the ribs. It was her way of saying thank you.

I was to dine out on Herb's theory thirty-six years later when "Roots" aired on television and a number of non-Southern friends asked me why the Sandy Duncan character seemed oddly "off." It's simple: she brought to the Virginia of Thomas Jefferson a giddy flutter that belonged in the Alabama of Jefferson Davis.

AT OUR PICNIC that afternoon, Dora Madison made a beeline for Herb and they fell to discussing the books they had been reading. Her girlfriends gathered round and gazed at him with an awe that hovered on the edge of romantic titillation. Here was the "real honest-to-God Englishman" Dora had promised them; a man who did not call them honey, who crossed his legs at the knee, who looked at a woman's face when she talked and actually listened to what she was saying. Seated in a row with their eyes locked on him, they looked as if they were watching a Ronald Colman movie.

After the picnic we all went down to the boardwalk. Granny bustled into the Bingo hall, bought five cards, and settled down to a serious evening of old-lady vice. She always stayed until they closed the doors so we used her as a rallying point to make sure we didn't lose any children. The rule was to report back to her at specified intervals, though whether her glassy gambler's eyes even recognized us remained in doubt.

Herb and Billy Bosworth went off to play darts and I went with Mama while she had her palm read. When Madame Zenia got to the finger sworls, she had to use a magnifying glass to penetrate the nicotine.

"I see a strange man," she rumbled in her whiskey voice.

"I see him every day."

Three hours later we were hungry again, so we found Charlotte and Dora and went to the crab shed. As we were about to enter, we heard a shriek behind us. It was Evelyn, waving frantically, pointing to her mouth and running sideways in imitation of a crab. It was her way of telling us that she was hungry, too.

She joined us and we took a big table in the middle of the restaurant. The waitress spread newspapers over it and we ordered a mess of softshell. When they came, we all fell to except Evelyn, who was staring at an empty pickle jar on the table.

"I'm going to steal that jar," she whispered.

"Why?" asked Charlotte. "There's nothing in it except juice."

"I know, that's why I want it. It's *pickle* juice."

She rolled her popping eyes around the room to make sure no one was watching; then she grabbed the jar, screwed the lid tight; and shoved it in her big straw handbag.

"It's so's I can catch my womb in case it falls out," she informed us.

"Oh, for Christ's sake!" Mama exploded. "How the hell can a womb fall out?"

"Aunt Lura said it could!" Evelyn wailed.

"Mother's full of shit!"

Evelyn's answer was a sob. Putting her fingers in her mouth, she emitted a long steady moan that made everyone turn around and stare at us. She sounded like a smoke detector.

"I think we'd better go," said Aunt Charlotte.

"Bring those crabs," Mama said to me.

They paid the check and hauled the weeping Evelyn to her feet. She cried all the way down the pier and across the boardwalk, sagging into Charlotte's arms while we followed behind with greasy newspapers full of our uneaten supper.

"Women!" Mama muttered.

The next night I ran into Evelyn at the cotton candy stand. I tried to escape her frantic company by saying that I had to report to Granny at the Bingo hall, but she grabbed my hand in her clammy grip and said she would go with me.

It was Saturday. The boardwalk was packed with Marines from Quantico, sailors from Anacostia, soldiers from Fort Belvoir, and defense workers from the shell factory at nearby Dahlgren. As we inched our way to the door of the Bingo hall, Evelyn screamed.

"Here it comes!"

Wrenching open her pocketbook, she tore madly through its chaotic contents, throwing combs, cosmetics, and old streetcar transfers in all directions until she found her pickle jar.

"Please!" she cried. "Please give me room! My womb's falling out!"

Her plea was instantly effective. As she squatted down and shoved the jar between her thighs, soldiers, sailors, Marines, brawny workingmen, the whole backbone of our nation moved as if impelled by some primitive religious instinct and formed a circle around her. Terror, disgust, and fascination bounced across their faces like the ball in a sing-along film. Were they Christians shrinking from a succubus, or Dionysian revelers admiring a maenad's cooch dance? Nobody knew. All certainties had vanished; the world was flat again and simple man was teetering on the abyss.

Attracted by the uproar, people poured out of the Bingo hall, among them Granny with a toaster and coffeepot clutched to her Daughterly bosom. She took one look at Evelyn and dropped both.

"Oh, Law!"

A vacationing doctor pushed his way through the crowd.

"Is she in labor?"

"Her womb's falling out! Her womb's falling out!" Granny cried, sounding just like Chicken Little. The doctor gave her an incredulous stare.

A few minutes later the police arrived. At first they thought

Evelyn was drunk and exposing herself. Nothing was showing, but her pornographic squat and the position of her hand made one of the cops mutter something about Spanish fly. They called for an ambulance and she was taken to the hospital in Fredericksburg, the rest of us following in several cars. The chief of gynecology examined her and said there was nothing wrong with her womb, but this only made her scream louder. She went on screaming until they had to put her under sedation.

Billy stayed with her and the rest of us drove back to Colonial Beach. The next day everyone was exhausted and Herb was in a foul mood. No one had ever seen him mad before; his equanimity was a family legend, especially to those who had lived with Granny. He spent most of the morning brooding alone on a sandbar. Later in the afternoon he came and got me and said we were going for a walk. It was not an invitation.

We walked nearly to Monroe Bay before he said what was on his mind.

"Don't you ever get like Evelyn."

"But suppose it runs in the family?"

"Bugger that! I am sick of this pelvic Shintoism." He pointed a finger in my face. "*You* decide what runs in you. Don't ever let anyone or anything else decide for you. Is that clear?"

I nodded.

"I've made a careful study of this family," he went on. "Evelyn is the creation of Aunt Nana and your grandmother, and they have created a Frankenstein. One of them wants her to go barmy and the other wants her crankcase to fall out, all for the sake of some outlandish vision of ideal womanhood the two of them have cooked up. *They are both wrong!* Don't forget that. Naturally you will continue to respect your grandmother and obey her in everyday matters, but *don't listen* to her madcap theories. Is that clear?"

"Yes. What does Shintoism mean?"

"Ancestor worship."

"What does bugger mean?"

A sheepish look crossed his face.

"It's something like what your mother means when she says 'shove it.'"

"You mean 'bugger' is British for 'shove it'?"

"Well, yes, you might say that."

We walked back to our cabin. Herb lapsed into another silence, his brows puckered in thought as if he wanted to say something else but wasn't sure how to put it. Finally he spoke again.

"Your grandmother and Aunt Nana really aren't the kind of women they would like to be, so they use Evelyn as a doppel-ganger."

"What's that?"

"German for substitute. You see, as long as Evelyn behaves in a feminine manner, Mrs. Ruding and Aunt Nana don't have to. All they need do is claim kinship with her, wait for her to col-lapse or abandon her wits, diagnose the problem as some quin-tessentially female plague, and then announce that she inherited it from them. That way, they can go on being autocratic without risking exposure. If Evelyn is weak, it follows that *they* are weak."

"What's autocratic?"

"Bossy."

"What's quin—quinner—"

"The highest example of something. As in, your mother is the quintessential baseball fan."

"Oh, I get it."

"You know," he said slowly, "this Evelyn business has been hard on your mother. Knowing that Mrs. Ruding would prefer Evelyn for a daughter has hurt her more than she lets on. If she seems brusque at times, try to understand her. Imagine how you would feel if you had a sister that everyone liked best."

"I don't want any goddamn sister."

"I believe you have taken the point," Herb said dryly.

I had. I was still half-afraid Mama would murder me, but I began, in a childish way, to grasp the basic family picture. And a small relief, like a single bead of sweat, rolled down my mind: I did not have to grow up to be like Evelyn.

Katharine Du Pre Lumpkin

(1897–1988)

A descendant of Georgia slaveholders, Katharine Du Pre Lumpkin made a break from the traditional values of her family and worked to bring racial equality to the South when few southern whites were involved in that movement. Lumpkin was born to a prestigious though only moderately prosperous family in Macon, Georgia, but moved to Columbia, South Carolina, while still very young. She returned to Georgia in 1912 when she enrolled in Brenau College in Gainesville, Georgia, where she experienced a religious rebirth that sensitized her to the contradictions between southern racial practices and the teachings of Christ. At Brenau, Lumpkin participated actively in the YWCA at a crucial juncture in that organization's history, when it was emerging as a force for moderate opposition to segregation. Her biography of the nineteenth-century abolitionist and feminist leader Angelina Grimké was published in 1974.

As the title of her autobiography, The Making of a Southerner *(1949), clearly suggests, Lumpkin rejected the notion that southernness constituted an essential identity. To illustrate her point, she employs an unusual though nonetheless effective method of describing the process by which she was "made" a southerner. By narrating her family and regional history from the antebellum period up through her young adulthood and repeating, as if she still accepted at face value, the confusing mixture of truths, half-truths, and outright lies she had been taught about the southern past, Lumpkin immerses her readers in the mythology of the Old South so that they can appreciate the difficulties she herself experienced in pulling away from those views. Like her contemporary Lillian Smith, she writes within the conventions of the spiritual autobiography, "confessing" her racial sins from the perspective of the penitent. In the following excerpt from "A Child Inherits a Lost Cause," a section of her autobiography, she describes her unquestioning acceptance of white supremacy and the necessity for segregation.*

FROM *The Making of a Southerner*

*T*HERE WAS the glamorous, distant past of our heritage. Besides this, there was the living, pulsing present. Hence, it was by no means our business merely to preserve memories. We must keep inviolate a way of life. Let some changes come if they must; our fathers had seen them come to pass: they might grieve, yet could be reconciled. It was inconceivable, however, that any change could be allowed that altered the very present fact of the relation of superior white to inferior Negro. This we came to understand remained for us as it had been for our fathers, the very cornerstone of the South.

It too was sanctified by the Lost Cause. Indeed, more than any other fact of our present, it told us our cause had not been lost, not in its entirety. It had been threatened by our Southern disaster (we would never concede the word "defeat"). No lesson of our history was taught us earlier, and none with greater urgency than the either-or terms in which this was couched: "Either white supremacy or black domination." We learned how Restoration—or the Redemption, as men still said in their more eloquent moments—had meant this as much as anything to our heritage. "The resounding defeat of the forces of darkness. The firm re-establishment of our sacred Southern principles." To be sure, we learned all this long after we had begun to behave according to the practical dictates of the "sacred principle" of white supremacy.

In the case of my particular generation, it seems that we first learned both behavior and belief at a time when those around us were peculiarly disturbed. I was born in 'ninety-seven. This was nearly in the midst of the main Populist years which spanned the 1890's. It is safe to say that no years since reconstruction's overthrow had been filled with so much belligerence and anxiety to Southerners of my people's kind. Even after the crisis passed there remained a tumultuous residue.

In Georgia, when I was born, Tom Watson was still surging along his unorthodox road, leading dissident farmers and workingmen into a separate People's Party. More than this, he had swelled his ranks by calling hitherto disfranchised Negroes—disfranchised not legally but in effect—to join his movement. They too, he told them, were being "fleeced" by greedy corporations; they too were being put upon, all the more so by the forces that kept them from making common cause with their poor white brothers. Nor did it reassure anyone who bitterly opposed Watson's course that he said plainly he had no use for "social equality." He frankly advocated "political equality." That sufficed for the predictions of disaster.

Conservative men would not, if they could prevent it, let overtake them this threat to the white South's solid front. It seems they saw white solidarity as their source of strength; they did not intend to let it be sapped away. All conservatives apparently felt this way, whether politically kin to the postwar New Departure men or Old South men like father. But some of them—not men of father's kind—took a peculiar course of action. (It used to seem peculiar to me when I heard of it in childhood; it was one piece of our history I felt slight shame about, although I would tell myself of the leaders' noble motives.) Some conservatives said, it seems, "If need be, we will fight fire with fire." This could mean, as in Georgia, planters and turpentine men taking their Negro hands to the polls and voting them in gangs. It could mean in some towns holding all-night revelries on election eve, serving barbecue, and beer and whiskey "by the barrel." Then marching the "voters" to the polls to the beat of drums—and the tramp of guards, lest some slip off to seek the fleshpots of the opposing side. For, it is said, the "regulars," the conservative men, were not alone in sinning; but they were "more resourceful," hence enjoyed "more success."

It was something that they were not voting Negroes "on principle." This may have comforted those who saw danger ahead. They did not offer "political equality." They opposed political equality as all men knew. This was frankly an expedient. They knew the People's Party had a large popular following, white and Negro. They countered with their own "popular following," by whatever means they could collect it. They were wise in the ways by which obscure voters could be found who responded to certain practical inducements. That is how the story went, and that they dealt out these several inducements with a generous hand.

At the same time, they seemed not unwilling to let the battle turn on the "race issue." The story goes that violence, bitterness, invective, hatred, became the almost daily portion of those Populist years. Here were white Southerners pitted not against outsiders, but battling among themselves.

The struggle did not relax until the late 1890's when People's Party strength had definitively waned. Then conservative men decided they should call a halt. On every side, white leaders began to speak and write of how wrong it had ever been to have brought the Negro back to the ballot box. He was virtually "eliminated from politics," they said, until this fight began. Now he must be "eliminated" once for all. He was, of course, but not without more struggle and especially not without a storm of speeches and writings and slogans rending the South. The battle had gone on in other Southern states. Everywhere they recited the woes that would befall us: at the worst, Negro domination, at the least, venal politics, if the Negro were not "eliminated." Precisely this was taking place in Georgia in my early childhood. In South Carolina this stage had been gone through shortly before I was born.

One is not guessing in telling of the tenseness of our home in the time of these election battles; how thick the air with talk of "black domination" and "white supremacy"; how sharp the criticism, to put it mildly, of the men responsible for such "unprincipled" actions; how "race" was the undercurrent and, sooner or later, the dominant note so much of the time. Of my parents' children I was the youngest. Our family circle had been in existence more than two decades when I was born. The older children were old enough in plenty to be listeners and even participants in all this exciting talk. We can be certain that from the time I could sit in my high chair at table or play about the parlor floor while others conversed, my ears were saturated with words and phrases at all times intimately familiar to Southern ears and in those years of harsh excitement carrying a special urgency: "white supremacy," "Negro domination," "intermarriage," "social equality," "impudence," "inferiority," "uppitiness," "good darkey," "bad darkey," "keep them in their place." As time passed, I myself would learn to speak these words, perhaps with special emphasis, given the times and the tones of others' voices saying them, even before I had the understanding to grasp all they stood for.

Of course I did come to comprehend. When I did, it was a sharp awakening. This was mere chance. Unless we may say it was hardly chance, since my father, although only a boy under slavery, yet had been reared to be a master; which in turn made me but one generation removed from the slave plantation; yet being removed—forty years had intervened—while Father had known Negro slavery at first hand, I knew only a child's dream replica of that alluring, bygone day.

Early in the century our family had gone to live on the outskirts of a small Carolina town some twenty-five miles from Columbia, a place to which we moved presumably for the summer but where we remained for more than a year. When I saw the place from a passing train almost a score of years after, it was sadly disillusioning. Perhaps it had been allowed to run down. Even so, there was no dislodging the pleasant memory I had cherished or the sense in which it realized ever so faintly an unfulfilled family dream.

I loved the house. It was a large brick place, square, and it may have been colonial in style, with wide, airy hallways down the center, and large square rooms. A long ell at back provided more, even larger rooms; the figure "forty feet long" remains in my mind. It was our custom to refer to the upstairs ell as the "ballroom," which it may or may not have been at some time; at any rate on rainy days it was a perfect playroom. The separate kitchen, even though we used in its place the more convenient room partitioned off in the house, gave us a warm sense of plantation authenticity.

Extensive grounds spread around the dwelling, shaded by fine old trees. We found a fenced-in vegetable garden, too huge for our family needs, which we planted half in cotton. Our generous pasture lay beyond, down the pinewoods slope and spreading away to how many acres I could not guess, so wide seemed its pleasant spaces to city children. Here was all the room our hearts could ask, for mountain climbing up and down the deep red gullies; or playing Indian in the woods; or hunting the nests of our recalcitrant far-flying guinea hens; or hurtling down the slope, thickly carpeted in pine needles, on sleds made at home of barrel staves.

Our place was located in an old part of town antedating the railroad but now bounded on one side by the tracks running parallel to our sidewalk. A few other houses stood on either side of us, wooden frame structures, less pretentious than ours. In one of them lived the sheriff of the county.

I have no recollection of the man. Possibly I rarely saw him. Certainly at my age I grasped little of what a sheriff was, except vaguely to connect him with the jail. In any small town a child would see the jail with its barred windows and usually the face of a Negro looking out. I knew the sheriff lived down the street in a house that we children held in some awe.

One summer morning I had gone aimlessly out into the yard before breakfast. In the kitchen breakfast-preparation had been stirring as I passed. Of a sudden in the house there was bedlam—sounds to make my heart pound and my hair prickle at the roots. Calls and screams were interspersed with blow upon blow.

Soon enough I knew someone was getting a fearful beating, and I knew full well it was not one of us: when we children were punished, it might be corporal, but it was an occasion of some dignity for all parties concerned. Carefully keeping my distance, I edged over so that I could gaze in through the kitchen window. I could see enough. Our little black cook, a woman small in stature though full grown, was receiving a severe thrashing. I could see her writhing under the blows of a descending stick wielded by the white master of the house. I could see her face distorted with fear and agony and his with stern rage. I could see her twisting and turning as she tried to free herself from his firm grasp. I could hear her screams, as I was certain they could be heard for blocks, "Mister Sheriff! Mister Sheriff! He's killing me! Help!" Having seen and heard, I chose the better part of stuffing my fists in my ears and creeping away on trembling legs.

The thrashing of the cook was not talked about, not around me at least. Nothing was said in the family, although a strained atmosphere was present all day—a tension one came to expect whenever slight incidents of race-conflict occurred. The neighbors said nothing. Although I waited with considerable trepidation—how unnecessarily I could not know—nothing was heard from the sheriff. To my hesitant question, "What had the cook done?" I was told simply that she had been very "impudent" to her mistress; she had "answered her back."

It was not the custom for Southern white gentlemen to thrash their cooks, not by the early 1900's. But it was not heinous. We did not think so. It had once been right not so many years before. Apparently it still could be. Given sufficient provocation, it might be argued: and what recourse did a white man have? All would have assumed, and no doubt did on this occasion, that the provocation on the Negro cook's part had been very great. Few Negro sins were more reprehensible in our Southern eyes than "impudence." Small child though I was, I had learned this fact. I knew "impudence" was intolerable. In this sense I had no qualms about what I had witnessed. But in another sense I did have, and this disturbed me. Naturally I had no explanation for these mixed feelings. I could merely try to forget the thing—a child wishing to feel at one with her surroundings.

We may assume this about it. It disturbed me because I saw it. If it had been remote, if I had merely heard it as a story as one did hear of similar acts toward Negroes in my childhood, if it had thus been completely removed from all sight and sound, surely I could have felt quite pleasantly *en rapport*.

In any event, this much I know. The inevitable had happened, and what is bound to come to a Southern child chanced to come to me this way. Thereafter, I was fully aware of myself as a white, and of Negroes as Negroes. Thenceforth, I began to be self-conscious about the many signs and symbols of my race position that had been battering against my consciousness since virtual infancy.

I found them countless in number. As soon as I could read, I would carefully spell out the notices in public places. I wished to be certain we were where we ought to be. Our station waiting rooms—"For White." Our railroad coaches—"For White." There was no true occasion for a child's anxiety lest we make a mistake. It was all so plainly marked. (Said the law, it seems, ". . . in letters at least two inches high.") Trains were plain sailing. One knew the "For Colored" coach would be up next the engine, and usually but half a car, with baggage the other half. Theaters were no problem. Negroes rarely went, and in any case "their place" was only a nook railed off far up in the "buzzard's roost." Street cars were more troublesome. Here too were the signs—"White" at the forward end, "Colored" at the rear. But no distinct dividing line, no wall or rail between. How many seats we occupied depended upon our needs. Sometimes conductors must come and shift things around in the twilight zone between. If whites were standing and Negroes not, it may be the latter were told to give up their seats. Conductors were the authority. They might handle the delicate rearrangement quietly by just a tap on the shoulder and a thumb pointing back—this to a Negro; but they might be surly or even belligerent, speak in a loud rough voice so all could hear—"Move back." A little white girl would rather stand, however much she knew it was her right to be seated in place of Negroes, than have this loud-voiced notoriety; and also, I think—it is ever so faint a memory—anything rather than have a fleeting glimpse of the still, dark faces in the rear of the car, which seemed to stare so expressionlessly into space.

We knew the streets were the white man's wherever he chose to walk; that a Negro who moved out into the gutter to let us pass was in our eyes a "good darkey." I could have been hardly more than eight when a little Negro girl of our age, passing a friend and me, showed a disposition to take her half of the sidewalk. We did not give ground—we were whites! Her arm brushed against my companion's. She turned on the Negro child furiously. "Move over there, you dirty black nigger!" I know why this recollection stayed with me while others did not. It outraged us so because this particular colored child did not shrink or run, but flared back at us with a stinging retort, remaining dead in her tracks, defying us, and we had no choice left us but to move on.

Less-than-proper humility from Negroes especially troubled our white consciousness. It was a danger signal and would never occur, we said, were it not for wrong policies. Nine times out of ten we linked it with education. Education was wrong. It made Negroes ambitious, impudent, wishing to "rise out of their place," we said. It was bound to result in intolerable situations.

I knew this was so. I myself had met it face to face. For example, when on Sunday mornings we would run into the line of college youths from Allen University, the Negro institution in our town. We were going to church. So were they. As was the custom for college boys and girls in my childhood, they walked to church in a line. We must cross the street they traversed on their way to church. We did not always meet them, but often we did, and there was always the possibility. What should we do? How comport ourselves? We had no precedent, save that of claiming our right to walk anywhere and Negroes to step aside.

But a whole line step aside for a family group, white though it was, or hold up its march, or break its ranks? Then should we walk through it, or should we wait? We might perhaps have said politely, "Excuse me, please. May I pass?" (Of course, if they had been white students going to church. . . .) It would be awkward merely to push through or try to. Suppose they did not make room. Being educated they might be "uppity"; it would be humiliating to let an incident occur; and there was the decorum due a Sunday morning. Must we then do that most galling thing, stand waiting in our places while "darkies" passed? It did not soothe us, but just the contrary, that they were nicely dressed, for it might mean, so we said, that they thought themselves as "good" as whites; or that they were "educated," they and their professors who accompanied them; much more than clothes, this could spell aspirations not encompassed in our beliefs about their "rightful place."

Often we spoke of the sin it would be to eat with a Negro. Next to "intermarriage" this was a most appalling thought. It was an unthinkable act of "social equality." To say the words, "eat with a Negro," stirred us disagreeably. In a sense, of course, it was no problem. How could it arise in our protected lives, and surrounded as we were by our racial barriers? It did, vicariously. We suspected Northerners of doing it upon occasion, and shuddered at the thought. We were sure Yankee teachers in Southern Negro institutions were guilty of the sin. That Republicans flaunted it was glaringly confirmed when one day our newspapers were filled with shocked accounts of President Theodore Roosevelt's entertainment of Dr. Booker T. Washington at luncheon in the White House. It was too much—this unpardonable "insult to the South" from the very seat of our national government, this fomenting in high places of "social equality." We were all aroused, on the streets, in our homes, at recess at school. We children talked of it excitedly, echoing the harshly indignant words and tones.

We often spoke of the peculiar inborn traits of this so peculiar race. For instance, the Negro's "thieving propensities."

White men stole too, but not "as a race." We verily believed that a Negro could not help but steal. So we acted accordingly. We must lock up our valuables. We children should never leave the key in the food pantry door, but turn it and put it back in its hiding place. Let something be missing; we suspected the cook, unless it was found; maybe even then, for she could have "got scared" and returned it. It was not serious with us; just a disability of the race, we said, that only we Southerners understood and took charitably. Of course in capacity they were different. This was the essence of our sense of difference—we superior, they inferior. But not merely that in their mental development none could ever go beyond say a child of ten or twelve (unless "they had white blood in them, of course"); they were qualitatively different, somehow, though we as children could not have explained wherein. We just used phrases such as "innately irresponsible," "love of finery," "not to be trusted," "slovenly," and a dozen more. To be sure, we would apply to special individuals contradictory attributes. But this made no difficulty about generalization. The innate traits, we said, applied to the race. To any doubting Thomases from the outside we had our irrefutable answer: "After all, we Southerners alone know the Negro."

At the club-forming age we children had a Ku Klux Klan. It was natural to do it, offspring of our warm Southern patriotism. We were happy in it for the aid and blessing it won from our adults. Our costumes, while made from worn-out sheets, were yet cut to pattern with help at home; they had fitted hoods, also, with tall peaks, and emblazoned across the front of the robes were red cheesecloth crosses. Constitution, by-laws, and ritual were something out of the ordinary. They were written, not on paper, but transcribed, as we supposed the original had been, on a long cloth scroll, at the top of which was a bright red cross. Our elders helped us write the ritual and rules and, true or not, we firmly believed that our laws and oaths were in some sense an echo from the bygone order.

It was certainly a game and fascinating as such. But it was much more besides. Its ritual, rolling off our tongues with much

happy gusto, was frequently interlarded with warm exhortations
to white supremacy. We held our meetings in the greatest
secrecy—so we pretended—in a friend's basement near our
home (our counterpart of a deep, silent forest around the hour
of midnight on a moonless night). A chief topic of business
when ceremonies had ended was the planning of pretended
punitive expeditions against mythical recalcitrant Negroes. And
while in one sense it never was real, in another it went far
beyond pretense. We vented our feelings. We felt glow in us an
indignant antagonism. These were real. We felt patriotic; so was
this real—this warm, pulsing feeling of Southern loyalty. We
told of our Cause and our Southern ideals which we were preserving. It was truly a serious game, and in a sense we were serious children bent on our ideals. We liked our clubs to have this
idealistic side. Witness the fact that the club to follow our Ku
Klux Klan was a "Knights of the Round Table," although it was
short-lived; it broke up over sharp competition for the post of
Sir Galahad.

Times would come when even we children must uphold our
beliefs in a serious public way. We rejoiced to do it. It made us
feel very worth while. So with me once in the sixth grade in
school. Our room was divided—"Busy Bees" on one side,
"Wise Owls" on the other. We were to have a debate. It was an
exceedingly strange query for a Southern schoolroom: "Are
Negroes Equal to White People?" It never would have been
proposed if we had not had in the room a little blond Northern
boy. He being a Yankee, he could with impunity be asked to
serve as the straw man for the rest of us to knock down. Patently,
his own side of the room could not support him, so it was all of
us against one. It was a strange debate. There were just the two
of us—the little Yankee boy and I who were actual participants.
My debate I can see now, carefully written down in my own
handwriting from the copy we had worked on with so much
earnestness in my family circle. His came first—one can guess
our scorn at the arguments that flowed from his Yankee home.
Then I argued mine. Of course I told of our history and how

the South had been saved by the courage of our fathers—we always told this. Probably I told of the Invisible Empire—we often did. Obviously, I recited all the arguments we had for Negro inferiority, and that this was why he must never be allowed to "rise out of his place." My peroration comes back to me in so many words, and how I advanced it with resounding fervor amidst a burst of applause from all the children in the room but my opponent: ". . . and the Bible says that they shall be hewers of wood and drawers of water forever!"

Ralph McGill

(1898–1969)

As the editor and publisher of the Atlanta Constitution *during a period spanning virtually the entire civil rights movement, Ralph McGill emerged as one of the most influential white southern liberals in the region, frequently placing his very life on the line by angering the proponents of racial violence. A farm boy, he was born and raised in the community of Igou's Ferry in East Tennessee, a section of the state composed primarily of yeoman farmers who had owned no slaves prior to the Civil War and who had openly sympathized with the Union. After graduating from a private academy in nearby Chattanooga in 1917, McGill enrolled in Vanderbilt University, but left shortly before the end of his senior year to work as a reporter for the Nashville* Banner, *never to return to school. In 1929 he took a job at the Atlanta* Constitution, *rising through the ranks to become chief editor and publisher in 1960. Because of his background, McGill never had to wrestle with the particular brand of guilt that Lumpkin and other liberal descendants of slave-owners describe in their autobiographies. Lacking the paternalism that motivated Will Percy to protect Greenville's African Americans from the Ku Klux Klan, McGill attributed his views on race to what he called his "Calvinist conscience." Although he certainly met a great deal of resistance to the opinions he expressed in his editorial columns, McGill took care not to be completely out of step with the beliefs of his readership. He argued in the forties for better educational facilities for African Americans as well as their more equitable treatment in courts and prisons, but waited until the years immediately preceding the 1954* Brown v. Board of Education *decision to openly advocate desegregation.*

In The South and the Southerner, *written in 1959, McGill intersperses personal recollections of youth and professional life with commentary on the character of the South and what he believed to be the best method of correcting its social ills. A gradualist, he displays considerable sympathy for members of the older generation of southern whites, whom he believed incapable of letting go of their racial prejudices. McGill ultimately places his faith in the South's redemption on "the younger generation" of southern whites and African Americans who will carry on the fight for racial justice. The selection that follows is from "Compensations," the narrative's concluding chapter.*

The South and the Southerner

O NE RAINY Saturday night about 11 o'clock, in the spring of 1961, my wife and I heard what sounded like a short, somewhat muted, string of firecrackers exploding. We wondered out loud what children in our neighborhood could possibly be out with firecrackers at that hour and at that time of year. We went on to sleep. But it so happened that across the street a young lady of fourteen, who, on the morrow, was to participate prominently in an outdoor school program, had at that moment awakened and gone hopefully to her upstairs bedroom window to see if the rain showed any signs of ending. Looking down into the well-lit street, she saw a cream-colored station wagon draw up by our mailbox and witnessed the flashes as a six-shooter was emptied into it.

The slugs cut six ugly gashes in the box and until a new one was installed, it was much admired by the neighboring children and visitors.

On other evenings garbage was dumped on the lawn or in the drive of our small brick house, which sits about one hundred twenty-five feet back from the street.

These were among the more curious revelations and reactions of the Klan and White Citizens Council mentality. One wondered without answer what they sought to demonstrate by firing into a mailbox or gathering up garbage and transporting it in boxes to be strewn on a lawn or drive.

On another occasion a .22 rifle was fired from a passing car. It put a neat hole in a window pane. No one was home when it happened and not until a window drapery one day was pulled back was the hole seen, and the bullet found in the back of a chair. This was a more serious thing, but still a puzzling, though somewhat revealing manifestation of the minds of the extremist groups which were, in many areas of the South, urging and employing violence as protests against the U.S. Supreme Court's decision banning segregation in the schools.

The anthropologist Margaret Mead has written that Americans join lodges and veterans organizations because there is created thereby a feeling of security by stressing a communal past. Status in our extremely fluid society, she concludes, depends not on birth, but on achievement. Social classes have been eliminated by highly temporary pecking orders.

The Klans and the various citizens councils in their beginnings attracted a gaggle of men whose sense of insecurity has remained embarrassingly obvious, as exposed by their publications, speeches, and deeds. Those organizations assuredly stressed a communal past which, if largely mythical and not therefore of their members' experience, nonetheless repeatedly was reasserted as a sacred tradition or way of life. Members could attain status by achievements such as dynamiting a school or home, by violent acts of terrorism, or by minor acts such as shooting into a mailbox or throwing garbage on a lawn. A fine manly council member might need to explode dynamite. His wife, on the other hand, would feel important if she shrieked curses and spat on school children and their mothers as did the harridans in New Orleans when the schools were desegregated there in the fall of 1961.

All too often in the years when fanatic adults set the ugly and irrational examples in the violence-ravaged cities seeking to obey court orders and desegregate their schools, one saw the sins of the fathers reflected in youthful efforts at emulating parental "achievement." One of the more dreadful features of Southern racial riots has been the high percentage of teenagers in brutal mobs—bent on injury and murder. On the summer night in 1961 when only the presence of federal marshals in Montgomery, Alabama, prevented a mass attack on a church filled with praying Negroes, thereby saving the lives of many, a local partisan source estimated that ninety per cent of the murder-minded mob of over two hundred persons was made up of teen-agers.

When the University of Georgia was desegregated in January, 1961, a shrieking mob enjoyed a few hours of infamy. (The shock of this was good therapy, enabling common sense to come into play.) This student-led demonstration was triggered by adults who assisted, financially and emotionally, the young men responsible. A leading merchant, from a town near the university, stood on the fringes of the riot, publicly encouraging the rioters and loudly offering to put up bond for any student arrested. The fact that the overwhelming majority of students at the university had not participated was largely overlooked.

Admission of Charlayne Hunter and Hamilton Holmes to the university became more than the story of the first Deep South state university to be integrated. It was, of course, compensation for much of the clamorous tirades of abuse which those who had supported the court orders had so long endured. But the mob made the two students and their admission into an exciting drama of America at its best, which was not at all what the rioters or the adults involved intended it to be.

All the university students, their parents, and the almost four million persons in the state, saw the Bill of Rights transformed, in the fast-driven drama of court tests, from printed words to action. The whole process of how our system works to protect and project the rights of the citizen was brought to focus in the swift series of events growing out of the desegregation order.

On Friday, January 6, 1961, the Georgia legislature, gathering in Atlanta for its annual session to begin on the following Monday, anticipated no emergency. It believed the severely restrictive segregation statutes enacted by previous legislatures made new action unnecessary. Had any person, in the hours before mid-afternoon of that day, suggested that before the legislature would be called to order two young, superiorly qualified Negro students would be sitting in classes at the university, he would have been dismissed as preposterous. Had it been further predicted that the legislature would remove all segregation laws from the books and enact legislation allowing local boards to desegregate or close schools, such a prophet would have been laughed down.

But even as the Assembly leaders were being interviewed and expressing their views the up-coming session would be a quiet one, a court case, long under consideration, was decided one hundred miles away.

At 3 o'clock that afternoon a law clerk in the District Court at Macon, Georgia, routinely released a judicial order. Reporters read its relatively brief content and excitedly telephoned newspapers and wire services. Bells soon began to ring in Atlanta hotel rooms where legislative leaders were registered, and at the governor's office.

The order said that Charlayne Hunter and Hamilton Holmes were qualified students and were being deprived of their constitutional rights by being denied admission to the university. They were, the court said, to be admitted at 9 o'clock on Monday, January 9, when the new term began.

A shocked and somewhat awed legislature found itself, to its own surprise, without words. There privately was general acknowledgment that an era had ended. Members met in quick caucuses. Save for a few die-hards, all recognized the fact they were up against the Constitution of their country and its guarantee of equal rights before the law for all citizens. For the legislators, too, the Constitution that day ceased to be merely words and was present in the form of physical meaning.

On Monday morning the two students dutifully were admitted. But at the same hour two automobiles hurried toward Macon. In one was a state attorney, who was to make one last face-saving effort. He asked for a delay in admitting the students so that an appeal could be made. The Negro attorney, who had been in the second car, opposed. The District Court reflected and then granted a delay. The two cars moved again. In Atlanta, a hundred miles north of Macon, an appeals judge heard the constitutional arguments. He ruled there was no constitutional basis for a delay, since the issue had already been covered in previous decisions. The students remained in school.

It was in the next act of the civil rights drama that "the bad ones" had their inning. The mob was organized. But of seventy-five hundred enrolled students less than five hundred participated. Among the mob were Klansmen, seven of whom were arrested. When order belatedly was obtained, the two Negro students, who had remained quietly in their rooms, were suspended because of the threat to law and order. By morning the drama was back in the courtroom. The Constitution was there, too. It presumed that law enforcement agencies would prevent violence. It further declared that the rights of some could not be suspended while the rights of others were maintained. So Charlayne Hunter and Hamilton Holmes went back to their classes.

The swift moves from court to court, the solemn arguments, the decisions based on the equality of citizenship, the acceptance of court order by the Georgia legislature, and the elimination of state segregation laws all combined to reveal the essential ingredients and meaning of our national principles. It did something else. It made plain the fact that under segregation the Negro citizen had been deprived of a just share in those principles.

In two great wars the American soldier was classified by many observers in Europe, Asia and Africa, as a confident, assured man—too damned much so, some said. He had grown up with no worry about liberty, individual rights, and full exercise of citizenship. It was a part of the national environment. We have been late to see that the American Negro has been excluded from the inspiring, developing psychology of American life. This exclusion was greatest in the South, though it existed everywhere. The school cases dramatized this fact. To see the Constitution function to give to the Negro citizen a chance to share in the assurance of the rights of citizenship was rewarding compensation.

The courage of the Negro children involved in the initial desegregations of schools was heartening. Many of them were too young to really comprehend the issues involved. But each knew enough to understand that something momentous was occurring and that they were a part of it. The first day in school is always a testing time for any child. But for those who had to go through police lines or be escorted by officers, the test was something more than going to school. It was an experience of very real courage and faith. The children in elementary and secondary schools and the young men and women who desegregated colleges and universities knew loneliness and hurt. But they stayed the course.

There has been criticism of what has been called "tokenism." Use of this word has cast a shadow over some of the school integrations. I do not agree that small beginnings were unwise or that they were in any sense tokens. What happened in Atlanta and other Southern cities where children were admitted in desegregation actions was that pupils selected under the placement acts had been carefully screened. It was important for them, and for those who would come after them, that they be children who would not fail. Had there been larger, unscreened admissions there inevitably would have been a number of failures. There would have been unavoidable charges of discrimination. Therefore, it seemed to me that it was the better part of wisdom to select students for the precedent-breaking changes who would be able to hold their own. In all Southern states where such admission policies were used the results have been good. It was possible then to build on this and to admit a larger number in the next year's classes. I have always regretted that the word "tokenism" came to be applied to many of the beginnings of school desegregation.

By 1962 there was evidence of some Southwide organization

of a hard-core hate group. Members of it seemed to be available on call to travel to distant states. Thus, when the Albany, Georgia, troubles reached the stage of violence in the late summer of 1962, Klan groups came from neighboring Alabama and South Carolina to participate in demonstrations. "Outsiders" were reported by police in almost every instance of racial violence in the South. This, of course, reached its climax in Oxford, Mississippi, when a considerable number of armed men appeared on the scene. Some of them were quoted as saying that they had come in response to General Edwin Walker's plea for supporters to join him there. Some of these men were found to have as many as three rifles in their cars.

Another melancholy development has been the mobility of teen-age toughs who have been on the move from state to state whenever violence seemed likely.

This fast-moving continuity of events has provided exciting experiences though, to be sure, there have been days of near-despair and sadness. The young toughs are perhaps the saddest of all spectacles.

Almost without exception the youngsters recruited into hate groups come from homes where they grew up hearing it. A ghastly sort of classroom for corrupting young minds exists, for example, in the homes of those adults, men and women, whose "achievements" are of the lowest grade—the anonymous telephone callers. They are so utterly common and vulgar, and so completely lacking in any quality save that of coarseness, that they become interesting because of their petty viciousness and the meagerness of their imagination and the poverty of their vile vocabulary.

They are, first of all, obsessed with sex. Females of this species, for example, regularly would telephone my home. If my wife answered they would speak in an absurd, stereotype Uncle Remus dialect and demand to know, with the most vulgar phrases, why I had not kept a date and was I coming. If I or my son answered, the approach was slightly varied. Often some of the men would call and, speaking in the preposterous phrases of the old minstrel show blackface acts of bygone generations, would say they had a daughter who wanted to marry a white nigger-lover. There were some who were simply psychopaths who spewed sex filth into the phone. A few who called dealt in threats of death and bombing. The mind pictured children listening to papa and mama, and the satisfaction of papa and mama over their "achievements."

There were those who telephoned at intervals all through the night. Pairs, or teams of them, harassed all those who publicly supported the courts and the morality of the school decision. Once during the desegregation of the University of Georgia, we had nineteen abusive calls between 7:30 and 9 P.M. In addition, there were those who saw in any effort to assist the Negro to have simple justice, the right to vote, and equal use of public services, a Communist plot. Some had to endure this idiocy in telephone calls and letters to the editor.

My experience with this sort of thing began in the early autumn of 1938. I had returned from Europe to be made executive editor. I was soon honored with a parade—about seventy-five or so robed and masked Klansmen paraded around the Constitution building one Saturday night carrying placards denouncing the paper and me.

From that time until the early spring of 1961, when my wife's increasing illness made an unlisted phone imperative, the number was in the book. In those years we were educated in how a Klansman, a White Citizens Council member, or plain vicious hater, attained status by achievement. For the more cretinlike, a filthy telephone call would suffice.

There were, of course, wonderful, warming, comforting, and strengthening compensations. One of these was almost weekly abuse by the Georgia equivalent of the White Citizens Council publication. It featured red and black type and its headlines were eighty-point bold and in the reddest of ink. I treasure, as a heritage for my son, certain copies of that paper. I knew we had it and its editor off balance and on the run as early as October, 1957, when the banner ribbon read: "Ralph McGill Menace to

Georgia: South's Worst Foe Since Thad Stevens." I was sure of it when the top red lines read "Ralph McGill Deliberately Lies Again; Tries To Scare South into Race Mixing" (Nov. 4, 1957); "McGill Continues to Deceive the People in Effort to Break Down Segregation" (Nov. 18, 1957); "People of Atlanta Will Not Be Tricked by Editor McGill." . . . (March 2, 1959); "Ralph McGill Is 'Just a Carpetbagger' Greensboro, Alabama Paper Charges" (March 9, 1959); "Georgia Politicians Had Better Beware the Siren Song of McGill, Hartsfield" (April 13, 1959); "Rastus McGill, Atlanta Constitution, Led People of Atlanta into a Boghole" (Jan. 11, 1960). In September of 1962 came the real accolade. The White Citizens Council choice for governor was defeated in the Georgia primary by a huge majority. Their headline, in red ink, read: "McGill's Race Mixing Philosophy Won Sweeping Victory Sept. 12." I had this issue framed as a sort of diploma.

There were other compensations. Letters of support and encouragement came, not too surprisingly, from small rural towns where the extremists ruled. Some were sent to neighboring towns to be mailed. Others were brought to Atlanta on a shopping tour and mailed there. One Thanksgiving eve a lady brought to my door a package of more than two hundred personal letters of thanks, and they were from white and colored citizens, teachers, professional and business people.

There were small, simple compensations which touched the heart with their sincerity. Frequently in restaurants an unknown Negro waiter or waitress would, in putting a plate of food on the table, whisper, "Thank you, sir, for what you write." Now and then a Negro cloakroom attendant would refuse the proffered tip, and say, "Please, sir. Let me do this for you."

There were compensations when the Atlanta bus lines were desegregated. To see the self-consciousness of most of those who boarded a bus and sat at the front or center, after a lifetime of going to the rear, was both an accusation and a compensation.

For some, the first experience of taking any available seat in a

trolley bus was one of intense excitement. A college professor
told me, "I was angry with myself for being self-conscious when
I took a seat midway up a bus. But unless you have lived all, or
most of your life, on a strictly segregated, separate basis, you
simply cannot comprehend what it means suddenly to be able to
sit in the middle of a bus."

John Hope, a distinguished member of Fisk University's faculty, said that he, and many of his friends, would now and then
take a plane to New York just to escape the pressurized chamber
of the South's segregation.

"I could never understand those white persons who would
say, with apparent sincerity, that they couldn't see why segregation really made much difference," said Hope. "It never seemed
to occur to them that a Negro might like to take his family out
to dinner or lunch at a decent restaurant. He could not do so in
the South. Or, he might wish to take his wife to a movie or concert without going down an alley to an entrance and climbing
two or three flights of stairs to a seat. The average nonhostile
white person never seemed to comprehend that his enjoyment
of such simple services might not be experienced by a Negro."

When the buses, the libraries, the department store restaurants, and golf courses were desegregated one could not avoid
the feeling of guilt which came with the knowledge that fellow
human beings had for so long been denied. There was an unexpected dividend for me in the desegregation of buses. Years ago
I gave up driving a car, and almost daily ride the bus some eight
miles to and from the office. In the first months after restrictions
ended, I usually was able to get a seat beside some Negro man or
woman. Some perplexed, or stubborn, white passengers would
be standing in the aisle, themselves self-conscious about the
change. This did not long endure. All too soon for my own selfish comfort, the old Southern custom lost out to tired feet and
weary legs. The sight of Negro and white persons sitting together ceased to be a novelty on my route. This, too, was a
compensation.

But greatest of all compensations was to be one of the many

who worked long and patiently at the arduous job of seeing to it that the people of Atlanta knew the facts and the alternatives. To see the golf courses, transportation, eating places, libraries and schools desegregated without an incident but rather with understanding and good manners was a warm and rewarding experience. There is almost an ecstasy which is quite indescribable, in seeing, and feeling, a city slowly but surely reach a decision and act on it. For a time, one lives a shared existence which is deeply rewarding.

Tim McLaurin

(1953–   )

Formerly known as Wild Man Mack *during his days as a carnival sideshow snake handler, Tim McLaurin was born and raised in the Fayetteville, North Carolina, area. He served in the U.S. Marines after graduating from high school, then returned to Fayetteville in 1975, where he worked as a driver/deliverer for Pepsi Cola before entering the carnival entertainment business. A Peace Corps volunteer for two years in Tunisia, he graduated from the University of North Carolina at Chapel Hill in 1986. His first novel,* The Acorn Plan, *was published in 1988 to favorable reviews, and was followed in 1989 by another novel,* Woodrow's Trumpet. *That year McLaurin was stricken by myeloma, but survived his bout with this deadly form of cancer after extensive chemotherapy and a bone marrow transplant. Like fellow North Carolinian Reynolds Price, who was prompted to engage in autobiographical reminiscence after surviving a near fatal struggle with cancer, McLaurin used his illness as an occasion to write his life story, resulting in the 1991 publication of* Keeper of the Moon: A Southern Boyhood. *McLaurin currently resides in Raleigh, where he continues to write. Recently, he has published two novels,* Cured by Fire *(1995), set in the tobacco fields of eastern North Carolina, and* The Last Great Snake Show *(1997), following the picaresque journey of a group of colorful social outcasts as they make their way from Carolina to Oregon.*

A truly memorable work, Keeper of the Moon, *from which the following excerpt is taken, ranges from fond memories of family bonds and boyhood adventures to relentlessly honest portrayals of human failures and wasted lives, from Sunday morning services at his grandpar-*

ents' Primitive Baptist Church to Saturday evening pit bull fights at all-night hog roasts. In the tradition of Harry Crews's A Childhood, Keeper of the Moon *strikes a balance between the gothic and the pastoral as it offers an unflinching and unapologetic account of life in the working-class South.*

FROM *Keeper of the Moon:*
A Southern Boyhood

L AWRANCE WILLIAMS STOOD to himself toward the back of the crowd, a single, lean black man, dressed in a black suit and white shirt. I had not seen him in years, but recognized him immediately. I was walking at the front corner of my father's coffin, a brother holding to each of the other corners, two uncles grasping the brass handles on each side. We were laying the old man to rest. One of his last requests had been that his sons carry him to the earth.

The grave was cut clean into the lawn: a green tarp had been fitted perfectly to cover the raw dirt. I knew we must set the coffin on top of the pulley structure, that I must not let my leg go into the hole, or trip and tip my end. I tried to ignore all the faces. Probably two hundred friends and family were gathered on that bright July day, but as I planted my feet carefully, I thought of Lawrance, remembered his son and how in my youth we had been close friends. It struck me that little had changed. We share the South now publicly, eat together, even marry, but there is still a distance, a final separation that will never end.

I CALLED HIM LJ, for Lawrance Junior, a wiry black kid who lived a half mile down the road. We were of the same age and grade. The Williamses lived in a rambling, wide-porched unpainted house that sat under a huge willow and several large oaks. Their seven kids rose in age like stair steps. Our fathers were both laborers by trade who worked farming on the side, our mothers about the same age, women who could wring a chicken's neck with a baby in one arm. Socially and economically, our families could not brag above each other, except for the fact that the Williamses were black. I called LJ's father Lawrance. LJ called my father Mr. Reese.

LJ lived just off the edge of civilized, white earth. The paved road stopped just beyond our house, and with the end of the tar stopped mail delivery, the telephone line, and school bus service. In the mornings in winter when the weather was good, we often met on the road beyond my house to wait for separate buses to the segregated schools we attended. Our ages were similar, Mabel the oldest sister, Sheryl an older brother, LJ, Kareen, Jackie, a baby or two that stayed home. We usually carried bag lunches to school, mine filled with a bologna sandwich on white bread, maybe a banana and vanilla wafers with peanut butter, a nickel buried in my pocket for milk. LJ's sack smelled of home-cooked biscuits split with salt pork. We wore clothes that looked similar, a match and mismatch of originals and hand-me-downs. Both our noses tended to run during cold weather, our lips would chap from the wind. I sometimes used a tube of Chap Stick, making ceremony as I coated extra on the corners of my mouth. I never offered him any and he never asked. We would talk, skip rocks, or hug ourselves for warmth until our separate buses came. His bus, a fixed-up hand-me-down from the white school system, usually came first, for it had a greater circuit to cover. The windows would be slam full of dark faces all pressed toward me when his bus stopped, all ages because the black school went from first to twelfth grade. He'd wave good-bye and step inside, jostle for seating along with his brothers and sisters. Winters we were only roadside acquaintances, both of us too busy staying warm to really be friends.

The coming of summer vacation brought down the barriers of clothes and color. As the sun deepened, my own skin turned darker like LJ's, both our heads were cut close of hair. The distinction of what bus we rode to school or the quality of our clothes lessened until a parity was reached where we were basically just two kids with idle time. Maybe it related to our common age and grade, maybe similar interests, but for several years, LJ and I were close friends. The other members of our families played together, but they were of mostly opposite sex, a barrier not tampered with in that era in the rural South. LJ and I roamed the woods and fields like wild creatures.

Neither of us cared to play the role of Jungle Jim when we were "natives" hunting wild game in the pine-thicket jungle that bordered my house. LJ, myself, my younger brothers, we'd strip down to only our briefs, and for hours we'd hunt the imaginary lion and rhino that inhabited those brushy twenty acres. We spoke in grunts and hand sign except for when only words would do, and were content to be equal warriors. In my mind, Jungle Jim was a sissy for wearing boots and a hat and I wanted no part of him.

Our weapon of choice was a spear cut from a reed. Sliced off at the base and trimmed of the leaves, the long, thin stems whistled a straight path through the air, and if honed with a pocketknife or piece of broken bottle, would stick end first into the ground. They were quite capable of putting out an eye.

Occasionally when game was scarce, we'd ambush the traffic that used the road through the pine thicket. In those days a car came along seldom, more likely a tractor or someone on foot. We'd follow at the woods edge, make noise, flash our spears, and then retreat. We were being unusually bold the day we spied a pickup coming, the four of us massing at the edge of the ditch, spears raised.

We were in full war paint. I had acquired a dog-eared copy of *National Geographic,* and we had used natural resources at hand to mimic the garb of a real African tribe. Red clay mixed with water, purple poke salad berries, a tube of old lipstick I'd found lying behind our couch, fresh skullcap haircuts—we looked as if pulled from under a log in the deepest jungle of Zaire. As the truck approached, we lifted our spears and crouched, and as it was passing, slung our arms forward, pretending we had launched our spears. We grinned broadly at a white man driving the truck.

Our arms had hardly stopped moving forward when the man driving the truck locked brakes and slid sideways in his effort to stop. He opened the door and stood on the running board. I recognized him as a man who lived a few miles down on the dirt roads beyond our house, the father of several ragged children who seldom got on the school bus. He glared at us for a moment, his jaw swelled with a plug of tobacco.

"You throw at my truck again, nigger, I'll cut your goddam throat," he said.

We all stood in silence.

"You hear me, jig? I seen you sling that rock."

LJ gave me a sidelong glance. "We didn't throw nothing, mister," I answered.

"That little nigger did. Rock or something. If it had dented my truck, I'd be rolling his black ass in the dirt right now."

"He ain't no nigger," I heard my voice say.

"He's blacker than the inside of my asshole. What y'all doing playing half-naked with a nigger, anyhow?"

For the life of me, I couldn't see a hair of difference between LJ and myself. Every exposed inch of skin was covered with either mud or berry juice. The man spit once on the road.

"You boys, I know your daddy. He wouldn't like you running around trying to act like a nigger. The nigger can't help it, but y'all can."

He slid back under the steering wheel and roared off. We never ambushed cars again.

At that early point in our lives, the end of the paved road between our houses seemed to divide our lives more than color. Not only did the mail service and telephone lines stop there, but so did the amenities that a few dollars a week difference in our fathers' salaries made possible. In the early years, I don't believe LJ envied my lighter shade of skin, but it was obvious he coveted

my access to a bologna sandwich on white, store-bought bread
with mayonnaise.

"It got to be on light bread," LJ stated emphatically. "Not no
corn bread or biscuit."

"We got three loaves of white bread," I assured him.

"Mayonnaise too," he continued. "You sure y'all got mayonnaise?"

"There's a jar full."

LJ's eyes sparkled as he reconsidered the proposal. A whole
bologna sandwich made with two slices of light bread and
plenty of mayonnaise, in exchange for mowing the grass in our
front lawn. Deal!

In a family blessed with an abundance of stale bread, sliced
bologna was a staple of life. The exchange of a second-class
sandwich for two hours of LJ's labor was an easy agreement for
me. I wondered at his eagerness: his own lunches of smoked
pork on homemade pan bread looked especially hot and crusty
and good.

"You got to cut close to the fence too," I reminded him. "So
the cows won't lean over the wire."

"I'll cut it. Let's go 'fore the sun gets any higher."

I studied the sun, and considered that my father didn't really
care who mowed the grass as long as it was done. He wouldn't
know, anyhow.

I'd stretch out in the shade of a tree while LJ labored behind
the splay-wheeled lawn mower, his dark skin running with
creeks of sweat. Occasionally I'd rise and direct him to a spot
he'd missed. The air would fill with the good smell of clipped
clover and fescue, toads and insects would flee the path of the
steel tornado. In the shortened grass, my brothers and I would
rediscover baseballs, dog-chewed Frisbees, a fork or spoon or
top. At last, LJ would mow over the last spot, he'd pull the
lever that shut off the gas, and again we'd hear birds, the whine
of the radio from where my older sister danced inside. He'd
brush off the grass that had clung to his sweaty legs, the crease of
a grin turning up the corners of his mouth. He wouldn't men-

tion the sandwich, and neither would I, but we'd start for the back door.

I think he enjoyed seeing the sandwich made almost half as much as eating it. He'd follow me as I took a loaf of bread from a shelf on the cabinet and laid it on the table, then to the refrigerator where a large jar of A&P mayonnaise sat cooling, the bologna one of those large economy packages, thick-sliced. He'd prop on his elbows and watch while I unscrewed the jar lid, laid out two slices of bread—never, never an end piece—took a spoon, and began lathering the mayonnaise on.

"Add little more to dat slice," he'd usually advise me.

When the proper amount of mayonnaise gleamed on each slice, I'd lift a piece of bologna from the package and peel off the casing around the edge. LJ savored the casing, would pull it between his teeth and scrape off the skim of bologna. He would insist that I center the slice of meat between the bread, no edges hanging off, and place the top slice of bread on carefully, not mash the imprint of my hand. The result wouldn't have excited a hobo, but LJ found it exotic.

He drank his water before eating, two glassfuls straight out of the cold water faucet in the kitchen. While I was the sandwich architect, drawing the water was his privilege. He was fascinated by the frothy water that gushed from the spigot. It tasted slightly of plastic pipe and had warmed in its long travel from the ground—in my opinion, it was a poor second to the pump water that gushed cold and clear in his backyard. He'd drink down two full glasses, never pausing while his throat pulsed. Then we'd go outside and sit in the shade, and he'd eat the sandwich slowly with small bites, rolling the sticky mass over his tongue, straining it well between his teeth and gums. The sweat would have dried now on his arms and legs like gullies cut through the film of dust. He'd chew slowly, thoughtfully. I'd feel guilty knowing that in an instant I would trade him two sandwiches for one of the fat, homemade biscuits filled with salt pork that he disdained.

AS THE WORLD MOVED into the sixties and our radio was replaced by a television, I became increasingly aware that a war was beginning between whites and blacks.

"You mark my words, somebody's gonna put a bullet through his head," my Uncle Jesse said. "People ain't gonna listen to such talk."

We were eating fried Virginia mullet, my dad and his older brother watching the television news as Martin Luther King paraded down a street backed by several hundred young blacks. The Porter Waggoner show had just ended, his twangy guitar and voice replaced by the oiled speech of a young Dan Rather. I was ten years old and stared uneasily at the television at signs and placards held aloft, demanding equal rights, blacks in clean, pressed clothes huddled together while surrounded by groups of angry white people.

"It ain't nothing but Communists," my father said. "Trying to stir up trouble. You look at Lawrance Williams right down the road there. Now, I respect that man. He works, looks after his family. You won't see him out there acting like that."

"The nigger needs a bullet," Jesse said, his eyes narrowing as King spoke into a microphone.

"Y'all hush that kind of talk in front of the children," my mother exclaimed.

"Well, it's the truth," my uncle continued. "Somebody'll get him."

After supper my brothers and cousins and I were herded out-side while the adults enjoyed a cup of coffee. Twilight was set-tling, doves beginning to call, a few early bats swooped for insects. One of my older cousins thought of the game, and soon we were all lined up, marched in goose step, chanting "Equal rights" over and over. The parade wound through the yard, cir-cling trees and moving along the edge of the road. Soon we were laughing so hard we could barely walk.

I spied LJ from the corner of my eye, and my laughter caught like a burr in my throat. He stood on the far side of the road, staring straight into my face, his arms straight by his side. I stopped, and the marchers passed me by and continued on, still goose-stepping, still shouting. LJ turned at that moment and began walking toward his house, but I ran to him and caught him by the arm.

"You want to cut the grass tomorrow?" I blurted. "The grass is getting high, and you can cut it if you want. We got plenty of bologna."

"Maybe I cut it," he said, staring at the line of marchers now rounding the corner of the house, their chant of "Equal rights" drowning out the animal calls of twilight.

"It needs cutting," I assured him. "My dad was complaining about it today. Mama brought home a new package of bologna just this afternoon."

We parted with goodbyes in the tepid air of that early evening, but a breach of trust had been committed and was the first crack in our union against time and change.

★   ★   ★

I THOUGHT OF LJ and of those simple early summers while the preacher spoke of my father and of the rewards of the dead. I avoided looking at the flower-draped coffin by staring at Lawrance. He shifted his weight from leg to leg, his eyes trained on a space of ground as if his thoughts too were remembering a better time. I made up my mind that I would go to him following the prayer and tell him how I appreciated him coming, inquire about LJ and the rest of his family. But when the final prayer ended, we were hustled toward the big black car. I reached out my arm and shook Lawrance's hand and said I was glad to see him. But I did not tarry, people were watching and waiting. I got in the limousine and closed the door against the world.

Anne Moody

(1940–   )

Born near Centreville, Mississippi, Anne Moody was one of many local volunteers who put their lives on the line by participating in the drive for voting rights and desegregation in her home state. She attended Natchez Junior College for two years before transferring to Tougaloo College in Jackson, where she became a worker in the NAACP, the Congress of Racial Equality, and the Student Non-violent Coordinating Committee. Through her involvement in those organizations, she was working closely with civil-rights leader Medgar Evers at the time of his assassination in 1963. (Evers's assassination and the eventual conviction more than thirty years later of white supremacist Byron de la Beckwith is the subject of the recent film Ghosts of Mississippi.) *The author of a book of short stories,* Mr. Death (1975), *she is best known for her autobiography,* Coming of Age in Mississippi (1969). *Her writings have appeared in* Ms. *magazine and* Mademoiselle. *A resident of New York City, she is currently at work on a novel.*

Coming of Age in Mississippi is a stirring and invaluable eye-witness account of some of the most important events of the civil rights movement's Mississippi campaign. In addition to her recollections of the more public battles fought in that epic struggle, she also recounts the more intimate conflicts she faced in dealing with family members and friends from home who were too intimidated by the threat of whites' retribution to force change in their own communities. In the following excerpt, Moody (called Essie at this time) describes her response to hearing, at age fourteen, of the killing of fourteen-year-old Emmett Till in a neighboring county.

NOT ONLY did I enter high school with a new name, but also with a completely new insight into the life of Negroes in Mississippi. I was now working for one of the meanest white women in town, and a week before school started Emmett Till was killed.

Up until his death, I had heard of Negroes found floating in a river or dead somewhere with their bodies riddled with bullets. But I didn't know the mystery behind these killings then. I remember once when I was only seven I heard Mama and one of my aunts talking about some Negro who had been beaten to death. "Just like them low-down skunks killed him they will do the same to us," Mama had said. When I asked her who killed the man and why, she said, "An Evil Spirit killed him. You gotta be a good girl or it will kill you too." So since I was seven, I had lived in fear of that "Evil Spirit." It took me eight years to learn what that spirit was.

I was coming from school the evening I heard about Emmett Till's death. There was a whole group of us, girls and boys, walking down the road headed home. A group of about six high school boys were walking a few paces ahead of me and several other girls. We were laughing and talking about something that had happened in school that day. However, the six boys in front of us weren't talking very loud. Usually they kept up so much noise. But today they were just walking and talking among themselves. All of a sudden they began to shout at each other.

"Man, what in the hell do you mean?"

"What I mean is these goddamned white folks is gonna start some shit here you just watch!"

"That boy wasn't but fourteen years old and they killed him. Now what kin a fourteen-year-old boy do with a white woman? What if he did whistle at her, he might have thought the whore was pretty."

"Look at all these white men here that's fucking over our women. Everybody knows it too and what's done about that? Look how many white babies we got walking around in our neighborhoods. Their mamas ain't white either. That boy was from Chicago, shit, everybody fuck everybody up there. He probably didn't even think of the bitch as white."

What they were saying shocked me. I knew all of those boys and I had never heard them talk like that. We walked on behind them for a while listening. Questions about who was killed, where, and why started running through my mind. I walked up to one of the boys.

"Eddie, what boy was killed?"

"Moody, where've you been?" he asked me. "Everybody talking about that fourteen-year-old boy who was killed in Greenwood by some white men. You don't know nothing that's going on besides what's in them books of yours, huh?"

Standing there before the rest of the girls, I felt so stupid. It was then that I realized I really didn't know what was going on around me. It wasn't that I was dumb. It was just that ever since I was nine, I'd had to work after school and do my lessons on lunch hour. I never had time to learn anything, to hang around with people my own age. And you never were told anything by adults.

That evening when I stopped off at the house on my way to Mrs. Burke's, Mama was singing. Any other day she would have been yelling at Adline and Junior them to take off their school clothes. I wondered if she knew about Emmett Till. The way she was singing she had something on her mind and it wasn't pleasant either.

> I got a shoe, you got a shoe,
> All of God's chillun got shoes;
> When I get to hebben, I'm gonna put on my shoes,
> And gonna tromp all over God's hebben.

When I get to hebben I'm gonna put on my shoes,
And gonna walk all over God's hebben.

Mama was dishing up beans like she didn't know anyone was home. Adline, Junior, and James had just thrown their books down and sat themselves at the table. I didn't usually eat before I went to work. But I wanted to ask Mama about Emmett Till. So I ate and thought of some way of asking her.

"These beans are some good, Mama," I said, trying to sense her mood.

"Why is you eating anyway? You gonna be late for work. You know how Miss Burke is," she said to me.

"I don't have much to do this evening. I kin get it done before I leave work," I said.

The conversation stopped after that. Then Mama started humming that song again.

When I get to hebben, I'm gonna put on my shoes,
And gonna tromp all over God's hebben.

She put a plate on the floor for Jennie Ann and Jerry.

"Jennie Ann! you and Jerry sit down here and eat and don't put beans all over this floor."

Ralph, the baby, started crying, and she went in the bedroom to give him his bottle. I got up and followed her.

"Mama, did you hear about that fourteen-year-old Negro boy who was killed a little over a week ago by some white men?" I asked her.

"Where did you hear that?" she said angrily.

"Boy, everybody really thinks I am dumb or deaf or something. I heard Eddie them talking about it this evening coming from school."

"Eddie them better watch how they go around here talking. Those white folks git a hold of it they gonna be in trouble," she said.

"What are they gonna be in trouble about, Mama? People got a right to talk, ain't they?"

"You go on to work before you is late. And don't you let on like you know nothing about that boy being killed before Miss Burke them. Just do your work like you don't know nothing," she said. "That boy's a lot better off in heaven than he is here," she continued and then started singing again.

On my way to Mrs. Burke's that evening, Mama's words kept running through my mind. "Just do your work like you don't know nothing." "Why is Mama acting so scared?" I thought. "And what if Mrs. Burke knew we knew? Why must I pretend I don't know? Why are these people killing Negroes? What did Emmett Till do besides whistle at that woman?"

By the time I got to work, I had worked my nerves up some. I was shaking as I walked up on the porch. "Do your work like you don't know nothing." But once I got inside, I couldn't have acted normal if Mrs. Burke were paying me to be myself.

I was so nervous, I spent most of the evening avoiding them going about the house dusting and sweeping. Everything went along fairly well until dinner was served.

"Don, Wayne, and Mama, y'all come on to dinner. Essie, you can wash up the pots and dishes in the sink now. Then after dinner you won't have as many," Mrs. Burke called to me.

If I had the power to mysteriously disappear at that moment, I would have. They used the breakfast table in the kitchen for most of their meals. The dining room was only used for Sunday dinner or when they had company. I wished they had company tonight so they could eat in the dining room while I was at the kitchen sink.

"I forgot the bread," Mrs. Burke said when they were all seated. "Essie, will you cut it and put it on the table for me?"

I took the cornbread, cut it in squares, and put it on a small round dish. Just as I was about to set it on the table, Wayne yelled at the cat. I dropped the plate and the bread went all over the floor.

"Never mind, Essie," Mrs. Burke said angrily as she got up and got some white bread from the breadbox.

I didn't say anything. I picked up the cornbread from around the table and went back to the dishes. As soon as I got to the sink, I dropped a saucer on the floor and broke it. Didn't anyone say a word until I had picked up the pieces.

"Essie, I bought some new cleanser today. It's setting on the bathroom shelf. See if it will remove the stains in the tub," Mrs. Burke said.

I went to the bathroom to clean the tub. By the time I got through with it, it was snow white. I spent a whole hour scrubbing it. I had removed the stains in no time but I kept scrubbing until they finished dinner.

When they had finished and gone into the living room as usual to watch TV, Mrs. Burke called me to eat. I took a clean plate out of the cabinet and sat down. Just as I was putting the first forkful of food in my mouth, Mrs. Burke entered the kitchen.

"Essie, did you hear about that fourteen-year-old boy who was killed in Greenwood?" she asked me, sitting down in one of the chairs opposite me.

"No, I didn't hear that," I answered, almost choking on the food.

"Do you know why he was killed?" she asked and I didn't answer.

"He was killed because he got out of his place with a white woman. A boy from Mississippi would have known better than that. This boy was from Chicago. Negroes up North have no respect for people. They think they can get away with anything. He just came to Mississippi and put a whole lot of notions in the boys' heads here and stirred up a lot of trouble," she said passionately.

"How old are you, Essie?" she asked me after a pause.

"Fourteen. I will soon be fifteen though," I said.

"See, that boy was just fourteen too. It's a shame he had to die so soon." She was so red in the face, she looked as if she was on fire.

When she left the kitchen I sat there with my mouth open and my food untouched. I couldn't have eaten now if I were starving. "Just do your work like you don't know nothing" ran through my mind again and I began washing the dishes.

I went home shaking like a leaf on a tree. For the first time out of all her trying, Mrs. Burke had made me feel like rotten garbage. Many times she had tried to instill fear within me and subdue me and had given up. But when she talked about Emmett Till there was something in her voice that sent chills and fear all over me.

Before Emmett Till's murder, I had known the fear of hunger, hell, and the Devil. But now there was a new fear known to me—the fear of being killed just because I was black. This was the worst of my fears. I knew once I got food, the fear of starving to death would leave. I also was told that if I were a good girl, I wouldn't have to fear the Devil or hell. But I didn't know what one had to do or not do as a Negro not to be killed. Probably just being a Negro period was enough, I thought.

A FEW DAYS LATER, I went to work and Mrs. Burke had about eight women over for tea. They were all sitting around in the living room when I got there. She told me she was having a "guild meeting," and asked me to help her serve the cookies and tea.

After helping her, I started cleaning the house. I always swept the hallway and porch first. As I was sweeping the hall, I could hear them talking. When I heard the word "nigger," I stopped sweeping and listened. Mrs. Burke must have sensed this, because she suddenly came to the door.

"Essie, finish the hall and clean the bathroom," she said hesitantly. "Then you can go for today. I am not making dinner tonight." Then she went back in the living room with the rest of the ladies.

Before she interrupted my listening, I had picked up the words "NAACP" and "that organization." Because they were talking about niggers, I knew NAACP had something to do with Negroes. All that night I kept wondering what could that NAACP mean?

Later when I was sitting in the kitchen at home doing my lessons, I decided to ask Mama. It was about twelve-thirty. Everyone was in bed but me. When Mama came in to put some milk in Ralph's bottle, I said, "Mama, what do NAACP mean?"

"Where did you git that from?" she asked me, spilling milk all over the floor.

"Mrs. Burke had a meeting tonight—"

"What kind of meeting?" she asked, cutting me off.

"I don't know. She had some women over—she said it was a guild meeting," I said.

"A guild meeting," she repeated.

"Yes, they were talking about Negroes and I heard some woman say 'that NAACP' and another 'that organization,' meaning the same thing."

"What else did they say?" she asked me.

"That's all I heard. Mrs. Burke must have thought I was listening, so she told me to clean the bathroom and leave."

"Don't you ever mention that word around Mrs. Burke or no other white person, you heah! Finish your lesson and cut that light out and go to bed," Mama said angrily and left the kitchen.

"With a Mama like that you'll never learn anything," I thought as I got into bed. All night long I thought about Emmett Till and the NAACP. I even got up to look up NAACP in my little concise dictionary. But I didn't find it.

The next day at school, I decided to ask my homeroom teacher Mrs. Rice the meaning of NAACP. When the bell sounded for lunch, I remained in my seat as the other students left the room.

"Are you going to spend your lunch hour studying again today, Moody?" Mrs. Rice asked me.

"Can I ask you a question, Mrs. Rice?" I asked her.

"You *may* ask me a question, yes, but I don't know if you *can* or not," she said.

"What does the word NAACP mean?" I asked.

"Why do you want to know?"

"The lady I worked for had a meeting and I overheard the word mentioned."

"What else did you hear?"

"Nothing. I didn't know what NAACP meant, that's all." I felt like I was on the witness stand or something.

"Well, next time your boss has another meeting you listen more carefully. NAACP is a Negro organization that was established a long time ago to help Negroes gain a few basic rights," she said.

"What's it gotta do with the Emmett Till murder?" I asked.

"They are trying to get a conviction in Emmett Till's case. You see the NAACP is trying to do a lot for the Negroes and get the right to vote for Negroes in the South. I shouldn't be telling you all this. And don't you dare breathe a word of what I said. It could cost me my job if word got out I was teaching my students such. I gotta go to lunch and you should go outside too because it's nice and sunny out today," she said leaving the room. "We'll talk more when I have time."

About a week later, Mrs. Rice had me over for Sunday dinner, and I spent about five hours with her. Within that time, I digested a good meal and accumulated a whole new pool of knowledge about Negroes being butchered and slaughtered by whites in the South. After Mrs. Rice had told me all this, I felt like the lowest animal on earth. At least when other animals (hogs, cows, etc.) were killed by man, they were used as food. But when man was butchered or killed by man, in the case of Negroes by whites, they were left lying on a road or found floating in a river or something.

Mrs. Rice got to be something like a mother to me. She told me anything I wanted to know. And made me promise that I would keep all this information she was passing on to me to myself. She said she couldn't, rather didn't, want to talk about these things to the other teachers, that they would tell Mr. Willis and she would be fired. At the end of that year she was fired. I never found out why. I haven't seen her since then.

Willie Morris

(1934–   )

The noted journalist, editor, novelist, autobiographer, and storyteller Willie Morris was born in Jackson, Mississippi, but moved before his first birthday to the town of Yazoo City on the edge of the Mississippi Delta. On the advice of his father, who wanted his son to see the world beyond the parochialism of small town Mississippi, he attended college at the University of Texas, where he got his first taste of journalism as the editor of the school newspaper. The recipient of a Rhodes Scholarship, he studied at Oxford for four years, earning a bachelor's and master's degree there before returning to Texas in 1961 to edit the Texas Observer *in Austin. In 1963 he was hired as an editor for* Harper's *magazine and soon became the youngest ever editor in chief of that publication. After an absence of twenty-eight years, Morris returned to his home state in 1980 as writer-in-residence at the University of Mississippi. He is the author of more than fifteen books, including* Yazoo: Integration in a Deep-Southern Town *(1971),* The Courting of Marcus Dupree *(1983),* Faulkner's Mississippi *(with photographs by William Eggleston [1990]), and, most recently,* The Ghosts of Medgar Evers: A Tale of Race, Murder, Mississippi, and Hollywood *(1998). His childhood memoir,* My Dog Skip *(1995), is currently being adapted into a motion picture. Morris lives in Jackson, Mississippi.*

During the civil rights era, many southerners living outside the region were at pains to distance themselves from the bigotry of the Ku Klux Klan and racist officials in the South. In the ironically titled North Toward Home *(1967), Morris used the autobiographical occasion to voice his disgust with the white South's refusal to abide by the decisions of the Supreme Court. Divided into three sections, "Missis-*

sippi," "Texas," and "New York," the narrative traces the author's gradual enlightenment on matters of race and his resulting sense of alienation from the place he once called home. In the first of those sections, from which the following excerpt is taken, Morris recounts his youth and adolescence in Yazoo City, taking care to describe the pervasive assumptions of white supremacy that were part of that world, even as he speaks nostalgically of the sense of community there. In the following selection, he invokes the confessional motif used by other white liberal southern autobiographers like Lillian Smith and Katherine Du Pre Lumpkin, describing his most shameful memories of the racism he once unquestioningly accepted and participated in so that he can more convincingly renounce his sins.

FROM *North Toward Home*

O NE SUMMER MORNING when I was twelve, I sighted a little Negro boy walking with a girl who must have been his older sister on the sidewalk a block from my house. The little boy could not have been more than three; he straggled along behind the older girl, walking aimlessly on his short black legs from one edge of the sidewalk to the other.

I hid in the shrubbery near the sidewalk in my yard, peering out two or three times to watch their progress and to make sure the street was deserted. The older girl walked by first, and the child came along a few yards behind. Just as he got in front of me, lurking there in the bushes, I jumped out and pounced upon him. I slapped him across the face, kicked him with my knee, and with a shove sent him sprawling on the concrete.

The little boy started crying, and his sister ran back to him and shouted, "What'd he *do* to you?" My heart was beating furiously, in terror and a curious pleasure; I ran into the back of my house and hid in the weeds for a long time, until the crying drifted far away into niggertown. Then I went into the deserted house and sat there alone, listening to every noise and rustle I heard outside, as if I expected some retribution. For a while I was happy with this act, and my head was strangely light and giddy. Then later, the more I thought about it coldly, I could hardly bear my secret shame.

Once before, when I had been a much smaller boy, I had caught a little sparrow trapped on my screen porch, and almost without thinking, acting as if I were another person and not myself, I had fetched a straight pin, stuck it through the bird's head, and opened the door to let him fly away. My hurting the Negro child, like my torturing the bird, was a gratuitous act of childhood cruelty—but I knew later that it was something else, infinitely more subtle and contorted.

For my whole conduct with the Negroes as I was growing up in the 1940s was a relationship of great contrasts. On the one hand there was a kind of unconscious affection, touched with a sense of excitement and sometimes pity. On the other hand there were sudden emotional eruptions—of disdain and utter cruelty. My own alternating affections and cruelties were inexplicable to me, but the main thing is that they were largely *assumed* and only rarely questioned. The broader reality was that the Negroes in the town were *there*: they were ours, to do with as we wished. I grew up with this consciousness of some tangible possession, it was rooted so deeply in me by the whole moral atmosphere of the place that my own ambivalence—which would take mysterious shapes as I grew older—was secondary and of little account.

One fact I took for granted was that Negro adults, even Negro adults I encountered alone and had never seen before, would treat me with generosity and affection. Another was some vague feeling for a mutual sharing of the town's past. (I remember going with one of my friends and her parents to take some food to an old Negro woman who lived alone in a cabin in the woods. The old woman told us about growing up in Yazoo, and of the day she saw the Yankee soldiers coming down the road in a cloud of dust. "I looked out the window," she said, "and there was the War, comin' at me from down the road.") Another assumption was that you would never call a Negro woman a "lady" or address her as "ma'am," or say "sir" to a Negro man. You learned as a matter of course that there were certain negative practices and conditions inherently associated with being a nigger. "Keeping a house like a nigger" was to keep it dirty and unswept. A "nigger car" was an old wreck without brakes and with squirrel tails on the radio aerial. "Behaving like a nigger" was to stay out at all hours and to have several wives or husbands. A "nigger street" was unpaved and littered with garbage. "Nigger talk" was filled with lies and superstitions. A "nigger funeral" meant wailing and shouting and keeping the corpse out of the ground for two weeks. A "white nigger store" was owned by a white man who went after the "nigger trade." There were "good niggers" and "bad niggers," and their categories were so formalized and elaborate that you wondered how they could live together in the same town.

Yet in the midst of all this there was the ineluctable attraction of niggertown, which enclosed the white town on all sides like some other world, and the strange heart-pounding excitement that Negroes in a group generated for me. I knew all about the sexual act, but not until I was twelve years old did I know that it was performed with white women for pleasure; I had thought that only Negro women engaged in the act of love with white men just for fun, because they were the only ones with the animal desire to submit that way. So that Negro girls and women were a source of constant excitement and sexual feeling for me, and filled my day-dreams with delights and wonders.

WHENEVER I GO back there and drive through niggertown, it is as if I had never left home. Few of the old shabby vistas seem changed, and time has not moved all these years for me: the strong greasy smells are the same, and the dust in the yards swirling around the abandoned cars, and the countless children with their glazed eyes on the porches and in the trees and in the road. The Negro grocery stores, the ones my dog and I drove

past in the summers, are still patched and covered with adver-
tisements, and the little boys still wait in front for a white man
with his golf clubs to drive up and shout, "Caddy!" The farther
one goes into niggertown, up Brickyard or down nearer the
town dump, the more dank and lean-to the structures: at first
there will be the scattering of big, almost graceful houses,
wholly painted or partially so, suggesting a slightly forbidding
affluence as they always had for me—but back along the fringes
of the town there remains that dreadful forlorn impoverish-
ment, those dusty and ruined wooden façades which as a child
would send me back toward Grand Avenue as fast as I could get
there.

In a small town like this one in the lower South, where the
population ran close to half and half, one of the simplest facts of
awareness was that Negroes were everywhere: they ambled
along the sidewalks in the white neighborhoods, they mowed
the grass and clipped the hedges in the broad green lawns, they
rode down the streets in their horse-drawn wagons, they were
the janitors and cleaning-women in the churches and schools
and the laundry-women coming to the back doors for the
week's wash. On the main street especially, on Saturdays, the
town was filled with them, talking in great animated clusters on
the corners, or spilling out of the drugstores and cafés at the far
end of the narrow street. Their shouts and gestures, and the loud
blare of their music, were so much a part of those Saturdays that
if all of them had suddenly disappeared the town would have
seemed unbearably ghostly and bereft. The different shades of
color were extraordinary, for they ranged from the whitest white
to the darkest black, with shades in between as various and distinct as yellows and browns could be. One woman in particular,
whom we saw walking through the crowds on Main Street on
Saturday nights, could have passed for a member of the women's
choir in the white Baptist church. "There's that white nigger
again," someone would say. "I wonder what the *others* think of
her?" Not until I was fourteen or fifteen did it begin to occur to
me to ask myself, "Are we *related*?" And it was about then that I

began hearing the story of the two white men who had Thanksgiving and Christmas dinner every year with three Negroes, who were the white men's half-brothers.

THERE WAS a stage, when we were about thirteen, in which we "went Negro." We tried to broaden our accents to sound like Negroes, as if there were not enough similarity already. We consciously walked like young Negroes, mocking their swinging gait, moving our arms the way they did, cracking our knuckles and whistling between our teeth. We tried to use some of the same expressions, as closely as possible to the way they said them, like: "Hey, ma-a-a-n, what you doin' theah!," the sounds rolled out and clipped sharply at the end for the hell of it.

My father and I, on Sundays now and then, would go to their baseball games, sitting way out along the right field line; usually we were the only white people there. There was no condescension on our part, though the condescension might come later, if someone asked us where we had been. I would say, "Oh, we been to see the nigger game over at Number Two."

"Number Two" was the Negro school, officially called "Yazoo High Number Two" as opposed to the white high school, which was "Yazoo High Number One." We would walk up to a Negro our age and ask, "Say, buddy, where you go to school?" so we could hear the way he said, "Number *Two!*" Number Two was behind my house a block or so, a strange eclectic collection of old ramshackle wooden buildings and bright new concrete ones, sprawled out across four or five acres. When the new buildings went up, some of the white people would say, "Well, they won't be pretty very *long.*"

Sometimes we would run across a group of Negro boys our age, walking in a pack through the white section, and there would be bantering, half-affectionate exchanges: "Hey, Robert, what you *doin'* theah!" and we would give them the first names of the boys they didn't know, and they would do the same. We would mill around in a hopping, jumping mass, talking baseball or football, showing off for each other, and sounding for all the world, with our accentuated expressions and our way of saying them, like much the same race. Some days we organized football games in Lintonia Park, first black against white, then intermingled, strutting out of huddles with our limbs swinging, shaking our heads rhythmically, until one afternoon the cops came cruising by in their patrol car and ordered us to break it up.

On Friday afternoons in the fall, we would go to see "the Black Panthers" of Number Two play football. They played in the discarded uniforms of our high school, so that our school colors—red, black, and white—were the same, and they even played the same towns from up in the delta that our high school played. We sat on the sidelines next to their cheering section, and sometimes a couple of us would be asked to carry the first-down chains. The spectators would shout and jump up and down, and even run onto the field to slap one of the players on the back when he did something outstanding. When one of the home team got hurt, ten or twelve people would dash out from the sidelines to carry him to the bench; I suspected some injuries might not have been as painful as they looked.

The Panthers had a left-handed quarterback named Kinsey, who could throw a pass farther than any other high school passer I had ever seen. He walked by my house every morning on the way to school, and I would get in step with him, emulating his walk as we strolled down to Number Two, and talk about last Friday's game or the next one coming up. We would discuss plays or passing patterns, and we pondered how they could improve on their "flea-flicker" which had backfired so disastrously against Belzoni, leading to a tackle's making an easy interception and all but walking thirty yards for a touchdown. "Man, he coulda *crawled* for that touchdown," Kinsey bemoaned. Once I said, "You got to get another kicker," and Kinsey replied, "Lord don't *I* know it," because in the previous game the Yazoo punter had kicked from his own twenty-yard-line, a high cantankerous spiral that curved up, down, and landed right in the middle of his own end zone. But this was a freak, because Kinsey and many of his teammates were not only superb athletes, they played with a casual flair and an exuberance that seemed missing in the white games. A long time after this, sitting in the bleachers in Candlestick Park in San Francisco, I saw a batter for the New York Mets hit a home run over the centerfield fence; the ball hit a rung on the bleachers, near a group of little boys, and then bounced back over the fence onto the outfield grass. Willie Mays trotted over and gingerly tossed the ball underhanded across the wire fence to the boys, who had been deprived of a free baseball, and that casual gesture was performed with such a fine aristocracy that it suddenly brought back to me all the flamboyant sights and sounds of those Friday afternoons watching Number Two.

On Friday nights, when the Yazoo Indians of Number One played, you could see the Number Two boys, watching with their girlfriends from the end-zone seats, talking plays and pointing out strategy. One night my father and I went to the hot-dog stand at halftime and saw Dr. Harrison, the Negro dentist who refereed the Number Two games, standing on the fringes of the crowd eating a hot-dog. My father drifted over his way and said, "How're you, Doc?" though not shaking hands, and they stood there until the second half started, talking about the virtues and shortcomings of the Yazoo Indians and the Yazoo Black Panthers.

CO-EXISTING WITH all this, in no conflict, were the hoaxes we would play on the Negroes, who were a great untapped resource. We would hide in the hedges in my back yard and shoot Negro men who were walking down the sidewalk, aiming BB's at their tails. We would throw dead snakes from the trees into their path, or dead rats and crawfish, or attach a long thread to a dollar bill on the sidewalk and, when the man stooped to pick it up, pull it slowly back into the bushes.

I took to phoning the Negro undertakers, talking in my flawless Negro accent, and exchanges like this would take place:

"Hello, this the undertaker?"

"Yes'm."

"This here's Miss Mobley, from out at Bentonia. I got me a problem."

"What's that?"

"Well, my cousin just died, and I wonder if I can bury him under the house."

"Bury him under the *house?*"

"That right. He never amounted to much to us, and we just want him out of the way quick."

"You can't do it. It's against the *law.*"

"But what if we don't tell nobody? Ain't nobody gonna miss him noway."

"Naw, you can't do it. You got to get a death certificate and things like that."

"Well, we still gonna put him under the house. Is Johnson's Baby Powder a good thing to sprinkle him with?"

"Johnson's *Baby Powder?* Lord no!"

"But it says on the can it's good for the body."

"Lady, you got to have your cousin buried *right.*" So I would give the undertaker the address, and then we would dash to the corner and watch the big black hearse come by on the way to Bentonia.

Or I would pick a Negro number at random from the telephone book, and phone it and say I was Bert Parks, calling from New York City on the Break-the-Bank program. Their number had been chosen out of all the telephones in the United States, and if they could answer three questions they would win $1000. "But I must warn you, Mrs. McGee, you are now *on the air,* and your voice is going into every home in America. Mrs. J. D. McGee, of Yazoo, Mississippi, are you ready for *question number one?*"

"Yessir, an' I hope I can answer it."

"Question number one! Who was the first President of the United States?"

"Why, George Washington was."

"That's absolutely correct, Mrs. McGee," as my fellow con-
spirators applauded in the background. "Now for question
number two, and if you answer it correctly you get a chance to
answer our big break-the-bank question. What is the capital of
the United States?"

"Washington, D.C. is."

"Very good!" (applause) "Now, Mrs. McGee, are you ready
down there in Yazoo for the big jackpot question?"

"Yessir!"

"Here it is. . . . *How many miles in the world?*"

"How many miles in the *world*?"

"That's right."

"The whole thing?"

"All of it."

"Oh Lord, I'll just have to guess. . . . One million!"

"One million? Mrs. McGee, I'm afraid you just missed! The
correct answer should have been one million and three."

SEVERAL TIMES I recall my father saying, when I was a small
boy, "I don't know why they treat these niggers so bad. They
pay taxes just like everybody else. If they pay taxes they oughta
get to vote. It's as simple as that. If they don't get to vote they
ought not to have to pay any taxes."

But one day the police finally caught Willie Johnson, a Negro
who had broken into a number of white houses on our street
and stolen everything he could carry away with him. He stole
my mother's engagement ring from our house, and several
pieces of family silver that the Harpers had buried in the dirt
floor of their smokehouse before the federal troops had arrived
in Raymond. The police brought Willie Johnson to the city hall
for questioning, and telephoned all the men whose houses had
been broken into to come down and question him. My father
took me with him.

It was a stifling hot summer day, so hot that all you had to do
was walk into the sun and your armpits and the hair on your

head would soon be soaking wet. The room at the city hall was a small one; it was crowded with white men, and several others peered through the open door from the hallway. The police chief was sitting behind a desk, and when he saw my father he shouted, "Come on in and let's talk to this boy." I found a place on the floor next to my father's chair, and then I saw the Negro, sitting in a straight chair, trussed up and sweating as much as I was. The other white men were looking at him, glowering hard and not saying a word. The police chief asked the Negro a few questions, and as I sat there taking it all in I heard a man I knew turn to Willie Johnson and say, in a strangely subdued voice, sounding not at all like himself: "Nigger, I just want to tell you one thing, and you better get it straight, because I ain't gonna repeat it. . . . If I so much as see you walkin' down the sidewalk in front of our house, I'll blow your head off."

A young boy grew up with other things: with the myths, the stories handed down. One of them concerned one of the town's policemen, a gnarled and skinny old man by the time I was growing up, who had shot a Negro on the sidewalk on the lower end of Main Street and stood over him with his pistol to prevent anyone from taking him away while he bled to death. Whether it was apocryphal or not was almost irrelevant, for the terror of that story was quite enough; we saw the policeman almost every day, making his rounds of the parking meters. "Don't fool with ol' ———," someone would say. "He'd just as soon shoot you as *look* at you," and then recount the legend in gory detail. There was the tale of the white planter, who owned one of the big plantations in the delta. When one of his Negro hands looked too closely at his wife one day, the man got his gun and killed him, and there was no trial.

There were a boy's recurring sense impressions of a hovering violence, isolated acts that remained in my memory long afterward, as senseless and unpatterned later as they had been for me when they happened:

. . . Some white men came to see my father, when I was six or seven years old. I heard them talking at the front door.

"We hear the niggers might cause trouble tonight," one of them said. My father went to town to buy some extra shotgun shells, and we locked all our doors and windows when the sun went down.

. . . A Negro shot and killed a white man at the honky-tonk near the town dump. When the time came for him to be executed, they brought the state's portable electric chair in a big truck from Jackson. We drove by and saw it parked in the back yard of the jail. The next day some older boys told me they had stayed up until midnight, with the lights on in their house, to watch all the lights dim when the nigger got killed.

. . . I was playing with some older boys behind the Church of Christ chapel. Three barefooted Negro children appeared in the alley and began rifling through the garbage can. One of them found a rotten apple core and started eating it. The other two stuck their heads inside the can looking for things. We stopped our game to look at them. One of the older boys I was playing with whispered, "Damn little bastards," then said in a loud voice, "What you boys *doin'*?" Before they could answer he ran at them and shouted, "Get outa here, you little coons!" and we all chased them away down the alley.

. . . One rainy night in September one of the Negro shacks in the river bottom near Mound Street toppled over. The shack belonged to a garrulous old Negro named Henry who worked on odd jobs for several white families. When my friends and I found out what had happened, we walked across town to take a look. One of the four stilts had broken, and the whole house had simply flopped down at an angle. Henry and his family had been listening to the radio in the front room, and had slid right into the kitchen. The family had moved out, but there was the house, tilted over at an impossible angle, its backside splintered and broken. A light drizzle was falling, and the more we looked through the rain at that crippled old house the less we could help laughing. The image of Henry, the radio, and the whole family sliding into the kitchen was too much. We laughed all the way home, and more the next day when we saw Henry and

Willie Morris　　　　　　　　　*201*

asked after his condition, and he said: "I picked up fifty splinters in my ass."

... I was walking up Grand Avenue to school. Just as I crossed the railroad track I heard a loud crash several hundred yards to the north. Looking in that direction I saw the early morning freight out of Memphis pushing the remnants of a car along the track on its cowguard. I ran up the track. The train had crashed into a Negro taxicab with a full load of passengers. Blood was everywhere; two people lay mangled and still inside the wrecked car. A third, a woman, straddled the car and the train. A carload of high school boys on their way to school screeched around the corner and the boys got out to look at the wreckage. The woman slowly regained consciousness, looked around her, and asked, "Where's the train?" One of the high school boys, the star tailback, replied: "Nigger, you sittin' right on it."

... One morning I awoke to hear that a neighbor had shot a Negro burglar. I ran down to his house, and a large crowd milled around on the porch and in the front room. Inside, the man was telling what had happened. He pointed to a bullet hole in the wall, and another in the leg of the table. He had awakened in the night and saw the nigger in the hallway. He pulled out his automatic and shot twice, and he heard a moan and saw the nigger running away. When he telephoned the police, all they had to do was follow the trail of blood to a house in niggertown. That morning we followed the blood ourselves, little drops and big ones in the dust of the alley and onto the concrete pavement. Then we came back and congratulated our neighbor on his aim. More people came in to hear the story, and he told them: "If that second shot had been two inches to the left, that woulda been one *good* nigger."

AS WE GREW OLDER, beyond puberty into an involvement with girls, it seemed as if our own acts took on a more specific edge of cruelty. On Canal Street, across from the old Greyhound station at the Bayou, there was a concrete bannister where the Negroes would sit waiting for the busses. On Saturday nights we would cruise down the street in a car, and the driver would open his door and drive close to the curb. We would watch while the Negroes, to avoid the car door, toppled backward off the bannister like dominoes. And the taunts and threats to the isolated Negroes we saw, on country roads and deserted white streets, were harder and more cruel than anything we had done as children.

Deeply involved with the unthinking sadism, and with the sudden curious affection, were the moments of pity and sorrow. One Fourth of July afternoon when we were in high school, we went in a large group to one of the lakes in the delta for swimming and a picnic. A Negro shack on the bank of the lake had burned to the ground the night before. The father had taken his wife and his several small children into a bare, floorless cabin nearby, alive with crawling things that came out of the rotten wood in the walls. All they had saved was the clothes on their backs. They sat around all day in front of their shack, watching us eat and swim; for hours, it seemed, they hardly moved. Finally my girlfriend and I walked over to them. We discovered that the children had eaten practically nothing in two days. The children sat there listlessly, not saying a word; the father said even the fish wouldn't bite for him. My girl started crying. We went back and told the others, and took up a collection that must have come to fifteen dollars, and gave them our hot-dogs and Cokes. The Negro family ate the food and continued to look at us down by the lake. Under their stolid gaze I felt uncomfortable; I wanted to head back to Grand Avenue again. We packed our things and went to the car, drove through the flat cotton country to town, and resumed our picnic on the back lawn of one of the big houses in our neighborhood.

Pauli Murray

(1910–1985)

A pioneer in many areas of the struggle for freedom and equality, Pauli Murray was a civil rights activist, feminist, lawyer, educator, autobiographer, poet, and member of the clergy. Born in Baltimore, Murray moved when she was young to Durham, North Carolina, where she was raised by her maternal grandparents, who proudly embraced both sides of their mixed racial background. After graduating from Hunter College in New York in 1933, she attempted to enroll as a graduate student at the University of North Carolina at Chapel Hill, but was denied entrance on the basis of race. In 1944, upon receiving her master's degree from Howard University, she sought enrollment into Harvard Law School but was once again denied admission—this time on the basis of her sex. She went on to earn a master's in law at the University of California at Berkeley and went from there to receive a Ph.D. at Yale. She has taught law at several prestigious universities in the United States and abroad. While at Howard in the forties she helped to integrate the nation's capital by participating in lunch counter sit-ins. Later, in the seventies, she played an active role in the formation of the National Organization for Women. After attending the General Theological Seminary in New York, Murray was ordained an Episcopal priest in 1977, becoming the first African-American woman ever to receive that honor.

Murray has written her life experiences in two memorable books. In Song in a Weary Throat *(1987), recently republished as* Pauli Murray: The Autobiography of a Black Activist, Feminist, Lawyer, Priest, and Poet *(1989), she details her social activism and meditates upon the significance of the events and movements into which she threw*

her energies. In Proud Shoes: The Story of an American Family
*(1956) the focus is on her family history, but much of the book is autobi-
ography, as well. In the selection from* Proud Shoes *that follows, we
witness Murray's devotion to her grandmother and her reaction to a
traumatic event that effectively ends her childhood innocence.*

FROM *Proud Shoes:*
The Story of an American Family

I WAS AT Pratt's well getting water for Grandmother the
day they found John Henry Corniggins near Vickers
Woods. It's strange how one thing leads to another and
how suddenly everything gets mixed up together. I hardly knew
John Henry. We inhabited different worlds. He was much bigger
than I was and until that day as remote as all the other neighborhood children. If Grandmother hadn't gotten sick I might not
have known about him at all. I saw him only once, but his name
and face have stuck in my memory longer than all the rest, more
real and haunting than those of any other child I ever knew.

John Henry Corniggins was one of the many boys who used
to roam through the Bottoms after school, whooping and hollering up and down the branch and making countless trips to
the trash pile over in Hesse's field. He lived a short way from
my house across Morehead Avenue in a hollow where the Bottoms continued southward through the edge of town. He had
a little brother named Leander who followed him everywhere.
The boys had no father and their mother worked all day in the
factory.

The trash pile in Hesse's field was a great eyesore to my
folks—it had the most awful smell of rotted garbage and drew
swarms of big green flies—but it was our neighborhood's greatest attraction for children. It substituted for everything—parks,
playgrounds, clubs or Scout troops—and it was a mine of innu-
merable treasures. I'd sit on the front porch after school and
watch the children rooting about in the big mound of tin cans,

broken bottles and discarded housewares. I'd hear their squeals of triumph whenever they'd fished something valuable from the debris. Pretty soon I'd see them coming back along the road in front of our house loaded with old wheels, wooden boxes, pieces of rope and other stuff. Later I'd catch glimpses of them clattering down Morehead Avenue and careening past our street corner in the lopsided wagons they'd built with various sizes of wheels—fruits of their forays. They'd shout hilariously when the overburdened vehicles capsized and dumped them in the middle of the road.

Grandmother thought the trash pile was the devil's workshop. When she was on the warpath lambasting the neighbors about their shortcomings, more than once she warned them against letting their children run wild.

"Snotty-nosed young'uns, tearing up and down these Bottoms like a spotted-rump bull that belongs to nobody," she'd yell. "You better keep them little urchins home and let 'em learn something that'll do 'em good. A colt needs a bit and bridle, and if you don't curb your young'uns now, they'll make you wish they'd never been born when they get a little older."

The neighbors were used to Grandmother's dire prophecies and few of them heeded her admonitions. Boys continued to roam the Bottoms and make expeditions to the trash pile. I envied their freedom. From my lookout on the porch steps, the trash pile seemed a mecca of childhood delights. I traveled the straight and narrow path to West End School and back home again. Aunt Pauline, who taught at the same school, kept me in tow both ways. Stopping to play or make detours past the trash pile was out of the question. "Mis' Dame" had been in the school system so many years she was no longer a mere teacher; she was a community institution inspiring an awe which attached to everything in her orbit. My schoolmates scooted past me, keeping a polite distance and leaving me to trail along in Mis' Dame's wake in lonely grandeur.

I don't know how long this isolation would have kept up if Grandmother hadn't come down with pellagra. We first noticed she was ailing when she suddenly stopped preaching at the neighbors that spring. It was a bad sign. Feuding with trespassers was like a tonic to Grandmother and it wasn't like her not to boil up and overflow upon them once in a while. When days passed and the astounded neighbors actually beat a footpath along the ledge in our field next to the road without getting a single sermon out of Grandmother, Aunt Pauline knew something was wrong.

"Mama, I don't like the way you're acting. You don't eat enough to keep a bird alive. Why don't you let me have Dr. Shepard come over here and take a look at you?" she pleaded.

"I don't have much for doctors to do," Grandmother told her. "They're ready to stick you in bed for everything. If I get down flat on my back while you're in school, who's gonna look out for your father? He's just like a little child. Wants his victuals on time and wants to know where I am every minute of the day. I've been catering to that man for nigh on to fifty years. Don't know what he'd do if I give out."

If Grandfather had heard her, he would almost have died of shame. He couldn't bear to think that anybody had to take care of him or that his blindness was a problem. He tried hard to manage by himself, and sometimes I thought he was needlessly harsh with Grandmother because he hated to admit how much he leaned upon her. For all her peppery tongue, she handled him very cautiously not to let him know the hundreds of little things she did to ease his way.

I had grown so accustomed to Grandmother's hollering spells the house was like a tomb when she wasn't shouting to the hilltop. We might as well have been living right inside the cemetery instead of a few steps away from it. The Bottoms was strangely still except when people lit up the hillside on Saturday nights. Aunt Pauline and Grandfather were solemn folk most of the time and there wasn't even Aunt Sallie's sudden burst of laughter or her hymn singing to liven up our place. She had been married to Reverend Small for almost a year and lived across town in St. Titus Rectory on Pine Street.

Grandmother began having vomiting spells and grew weaker and weaker. She got so thin her body had shriveled to skin and bones. Then the skin cracked open between her fingers and we could see the raw angry flesh eaten away almost to the bone. She tried various salves on them but they got worse and sores spread all over her body. She hung on until school was out, treating herself, and then she gave up and went to bed. She could hardly lift her head from the pillow to speak above a whisper. She looked awful. Grandmother was such a whirlwind of energy it was pitiful to see her so silent and still, lying upstairs in the big wooden bed in her miserably hot, low-ceilinged bedroom over the parlor. It was worse to see tears rolling down her bony cheeks when she clawed at her sores.

I had never seen Grandmother helpless before and my universe tottered. She was my buffer at home. She never scolded me and she petted me a great deal. We understood one another. Aunt Pauline and Grandfather were much alike. They issued orders like generals on a battlefield, were inflexible about them and tolerated no weaknesses or excuses. Aunt Pauline had been serious-minded all her life. In times of stress Grandfather's mantle fell upon her shoulders as the oldest Fitzgerald daughter. She was heavy handed and gloomy, but she was cool and dependable in emergencies. She took charge, rode out storms and seemed completely above any human deficiency, I thought.

Grandmother and I were different. We were nervous and excitable, easily stampeded, as vulnerable to imaginary terrors as we were to real dangers. We were the sensitive exposed ones who couldn't stand pressures, took everything to heart, were torn by conflicts and cried out in protest when we were wronged or hurt, whether anyone heeded or even heard us. Grandmother must have known this about me even then. She tried to make it easy for me. She'd slip me little sweets behind Aunt Pauline's back like a fellow conspirator. And she'd make fun of Aunt Pauline's stern ways.

"I declare, Old War Horse, you act more like Miss Mary Ruffin Smith the older you get," she'd tell her.

Aunt Pauline puffed up angrily at this, but I think it gave her a bit of satisfaction. She knew that for all of Grandmother's fun-making it was meant as a backhanded compliment. When Grandmother took to her bed she took charge and sent for Dr. Shepard right away. He had been her physician for years. She doted on him and thought there was little in the way of sickness that he couldn't handle. He was a dapper little man, brown as gingerbread and neat as a pin, who wore gold-rimmed glasses. It was a great shock to Aunt Pauline when he examined Grandmother and said he couldn't take her case.

"I think your mother's got pellagra, Mrs. Dame," he said. "I'd like to treat her but that's out of my line. The best thing for you to do is send for Doc Caldwell in Chapel Hill. They say he's had a lot of success with these cases. And you'd better get him over here right away."

Down our way, having pellagra was only a little less disgraceful than having "the bad disease," as folks called gonorrhea and syphilis. People thought it came from dirt and filth and that only ignorant poverty-stricken country folks got it. They considered it highly contagious and avoided those who had it as they would lepers or smallpox cases. It was a great comedown for us. For folks to know the Fitzgeralds had pellagra at their house was almost as calamitous as the disease itself.

Aunt Pauline was mortified, but Grandmother took the news in stride. She'd had too many troubles in her seventy-three years to get steamed up over pellagra. She actually took heart at mention of Doc Caldwell.

"They don't come no smarter than Wilson Caldwell's boy," she said. "I've known him since he was knee high to a duck. Folks call him a quack doctor, but he's got good horse sense. I'd trust that big, fussikin Doc quicker'n I would all these hifalutin Durham doctors put together. There's no put on to him. He's just a diamond in the rough."

Grandmother was very loyal to her Chapel Hill folks. I'd heard her speak many times of the Caldwells. She said they came from some of the finest stock in Orange County and that their people had helped to build the University of North Carolina. She seldom made distinctions between white and colored families of the same name from Orange County. They were all kinfolks to her.

When Doc Caldwell came back from medical school, he went quietly about the county treating folks without pay, taking cases which stumped other doctors and using methods others of his profession had never heard of. He'd sit up until all hours poring over medical journals his father had slipped him overnight from the University library, where Wilson Caldwell was the janitor. Folks laughed at him at first when he concentrated on diets instead of pills in cases of hookworm and pellagra which were so prevalent among the rural folk. But when he began curing cases among the colored people, the white folks sat up and took notice. Before long they were sending for him to come to their places after dark, and although they tried to keep it quiet Doc was said to have as many pellagra patients among the white folks around Orange and Chatham counties as he had among the colored.

He drove over the twelve miles from Chapel Hill to see Grandmother one night in his mud-spattered old buggy behind a big rawboned nag. He didn't look much like a doctor to me. He was a mountainous, coconut-brown, barrel-stomached man who had several chins, big calloused hands, a face that was all wrinkles and creases, and he smelled strongly of horses and raw tobacco. He bulged from his ill-fitting clothes that stretched over his bulky frame tight as a ship's hawser in port at high tide. His coat seemed bursting at the seams and his vest and pants had parted company, exposing a vast expanse of rumpled shirt which billowed about his suspenders. From time to time he took out his big dingy handkerchief and mopped the great drops of sweat which rolled down the creases and dripped onto his damp frayed collar. He seemed to fill the room, and when he dropped into a chair at Grandmother's bedside the floor shuddered from the shock and the oil lamp on the mantelpiece trembled violently. But when Doc spoke, his deep gentle voice was so full of reassurance you knew right off everything was going to be all right.

"It's an advanced stage of pellagra," he announced as soon as he had examined Grandmother, "but I think we can get it under control."

"Any danger of catching it?" Aunt Pauline asked him.

"You don't 'catch' pellagra. That's a notion folks have," Doc said.

He explained that pellagra came from eating the same kind of food and having a deficiency in the diet. He said when people ate cornmeal and grits, fatback and molasses over many years and didn't get enough other foods in their system, their bodies lacked nourishment and pellagra attacked. He told Aunt Pauline the best way to treat it was to change Grandmother's diet to plenty of red lean meat, fresh vegetables and milk. He prescribed frequent Epsom salts baths and some powders for the itching and burning but no other medicines.

"I'm depending mainly on your diet and on limestone water to cure you, Mrs. Fitzgerald," he told Grandmother. "Know anybody around here who has a deep limestone well that's kept clean?"

The only one we knew of was Pratts' well at the top of Morehead hill. Doc Caldwell said that was fine because he wanted all of Grandmother's food prepared with limestone water and that she must drink at least two glassfuls of it fresh from the well three times a day. This created a crisis because there was no one to get the water.

"I don't know how we'll manage it," Aunt Pauline said. "I could get it myself but with Mama so helpless right now and Papa not being able to see, I'd hate to be out of the house that often."

"Can't you pay some child to make regular trips? One you could trust not to set the water down and let dirt get into it?"

"When the neighbors find out Mama's got pellagra they won't come near us, let alone send their children."

"You could explain that pellagra's not catching."

"I guess I could, but it's a little more than that. You see, when some of the neighbors walk on Mama's land, she blesses them out and says some mighty harsh things to them sometimes. It's times like this we need friends, but after the way Mama has preached to some of these folks, I'd be downright ashamed to go to any of them for favors."

Grandmother raised up a little.

"Don't be signifying at me. I don't bite my tongue and everybody knows it. I'll do without the limestone water. And if the Lord sees fit to raise me up from this sickbed and folks don't treat me right, I'll tell 'em about it same as ever."

"Now, Mrs. Fitzgerald, don't fret yourself," said Doc. "We'll work it out somehow."

I was anxious for Grandmother to hurry up and get well so I said I could go for the water if Aunt Pauline would let me. She said she couldn't turn me loose to run wild through the Bottoms after all Grandmother's talk about other folks' children and that if anything happened to me she'd never hear the end of it. Grandmother said bless my heart but I was too little to lug water all the way down the hill from Pratts'. Doc Caldwell looked as if he thought it was a good idea.

"How old are you, little one?" he asked me.

"Six and a half going on seven," I replied.

"Oh, then you go to school?"

"Yes, I'm in high second."

"How young are you then?"

"Six and a half."

Doc's rumbling laugh shook the furniture and the lamp danced dangerously near the edge of the mantlepiece.

"You're as quick on the trigger as your grandma. I've caught many a youngster on that one."

"She'll do pretty well," said Aunt Pauline. Like Grandfather, she was very sparing with her praise.

"I wouldn't worry about her if I were you, Mrs. Dame. She can take care of herself. I'd let her get the water."

And so it was settled that I'd make the three trips a day to Pratts' well for the limestone water. I'd take two little lard pails with me so I could bring back a gallon each trip. It was a good thing Aunt Pauline decided to let me do it because there wasn't anyone else to do anything for us. As she said, folks wouldn't come near the house. It was like a quarantine. The postman got away as fast as he could and the newspaper boy stood down in the field and heaved our newspaper over the hedge. Neighbors who stopped past the yard to ask how Grandmother was stood far off from the porch and hurried away again without coming in.

Aunt Pauline was on her feet all day running up and down the stairs, changing Grandmother's bed linens several times a day, emptying bedpans, giving her salts baths, putting on gauze dressings, washing sheets, scrubbing, disinfecting, cooking meals and keeping an eye on Grandfather. He was miserable without Grandmother to fuss at him. He'd sit on the porch all day looking forlorn and hardly saying a word. Aunt Pauline kept me too busy doing chores and running errands for me to read him the morning newspaper. Every evening after supper he'd go upstairs and sit with Grandmother, combing her hair while Aunt Pauline and I worked in the garden. There was nothing Grandmother loved more than having Grandfather comb her hair.

I learned to do many things that summer—to chop kindling, stack firewood, feed the chickens, gather eggs, clean the ashes from the stove grate, fill the kerosene lamps, polish the lamp chimneys and trim the wicks, and hoe weeds from the garden. I also graduated from the porch steps and became a person of affairs in the neighborhood. Aunt Pauline began sending me to the grocer's and the drugstore. Running errands wasn't quite as good as being free to roam and visit the trash pile. I was always in a hurry and had to carry things on my way back, but I learned to play on the wing. Aunt Pauline knew exactly how long each errand ought to take and she expected me to go and come without stopping. On my way to the store, I'd shave off a few precious minutes for a game of hopscotch or marbles and then I'd run all the rest of the way there and back on the double trot. I'd arrive home breathless and covered with fine dust but well within my time limit.

My reward was going barefoot that summer, a privilege which placed me on an equal footing with other neighborhood children. It was a privilege I was allowed to keep. I never associated going barefoot with being poor. It was a significant event, like seeing the first robin or dandelion in spring or going to the parade when the circus came to town. We waited all winter for that memorable first warm spring day when we were allowed to take off our shoes and stockings. We'd rush home from school, discard them and plunge our toes into the soft cool earth. We vied with one another to see who could shed his shoes earliest in spring and keep them off longest in fall. We loved to pick up little blobs of damp sand in our toes, to tramp about in the mud on rainy days and to splash through the branch. We were always running nails in our feet or cutting them on sharp weeds and having our folks worried that we would get lockjaw, but we went about proudly displaying our cuts and bruises like battle ribbons. The child with the dirtiest feet and the most scars had high standing among the others.

I suppose there was so little to brag about in the Bottoms we made a lot of fuss over little things—like my going to Pratts' well. People who didn't have city plumbing carried water all the time, but my trips made me feel especially important. Everybody knew my grandmother had pellagra and that I was carrying water for her. To and from the well I traveled in a circle where I could say howdy to all the neighbors on the two streets which bounded the Bottoms and let them see we were getting along all right over there by ourselves.

It wasn't a very long trip—you could see Pratts' chimney through the trees from our house—but I made the most of it. Every morning before breakfast, at noon and in the evening around sunset, I'd take off down the wagon track through our field, a small lard pail stuck on each shoulder like a pair of bulbous wings and Grandmother's big sun straw pulled down over my ears. I'd cross the road and follow the footpath along the Bottoms to the branch. When the water was shallow I crossed on a log, but when the stream was angry and swollen from rains

I'd scamper along the banks to a spot where I could hop across on the flat moss-covered rocks. I had to keep a sharp lookout for snakes in the tall weeds but there was always a chance I'd see a terrapin or a bullfrog near the bank.

Once across the branch, I'd loiter along the cowpath up the hill searching for four-leaf clovers or digging my toes into a mole tunnel. When I looked back across the Bottoms to my house from the pine grove, the cemetery behind our house spread out as far as I could see, but the tombstones had shrunk and did not seem nearly so ready to topple down on us as they did from our back fence at home.

The Pratts lived high above the street level in a two-story frame house with a separate one-room kitchen joined at the back by a shed and a pair of low steps. The wellshed stood in the center of their wide sandy yard and a giant persimmon tree towered above it. Their place was the dividing line between the white and colored families who lived on Morehead Avenue. East of Pratts', the tree-arched avenue sloped gently toward town through "Swellton Heights" and the fine old homesteads and spacious lawns of Durham's oldest families. West of Pratts' were the Negro factory and mill workers who lived in tiny cottages or little unpainted three-room dwellings. Here the street had been widened, leveled off and paved in such a way that the small houses either teetered on a high ledge above it or sank to their rooftops below it. There were no sidewalks and not a single shade tree. Down in the hollow where Cameron Street crossed Morehead and ran into Shaw Street, the back porches on both sides of the avenue faced the Bottoms.

I envied the Pratts high on their hilltop. Their house faced east toward the beautiful estates and they could sit on their front porch at night under the protective glow of the street lamp at their intersection. They were sheltered from the Bottoms by the pine grove behind their house. There were no children in their home but their big persimmon tree drew all the neighborhood children on the hillside. Their well made them the most popular family on Morehead hill. Dug fifty feet deep and lined with brick, it surpassed all other wells. The water was ice cold and people came from everywhere to get a drink and pass the time of day. Folks said limestone water purified the blood. They'd stand about waiting their turn at the big tin dipper which hung on the wellshed and gossiping with one another. The Pratts were great talkers, and through their well they kept up with everything that happened.

If they were busy when I arrived with my pails, I'd roam the yard hunting ripe persimmons or play marbles with the Wilson children who lived next door or stand around listening to the gossip. They never allowed me to draw the water myself because they were afraid the heavy bucket might pull me down into the well. I had to content myself with standing on tiptoe and peeping over the side of the shed down the mysterious, dark hole to the threatening water below. As the bucket hurtled downward, I'd peer into the depths looking for stars people said you could see in broad daylight down a well, but all I ever saw was my own scared face looking up at me. When the bucket hit the water with a big plop and sank out of sight, the strange mirror shattered and the angry water churned against the mossy sides until the brimming bucket rose to the surface and was pulled up again hand over hand on the creaking chain.

Miss Sarah Pratt, the oldest daughter, who taught one of the lower grades at West End School with Aunt Pauline, and Miss Mary Lawson, a county schoolteacher who lived with the Pratt family, were usually in the kitchen when I arrived. They were wonderful cooks and there was always a smell of spices or chopped onions or frying chicken or ham when I came up. Almost every noon they did their baking for supper. If they were taking it out of the oven around the time I came along, they'd offer me a little sample of hot rolls and butter, or apple pie, blackberry cobbler, peach dumpling, cherry mash or something equally tasty. When it was raining, they'd invite me into the kitchen to wait and I'd sit on a little stool talking to them, my eyes glued to the oven door of the big black iron stove. Miss Mary and Miss Sarah were such jolly souls, always so full of news and merriment, I liked them as much for themselves as for their pies and dumplings.

When my pails were filled, I'd start home again down Morehead Avenue, my head bobbing up and down in continual greeting to all the neighbors. The older folks called me "that Fitzge'l child" and the younger ones "Mis' Dame's girl." Nobody remembered my own name. Everybody would ask me how Grandmother was and I'd keep them posted on her progress. I was especially polite to those folks who never harassed her when they went through the Bottoms. It was my way of thanking them. The others got distant politeness. I never stopped on the way home because I couldn't set Grandmother's water down and I had to hurry to get it to her while it was cool.

I usually came in stuffed with information about all of the neighbors. I knew who was getting married, or had a baby, or was on the sick list, or got sent "to the roads." I'd make a beeline to Grandmother's room as soon as I put down the pails in the kitchen and I'd spill out all my news. I think the gossip I picked up at the well did her as much good as the limestone water. She'd laugh and say I was better than a local newspaper and she'd perk up afterward.

That's how I came to find out about John Henry Corniggins. It was around noon when I made my second trip to the well that day. The Carolina heat poured down on everything and there wasn't a breath of air stirring. It was quiet all over the hillside. It wasn't a day for visiting or trading gossip. The porches were empty. People who weren't at work had gone inside their houses out of the hot sun and the neighborhood dogs had crawled beneath the houses to lie panting in the dust.

The well was deserted when I arrived at Pratts' yard but I saw a thin curl of smoke coming out of the kitchen chimney. I set down my pails at the wellshed and knocked on the screen door. Miss Sarah Pratt came out wiping her steaming face on her apron. Behind her floated the smell of burning sugar, melted butter and cinnamon.

"Hello there," she said. "You're a little late, aren't you?"

"How you, Miss Sarah? I had to help Aunt Pauline wash clothes."

"Don't tell me you can wash clothes."

"I can't do the big things but Aunt Pauline lets me rinse out the little ones and spread them on the grass."

"Mrs. Dame has to do all that washing by herself?" Grandmother would call this "picking you."

"Yes Ma'am, but we're making out."

Miss Sarah let down the bucket. I squashed a rotten persimmon between my toes and wondered what she had in the oven. The sunlight filtered through the persimmon boughs and little rainbows appeared on her coffee-brown face. I wondered why some people were called white and some called colored when there were so many colors and you couldn't tell where one left off and the other began. Some folks were Aunt Pauline's color— strawberries and cream—and some were like licorice. Some were cream chocolate and some were dark chocolate. Some were caramel and some were peanut butter. Some were like molasses taffy after it has been pulled awhile and some were like gingerbread. I'd heard somebody say colored people were like a flower garden but I thought they were more like good things to eat.

Miss Sarah pulled up the bucket and was just pouring my water when Lizzie Jones, who lived on Morehead Avenue just below the Pratts, came running up the back path from her porch. I liked Lizzie. She was a plump, round-faced, smiling girl who reminded me of peanut butter. She had sweet ways and never teased Grandmother. She had always seemed very fond of Aunt Pauline, who had taught her when she was a little girl. Now she was nearly grown.

Lizzie stopped just long enough to dipper a drink from what was left in the bucket.

"Haven't got time to stop, Miss Sarah," she gasped between swallows. "I just heard something's happened to one of those Corniggins boys out yonder in Vickers Woods."

"Mercy me! Which one? What happened?"

"I don't know yet. I'm on my way out there now to see."

"I'd go along with you but I've got a pie in the oven."

"I'll see if Rosa Hogans will go. Tell you what I find out when I get back," said Lizzie disappearing around the corner of Pratts' house.

The neighborhood houses suddenly came alive. There was a sound of running feet and shouting. I picked up my pails and edged away from the well.

"Much obliged for the water, Miss Sarah."

"You're not coming in to taste my peach pie? I'm taking it out in a minute."

"No ma'am. I better be getting on."

I rushed around the house looking for Lizzie. She was standing on the opposite corner in front of Rosa Hogans' house. From everywhere people were streaking along several paths toward the heavy woods beyond where Arnette Avenue ended abruptly in a dump heap. Many of them were factory workers who had worked a half day and still had on their bright blue hoover aprons with white collars and cuffs. Rosa came out of her door and knelt down to tie her shoes. She was a tall, pretty, hazel-nut-colored girl about Lizzie's age.

I struggled up the slope with my pails to the ledge where Lizzie was standing.

"May I go too, Lizzie?"

"Oh, honey, I don't mind taking you but I don't want to get in Dutch with Mis' Dame. She'd get down on me sure if I took you over there in those woods without her say-so."

"You better go on home, sugar," Rosa told me. "Mis' Dame don't stand for any foolishness."

"Couldn't I just go and see and come right back?"

Lizzie looked at Rosa.

"I'm not telling you to go," she said, " 'cause I don't want to get on the bad side of Mis' Dame. But if you do go, you got to hold my hand every step of the way."

I forgot all about Grandmother's water. I set the pails down under the broiling sun in the middle of the path and took Lizzie's hand.

"Lord, if Mis' Dame ever finds out about this," she groaned.

We started for the woods, half running, half stumbling along the footpath past a big billboard, through a field of sumac and weeds higher than my head and on through a bramble thicket. The heavy weeds struck me in the face, the brambles tore at my clothes and ripped my bare legs and the sharp stones bruised my feet, but I knew better than to cry after begging to go along. I clung to Lizzie's hand and kept up the best I could. From the far side of the field we followed the path through a heavy pine forest. Now we could hear somebody crying, hacking little cries like a child with whooping cough. The woods fell away sharply into a clearing on low marshy ground. We ran down the bluff, waded through black mud to our ankles and joined a little half circle of people who stood transfixed staring at something in the bushes.

Then I saw John Henry Corniggins lying in the tall grass close to a briar patch. I saw his feet first, the white soles sticking out of the grass and caked with mud, then his scratched brown legs. He lay on his side, his legs twisted around one another, one hand flung over his head clutching at a clump of earth, the other crumpled under his body. A dirty cap lay near him and huddled beside him was a little boy no bigger than I in ragged knee pants which swallowed his scrawny body. The little boy cried in jerky sobs.

For one long awful moment there was no other sound except the rending sobs. Everything seemed frozen. Not a leaf quivered; not a bird called. John Henry lay so still he did not even move to shoo away the large green fly that settled on his face and crawled over his cheek. Another lighted on his lips and crawled inside his mouth. Overhead a lone buzzard circled toward earth.

The woods stirred and moaned behind us and a rush of air came down the hill. The bushes swayed slightly and a heavy dark shadow moved across the clearing and fell over the spot where

John Henry lay. Thunder rumbled off in the distance. The half circle grew larger and began to babble. Scared questioning voices melted into one another in a single muttering voice.

"It's John Henry, that Corniggins boy. I seen him pass my house with Leander not an hour ago."

"He's dead all right. Deader'n a doornail."

"Oh my God! Pore Mis' Corniggins."

"She know yet?"

"Somebody's gone to fetch her from the fact'ry."

"It's gonna be a terrible blow to that pore woman. She's had such a time trying to raise her young'uns."

"Ain't it a shame?"

"How'd it happen?"

"Say that WHITE man shot him."

"WHITE man?"

"Yeah. The one got that watermelon patch up there back of Vickers Avenue."

"How he come to shoot him?"

"Say he been threatening shoot niggers stealing his watermelons."

"Yeah?"

"Well, say he shot John Henry."

"John Henry stealing watermelons?"

"Can't tell."

"What Leander say?"

"Leander so scared you can't hardly make heads or tails outta what he say."

"Doan Leander know who shot his brother?"

"Leander say they was playing dogs and rabbit and run right 'cross the end of the white man's watermelon patch. He say the white man hollered at 'em and they kept on running."

"What else Leander say?"

"Say John Henry was running when he fell."

"I doan see no watermelon down here near him and that watermelon patch is 'way off up that hill. Looks mighty doggone funny to me. Looks like that white man shot this boy outta pure down meanness."

"Thass what I say."

"Oh, dear Jesus! It coulda been my Rufus. He hangs out with John Henry all the time."

"Thass what I tell these chillun 'bout going round white folks' neighborhoods. I'll be plumb scared to let mine out of my sight after this."

"It ain't right. Shooting him down like a dog. If 'twuz my chile, I'd put the law on him, WHITE man or no WHITE man."

"Now you talking. This ain't no Jawjuh."

"Might not be Georgia, but how's anybody gonna prove the white man done it? No witnesses but Leander. It'll be *his* word 'gainst Leander's and Leander ain't nothing but a chile."

"Doan matter. I'd put the law on him all the same."

"Yeah, me too. It's time *somebody* put a stop to shooting up colored folks."

"Well, if a WHITE man done it, you can betcha bottom dollar that's the end of it."

Somebody screamed in the woods behind us.

"Lawd, that must be his mother now. Don't let her come down here and see him like this."

"Somebody take him up there on high ground."

"Here comes Dick Banks. Let him through."

Tall, amber, gray-eyed Dick Banks, the painter and plasterer, who lived on Shaw Street just above John Henry's house, shouldered through the crowd. Without a word he strode into the bushes, knelt down and picked John Henry up in his arms. He carried him out of the marsh and up the slope. John Henry's skinny arms flopped up and down like a dead turkey's wings. A woman put her arms about Leander's shoulders and urged him forward.

"Come on, honey. I'm gonna take you up there to your mama."

Leander whimpered up the path. A silent queue single-filed

behind Dick Banks and his burden. He stopped at the edge of the woods and laid John Henry on his back under a tall pine tree. I saw his eyes now for the first time. They were wide open and staring into the sky. They were fixed and shiny like two glass beads. Across his lean brown face gleamed two livid stripes where his cheek had lain against blades of grass. A small hole blackened about the edges showed on his shirt front over his heart.

The sky was so dark overhead now that it looked like night in the woods. A few drops of rain spattered against the pine needles and the thunder rolled nearer. The screams we had heard grew louder and more piercing. I suddenly felt cold and began to tremble although my clothes were dripping wet from sweat. I remembered Grandmother's pails of water sitting on the path.

"I gotta go, Lizzie," I whimpered. "I left Grandma's water and a big storm's coming up."

"Guess we'd better," she said in a queer frightened voice. My hand burned in hers. She had never let go of it.

I could hear Aunt Pauline calling me as I hurried down Morehead hill a short while later. She was walking the porch when I came up.

"Where on earth have you been?" she began. "I'm almost out of my mind. I heard screaming and thought something had happened to you. Just look at your clothes and that mud on your feet!"

I burst out crying as soon as I reached the steps.

"A WHITE man shot John Henry Corniggins," I sobbed, "and I saw him DEAD over there in the woods."

Aunt Pauline did not whip me when she heard my story. Her face just looked sterner and her thin lips more set. Grandmother's water wasn't fit to drink and we had to boil it. But I could think of nothing except John Henry Corniggins. It was the first time I could remember seeing death. All the rest of that day and the next I kept asking the same question over and over again.

"Why, Aunt Pauline? Why did the WHITE man shoot John Henry?"

"I can't tell you, child. There are some things you'll understand better when you get older," was all she would say.

Doc Caldwell had Grandmother up again by fall. I no longer had to go to the well. We never found out who killed John Henry. Somebody later said a colored outlaw from the Bottoms had shot him, but nobody believed that story. Everybody thought it was the white man. Nothing was done about it and after a while people stopped talking.

William Alexander Percy

(1885–1942)

Will Percy was born into one of the most prominent families of the Mississippi Delta and spent much of his young adulthood vacillating between the desire to pursue his literary ambitions or to enter into public service as his father, U.S. Senator Leroy Percy, and grandfather had done. Percy was educated at home, then at the University of the South in Sewanee, Tennessee, to which he returned as an instructor for a year. The author of three volumes of poetry, he was temperamentally predisposed to the cosmopolitan life and spent many of his summers vacationing among the wealthy American and European expatriates in the Italian resort communities of Taormina and Capri. At his father's insistence, Percy studied law at Harvard, then returned to practice law in his hometown of Greenville, Mississippi, where he also served as a civic and cultural leader and manager of a three-thousand-acre cotton plantation. When his cousin Leroy Pratt Percy committed suicide in 1929, he adopted his deceased kinsman's three boys, one of whom was future novelist Walker Percy, who wrote of his adoptive father, "he was the most extraordinary man I have ever known."

Lanterns on the Levee: Recollections of a Planter's Son, *published in 1941, may be the most impassioned and articulate defense of southern paternalism ever penned. For all his eloquence, though, Percy's views on race relations have been so thoroughly discredited that contemporary readers may be tempted to dismiss him completely, overlooking the value of* Lanterns *as a window into a receding worldview that shaped the South we have inherited today. In much the same vein as* The Education of Henry Adams, *Percy presents a heavily ironic autobiographical persona that is cast as an anachronism, alienated by his outmoded worldview and ill-suited to the corrupt and chaotic world of modernity. Despite this rhetorical posture, however, Lanterns also reveals a man who was very much a part of the world he inhabited.*

In the following excerpt, Percy draws a character sketch of his servant, Ford, that reveals much more about himself than his purported subject. Patently racist, it attempts to portray "Fode" as a representative African American, childlike, one wrong step away from total disaster, and ultimately dependent on his master's good graces. Beyond this distorted caricature, though, lies a brutally self-honest description of a very close relationship whose intimacy is built upon the master's vulnerabilities. Other chapters from Lanterns might present Percy in a better light, but I include it because it shows the extent to which privileged southern whites constructed their own sense of selfhood in relation to their racial other.

FROM *Lanterns on the Levee: Recollections of a Planter's Son*

PEOPLE ARE DIVIDED into Leaners and Leanees: into oaks more or less sturdy and vines quite, quite clinging. I was never a Leaner, yet, although seldom mistaken for one, I find people are constantly feeling impelled to protect me. Invariably they are right and I accept their proffered ministrations gratefully. I cannot drive a car or fix a puncture or sharpen a pencil or swim or skate or give a punch in the jaw to the numerous parties who need punching. My incompetency is almost all-inclusive, but it must have a glow, for it attracts Samaritans from miles around. I have been offered a very fine, quick-working poison for use on my enemies or myself; I have had my rifle carried by a soldier who disliked me, just because I was all in; a bootlegger once asked me to go partners with him because I looked seedy; a top sergeant, icy with contempt, put together my machine-gun when its disjecta membra unassembled would have returned me in disgrace to America; a red-headed friend of mine had to be restrained from flinging a red-headed enemy of mine into the river for some passing insolence; an appreciable percentage of the hard-boiled bastards of the world have patched tires, blown life into sparkplugs, pushed, hauled, lifted, hammered, towed, and sweated for me because they knew that without their aid I should have moldered indefinitely on some wretched, can-strewn landscape. If you mix incompetency with a pinch of the wistful and a heap of good manners, it works pretty well. Men of goodwill are all over the place, millions of them. It is a very nice world—that is, if you remember that while good morals are all-important between the Lord and His creatures, what counts between one creature and another is good manners. A good manner may spring from vanity or a sense of style; it is a sort of pleasant fiction. But good manners spring from well-wishing; they are fundamental as truth and much more useful. No nation or stratum of society has a monopoly on them and, contrary to the accepted estimate, Americans have more than their share.

The righteous are usually in a dither over the deplorable state of race relations in the South. I, on the other hand, am usually in a condition of amazed exultation over the excellent state of race relations in the South. It is incredible that two races, centuries apart in emotional and mental discipline, alien in physical characteristics, doomed by war and the Constitution to a single, not a dual, way of life, and to an impractical and unpracticed theory of equality which deludes and embitters, heckled and misguided by pious fools from the North and impious fools from the South—it is incredible, I insist, that two such dissimilar races should live side by side with so little friction, in such comparative peace and amity. This result is due solely to good manners. The Southern Negro has the most beautiful manners in the world, and the Southern white, learning from him, I suspect, is a close second.

Which reminds me of Ford. (He pronounces his name "Fode" with enormous tenderness, for he is very fond of himself.)

In the South every white man worth calling white or a man is owned by some Negro, whom he thinks he owns, his weakness and solace and incubus. Ford is mine. There is no excuse for talking about him except that I like to. He started off as my caddy, young, stocky, strong, with a surly expression, and a smile like the best brand of sunshine. For no good reason he rose to be my chauffeur; then houseboy; then general factotum; and now, without any contractual relation whatever, my retainer, which means to say I am retained for life by him against all disasters, great or small, for which he pays by being Ford. It was not because of breaking up the first automobile, coming from a dance drunk, or because of breaking up the second automobile, coming from a dance drunk, that our contractual relation was annulled, but for a subtler infamy. I was in the shower, not a position of dignity at best, and Ford strolled in, leaned against the door of the bathroom, in the relaxed pose of the Marble Faun, and observed dreamily: "You ain't nothing but a little old fat man."

A bit of soap was in my eye and under the circumstances it was no use attempting to be haughty anyway, so I only blurted: "You damn fool."

Ford beamed: "Jest look at your stummick."

When one had fancied the slenderness of one's youth had been fairly well retained! Well, taking advantage of the next dereliction, and one occurred every week, we parted; that is to say, I told Ford I was spoiling him and it would be far better for him to battle for himself in this hostile world, and Ford agreed, but asked what he was going to do "seeing as how nobody could find a job nohow." As neither of us could think of the answer, I sent him off to a mechanics' school in Chicago. He returned with a diploma and a thrilling tale of how nearly he had been married against his vehement protest to a young lady for reasons insufficient surely in any enlightened community with an appreciation of romance. With Ford's return the demand for mechanics fell to zero—he always had an uncanny effect on the labor market—so he took to house-painting. His first week he fell off the roof of the tallest barn in the county and instead of breaking his neck, as Giorgione or Raphael would have done, he broke only his ankle and had to be supplied with crutches, medical care, and a living for six weeks. It was then that I left for Samoa.

But I should not complain. Ford has never learned anything from me, but I am indebted to him for an education in more subjects and stranger ones than I took at college, subjects, however, slightly like those the mock-turtle took from the Conger eel. The first lesson might be called "How Not to Faint in Coils." Ford observed:

"You don't understand folks good as I does." I was appalled. "You sees what's good in folks, but you don't see what's bad. Most of the time I'se a good boy, then I goes nigger, just plain nigger. Everybody do that, and when they does, it hurts you." I was pulverized. It may not have taken a wicked person to think that, but it certainly took a wicked one to say it.

That I have any dignity and self-respect is not because of but in spite of Ford. We were returning from a directors' meeting in a neighboring town and he was deeply overcast. At last he became communicative:

"Mr. Oscar Johnston's boy says Mr. Oscar won't ride in no car more'n six months old and he sho ain't goin' to ride in nothin' lessen a Packard."

I received this calmly, it was only one more intimation that my Ford was older than need be and congenitally unworthy. Ford continued:

"He says Mr. Oscar says you ain't got near as much sense as your pa." I agreed, heartily. "He says you ain't never goin' to make no money." I agreed, less heartily. "En if you don't be keerful you goin' to lose your plantation." I agreed silently, but I was nettled, and observed:

"And you sat there like a bump on a log, saying nothing, while I was being run down?"

"Well, I told him you had traveled a lot, a lot more'n Mr. Oscar; you done gone near 'bout everywhere, en he kinder giggled and says: 'Yes, they tells me he's been to Africa,' en I says: 'He is,' en he says: 'You know why he went Africa?' en I says: ''Cause he wanted to go there,' en he says: 'That's what he tells you, but he went to Africa to 'range to have niggers sent back into slavery.'"

I exploded: "And you were idiot enough to believe that?"

"I'se heard it lots of times," Ford observed mildly, "but it didn't make no difference to me, you been good to me en I didn't care."

Having fancied I had spent a good portion of my life defending and attempting to help the Negro, this information stunned me and, as Ford prophesied, it hurt. But hiding my wounded vanity as usual in anger, I turned on Ford with:

"You never in your life heard any Negro except that fool boy of Oscar Johnston's say I was trying to put the Negroes back in slavery."

"Lot of 'em," reiterated Ford.

"I don't believe you," I said. "You can't name a single one."

We finished the drive in silence; spiritually we were not en rapport.

The next morning when Ford woke me he was wreathed in smiles, suspiciously pleased with himself. He waited until one eye was open and then announced triumphantly:

"Louisa!" (pronounced with a long *i*).

"What about Louisa?" I queried sleepily.

"She says you'se goin' to send the niggers back into slavery!"

Louisa was our cook, the mainstay and intimate of the household for fifteen years.

"God damn!" I exploded, and Ford fairly tripped out, charmed with himself.

I dressed thoughtfully and repaired to the kitchen. My intention was to be gentle but desolating. Louisa weighs over three hundred, and despite a physical allure I can only surmise from the stream of nocturnal callers in our back yard, she distinctly suggests in her general contour a hippopotamus. When I entered the kitchen I found her pacing ponderously back and forth through the door that opens on the back gallery. It seemed a strange procedure—Louisa was not given to exercise, at least not of that kind. The following colloquy ensued:

"Louisa, what are you doing?"

"I stuck a nail in my foot."

"Why don't you go to the doctor?"

"I'se gettin' the soreness out."

"You can't walk it out."

"Naw, suh, the nail is *drawing* it out."

"What nail?"

"The nail I stepped on."

"Where is it?"

Louisa pointed to the lintel of the door. A nail hung from it by a piece of string; under it Louisa was pacing. I left her pacing. I didn't mention slavery then or later.

My bitter tutelage didn't conclude here. In late autumn we drove to the plantation on settlement day. Cotton had been picked and ginned, what cash had been earned from the crop was to be distributed. The managers and bookkeeper had been hard at work preparing a statement of each tenant's account for the whole year. As the tenant's name was called he entered the office and was paid off. The Negroes filled the store and over-flowed onto the porch, milling and confabulating. As we drove up, one of them asked: "Whose car is dat?" Another answered: "Dat's *us* car." I thought it curious they didn't recognize my car, but dismissed the suspicion and dwelt on the thought of how sweet it was to have the relation between landlord and tenant so close and affectionate that to them my car was their car. Warm inside I passed through the crowd, glowing and bowing, the lord of the manor among his faithful retainers. My mission concluded, I returned to the car, still glowing. As we drove off I said:

"Did you hear what that man said?"

Ford assented, but grumpily.

"It was funny," I continued.

"Funnier than you think," observed Ford sardonically.

I didn't understand and said so.

Ford elucidated: "He meant that's the car *you* has bought with *us* money. They all knew what he meant, but you didn't and they knew you didn't. They wuz laughing to theyselves."

A few days later the managers confirmed this version of the meaning of the phrase and laughed. I laughed too, but not inside.

Yet laughter singularly soft and unmalicious made me Ford's debtor more even than his admonitions and revelations. I still think with gratitude of an afternoon which his peculiarly Negro tact and good manners and laughter made charming. I was in what Ford would call "low cotton." After a hellish day of details and beggars, my nerves raw, I phoned for Ford and the car. On climbing in I asked dejectedly:

"Where shall we drive?"

Ford replied: "Your ruthers is my ruthers" (what you would rather is what I would rather). Certainly the most amiable and appeasing phrase in any language, the language used being not English but deep Southern.

"Let's try the levee," I suggested.

Although nothing further was said and Ford asked no questions, he understood my depression and felt the duty on him to cheer me up. He drove to my favorite spot on the levee and parked where I could watch across the width of waters a great sunset crumbling over Arkansas. As I sat moody and worried, Ford, for the first and only time in his life, began to tell me Negro stories. I wish I could imitate his exact phrases and intonations and pauses, without which they are poor enough stories; but, in spite of the defects of my relaying, anyone can detect their Negro quality, care-free and foolish and innocent—anyone, that is, who has lived among Negroes in the South.

Here are the three I remember in something approximating Ford's diction:

"THERE WUZ a cullud man en he died en went to hevven en the Lawd gevvum all wings, en he flew en he flew" (here Ford hunched his shoulders and gave a superb imitation of a buzzard's flight). "After he flew round there fur 'bout a week he looked down en saw a reel *good*-lookin' lady, a-settin' on a cloud. She wuz *reel* good-lookin'. En he dun the loop-the-loop.

"The Lawd cum en sez: 'Don't you know how to act? There ain't nuthin' but nice people here, en you beehavin' like that. Git out.' But he told the Lawd he jest didn't know en he wuzzent never gonner do nuthin' like that no mo', en please let him stay. So the Lawd got kinder pacified en let him stay. En he flew en he flew. En after he had been flying round fur 'bout a week, he ups en sees that same good-lookin' lady a-settin' on a cloud en he jest couldn't hep it—he dun the loop-the-loop.

"So the Lawd stepped up en he sez: 'You jest don't know how to act, you ain't fitten fur to be with decent folks, you'se a scanlus misbeehavor. Git out.' En he got.

"He felt mighty bad en hung round the gate three or four days tryin' to ease up on St. Peter, but St. Peter 'lowed there wuzn't no way, he jest couldn't let him in en the onliest way he might git in wuz to have a *conference* with the Lawd. Then the man asked if he couldn't 'range fur a conference en they had a lot of back-and-forth. En finally St. Peter eased him in fur a conference." (Ford loved that word, it made him giggle.) "But the Lawd wuz mad, He wuz mad sho-nuff, he wuz hoppin' mad en told him flat-footed to git out en stay out. Then the cullud man sez:

"'Well, jest remember this, Lawd: while I wuz up here in yo' place I wuz the flyin'est fool you had.'"

Since the thirteenth century no one except Ford and his kind has been at ease in heaven, much less confident enough of it to imagine an aeroplane stunt there. And I do hope that good-looking lady saw the loop-the-loop.

THE SECOND STORY is just as inconsequential:

"A fellow cum to a cullud man en promised him a whole wagen-load of watermelons if he would go en set by hisself in a hanted house all night long. Well, the man he liked watermelons en he promised, though he sho didn't like no hanted house, en he sho didn't wanter see no hants. He went in en drug up a cheer en set down en nuthin' happened. After so long a time, in walked a black cat en set down in front of him en jest looked at him. He warn't so skeered because it warn't much more'n a kitten, en they both uvvem just set there en looked at each uther. Then ernurther cat cum in, a big black 'un, en he set by the little 'un en they jest set there lookin' at him, en ain't sed nothin'. Then ernurther one cum en he wuz big as a dawg en all three uvvem jest set there en looked at him en sed nuthin'. Ernurther one cum, still bigger, en ernurther, en ernurther, en the last one wuz big as a hoss. They all jest set there in a row en sed nuthin' en looked at him. That cullud man he wuz plum skeered en he had ter say sumpin so he 'lowed all nice en p'lite:

" 'What us gwiner do?'

"En the big 'un sed: 'Us ain't gwiner do nuthin', till Martin comes.'

"The cullud man says reel nice en p'lite: 'Jest tell Martin I couldn't wait,' en he busted out the winder en tore down the big road fast as he could en faster, en he ain't never taken no more interest in watermelons since."

"But, Ford," I asked, "who was Martin?"

"I dunno," said Ford and chuckled, "but I reckon he wuz big as er elly-fant."

I reckon so too, and twice as real, so far as I am concerned.

AND NOW the last:

"A cullud man cum to the white folks' house in the country en sed to the man:

" 'Boss, I'se hongry; gimme sumpin t'eat.'

"The man sed: 'All right, go round to the back do' en tell the cook to feed you.'

"The cullud man sed: 'Boss, I'se neer 'bout starved, I ain't et fur a whole week.'

"The man sed: 'All right, all right, go round to the kitchen.'

"The cullud man sed: 'Boss, if you gimme sumpin t'eat I'll split up all that stove wood you got in yo' back yard.'

"The man sed: 'All right, all right, go en git that grub like I tole yer.'

"So he went. After 'bout three hours the man went to his back yard en saw the cullud man, who wuz jest settin'. So he sed:

"'Has you et?'

"En he sed: 'Yassir.'

"En he sed: 'Has you chopped up that wood-pile?'

"En he sed: 'Boss man, if you jest let me res' round till dinner time, after dinner I'll go en chop out that patch of cotton fur you.'

"So the man sed: 'All right, but don't you fool me no more.'

"After the cullud man had et him a big dinner he started out to the cotton patch en he met him a cooter [a mud-turtle] en the cooter sed to him:

"'Nigger, you talks too much.'

"The nigger goes tearin' back to the big house en when he gits there the man cums out en sez:

"'Nigger, has you chopped out that cotton?'

"En the nigger sez:

"'Lawd, boss, I wuz on my way, fo' God I wuz, en I met a cooter en he started talkin' to me en I lit out from there en here I is.'

"The boss man was plenty riled and he sez:

"'Nigger, take me to that cooter en if he don't start talkin', I'se goin' to cut your throat frum year to year.'

"So they bof uvvem started fur the cotton patch en there in the middle of the big road set that cooter. En he never opened his mouth, he ain't sed nuthin'. So the man hopped on the nigger en whupped him sumpin' scand'lous en left fur the big house mighty sore at niggers en cooters. Well, the cullud man wuz neer 'bout through breshing hisself off en jest fo' moseying on off when the cooter poked his head out en looks at him en sez:

"'Nigger, I tole you you talks too much.'"

CAN IT BE wondered at, now that Ford is sojourning in the North beyond the infamous housing conditions of the South, comfortable and healthy in his own little room with four young Negro roommates, a single window to keep out the cold and a gas burner for cooking and heat—can it be wondered, if now when the phone rings and the operator's voice says: "Detroit, calling collect," that I accept the charge, although I know who it is and why he is calling? It is Ford and he is drunk and he is incoherently solicitous for me and mine and for his mother and wants to come home and needs five dollars. I reply I am glad to hear his voice, which is true, and hope he is well, and advise him to be a good boy and stick to his job, and a letter will follow or shall I wire? Of course, he has no job, except with the W.P.A., to which he has attached himself by fictions and frauds with which all good Southern darkies with itching feet are familiar. I hope the government supports him as long and as loyally as I did, because if it doesn't, I must. I must because Ford is my fate, my Old Man of the Sea, who tells me of Martin and admonishing cooters and angels that do the loop-the-loop, my only tie with Pan and the Satyrs and all earth creatures who smile sunshine and ask no questions and understand.

I wish my parting with him could have been happier or that I could forget it. He had abandoned his truck in a traffic jam and forfeited his job, one that I had procured for him with much difficulty and some misrepresentation. Then he had got looping drunk and last, against all precedent and propriety, he had come to see me; it was late at night when he arrived, stumbling and weeping. He threw himself across the couch and sobbed without speaking. I could not get him up or out, and he wouldn't explain his grief. At last he quieted down and, his face smeared with tears, managed to gasp:

"You can't do no good, Mr. Will. It don't make no difference how hard I tries or how good I bees, I ain't never gonner be nuthin' but jest Fode."

I wish I had never heard him say that. There are some truths that facing does not help. Something had brought home to Ford the tragedy of himself and of his race in an alien world. Had he been in South Africa or Morocco or Harlem or Detroit, his pitiful cry would have been equally true, equally hopeless and unanswerable. What can we do, any of us, how can we help? Let the man who has the answer cry it from the house-tops in a hundred languages. But there will be no crier in the night, and it is night for all the Fords of the world and for us who love them.

Reynolds Price

(1933-)

One of the most gifted and prolific writers in the history of southern literature, Reynolds Price has published twenty-eight books, including ten novels, six collections of poems, four collections of short fiction, and two memoirs. Born in Macon, North Carolina, he attended Duke University, graduating in 1955, then was a Rhodes Scholar at Merton College at Oxford University. He returned to his alma mater in 1958 as a member of the English faculty, where he still teaches. When his novel A Long and Happy Life appeared in 1962, Price was heralded as the most promising literary successor to William Faulkner, who died that same year. While providing him some attention, the comparisons to Faulkner may have led reviewers of his early works to overlook Price's own distinctive qualities as a writer. By the late seventies, however, he had established his mastery of the novel, and his critical reputation has grown steadily since. In 1984, he was stricken with a near-fatal case of spinal cancer, resulting in almost total paralysis and considerable pain. Miraculously, his bout with cancer, currently in remission, marked the beginning of the most productive and arguably most artistically successful period of his rich literary career. His most recent novel is Roxanna Slade (1998).

   Although his critical reputation rests deservedly on his novels and, to a lesser extent, on his short fiction and poetry, Price's skill as a memoirist is exceptional. In A Whole New Life (1994), he writes with astounding and sometimes graphic clarity of his struggle with cancer and the spiritual renewal he experienced during the darkest days of his chemotherapy. Clear Pictures: First Loves, First Guides (1989), from which the following selection is taken, is a memoir of family members and childhood friends that allows him to display his remarkable powers of recall.

FROM *Clear Pictures: First Loves,*
First Guides

I'M LYING in dry sun, alone and happy. Under me is a white blanket. I'm fascinated by the pure blue sky, but Topsy the goat is chained to my right—out of reach they think. The sound of her grazing comes steadily closer. I've sat on her back, she pulls my cart, I'm not afraid. Suddenly though she is here above me, a stiff rank smell. She licks my forehead in rough strokes of a short pink tongue. Then she begins to pull hard at what I'm wearing. I don't understand that she's eating my diaper. I push at her strong head and laugh for the first time yet in my life. I'm free to laugh since my parents are nearby, talking on the porch. They'll be here shortly, no need to cry out. I'm four or five months old and still happy, sunbathing my body that was sick all winter.

THAT SCENE is my earliest sure memory; and it poses all the first questions—how does a newborn child learn the three indispensable human skills he is born without? How does he learn to live, love and die? How do we learn to depend emotionally and spiritually on others and to trust them with our lives? How do we learn the few but vital ways to honor other creatures and delight in their presence? And how do we learn to bear, use and transmit that knowledge through the span of a life and then to relinquish it?

I've said that all but one of my student writers have located their earliest memory in the third or fourth year. My own first memory appears to be a rare one. The incident was often laughed about in my presence at later gatherings—the day poor Topsy went for Reynolds's diaper, got a good whiff and bolted. So I might have built a false memory from other people's narratives. But I'm still convinced that the scene I've described is a fragment of actual recall, stored at the moment of action. If it wasn't I'd have embellished the scene further—adding clouds to the sky, a smell to the grass, the pitch of my parents' voices. What I've written is what I have, an unadorned fragment that feels hard and genuine. And the only trace of emotion is my lack of fear, my pleasure, both of which produced my first awareness of dependency—the goat won't eat me; help is near.

From the presence of Topsy, I know I'm in Macon, North Carolina. She was born, the same day as I, on my Uncle Marvin Drake's farm up near the Roanoke River. My father has had a small red goat-cart built, big enough for me and one child-passenger; and Topsy is already strong enough to pull us. Since we left Macon before I was a year old, then the memory comes from my first summer in 1933. That February 1st, I'd been born in the far west bedroom of my mother's family home in Macon.

MACON WAS then a village of under two hundred people, black and white. Because it was an active station on the Seaboard Railroad's Raleigh-to-Norfolk line, it had grown north and south from the depot in the shape of a Jerusalem cross—a north-south dirt street, an east-west paved road parallel to the train tracks and a few dirt streets parallel still to both axes.

There was a minuscule but thriving business district—three grocery and dry-goods stores, a gas station and a post office. There were two brick white churches, Methodist and Baptist, and two frame black churches, one on the west edge and one in the country. There were fewer than forty white households, mostly roomy but unpretentious frame houses, no pillared mansions. A few smaller black houses were set in the midst of town with no hint of threat or resentment; but most black families lived on the fringes of town—some in solid small houses, some in surprisingly immortal-seeming hovels. And on all sides, the sandy fields of tobacco and cotton lay flat and compliant, backed by deep woods of pine and cedar and big-waisted hardwoods.

Almost every white family employed one or more black women, men and children as farm hands, house servants, yard-men, gardeners and drivers. With all the deep numb evil of the system (numb for whites)—slavery and servitude did at least as much enduring damage to whites as to blacks—those domestic relations were astonishingly good-natured and trusting, so deco-rous that neither side began to explore or understand the other's hidden needs. When they'd granted one another the hunger for food, shelter and affection, their explorations apparently ceased; and the ancient but working standoff continued.

Yet a major strand of the harmony of all their lives consisted of the easy flow of dialogue expressive of mutual dependency, jointly sparked fun and the frequent occasions of mutual exas-peration. There were even glints of rage from each side; but in our family homes at least, there was never a word about the tragic tie that bound the two peoples. And if a cook or yardman mysteriously failed to appear on Monday morning, even the kindest white employer was sure to foment angrily on the bla-tant no-count ingratitude—no trace of acknowledgement that a bone-deep hostile reluctance might be fuming.

SINCE THE FAMILY TREES of strangers are high on any-one's boredom scale, I'll limit the following to what seems bare necessity if I'm to track these mysteries. My mother Elizabeth Martin Rodwell was born in 1905 and reared in Macon in the oak-shaded rambling white seven-room house built by her father in the mid-1880s. He was John Egerton Rodwell, station master of the Macon depot. He'd grown up in a big nest of brothers on a farm, some four miles north, between Macon and Churchill. His mother Alice Egerton, whether she knew it or not, could have claimed descent from the English family that commissioned John Milton to write his masque *Comus* in 1634 to celebrate the elevation of John Egerton, Earl of Bridgewater, to the Lord Presidency of Wales (the leading player in *Comus* was his daughter Alice Egerton, age fifteen). While the memory of such a standing was retained by a few of the deep-country farmers my Egertons had become, after two centuries in slave-holding Virginia and North Carolina, they seldom bragged on their blood.

My mother Elizabeth's mother was Elizabeth White—called Lizzie, even on her gravestone—from the oldest continuously settled part of the state, Perquimans County in the northeast corner, eighty miles east of Macon. Lizzie's mother had died in Lizzie's infancy, and she had been reared by her storekeeper father and an agreeable stepmother. On a visit to friends in Macon, she met black-haired, brown-eyed funny Jack Rodwell; and she married him soon after. She was all of sixteen, mirthful and pleasantly buxom (a later problem), not pretty but widely loved for her good talk, her endless self-teasing and much ready laughter.

She was fated to bear eight children in twenty years, seven of whom survived her. One boy died in his first year; the other three left home early, in the common Dickensian fashion. They packed their small belongings, kissed their parents (all my kin flung themselves on kisses with the recklessness of Russian premiers), flagged the train and headed up the line for railroad jobs in Norfolk, already a teeming port of the U.S. Navy. Of the four daughters, my mother Elizabeth was the youngest. Lizzie used to claim that Elizabeth was conceived because, well after Lizzie thought she was done, the Seaboard added a four a.m. express. Its window-rattling plunge through the heart of Macon would wake Jack nightly and leave him with nothing better to do in the dark than turn to his mate.

My father William Solomon Price was born in 1900 in War-renton, the small county-seat five miles from Macon. Before the Civil War, the town was a social and political center of the state (a local statesman Nathaniel Macon was Speaker of the House of Representatives in the presidency of Thomas Jefferson). As such it was the home of wealthy slaveholding planters, many of whose elegant houses have lately been refurbished, though Warrenton now shares the sad lot of all bypassed farm towns—its children leave.

Will's father—Edward Price, a famed dry wit—was a son of the town carriage-maker, of Welsh and Scottish stock; Edward's mother was a Reynolds from Perth, Scotland. Barely out of boyhood and balked by Reconstruction poverty from his hope to study medicine, Edward avoided the family business and clerked for the remainder of his life in the county's Registry of Deeds. Will's mother was Lula McCraw, also of Warrenton and the descendant of Scottish, English and French Huguenot immigrants. One of her third-great-grandfathers was James Agee, a Huguenot whom we share with our Tennessee cousin, the writer James Agee. Lula Price was small, with a bright voracious mind, watchful as a sparrow and capable of winging a startlingly ribald comment from behind her lace and cameo with such swift wit as to leave the beauty of her face unmarred. Her short narrow body bore six strong children, all of whom survived her; yet she found the energy to run a ten-room house generously, almost lavishly, on her husband's modest income with a strength of mind and hand that, again, her white-petal beauty belied.

MY PARENTS MET six years before their marriage. The meeting was in 1921 when Will was twenty-one and Elizabeth sixteen. They'd each gone to a dance at Fleming's Mill Pond, with other dates—Will with Sally Davis, Elizabeth with Alfred Ellington. Elizabeth's date introduced her to Will; and despite Sally Davis's beauty and wit, an alternate circuit at once lit up. First, both Will and Elizabeth looked fine and knew it, within reason. Second, they were both storage batteries of emotional hunger and high-voltage eros. And third, their short pasts— which felt like eons—had left each one of them craving the other's specific brand of nourishment.

Will had graduated from high school four years earlier and had since held easy jobs, none of which required him to go more than a few hundred yards from his family home, while continuing to sleep and board with his parents. His two elder brothers had gone as far as was imaginable then, to Tennessee; but all three of his witty and unassuaged sisters were still in place—the eldest having left her husband and returned unannounced at the age of twenty with a young son to live for good in the shadow of her father, whom she loved above all and whose deathbed pillows were found in her cedar chest at her own death, more than fifty years later. Both Will's parents were in hale, testy, often hilarious control; so the house contained eight Prices in five bedrooms, plus at least one cook and a handyman.

I can hardly think how a healthy young man, between the ages of seventeen and twenty-seven, can have stood to inhabit such a crowd of watchers and feeders—and stood them, day and night, for ten years after finishing high school—but stand them he did. As the youngest son, Will was his mother's "eyeballs." And later evidence suggests that she unconsciously mastered his growing dependence on alcohol to keep him close to an all-forgiving bosom (Elizabeth told me, late in her life, that "Will's mother would ride with him to the bootlegger when no one else would go").

For whatever reasons, Will's extrication from the grip of such a rewarding and demanding mother—and from his fondness for Sally Davis—took him six long years of fervent courting. And once he and Elizabeth had steeled themselves, they married as far from Warren County as they could go and still be sheltered by kin. Elizabeth's next-oldest, and favorite, brother Boots gave her away in Portsmouth, Virginia; and in Warrenton, Will's sisters rose at dawn to set all the clocks in the Price house an hour ahead. Then at "noon"—as the distant vows seemed imminent and their mother announced her imminent heart-spell—they could say "Just calm yourself, Muddy; it's too late now. Will and Elizabeth are a whole hour married and on the *train*." And so they were—the Orange Blossom Special, in a "drawing room" suite (courtesy of Elizabeth's Seaboard brothers) and bound for Florida, one of the gorgeous ends of the Earth in those grand days.

ELIZABETH'S PARENTS had died young. When my mother was eleven, Lizzie's kidneys failed; and Elizabeth was led to her mother's deathbed—surrounded by galvanized tubs of ice to cool the fierce heat—for a final goodbye. Three years later, sitting on her own porch, Elizabeth looked up the dirt road to see a mail cart from the depot roll toward her. It bore her last anchor—Jack Rodwell her father, dead of his second stroke at fifty-eight.

From the age of eleven, Elizabeth and her sister Alice, called Britsy and five years older, were mothered by their kind sister Ida. Ida was eighteen years older than Elizabeth; and with her came her then-volatile husband Marvin Drake and their three boys. Though they were Elizabeth's near-contemporary nephews, they quickly became her surrogate brothers, foster sons and chief playmates.

The Drakes had moved in at Lizzie's death to keep house for Jack and the girls; and once Jack died, they stayed for good. Ever after, Elizabeth's feelings about the years of at-home orphanhood were understandably mixed. She was grateful for the chance to remain in her birthplace with mostly well-intentioned kinfolk. But on rare occasions in my own childhood, I'd see her ambushed by sudden resentment. In those short forays, she'd glimpse the worst—she'd been dispossessed in her rightful place by an interloper with a cold eye for gain, a brother-in-law (who would ultimately purchase the Rodwell children's shares in the home and will it and all its Rodwell contents to his Drake heirs). In a few days though, I'd hear her say "Let's drive up home and see Ida and Marvin." In her best mind, my mother knew they'd kept her alive.

WILL AND ELIZABETH WERE reared then in classic, though healthily honest, family situations where blood-love, or at least loyalty, was the binding principle of a majority of the by-no-means happy populace. As an inevitable and paradoxical result, my young parents were primed for another love, private but transcendent, that would lead them out of the blighting shadows of their homes into the glare of their own graceful bodies in one another's hands, worked as they were by aching need.

The repeatable public stories of their courtship were among my own favorites from their long repertoire. There was the night when, returning from a performance of *The Merry Widow* in Henderson, Will left his Model A Ford for a moment to buy cigarettes; and Elizabeth, still too well-mannered to mention a body-need, was forced to lift the floorboard and pee quickly on the hot gear box. It reeked mysteriously through the rest of Will's evening. Or the time the same car got bogged in quicksand and almost sank them. Or the hard days of Will's terror when Elizabeth suffered a ruptured appendix, twenty years before the discovery of antibiotics, and was rushed in agony from Macon to Norfolk on a stretcher in the baggage car of a train—the only place she could ride flat—for six weeks of desperate but successful remedies. Or Elizabeth's happiest memory of her strongly ambivalent mother-in-law—the time they were driving alone together, struck a turkey, killed it neatly and brought it home to eat. Or the lovers' own mutual fits of jealousy and their laughing reconciliations, alone in the woods by the sandy creek in Macon or at big late dances in the open pavilion at Fleming's Mill Pond or a place in the woods called Largo.

WELL BEFORE I was in school, I came to realize that they'd been together twelve years before my birth—six years of courtship and six of marriage. And with that realization came a kernel of bitterness that I'd missed so much of them, that they'd had so much without me. Knowing nothing of the mechanics of reproduction, I lamented my absence from so much fun and from all the magical snapshots in their albums. Why hadn't they wanted to bring me in sooner?

The kind of merciless consolation available only to children and madmen came in my realizing simultaneously that those twelve years broke into two pieces, good and bad. The courtship was happy, though subject to the clouds I've mentioned (Sally Davis took a long time resigning her hold on Will, and Elizabeth ran an unpredictable sideline in other beaux). But the six years of marriage before my birth were all but tragic. Will's boyish taste for bootleg liquor—the fuel of so much of his early fun— became a nightmarish and paralyzing thirst.

The drunkenness, and all the missed work-days, led to aimless dangerous roving with his bachelor best-friend and fellow-soak, whom I'll call Alec, while Elizabeth waited—sober and wretched in whatever room they'd rented that month. And all round, the troubles of an always-poor state grew as the Great Depression plummeted. Even Will's sisters, two of whom by then had suffered disastrous marriages, told Elizabeth that they couldn't fault her if she left for the sake of her own self-respect and sanity. She later admitted that, in their courtship, she drank her own share of bathtub gin, especially at Boots's nonstop party in Norfolk. But now, avid as she was for her own chance at life but devoted to Will in his pitiful baffling thirst, she was sober in earnest. And she stayed. Long after his death, she said to me "The thing was, he always came back late to me, so sick and helpless, saying I was all he had. I wanted to doubt him, but I knew it was true."

With all their other troubles, living near their families in a fruitful farming county, they never went cold or hungry, though I've heard Mother say "With one dollar bill you could pack the car with groceries; the only trick was finding that dollar." More than once she was forced to down her pride, approach her solvent brother-in-law, who owned the local feed-and-seed store; beg for a dollar and endure his asking "Why in the world?—to buy Will's liquor?"

Will's constant worry, beyond a drunkard's guilt, was jobs and income. Like his father and two older brothers, he'd never really thought of college; and he was skilled in nothing more saleable than wit, charm and a generous heart. As a boy and a youth, he'd sold newspapers, clerked in the freight office of the Warrenton Railroad's depot. He even rode as conductor on that lightly traveled, remarkably short line—less than five miles out to Warren Plains and back. The only job I recall his mentioning from those first married years was door-to-door life-insurance sales. At least it wasn't office work. With his own Ford, and without the cold-eyed scrutiny of a boss, Will could roam the backroads of Warren and Vance counties, canvassing hard-up farmers. I never heard tales of his drinking at work but he must have. For whatever reason, the jobs were short and unambitious; and he and Elizabeth moved restlessly from rented room to rented room, all within a fifteen-mile radius of their family homes.

PICTURES OF WILL PRICE in youth show a strong up-turned face with a radiance almost better than beauty, a heat centered in the gray eyes that burn with what seems fervor—where does it come from; what fuel does it take? A few years later, the courtship pictures still show him as a trim dapper man with splendidly live eyes, an upright carriage of his medium frame and with always the threat of a smile on his mouth. But I've found no pictures of him from those hard first six years of marriage; and surely that gap in the record can't be accidental (thirty years later when I got a home-movie camera, he was openly fascinated with his own walking likeness; and he often said he was going to buy a whole reel and get me to use it all on him, though sadly he never did).

It's only with my birth that he appears in the albums again, holding me with the winning edginess of a fledgling member of the bomb-disposal squad. But by then, in his early thirties, he's taken on weight. It looks like bloat and, worse, there's a blurring glaze on the once-hot eyes. Half-smiling still, thoughtful and protective as he is, by now there's a presence in his life even more demanding than his wife and first son.

I also have no pictures of Elizabeth from those six years. But her long absence from the record of an eagerly snapshooting family is also eloquent, though I recall only two occasions when she mentioned the slow pain. In 1961, seven years after Will's death, I was living in England and working on an autobiographical story called "Uncle Grant." It was about a black man who worked for us in those early years; and I wrote to ask Mother if Grant, in his devotion to Will, had ever drunk with him. She answered quickly; no, Grant "never took a drink with Will that I know of." And then, for the only time in all her relations with my writing, she hinted at a possible suppression—"I don't know, but maybe 'twould be better not to bring in the drinking days, they were so horrible" (that instinctive slide into the poetic *'twould* still sounds its desolation). When she reappears in my baby pictures, it's clear that she's fared much better than Will. In her late twenties now, she's lost her baby fat but is still a good-looking woman ("a well set-up girl, I can tell you," as Will might have said). Whatever pain those dark eyes have eaten has left no trace, not yet.

In the face of their own problems, and the economic world-maelstrom in which they were helpless floaters, it's hard to guess why in early May of 1932 they conceived a first child. Once I was grown, Will told me of the pains he took in those years to preserve a single washed condom in a box of powder for numerous uses, but he didn't connect the fact with my conception. I may have been an accident, and few of us want that; but it feels at least possible from here that Elizabeth, justifiably leery of childbearing, arranged to conceive as a last hope of braking Will's rush to drown. She'd tried every other way she knew. Maybe a child would get his attention where all else had failed; he had seemed to enjoy his nearest nephew and niece.

————

PHYSICALLY, the pregnancy was uncomplicated. They were living in Henderson as the day approached, again in a rented room with a cranky widow who monopolized the bathroom. The intention was, though, that I should be born in Elizabeth's home in Macon. I've said that it was her birthplace and that of her brothers and sisters; it had also seen the deaths of one of her brothers and both her parents. No Rodwell or Price of their generations had yet been born or died elsewhere. Will's boyhood friend Dr. Pat Hunter supervised the pregnancy; and when Elizabeth felt contractions in the late afternoon of January 31st, she and Will lit out for Macon. (Earlier in the day Adolf Hitler had assumed dictatorial powers in Germany, but they wouldn't have known or cared.) Elizabeth's water broke before they arrived; but she walked from the car into the house, to find Ida and Marvin playing rummy with friends. There was no telephone; a cousin drove to Warrenton to fetch Pat Hunter; someone else went for Betty Lyons the black midwife. And soon after they arrived, labor set in.

In the living room Marvin, Will and the friends tried to wait it out. They scrambled eggs and played more cards by the hot woodstove, though Will was far too scared to concentrate. By midnight nothing had come from the bedroom but cries from Elizabeth. The friends left; Marvin tried to sleep. But Will lurked helpless at the edge of the hardest birth ever suffered on the place.

It was remembered as that, even by the other women present—black Betty Lyons with Ida and Cousin Joyce Russell, who administered ether on a clean cotton pad till she herself was nearly unconscious. By the time I began to listen, that night was one of the epic family tales, a ghastly double-death turned back as cold morning broke. In the far west room on a white iron bed six feet from a woodstove, Elizabeth worked for twelve hours. I was breeched—turned backward, stalled defiant—in the womb; and since antibiotics were twelve years off and a caesarean was all but unthinkable, Pat Hunter struggled to turn me.

No luck. Near day when Will peered in again, Pat looked up and said "I'm losing them both." It was all Will needed. More than once in later years, I watched him hear the story of his next act from others; but I never heard him tell it. Even for a narrator as driven and dazzling as he, it was far too weighty for public performance.

He fled the house in the freezing dawn, went out to the woodshed; and there he sealed a bargain with God, as stark and unbreakable as any blood pact in Genesis—if Elizabeth lived, and the child, he'd never drink again.

By the time he was back in the house, Pat had finally turned me, clamped forceps to my pliant skull, braced his feet on the rail of the bed and pulled me out by main force. My rubbery skull was dented, and one ear was torn; but once I'd wailed and been handed to a revived Joyce for bathing, Pat went to tell Will. Elizabeth was alive, exhausted but safe. And plainly I was there too, the first of their sons.

No one recalled, in my presence, what either Will or Elizabeth said to Pat or to one another, nor did anyone say when Will told her of his solemn deal. Likely the first words, after endearments, were my name—*Edward* for Will's dead father, *Reynolds* for his Scottish grandmother. Will's elder brothers had so far produced three girls and a boy, none of whom bore their grandfather's name. My guess is that it meant much to Will to go to his mother with the news of a boy named Edward Price—again. There seems to have been no question of a name from the Rodwell side, though Elizabeth often told me "Will put his foot down—you couldn't be a junior." That was saved for another boy years later, when Will may have loathed his own name less.

He must have told Elizabeth his hopeful news soon because, obedient to medical wisdom at the time, she spent the next three weeks in bed (or near it) and would have needed cheering. For the remainder of his life, he teased her about the long rest—"I thought we'd have to hire a damned steam shovel to get you up. You were that scared of touching your foot to the floor." She had been badly torn and would need surgical repair years later.

GOD HAD KEPT his half of the bargain. The family myth had it that Will Price kept his half. The fact is, in time he did but not at once—and no wonder. In the upper South in the 1930s, the help available to a drunk who hoped to quit was no more unusual than prayer and no more imaginative then the standard injunction to buck up, be a man and do the manly thing. Professional help was limited to small private clinics for the discreet sobering up of drunks who could pay for weaning, "vitamin" shots and a dollop of scoutmasterly advice; but one and all, the clinics were notoriously unsuccessful in long-range help. It's now conceded that the majority of enduring recoveries in America are achieved through membership in Alcoholics Anonymous, but A.A. had not been organized in 1933. It was one year off and nearly twenty years before its groups appeared in the smalltown South.

So Will was all but on his own. His mother and sisters were slim help; the middle sister was involved in her own sad marriage to a charming drunk who would soon kill himself, leaving her and a young daughter to return to the Warrenton home. Both Will's brothers, by then in Tennessee, were also drinkers—as were all three of Elizabeth's and ultimately all her nephews. Whether or not Will's mother unconsciously fostered his thirst, there's no doubt that in his cups he often resorted to the tiny glistening face of his mother, so ready to forgive and provide what an interloping wife was baffled to find.

The interloper though was the stronger prop, the wife he'd courted so hard for years. Elizabeth was no more a trained alcoholic counselor than anyone else in the South of those days; but she was passionately ready to help, to nurse him in his sickness and to wait in hope. Once she told me "The help was seldom more than waiting, then fixing him soft-boiled eggs with butter in a glass." Years later Will also acknowledged the spiritual guidance of Robert Brickhouse, his Baptist minister in Warrenton; and he had the bald enormous fact of a mortal deal with the

God he never questioned. If Will Price couldn't keep his half of the bargain, then in his mind the unquestioned corollary was that God had every right to reclaim Elizabeth and Reynolds. And given the Old Testament tally of God's response to such defaults, the corollary surely stood cocked and ready to seize its double blood-due.

I stress that I never heard my father mention the deal and its terrors; he was no chattering fundamentalist but a silent wrestler in the scalding dark. In the first two years of my life, we continued to camp out—first in Henderson, fifteen miles southwest; then around Warren County with relatives and in rented rooms; so I spent many hours in the close company, not only of my housewife-mother but with Will. I remember frequent bearhugs and the scrape of a beard that could never quite be shaved; I can see flashes of my first Christmas; I have a glimpse of his delight when I took a first step on my first birthday. But I have no memory of seeing him high or loud or abusive.

Will and Elizabeth were long dead and I was in my forties before I learned from Lulie, the sister nearest Will in age, that Will concluded the deal more gradually than legend records. Admitted, at once he began to quit or *taper off*, as drunks still say. There were no more long nights of aimless driving through the county, no more work-days missed as he slept comatose at home or hid beside the loyal Elizabeth in self-hating self-pity. There was nonetheless still a fair amount of beer. According to Lulie, the real end did come suddenly but not till I was three.

THOSE FIRST THREE YEARS were dogged by illness— allergic rashes so severe that Mother pinned my arms to the sheets at night to prevent gouging, a winter-long bout of whooping cough and then a mysterious succession of frightening seizures. Without warning, my fever would soar; and in a matter of minutes, I'd rush into racking board-stiff convulsions. Only fast plunges in cold water and quickly administered enemas appeared to help. The doctors were helpless; maybe I was allergic to egg. (By age five however, I was eating egg with impunity. All my life I've been subject to sudden allergies that vanish as suddenly; but I now strongly suspect that in infancy I was showing first signs of the often congenital type of spinal tumor that would not fully manifest till I was fifty-one.)

Whatever the cause, everyone agreed that my seizures were dreadful to watch. Elizabeth would spring into purposeful action; Will would stand by, anguished and unmanned. At their height I appeared to be dead; when they passed I would sleep exhausted through whole days and nights. And all that I later knew of Will Price affirms that, early in the course of my afflictions, he'll have sighted the link between their threat and his continued cheating on a dead-earnest deal.

IN 1935 HE GOT the first good job of his life, as a salesman of electric appliances for Carolina Power and Light Company; and we moved forty miles to the small mill-town of Roxboro where finally we had a rented house to ourselves. An imperious surviving letter from Will's mother—clubbing him, in a potent tall script, for negligence and ordering him to see that she got "toe pads" before the week was out—suggests how short a hyphen fifty miles could be, even in slower days. But at least he wasn't in five-mile reach of that brand of vampire whim.

The year I was three, his oldest sister Mary Eleanor was visiting us. Late one afternoon she and Will walked up the slope behind our house to a neighborhood curb-market for a loaf of bread. While there, for whatever reason, Will chose to drink a bottle of beer. When they ambled down to the house twenty minutes later, I was in the grip of the hardest seizure yet. Elizabeth had failed to reach Dr. Gentry, so she'd called the black doctor, but he still hadn't come. And with all their efforts, I was borne further off—eyes rolled back white, skin purple, hands clenched so tight my palms were cut. Lulie said "Will knew you were dying, he knew he had caused it, and he quit then and there."

Such a mortal dare would have come at Will as no shock at all, no ambush. He trusted, and his sons do, that even a life as low to the ground, as wasteful and destructive as his own, was of serious weight in the hand of God. In his own head, then, he earnestly swore to redeem his pledge.

In half an hour both doctors were gone, I was cool and sleeping, and Elizabeth could finally start cooking supper. According to Lulie, it was my last seizure. In any case, Will Price lived another eighteen years and never again drank so much as a spoonful of alcohol. His quitting was as graceful as his jokes. He could watch kin and friends drink with no apparent temptation, and he always kept a pint of bourbon far back on the top pantry-shelf (and a four-ounce bottle in his suitcase)—for emergencies with the heart he believed to be weak, though it beat like a perpetual piston through the worst of his end at fifty-four. Even more importantly, I suspect, the stored bottle was also an emblem—the old demon, captive and harmless on a shelf.

Evelyn Scott

(1893–1963)

Although novelist and poet Evelyn Scott was praised by critics as a genius of rare talent, and circulated among the most highly recognized poets and novelists in America during the 1920s, few readers today have heard of her, let alone read her works. Born Elsie Dunn in Clarksville, Tennessee, Scott belonged to a prestigious family that had made its fortune in the railroad business but lost it in the years following the Civil War. She was an avid reader who began writing at age seven and produced a novel at age fifteen. When her family moved to New Orleans, she became the youngest student to attend Tulane. However, instead of completing her course of study there she developed a romantic relationship with Frederick Wellman, a married man and one of the college's academic deans, with whom she fled the country in 1913. The couple, who assumed the new names C. Kay-Scott and Evelyn Scott, eventually ended up in Brazil for nearly six years, a period she wrote about in her autobiographical novel Escapade *(1923). The author of twenty books, Scott received her greatest critical acclaim for* The Narrow House *(1921), the first volume of a trilogy about a middle-class southern family, and* The Wave *(1929), a panoramic novel of the Civil War. Along with Faulkner, Scott was one of the first southern practitioners of literary modernism, employing stream-of-consciousness techniques and fragmented narrative structures that placed unusually high demands on readers of the day. She was also an outspoken feminist who had no qualms about using her art as a vehicle for the advancement of her sexual politics.*

At the time of her death, Scott left behind an unfinished manuscript of a formal autobiography, which remains unpublished. However, Background in Tennessee, *published in 1937 and reprinted in 1980, recounts in great detail her early years and growing rebelliousness against the conventions of southern gentility. Combining personal reminiscences of life in the community of Clarksville with an objective history of the state's settlement and gradual cultural development, the structure of* Background in Tennessee *illustrates the interrelationship among personal, family, and regional identity that characterizes southern autobiography in general. In the following selection, Scott playfully describes her gradual disengagement from the rituals of coquetry that southern belles in the traditional South were expected to master.*

FROM *Background in Tennessee*

HOWEVER, I did, at any rate, emancipate myself from further obligations to that relic custom of feudal pioneering which ordains it that marriageable girls in the South pass their time, year in and year out, in rounds of exchange visiting! No more for me either the penalties of the benefits of a species of co-operating matchmaking, exemplified in such hospitality as will test the endurance of both hosts and guests! In the rural, and semirural South, a visitor invited to your house for a fortnight may linger for months! There can be no complaint! Reciprocity may be valuable, and has been taken for granted! The father and mother of the girl from Texas who has decided to make Tennessee her hunting ground for a winter will do as much for your own daughter when the time arrives!

At my aunt's (for we, as city people, were never typical), where the normal composition of the family included eleven souls, there was rarely a meal for which housegirl and houseboy were not required to provide seats for from fifteen to eighteen persons—the extras being, for the most part, impromptu additions to the company; though there would be among them, also, the young lady from Georgia, Alabama, or "The Lone Star State," who had arrived for Christmas eggnog and holiday junketing and might remain until the dog days of August, should it be her whim to do so.

I recollect but a single outburst protesting this presumed right of any female after a husband to seize on board and lodging in whatever quarter she considered convenient, and stay on where she willed for as long as her optimism endured. Then it was my uncle who exploded one day in disgust, admitting himself, in a rare moment of privacy, sick to death of a particular perky face and inane giggle, that had come together in the spring when swallows were being welcomed, and had been present for ten months! He never, he said, hoped to be able to enjoy a meal exclusively with his family, but he *did* ask for variety!

I don't remember when the visitor left, or how she was finally got rid of; but I suspect nothing could really be done about it until she had run through her wardrobe—the clothes she had bought and brought, and an equal number of borrowed dresses. With a risk before her of having to wear the same party frock three times in succession, she may have become suddenly amenable; or may even have resolved, of her own accord, to transfer her activities to another place. In the matter of costume, it was regarded as hardly less than disgraceful for a girl to reproduce her own effects too frequently and obviously. So travel became a double economy, a change of venue sometimes equivalent to an entirely new wardrobe. It was all made easier, too, by the freemasonry existing among girls, who agreed liberally to appropriate one another's belongings, often for weeks at a time. Probably it was the constant stressing of the dramatic importance of physical appearances, which caused me to supplement preparations following a first permission to attend an evening party for children, with a trip to the florist's, from whom I ordered red carnations, sent to myself with seemly greetings from myself, signed "John." (I was twelve.) I wore my flowers, not too certainly, with a new scarlet point d'esprit.

Not (I must add hastily) that I commanded only invented tributes! One of the privileges of old age I have noticed (and they are few enough!) is a shameless dilation on the flattering aspects of the personal past—a habit of retrospective boasting that the more self-respecting modesty of youth would abhor. However, after my own fortieth birthday, I decided every woman able to survive such an ordeal was completely justified in claiming for herself, as an inalienable right, a share in contributing to complimentary legends (in memoriam) of "the glorious dead." I was not a beautiful child, but neither was I stupid, except as I reacted with blind impressionableness to demands made by southern custom upon the vanity of womanhood. It seems improbable that a child in the North would have been aware, as I was before I was seven, that Santa Claus, for example, though his supernatural powers elevated him to the status of the angels, was, also, a man. Yet I remember clearly a Christmas Eve after the sacrifice of my chief adornment to malaria, when my mother, in despair over my appearance and anxious to have me shine at the next day's festivities, sent me to bed with my hair done in curlers improvised from strips of soft rag. Something warned me not to object openly against the libellous effect she was willing to let me make on Saint Nicholas; but I had in mind the jacket design on *The Night Before Christmas,* and, while I hung up my stocking, rebelled privately against an invidious comparison the expected nocturnal visitor was bound to make between a little girl whose head was encircled by disgusting humps and knobs, and that chubby-cheeked, golden-orioled sum of infant perfections depicted by an artist. And as soon as my mother, ingenuously oblivious to the havoc she had wrought, had kissed me and left me to what she imagined would be innocently selfish dreams of gifts, I snatched off the curlers, and, settling myself upon the pillow carefully, arranged my locks in such a fashion as to make the utmost of their temporary paucity. In my realistic conception of things, I was rewarded for my cautious foresight—it was the Christmas I received a dollhouse which, to this very moment, seems to me like the apotheosis of all dollhouses, and even far superior to the Queen's.

Such premature concern for male opinion may strike the Yankee as only idiosyncratic and perverse; and it may well be

that I was abnormally sensible of what was expected of a little
girl. But the background for my behaviour was general sugges-
tion, which affected other children, too. For me, pervasive innu-
endoes were embodied in a jovial, portly bachelor called Mr.
Blakeman, who had claimed me as his sweetheart from the age
of three. He owned a dry goods store; and when my mother
took me with her on a shopping tour, would pounce upon me
from the door of his emporium, decoy me in with gifts of
chocolates and peppermints, swing me to a vacant counter, and
entice me into giving recitations from the works of Eugene
Field, before an audience of males who always laughed uproari-
ously. The pact between us was sealed finally when I received
from him a little silver "friendship bracelet" with a jewelled,
heart-shaped lock engraved: "with Blakeman's love." And once,
on Sunday, he invited me to drive with him behind a tandem
pair which he manipulated dashingly. I wore a new blue cash-
mere frock from New Orleans, and carried, for the first time, a
small blue silk parasol with pale pink frills; and proudly, almost
suffocated by the steaming bulk which towered beside me in the
narrow seat of his smart vehicle, endured an ordeal of discomfort compensated for by the display.

Though I may have represented an extreme, all little southern
girls, as I remember them, were almost frighteningly precocious
in developing sex-consciousness. For one thing, constant contact with the coloured race both stimulated and informed them
about matters veiled by late-Victorian, white taboos. And in the
case of boys, strictly conventional white parents were incredibly
obtuse, often employing, as a paid companion for a lonely child,
some small Negro, who was called "a play boy." At ten, we
priggishly reared daughters of "first families" were familiar
with a language we half comprehended which would have been
proper for a bawdyhouse. It seeped in from untrammelled sources
with a curious, poisoning incongruity that made our natural
guardians into egregious hypocrites. While we tripped forth
politely, with our miniature cardcases, and, under adult supervi-
sion, called on one another formally, like polite "little ladies,"

we adventured, simultaneously, into forbidden territories we found terrible and strange. Odd indeed it is to think that such tender maidens as we were, occasionally escaped in a nursery pony cart into a province perilously near the sort exposed by Brand Whitlock in one of the earliest of "muckraking" novels: *The Thirteenth District*!

We were attracted there by a large, drably unimposing frame house, which was a conspicuous salient for our expeditions because, extraordinarily, though it was on the fringes of a Negro settlement, it was inhabited by white women. On this account, and by reason of numberless semi-intelligible explanations of its significant repute, it fascinated us as if it had been a Castle of Otranto, or the villa into which Count Dracula descended from his mountain stronghold for variety in summer months. And every now and then, quaking, but gleeful over our own daring, we would turn the pony from the main road, and make a detour by this awesomely mysterious place. Y., the mistress of the diminutive vehicle in which we crowded, cowering, would then try to put a brave front on her own timidity and defiantly curb the pony's trot until it became a walk. Then we could covertly and deliberately survey a seedy yard containing poor grass and a few shrivelling cannas; or scrutinize the dirty curtains before upper windows where the blinds, even at midday, always seemed to be drawn. I remember, once, a sharp glance given us by a thin-featured girl in a wrapper, who, as we passed, stared at us from a lawn swing in which she was idly enjoying the sun; and that the casual look she bestowed upon us turned back on me like a weapon the dangerous feeling of my own guilt. As Y. lashed the pony into a gallop, it produced in a lot of us an explosion of hysteria; and as we rattled on along the regained public thoroughfare, we might have been fleeing for our lives.

What had must amazed me in this exploration of a demi-monde had been the evidence of poverty. From a House of Usher, bound to fall in the end, I had anticipated sinister grandeur. Instead—shockingly!—we had discovered only a shabby dwelling, in need of paint and repairs! Why, *anybody* might have lived in it! And the girl in the swing—not pretty, with a slovenly air of discouragement and languor, her clothes without a single touch of luxury! By her mere appearance, she annihilated forever the "romance of vice."

The stories whispered surreptitiously by little coloured children had primed all of us, voluptuously, for horror; but, actually, quite simply, I remembered Mary; and my heart was sick. Before this, in *Eva Gay*, I have tried to write of Mary—she was one of three or four literal ingredients among the many fictional elements in that novel—one people not initiate have questioned on the score of plausibility. Though I have frequently, indignantly, protested against such an interrogation of corroboratable plain fact, I incline, now, to accept the aesthetic basis for these objections. After all, though I am telling the precise truth when I say I, at seven, loved Mary, who was fourteen, more than I have ever loved anyone else; I know, also, that, when she fell into disgrace and was carried off into concealment, so that I never heard of her again—ever!—certain feelings she engendered, which belonged to her, and to no other being, were forced so deep underground they cannot be brought to the surface again. As well insist a dumb animal eloquently articulate devotion to a lost master, as ask me to express, today, what Mary used to mean to me. Yet she belongs here, in a chapter which might be fittingly concluded with a discourse on chivalry, which, it is reputed, flowered in the South in the early nineteen hundreds as never elsewhere since the disbanding of the Round Table! It is particularly appropriate to mention her, not only because she was physically beautiful (with a profile like that of Henny Porten, a German cinema actress, now retired I believe, and the loveliest human object I ever saw in this world), but, more notably, considering her tragedy, because she was such a *good* little girl— docile, dutiful, as instinctively housewifely as Meg in *Little Women*! As naturally domestic and "normally" kindly as little Daisy in *Jo's Boys*! Indeed Mary was as lacking in those impulses which make for sexual precocity—as really stupid, in one way of looking at such things!—as Louisa M. Alcott herself!

And why didn't they take *that* into account? I used to wonder; after I was commanded to forget her; after I was told—
incredible!—she had become a *bad* girl! Because, if you please,
she had had a baby—and it took three years to ferret *that* out!
And three years more to make literally certain the baby had
come into the world with a father, who went about uncastigated
(appearances deceived me then) by what, for her, had been
calamity no one could mend! And whether or not those militant
feminists who, for a while, during my adolescence, commanded
my admiration and respect, in the end, made it impossible for
any little girl to share Mary's fate, I don't know even yet. Mary
was a Kentuckian—as victim, she was universal. As universal,
and as much a victim as so many of her male contemporaries—
poor romance-starved and semiliterate little adolescents, would-
be profligates in southern towns and villages!

The Portuguese tell an apocryphal tale of Dom Pedro
Segundo, whose beloved mistress, Inez de Castro, was hounded
to her death by the jealousies of a political opposition which had
refused to recognize her as his Queen. And when he came into
power, he set her corpse upon the throne, called an audience of
those servile courtiers who were her murderers at heart, and
standing, lash in hand, beside her body, gloatingly exacted genu-
flections to her from her erstwhile enemies. For years, when I
remembered Mary, it was with an indignation as intense, and as
magniloquent as this attributed to "mad" Dom Pedro. An inap-
propriate indignation, misdirected against poor, blind sheep! I
had not then accepted it that force is wasted—illustrated fittingly
by Andrew Jackson's too impetuous propensity for futile duel-
ling, intended to defend Mrs. Jackson's fame! As for arguments,
I had to learn that they are never useful to convince, and serve
their one sound purpose by providing common speech for those
already in agreement on the basis of coincident emotional experiences.

And anyhow, between the ages of seven and thirteen, for all
my festering wounds of a moralist, I continued, unabatingly, to
be interested in manifestations of what I believed lay before me,

as I advanced toward the threshold of woman's only serious career. Indeed I and my little friends awaited fretfully the passage of the time required to accomplish our liberation to a share in important prerogatives which included dancing nightly until daylight, lying abed until noon, and sanction to spend as much of the remaining hours as we did not dedicate to card parties in the rites of the toilet.

Lillian Smith

(1897–1966)

An outspoken opponent of segregation at a time when other white southern liberals were only cautiously advancing modest improvements in race relations, Lillian Smith pursued her cause in relative isolation, shunned by mainstream organizations for her zealous condemnation of the South's racial sins. Smith was born in Jasper, Florida, a mill town just below the Georgia line, where her father, a textile manufacturer, was one of the principal employers. When his businesses suffered at the onset of World War I, her father liquidated most of his assets and moved the family to their mountain retreat near the North Georgia town of Clayton, where they eventually opened the Laurel Falls Camp for Girls. Smith studied music at the Peabody Conservatory in Baltimore, then taught music for three years at a missionary school in China before returning permanently to Georgia in 1925 to operate the Laurel Falls Camp. Under Smith's direction, the camp became a kind of testing ground for her social theories, where the daughters of wealthy southerners were exposed through creative learning experiences to remarkably progressive ideas about religion, race relations, and sexuality. Amazingly, the operation was a financial success and never suffered from a lack of enrollment. In 1935, Smith and Paula Snelling, her assistant and lifetime partner, published the first edition of the literary and social commentary journal Pseudopodia *(later changed to* North Georgia Review, *and later again to* South Today*). Unable to secure outside funding for the journal, Smith folded* South Today *in 1945. By then, however, she was enjoying international celebrity as the author of* Strange Fruit *(1944), a novel about an interracial love affair that ends in violence. In addition to* Strange Fruit, *Smith wrote seven books,* *including* Killers of the Dream *(1949)*, Now Is the Time *(1955)*, *and* Memory of a Large Christmas *(1961)*. *After her death, the Southern Regional Council, the South's oldest interracial organization, created the Lillian Smith Book Award, given annually to authors who write about social reform and racial issues in the South.*

Arguably Smith's most powerful work, Killers of the Dream *is a collection of personal essays that explore the psychological, social, and moral consequences of slavery, miscegenation, and segregation—what she refers to as the "race-sex-sin spiral"—that haunted the South and created deep divisions in the hearts of whites and African Americans alike. Though her thinking in* Killers of the Dream *shows a strong, perhaps reductive, Freudian influence, her views are based primarily on intuitive insights and religious conviction rather than scientific principles of analysis. The following selection, "When I Was a Child," the opening essay of the book, describes a long repressed memory of an incident that first made her aware of the tremendous significance her elders attached to "color."*

FROM *Killers of the Dream*

EVEN ITS CHILDREN knew that the South was in trouble. No one had to tell them; no words said aloud. To them, it was a vague thing weaving in and out of their play, like a ghost haunting an old graveyard or whispers after the household sleeps—fleeting mystery, vague menace to which each responded in his own way. Some learned to screen out all except the soft and the soothing; others denied even as they saw plainly, and heard. But all knew that under quiet words and warmth and laughter, under the slow ease and tender concern about small matters, there was a heavy burden on all of us and as heavy a refusal to confess it. The children knew this "trouble" was bigger than they, bigger than their family, bigger than their church, so big that people turned away from its size.

They had seen it flash out and shatter a town's peace, had felt it tear up all they believed in. They had measured its giant strength and felt weak when they remembered.

This haunted childhood belongs to every southerner of my age. We ran away from it but we came back like a hurt animal to its wound, or a murderer to the scene of his sin. The human heart dares not stay away too long from that which hurt it most. There is a return journey to anguish that few of us are released from making.

We who were born in the South called this mesh of feeling and memory "loyalty." We thought of it sometimes as "love." We identified with the South's trouble as if we, individually, were responsible for all of it. We defended the sins and the sorrows of three hundred years as if each sin had been committed by us alone and each sorrow had cut across our heart. We were as hurt at criticism of our region as if our own name had been called aloud by the critic. We knew guilt without understanding it, and there is no tie that binds men closer to the past and each other than that.

It is a strange thing, this umbilical cord uncut. In times of ease, we do not feel its pull, but when we are threatened with change, suddenly it draws the whole white South together in a collective fear and fury that wipe our minds clear of reason and we are blocked from sensible contact with the world we live in.

To keep this resistance strong, wall after wall was thrown up in the southern mind against criticism from without and within. Imaginations closed tight against the hurt of others; a regional armoring took place to ward off the "enemies" who would make our trouble different—or maybe rid us of it completely. For it was a trouble that we did not want to give up. We were as involved with it as a child who cannot be happy at home and cannot bear to tear himself away, or as a grownup who has fallen in love with his own disease. We southerners had identified with the long sorrowful past on such deep levels of love and hate and guilt that we did not know how to break old bonds without pulling our lives down. *Change* was the evil word, a shrill clanking that made us know too well our servitude. *Change* meant leaving one's memories, one's sins, one's ambivalent pleasures, the room where one was born.

In this South I lived as a child and now live. And it is of it that my story is made. I shall not tell, here, of experiences that were different and special and belonged only to me, but those most white southerners born at the turn of the century share with each other. Out of the intricate weaving of unnumbered threads, I shall pick out a few strands, a few designs that have to do with what we call color and race . . . and politics . . . and money and how it is made . . . and religion . . . and sex and the body image . . . and love . . . and dreams of the Good and the killers of dreams.

A southern child's basic lessons were woven of such dissonant strands as these; sometimes the threads tangled into a terrifying mess; sometimes archaic, startling designs would appear in the weaving; sometimes, a design was left broken while another was completed with minute care. Bewildered teachers, bewildered pupils in home and on the street, driven by an invisible Authority, learned their lessons:

The mother who taught me what I know of tenderness and love and compassion taught me also the bleak rituals of keeping Negroes in their "place." The father who rebuked me for an air of superiority toward schoolmates from the mill and rounded out his rebuke by gravely reminding me that "all men are brothers," trained me in the steel-rigid decorums I must demand of every colored male. They who so gravely taught me to split my body from my mind and both from my "soul," taught me also to split my conscience from my acts and Christianity from southern tradition.

Neither the Negro nor sex was often discussed at length in our home. We were given no formal instruction in these difficult matters but we learned our lessons well. We learned the intricate system of taboos, of renunciations and compensations, of manners, voice modulations, words, feelings, along with our prayers, our toilet habits, and our games. I do not remember how or when, but by the time I had learned that God is love, that Jesus is His Son and came to give us more abundant life, that all men are brothers with a common Father, I also knew that I was better than a Negro, that all black folks have their place and must be kept in it, that sex has its place and must be kept in it, that a terrifying disaster would befall the South if ever I treated a Negro as my social equal and as terrifying a disaster would befall my family if ever I were to have a baby outside of marriage. I had learned that God so loved the world that He gave His only begotten Son so that we might have segregated churches in which it was my duty to worship each Sunday and on Wednesday at evening prayers. I had learned that white southerners are a hospitable, courteous, tactful people who treat those of their own group with consideration and who as carefully segregate from all the richness of life "for their own good and welfare" thirteen million people whose skin is colored a little differently from my own.

I knew by the time I was twelve that a member of my family would always shake hands with old Negro friends, would speak graciously to members of the Negro race unless they forgot their place, in which event icy peremptory tones would draw lines beyond which only the desperate would dare take one step. I knew that to use the word "nigger" was unpardonable and no well-bred southerner was quite so crude as to do so; nor would a well-bred southerner call a Negro "mister" or invite him into the living room or eat with him or sit by him in public places.

I knew that my old nurse who had cared for me through long months of illness, who had given me refuge when a little sister took my place as the baby of the family, who soothed, fed me, delighted me with her stories and games, let me fall asleep on her deep warm breast, was not worthy of the passionate love I felt for her but must be given instead a half-smiled-at affection similar to that which one feels for one's dog. I knew but I never believed it, that the deep respect I felt for her, the tenderness, the love, was a childish thing which every normal child outgrows, that such love begins with one's toys and is discarded with them, and that somehow—though it seemed impossible to my agonized heart—I too, must outgrow these feelings. I learned to use a soft voice to oil my words of superiority. I learned to cheapen with tears and sentimental talk of "my old mammy" one of the profound relationships of my life. I learned the bitterest thing a child can learn: that the human relations I valued most were held cheap by the world I lived in.

From the day I was born, I began to learn my lessons. I was put in a rigid frame too intricate, too twisting to describe here so briefly, but I learned to conform to its slide-rule measurements. I learned it is possible to be a Christian and a white southerner simultaneously; to be a gentlewoman and an arrogant callous creature in the same moment; to pray at night and ride a Jim Crow car the next morning and to feel comfortable in doing both. I learned to believe in freedom, to glow when the word *democracy* was used, and to practice slavery from morning to night. I learned it the way all of my southern people learn it: by closing door after door until one's mind and heart and conscience are blocked off from each other and from reality.

I closed the doors. Or perhaps they were closed for me. One day they began to open again. Why I had the desire or the strength to open them, or what strange accident or circumstance opened them for me would require in the answering an account too long, too particular, too stark to make here. And perhaps I should not have the wisdom that such an analysis would demand of me, nor the will to make it. I know only that the doors opened, a little; that somewhere along that iron corridor we travel from babyhood to maturity, doors swinging inward began to swing outward, showing glimpses of the world beyond, of that bright thing we call "reality."

I BELIEVE there is one experience which pushed these doors open, a little. And I am going to tell it here, although I know well that to excerpt from a life and family background one incident and name it as a "cause" of a change in one's life direction is a distortion and often an irrelevance. The hungers of a child and how they are filled have too much to do with the way in which experiences are assimilated to tear an incident out of life and look at it in isolation. Yet, with these reservations, I shall tell it, not because it was in itself a severe trauma, but because it became a symbol of buried experiences that I did not have access to. It is an incident that has rarely happened to other southern children. In a sense, unique. But it was an acting-out, a private production of a little script that is written on the lives of most southern children before they know words. Though they may not have seen it staged this way, each southerner has had his own private showing.

I should like to preface the account by giving a brief glimpse of my family, hoping the reader, entering my home with me, will be able to blend the edges of this isolated experience into a more full life picture and in doing so will see that it is, in a sense, everybody's story.

I was born and reared in a small Deep South town whose population was about equally Negro and white. There were nine of us who grew up freely in a rambling house of many rooms, surrounded by big lawn, back yard, gardens, fields, and barn. It was the kind of home that gathers memories like dust, a place filled with laughter and play and pain and hurt and ghosts and games. We were given such advantages of schooling, music, and art as were available in the South, and our world was not limited to the South, for travel to far places seemed a natural thing to us, and usually one of the family was in a remote part of the earth.

We knew we were a respected and important family of this small town but beyond this we gave little thought to status. Our father made money in lumber and naval stores for the excitement of making and losing it—not for what money can buy nor the security which it sometimes gives. I do not remember at any time wanting "to be rich" nor do I remember that thrift and saving were ideals which our parents considered important enough to urge upon us. In the family there was acceptance of risk, a mild delight in burning bridges, an expectant "what next?" We were not irresponsible; living according to the pleasure principle was by no means our way of life. On the contrary we were trained to think that each of us should do something of genuine usefulness, and the family thought it right to make sacrifices if necessary, to give each child preparation for such work. We were also trained to think learning important, and books; but "bad" books our mother burned. We valued music and art and craftsmanship but it was people and their welfare and religion that were the foci around which our lives seemed naturally to move. Above all else, the important thing was what we "planned to do." That each of us must do something was as inevitable as breathing for we owed a "debt to society which must be paid." This was a family commandment.

While many neighbors spent their energies in counting limbs on the family tree and grafting some on now and then to give symmetry to it, or in licking scars to cure their vague malaise, or in fighting each battle and turn of battle of that Civil War which has haunted the southern conscience so long, my father was pushing his nine children straight into the future. "You have your heritage," he used to say, "some of it good, some not so good; and as far as I know you had the usual number of grandmothers and grandfathers. Yes, there were slaves, too many of them in the family, but that was your grandfather's mistake, not yours. The past has been lived. It is gone. The future is yours. What are you going to do with it?" He asked this question often and sometimes one knew it was but an echo of a question he had spent his life trying to answer for himself. For the future held my father's dreams; always there, not in the past, did he expect to find what he had spent his life searching for.

We lived the same segregated life as did other southerners but our parents talked in excessively Christian and democratic terms. We were told ten thousand times that status and money are unimportant (though we were well supplied with both); we were told that "all men are brothers," that we are a part of a democracy and must act like democrats. We were told that the teachings of Jesus are important and could be practiced if we tried. We were told that to be "radical" is bad, silly too; and that one must always conform to the "best behavior" of one's community and make it better if one can. We were taught that we were superior to hate and resentment, and that no member of the Smith family could stoop so low as to have an enemy. No matter what injury was done us, we must not injure ourselves further by retaliating. That was a family commandment.

We had family prayers once each day. All of us as children read the Bible in its entirety each year. We memorized hundreds of Bible verses and repeated them at breakfast, and said "sentence prayers" around the family table. God was not someone we met on Sunday but a permanent member of our household. It never occurred to me until I was fourteen or fifteen years old that He did not chalk up the daily score on eternity's tablets.

Despite the strain of living so intimately with God, the nine of us were strong, healthy, energetic youngsters who filled days with play and sports and music and books and managed to live most of the time on the careless level at which young lives should be lived. We had our times of anxiety of course, for there were hard lessons to be learned about the soul and "bad things" to be learned about sex. Sometimes I have wondered how we learned them with a mother so shy with words.

She was a wistful creature who loved beautiful things like lace and sunsets and flowers in a vague inarticulate way, and took good care of her children. We always knew this was not her world but one she accepted under duress. Her private world we rarely entered, though the shadow of it lay heavily on our hearts.

Our father owned large business interests, employed hundreds of colored and white laborers, paid them the prevailing low wages, worked them the prevailing long hours, built for them mill towns (Negro and white), built for each group a church, saw to it that religion was supplied free, saw to it that a commissary supplied commodities at a high price, and in general managed his affairs much as ten thousand other southern businessmen managed theirs.

Even now, I can hear him chuckling as he told my mother how he won his fight for Prohibition. The high point of the campaign was election afternoon, when he lined up the mill force of several hundred (white and black), passed out a shining silver dollar to each one, marched them in and voted liquor out of our county. It was a great day. He had won the Big Game, a game he was always playing against all kinds of evil. It did not occur to him to scrutinize the methods he used. Evil was a word written in capitals; the devil was smart; if you wanted to win you outsmarted him. It was as simple as that.

He was a hardheaded, warmhearted, high-spirited man born during the Civil War, earning his living at twelve, struggling through decades of Reconstruction and post-Reconstruction, through populist movement, through the panic of 1893, the panic of 1907, on into the twentieth century accepting his region as he found it, accepting its morals and its mores as he accepted its climate, with only scorn for those who held grudges against the North or pitied themselves or the South; scheming, dreaming, expanding his business, making and losing money, making friends whom he did not lose, with never a doubt that God was by his side whispering hunches as to how to pull off successful deals. When he lost, it was his own fault. When he won, God had helped him.

Once while we were kneeling at family prayers the fire siren at the mill sounded the alarm that the mill was on fire. My father did not falter. The alarm sounded again and again—which signified the fire was big. With dignity he continued his talk with God while his children sweated and wriggled and hearts beat out of their chests in excitement. He was talking to God—how could he hurry out to save his mills! When he finished his prayer, he quietly stood up, laid the Bible carefully on the table. Then, and only then, did he show an interest in what was happening in Mill Town. . . . When the telegram was placed in his hands telling of the death of his beloved favorite son, he gathered his children together, knelt down, and in a steady voice which contained no hint of his shattered heart, loyally repeated, "God is our refuge and strength, a very present help in trouble. Therefore will we not fear, though the earth be removed, and though the mountains be carried into the midst of the sea." On his deathbed, he whispered to his old Business Partner in Heaven: "I have fought a good fight . . . I have kept the faith."

AGAINST THIS BACKDROP the drama of the South was played out one day in my life:

A little white girl was found in the colored section of our town, living with a Negro family in a broken-down shack. This family had moved in a few weeks before and little was known of them. One of the ladies in my mother's club, while driving over to her washerwoman's, saw the child swinging on a gate. The shack, as she said, was hardly more than a pigsty and this white child was living with dirty and sick-looking colored folks. "They must have kidnapped her," she told her friends. Genuinely shocked, the clubwomen busied themselves in an attempt to do something, for the child was very white indeed. The strange Negroes were subjected to a grueling questioning and finally grew evasive and refused to talk at all. This only increased the suspicion of the white group. The next day the clubwomen, escorted by the town marshal, took the child from her adopted family despite their tears.

She was brought to our home. I do not know why my mother consented to this plan. Perhaps because she loved children and always showed concern for them. It was easy for one more to fit into our ample household and Janie was soon at home there. She roomed with me, sat next to me at the table; I found Bible verses for her to say at breakfast; she wore my clothes, played with my dolls and followed me around from morning to night. She was dazed by her new comforts and by the interesting activities of this big lively family; and I was as happily dazed, for her adoration was a new thing to me; and as time passed a quick, childish, and deeply felt bond grew up between us.

But a day came when a telephone message was received from a colored orphanage. There was a meeting at our home. Many whispers. All afternoon the ladies went in and out of our house talking to Mother in tones too low for children to hear. As they passed us at play, they looked at Janie and quickly looked away again, though a few stopped and stared at her as if they could not tear their eyes from her face. When my father came home Mother closed her door against our young ears and talked a long time with him. I heard him laugh, heard Mother say, "But Papa, this is no laughing matter!" And then they were back in the living room with us and my mother was pale and my father was saying, "Well, work it out, Mame, as best you can. After all, now that you know, it is pretty simple."

In a little while my mother called my sister and me into her bedroom and told us that in the morning Janie would return to Colored Town. She said Janie was to have the dresses the ladies had given her and a few of my own, and the toys we had shared with her. She asked me if I would like to give Janie one of my dolls. She seemed hurried, though Janie was not to leave until next day. She said, "Why not select it now?" And in dreamlike stiffness I brought in my dolls and chose one for Janie. And then I found it possible to say, "Why is she leaving? She likes us, she hardly knows them. She told me she had been with them only a month."

"Because," Mother said gently, "Janie is a little colored girl."
"But she's white!"
"We were mistaken. She is colored."
"But she looks—"
"She is colored. Please don't argue!"
"What does it mean?" I whispered.
"It means," Mother said slowly, "that she has to live in Colored Town with colored people."

"But why? She lived here three weeks and she doesn't belong to them, she told me so."

"She is a little colored girl."

"But you said yourself she has nice manners. You said that," I persisted.

"Yes, she is a nice child. But a colored child cannot live in our home."

"Why?"

"You know, dear! You have always known that white and colored people do not live together."

"Can she come to play?"

"No."

"I don't understand."

"I don't either," my young sister quavered.

"You're too young to understand. And don't ask me again, ever again, about this!" Mother's voice was sharp but her face was sad and there was no certainty left there. She hurried out and busied herself in the kitchen and I wandered through that room where I had been born, touching the old familiar things in it, looking at them, trying to find the answer to a question that moaned like a hurt thing. . . .

And then I went out to Janie, who was waiting, knowing things were happening that concerned her but waiting until they were spoken aloud.

I do not know quite how the words were said but I told her she was to return in the morning to the little place where she had lived because she was colored and colored children could not live with white children.

"Are you white?" she said.

"I'm white," I replied, "and my sister is white. And you're colored. And white and colored can't live together because my mother says so."

"Why?" Janie whispered.

"Because they can't," I said. But I knew, though I said it firmly, that something was wrong. I knew my father and mother whom I passionately admired had betrayed something which they held dear. And they could not help doing it. And I was shamed by their failure and frightened, for I felt they were no longer as powerful as I had thought. There was something Out There that was stronger than they and I could not bear to believe it. I could not confess that my father, who always solved the family dilemmas easily and with laughter, could not solve this. I knew that my mother who was so good to children did not believe in her heart that she was being good to this child. There was not a word in my mind that said it but my body knew and my glands, and I was filled with anxiety.

But I felt compelled to believe they were right. It was the only way my world could be held together. And, slowly, it began to seep through me: *I was white. She was colored. We must not be together. It was bad to be together. Though you ate with your nurse when you were little, it was bad to eat with any colored person after that. It was bad just as other things were bad that your mother had told you. It was bad that she was to sleep in the room with me that night. It was bad. . . .*

I was overcome with guilt. For three weeks I had done things that white children were not supposed to do. And now I knew these things had been wrong.

I went to the piano and began to play, as I had always done when I was in trouble. I tried to play my next lesson and as I stumbled through it, the little girl came over and sat on the bench with me. Feeling lost in the deep currents sweeping through our house that night, she crept closer and put her arms around me and I shrank away as if my body had been uncovered. I had not said a word, I did not say one, but she knew, and tears slowly rolled down her little white face. . . .

And then I forgot it. For more than thirty years the experience was wiped out of my memory. But that night, and the weeks it was tied to, worked its way like a splinter, bit by bit, down to the hurt places in my memory and festered there. And as I grew older, as more experiences collected around that faithless time, as memories of earlier, more profound hurts crept closer, drawn to that night as if to a magnet, I began to know that people who talked of love and children did not mean it. That is a hard thing for a child to learn. I still admired my parents, there was so much that was strong and vital and sane and good about them and I never forgot this; I stubbornly believed in their sincerity, as I do to this day, and I loved them. Yet in my heart they were under suspicion. Something was wrong.

Something was wrong with a world that tells you that love is good and people are important and then forces you to deny love and to humiliate people. I knew, though I would not for years confess it aloud, that in trying to shut the Negro race away from us, we have shut ourselves away from so many good, creative, honest, deeply human things in life. I began to understand slowly at first but more clearly as the years passed, that the warped, distorted frame we have put around every Negro child from birth is around every white child also. Each is on a different side of the frame but each is pinioned there. And I knew that what cruelly shapes and cripples the personality of one is as cruelly shaping and crippling the personality of the other. I began to see that though we may, as we acquire new knowledge, live through new experiences, examine old memories, gain the strength to tear the frame from us, yet we are stunted and warped and in our lifetime cannot grow straight again any more than can a tree, put in a steel-like twisting frame when young, grow tall and straight when the frame is torn away at maturity.

AS I SIT HERE writing, I can almost touch that little town, so close is the memory of it. There it lies, its main street lined with great oaks, heavy with matted moss that swings softly even now as I remember. A little white town rimmed with Negroes, making a deep shadow on the whiteness. There it lies, broken in two by one strange idea. Minds broken. Hearts broken. Conscience torn from acts. A culture split in a thousand pieces. That is segregation. I am remembering: a woman in a mental hospital walking four steps out, four steps in, unable to go further because she has drawn an invisible line around her small world and is terrified to take one step beyond it. . . . A man in a Disturbed Ward assigning "places" to the other patients and violently insisting that each stay in his place. . . . A Negro woman saying to me so quietly, "We cannot ride together on the bus, you know. It is not legal to be human down here."

Memory, walking the streets of one's childhood . . . of the town where one was born.

Clifton Taulbert

(1945–)

Clifton Taulbert was born in the Mississippi Delta town of Glen Allan, where he spent most of his youth. After graduating valedictorian of his class in Greenville, Mississippi, he served in the U.S. Air Force before attending college in Maine and Maryland and finally earning a B.A. in history and sociology at Oral Roberts University in Tulsa, Oklahoma. A successful businessman in Tulsa, he has also written four books: Once Upon a Time When We Were Colored *(1989),* The Last Train North *(1992),* Watching Our Crops Come In *(1997), and* Eight Habits of the Heart *(1997). In 1996, Tim Reid directed a critically acclaimed film adaptation of* Once Upon a Time When We Were Colored.

Unlike fellow Mississippi autobiographer Richard Wright, who shows in Black Boy *considerable disdain for the South and for his family and neighbors whom he believed acquiesced too easily to their mistreatment by whites, Clifton Taulbert writes fondly of his childhood environment, even as he calls attention to the ever-present danger of racial intimidation and violence. Although* Once Upon a Time When We Were Colored *ends in much the same way as the 1945 version of* Black Boy, *with the young narrator looking with hope to a new beginning as he leaves the South, Taulbert makes it clear that his attachments to kinfolks and friends in Glen Allan are deep and profound, and that his actions in the North will be shaped in large part by the positive lessons he learned from them. In the following chapter from* Once Upon a Time, *"Some Glad Morning, Some Glad Day, I'll Fly Away," Taulbert recalls the preeminent position of the church in the African-American community.*

FROM *Once Upon a Time*
When We Were Colored

IT WAS CLOSER to our hearts than our homes—the colored church. It was more than an institution, it was the very heartbeat of our lives. Our church was all our own, beyond the influence of whites, with its own societal structure.

Even when colored people moved north, they took with them their church structure. The Baptist church, of which my family was a part, had (and has) a big network under the auspices of the National Baptist Convention. A small colored Baptist church in Glen Allan, Mississippi, and a large colored Baptist church in Saint Louis, Missouri, had the same moderator, used the same Sunday-school books, and went to the same conferences. And whether north or south, large or small, the colored church was a totally black experience.

Ma Ponk made sure I was regularly immersed in the colored-church world. As early as I remember, I spent my Sundays, both night and day, attending church with Ma Ponk. No matter the hard workweek, we all looked forward to Sunday when we would dress in our best and meet our friends.

Sunday morning came in easy and Ma Ponk would let me sleep late. The smell of hotcakes and homemade pork sausages fried in lard would float through the house. Ma Ponk only had to call once.

When I got to the kitchen Ma Ponk would be moving around the black iron stove in her starched white dress. She was on the Mothers' Board of the church, and as a church mother, she was required to wear white to Sunday services. Ma Ponk made sure her dress was hand starched and washed in rainwater to ensure that extra whiteness. She was careful not to get any spots on her dress as she skillfully turned the hotcakes and brewed her Maxwell House drip coffee.

"Don't git in my way. Now, you jes' sit down on the back porch and eat your food. We got to leave for church pretty soon," Ma Ponk said.

She began to pin up her hair. She had extra long silky black hair, but she felt it was unchristian to wear it down, so she would plait her hair into long braids and wrap those braids around her head. Finally to ensure her hairpins held safely, she would wrap her head in a white scarf.

In white shoes, silk stockings, starched white dress and her white scarf, Ma Ponk was ready for church. Ma Ponk's parents and grandparents were founding members of Saint Mark's Missionary Baptist Church and she was considered one of the leaders. It was the fourth Sunday, Pastoral Day, and our little colored neighborhood was all abuzz as the gravel roads were filled with people dressed in their best, laughing and joking on the way to the sanctuary, our church.

Pastoral Sunday was the one day a month when our official elected pastor would be there to deliver the message. Other Sundays, he would be at one of the other churches he served, and Saint Mark's would have to make do with a pinch hitter. It was no great honor to be asked to speak on those off Sundays, because everybody knew that the crowd would be small and the offering (from which preachers were paid) would be low. People who felt the call to preach and positioned themselves to fill in on off Sundays were called jackleg preachers, because they had no churches of their own.

Today, however, there would be no jackleg preacher. It was Pastoral Sunday, and there was a great feeling of togetherness as we neared the church. Women in their white dresses and black Sunday hats and men in their Sunday suits with their best brightly colored ties and shined shoes were shaking each other's hands, hugging and kissing the children as we took our turns climbing the steps into the main sanctuary.

Today, field hands were deacons, and maids were ushers, mothers of the church, or trustees. The church transformed the ordinary into an institution of social and economic significance. A hard week of field work forgotten, the maid's aprons laid to rest, and the tractors in the shed, these colored men and women had entered a world that was all their own. Rough hands softened with Royal Crown grease were positioned to praise. As a young boy, I sat quietly in my seat and waited for the services to start. The church was designed for us children to be seen and not heard, and if by chance we talked or got caught chewing gum, Miss Nola or one of the ever-present ushers would take a long control stick and crack us on the head. The church rules were strict, and the ushers made sure nothing interfered with the high spirit of the service.

While the ushers proceeded to order the crowd, three of the deacons would place their chairs in front of the altar, for they were charged with starting the service. As I watched the activity of the church, my eyes fell on Mother Luella Byrd. Mother Byrd was not only head of the Mothers' Board, but basically in charge of the church. There she sat, dressed in white with her black cape draped over her shoulders, her arms folded and her face set. Once Mother Byrd had taken her position, God could begin to move. Ma Ponk reluctantly paid homage to Mother Byrd, but under her breath she could be heard saying, "Byrd acts like she owns Saint Mark's."

And it was true; Mother Byrd was without question the matriarch of the church. Not only was she an influencing and stabilizing factor for Saint Mark's, but her demand for perfection and self-respect and her high hopes for the colored race will always be with me. She was slightly overweight and walked with her left foot turned outward. When she walked, her hands would be clasped behind her back, and whatever the day, she was dressed as if she were in charge.

Mother Byrd was known for her Easter program which was a must for all the children of the church. We were expected to know our parts to perfection. Securing a commitment from the parents, she would give us our speeches one month in advance and hold practices weekly. Our limited resources never bothered her, only spurred her on to pull out of us the best she knew to be there. For her, Saint Mark's Missionary Baptist Church was Washington Cathedral and we, her pupils, were the cream of the crop. With determination, she'd take our unorganized minds, lack of ambition, and bad grammar and create a top-quality program. Mother Byrd had no formal education herself, but she encouraged us to work hard and get an education. She was a proponent of black pride long before it became fashionable as she tuned out our excuses and channeled our efforts.

Every Sunday morning, Mother Byrd was seated front and center at Saint Mark's by the time the singing began. As the song "I'll Fly Away" rang throughout the building, she rocked back and forth while the congregation rocked from side to side. While they sang, Elder Thomas began to preach. The singing and the preaching would blend and build together to a fever pitch. Elder Thomas, like an athlete at peak performance, paced the front of the church and preached until he was covered with sweat and the entire congregation was caught up in the spiritual fervor.

By contrast with Sunday morning, Sunday night was rather dull in Glen Allan unless we were lucky enough to have a "singing" at one of the neighboring churches. Ma Ponk always went to the Sunday-night singing. She felt that one could never get enough of God. A good cowboy movie or a chance for me to play softball would not override her decision to go to a singing. Of course she knew the dates, places and times for each one, because announcements were tacked on every electrical pole in town and lying in every ditch.

Quartet singers represented more than colored harmonizing; they were examples of the good life. If those singers happened to have come from Memphis, our excitement could not be contained. You see, we knew that all the really good singers lived in Memphis. If the singers were coming from Memphis, Saint Mark's wasn't good enough for them. They would sing at Mount Zion Baptist Church. While most of the colored churches in our small town were wood shingled, Mount Zion was covered with white asbestos siding and had concrete steps leading into the main sanctuary.

I remember the Sunday after church at Saint Mark's when Ma Ponk and her friend Miss Doll decided we'd go to the big quartet singing at Mount Zion. Every colored person in Glen Allan wanted to be part of the Mount Zion singing. Ma Ponk didn't wear white because tonight she would not be on the mothers' bench. Tonight, she dressed in her best, a multicolored jersey dress, and wore her black straw hat. I wore my one good outfit, my brown gabardines and a plaid shirt.

The Memphis singers, usually all men, were role models of sorts for the young colored males and objects of fantasy for the women. These singers were dressed in the latest northern fashions, and their hair was ironed to their heads. Their shiny straightened hair would glisten under the exposed sixty-watt bulbs. The women idolized them, and the young black males would come out in droves.

According to Ma Ponk, you couldn't get these people out for real church, but at a singing they'd take up good seats and the Christians would have to stand. There they'd be, the young male field hands dressed in gabardines and nylon puckered shirts. The more fortunate ones wore suits and pointed-toe shoes. For the women, this singing brought out more fishnet and taffeta material than any other event. Their hair would be tightly curled and pressed to their heads, held in place by rhinestone combs. The ladies—young and old—would come early to get a front seat so they could reach out and touch their perspiring idols and occasionally faint and very innocently fall into the arms of the lead singer.

And the singers would sing until their clothes were dripping with perspiration and their guitar strings were begging for mercy. Once the singing got going good, they'd rip off their ties and coats and throw them to the crowd. We were all enthralled by the Memphis sound. Even Ma Ponk, not known for unnec-

essary emotion, would rock back and forth while making sure
her hands remained tightly folded. Mount Zion hosted all the
Memphis singing stars of those years, even the late great Sam
Cooke.

As the last encore ended and the applause became part of the
night, we left Mount Zion with new conversation good for at
least three working days. The week's field work would go easier
now because the colored quartet had come to town.

We spent most of the summer working hard in the fields and
relishing the interruptions brought by the church. As the summer came to its end, Ma Ponk, our family, our friends and our
town began preparing for the social events that usually took
place this time of year. High on the list of such social events was
the Annual Sister-workers Day.

I had heard about the sister-workers all my life. Nearly
everyone I knew was a member, and Cousin Lulu Harris from
the colored colony was the treasurer of one of the larger
"works." Ma Ponk paid her dues religiously and ensured that her
family was doing the same. The sister-workers was an auxiliary
to the colored church. Its primary purpose was to provide funds
to families of its members on the deaths of loved ones. Even
though it was organized, operated and staffed by women, membership was open to all. The monthly fee was less than a dollar
per person, and at death, sixty dollars would be given to the
deceased person's family. Ma Ponk belonged to five works as
they were collectively called.

Once yearly, the local sister-workers would have their year-
end conference, commonly called Annual Day. Annual Day centered around friends and baskets of individually prepared food.
Even people who had moved north would arrange their yearly
visits to coincide with this day. They would come back to Glen
Allan to pay their annual assessment in person and, of course,
visit their many friends and relatives. It was a much-needed and
well-attended social event.

I have fond memories of the sweet-potato pies Cousin
Beauty baked for the Annual Day, and of Cousin Savannah's

famous pound cake. Although Ma Ponk was a member in good standing of several works and never missed an Annual Day, she and her older sister Aunt Lurlean were never known for their fancy cooking. Ma Ponk fixed a basket of food which consisted of plain store-bought cake and chicken fried by my mother, Mary. Aunt Lurlean, who was treasurer of the Saint Mark's work, prepared a basket of store-bought food. All Saturday morning everybody else in Glen Allan was cooking. The smells of cakes, pies and fried chicken mingled in the streets. Finding the right-sized cardboard boxes to make our baskets was my job. I'd make numerous trips to the Chinaman's store to get my arm load of boxes, big enough to hold all the food without the tops pressing down. I could hardly wait for 2:30 p.m. For eleven months, we had all looked forward to this day. The Annual Day meant the best food ever.

We'd get to church early, because Ma Ponk was responsible for making sure the aluminum water bucket was filled with water and ice and there were at least two drinking glasses. Of course Ma Ponk always brought her own glass. Under no circumstances would she drink from the community cup. After getting the bucket filled with cold water, we went around the church, opened all the windows and placed the funeral home fans in each seat. As we put out the paper fans, we could see people beginning to arrive.

All the neatly tied pasteboard boxes of food were placed in the communion room until it was time to serve: Sweet-potato pies, jelly cakes, chocolate cakes, fried chicken, baked rabbit, fried pork chops and pork-sausage sandwiches. I just prayed that Mother Byrd would not talk forever. Eventually, the last song was sung, the last prayer prayed, and I was ready to sample as much as Ma Ponk would let me.

Ma Ponk never ate while there, but she enjoyed the fellowship. Everybody else feasted and talked for hours until at last it was time to leave. We both laughed as we saw some people who had come with no boxes, leaving with full loads. As the Annual Day ended, Ma Ponk and I stayed behind to close the windows and lock the church. A soft wind came along to blow away the used paper napkins, and neighborhood dogs gathered to enjoy the scraps. Ma Ponk was tired, but her dues were paid for another year, and between the money from her works and her burial policy, she would not be ashamed to die.

Not only did the colored church prepare us for death financially, it made sure our souls were prepared as well, because every year Saint Mark's revival came on the heels of Annual Day. Ma Ponk, as one of the church's mothers, was intimately involved in the yearly revival.

It seemed as if God always waited until the end of the cotton-chopping season and right before the picking started to prompt the church to get the revival fires started. All the small colored churches around Glen Allan and neighboring plantations were getting ready for revival. The sinners had been notified. God was coming to town, and his front men were filled with holy indignation. They gave the sinners warning that this year's revival might be their last chance to miss hell's fury.

Handbills with misspelled words were passed out. Ma Ponk, Mother Byrd and all the soldiers of the church began to pick sinners for which they would especially pray. Seven days had been set aside for the Saint Mark's revival, starting on Monday and ending on Sunday with a public baptismal service at Lake Washington. Ma Ponk was happy that the Reverend Thomas would be preaching this year's revival, because he was her pastor whom she had elected. "Look out, Satan! God's man's entering your territory." Ma Ponk couldn't wait until the ending Sunday when the Rev. Thomas would march the candidates (the newly saved sinners) right down the main street of Glen Allan so the Devil could see them with his own eyes.

This would be a good year for souls, according to Ma Ponk and Cousin Lulu Harris. They had just finished having a big revival in the colored colony. Cousin Lulu always came to town to visit Ma Ponk and to keep her informed on the Lord's work. Ten souls were saved in the colony, then brought to Glen Allan to be baptized. But nothing would compare with the Reverend

Thomas' revival. This would be the big one. This would be the one where I would get a chance to be saved.

It was Monday night. The revival had started. Saint Mark's was packed with people, all fanning themselves with paper funeral home fans in the hot one-room church. As the singing began, the deacons and mothers of Saint Mark's lifted their voices to the Lord, filling the rafters with song. Aunt Willie Mae, a good singer with a strong voice, was leading the congregation.

"I'll fly away. I'll fly away. Some glad morning, I'll fly away."

As they rocked and clapped, their spirits seemed to have soared to heights unknown. And in the midst of this fervent praise, the Reverend L. T. Thomas, an imposing colored preacher, rose from behind the altar and lifted his voice to start the revival. He had a voice as deep as a well and as clear as a noon bell. The Reverend Thomas' eyes seemed to focus directly on me, my cousin Bobby, and my Uncle Eugene.

"Can you fly away? Will you have a glad morning someday?" The Reverend Thomas bellowed over the singing. As the congregation sang more softly, the Reverend Thomas asked the deacons to set up the mourners' bench, a place designated in the front of the church for sinners to come, sit and be surrounded by praying church folk.

This was our year. We had been an embarrassment to our families too long. So without much coercion from the pulpit, the three of us led the way to the mourners' bench. As we took our seats and others joined us, there were shouts of acclamation, "Amen!" and "Praise God!" all over the church. Once seated up front, we were soon forgotten. The services went on at a high-fevered pitch while we, the town sinners, just sat and looked.

The mourners' bench was a world unto itself. While sitting on the bench, we would try to make each other laugh while the preaching and singing was going on around us. My cousin Bobby was chewing bubblegum. I was trying to concentrate on my lost soul when Bobby tapped me on the shoulder. Just as I turned to look a huge pink bubble burst all over his face. Nearing the end of the service, the Reverend Abe Brown, who was my great uncle and Bobby's great-grandfather, was asked to pray the salvation prayer for the mourners' bench. On request, we all fell to our knees. As we knelt there, Bobby reached over and pinched me, and before I could pinch him back I felt Uncle Abe's hot breath on my neck. He laid hands on me and Bobby and began to pray:

"Lord, look on these sinners. Look on my grandson Bobby and my nephew Cliff. They is good boys, but they don't know you. . . ."

As Uncle Abe prayed, we buried our heads in our hands and prayed not for our salvation, but rather that Uncle Abe would not pray all night. Finally, the services came to an end and we were instructed to find a quiet secluded place to pray during the day and to make sure we asked God to give us a sign of significance that our lives had been changed.

The week's revival was coming to an end; true to his reputation, the Reverend Thomas had cracked the ranks of Satan's army. More than one dozen people had come to the Lord. Both Bobby and Eugene were saved, but for some reason, in spite of my praying and finding my secluded spot, I did not get saved that year.

Even though I didn't confess religion, Ma Ponk and the whole church were overjoyed. Their prayers were answered. Their revival had saved more souls than the one in the colored colony. By now everyone knew who was saved and the colored section of Glen Allan was preparing for the big baptismal service.

The revival services ended on the Saturday night before the fourth Sunday. This would be the day to baptize. The Reverend Thomas had requested the deacons and the mothers and the candidates for baptism to meet at the church at least one hour prior to the time to march to Lake Washington. Ma Ponk, being one of the head mothers of the church, was among the ones requested. She would assist the female candidates in dressing. Today, Ma Ponk was all dressed in white from head to toe. This was a sacred responsibility; she had even left her snuff behind. My grandfather Julius was responsible for getting the men ready. Their goal was to create a visible difference between those new initiates of the Kingdom and the rest of the world. The candidates, both men and women, were dressed in long white gowns and their heads were covered with white caps. Except for the color of their skin, hair, and shoes, the baptismal party was an army of walking whiteness. With the Reverend Thomas leading the group, they marched from Saint Mark's church down the middle of the paved road and right through the uptown section of Glen Allan to the lake. With singing and clapping, crying and praising, the baptismal procession began. Everybody was arranged in order of importance, with the Reverend Thomas in the front of the parade and the deacons behind him. The candidates followed, with the mothers of the church walking religiously behind, their arms loaded with towels and sheets.

As they marched, they sang, "Take me to the Jordan, take me to the Jordan, I want to be baptized." In ones and twos, others of us joined in the march. By the time we were passing the local juke joints, we had begun singing, "Lord, wash me whiter than snow." While the Lord was washing us whiter than snow, we were preparing to walk through the residential part of town where Glen Allan's whites lived. When we got close to their homes, the Reverend Thomas would say, "Look to God, pay no attention to the peckerwoods. They don't respect nothin'." He talked, we marched, we sang and we looked straight ahead and paid no attention to the teenage white boys who looked on and laughed.

The crowds had grown, and when the procession reached the banks of the lake, there were scores of people sitting on their cars waiting to see the candidates go under the water and come up. At the lake, the singing slowed and we watched where we were walking, because the rumor had started that Deacon Roy had killed a rattlesnake while cutting a path down the hill to the bank so he could set the stakes out in the lake. The water was crystal clear and the air was filled with low humming sounds coming from the church members and visitors. Everybody was just waiting on the signal to burst out in the favorite baptismal song, "Wade in the Water, Children."

With his hands uplifted and flanked on either side by his deacons, the Reverend Thomas offered prayer and called for the first candidate. It was a man; the town drunk had come to Christ. He told about his troubles, the religious dreams he had experienced while on the mourners' bench, and those left standing on the banks began to cry and raise their hands in agreement with the candidate's testimony.

"On the banks of stormy Jordan I stand. . . ."

Lake Washington wasn't Jordan, but it served as a good substitute. When the baptism was over and the fervor had died down, when the soaked bodies were wrapped in the big towels, we all began to leave. Those of us who had marched through the city in triumph were now left to thumb a ride home. It was a good revival, even though I probably let Ma Ponk down by not getting saved. She just nodded and said, "Maybe next year."

Our lives centered around the colored church. It provided the framework for civic involvement, the backdrop for leadership, a safe place for social gatherings, where our babies were blessed, our families married and our dead respected. Yes, the colored church became the sanctuary for our dreams and the closet for our secrets, and even the funerals were representative of all we were, and what we hoped to become.

One of the funerals I remember was that of Miss Hester. When Miss Hester died, it was late at night, but somehow Granddaddy Julius knew, and the church bells tolled. Ma Ponk always heard the bells. She always listened for the midday crowing of the roosters, and during this particular week, the roosters had crowed continuously, so Ma Ponk knew someone would die, but she didn't know who it would be. As the bell tolled, she got up and looked out the window, trying to determine which house had lights on. It would be hard to sleep, not knowing who had passed away.

The next morning early, Ma Ponk went out to her backyard,

talked across the fence to her neighbor, and found out Miss Hester had died. Miss Hester, like some others in our town, was a mulatto. She was nearly white. Her mother was colored and her father was a white farmer. She kept a big picture of her father on horseback hanging in her parlor. Oftentimes she and Ma Ponk, who was part Jewish, would spend hours arguing about the amount of blood required to make them totally white. Even though strict racial segregation was the order of the day, it somehow seemed to have slipped at night, because throughout our colored community were numerous men, women and children who were called "high yaller." Ma Ponk, herself being one, always said, "nearly ever' peckerwood got a nigger in his closet." Ma Ponk always liked to tell about the time the colored soldier came to town after the war to visit his white uncle who lived across the field from us. According to her, he was received well and spent the day with them. After that, he left, went north and never returned.

Miss Hester's death brought up a flood of such conversations, because all her near-white sisters and brothers from around Jackson would be coming to the funeral. It would be a big funeral, held at Mount Zion Baptist Church, so Miss Doll, Ma Ponk and I went early to get good seats.

While waiting for the family processional to begin, I recall Ma Ponk and Miss Doll reminiscing about the time another high yaller lady had died. During that funeral, a well-dressed lady walked in. She had red hair, and her freckled face was partially veiled. As she walked up near the front, the ushers were confused. They didn't know if she was white or colored. Ma Ponk recalled that as the lady walked by she recognized her. It was her childhood friend Lizzie who had not been to Glen Allan for more than forty years. In those days, many high yaller colored chose to move north and live a white life.

Ma Ponk and Miss Doll probably would have unlocked every closet in town had it not been for the preacher asking the church to rise. The body was being brought in, with all of Miss Hester's nearly white relatives following close behind.

The choir began singing and the funeral directors busied themselves arranging the flowers on the casket. The choir led us in singing "Farther Along," then the mistress of ceremonies came to the front and began the program that would provide opportunity for Miss Hester's neighbors and church members to speak about her and pay their last respects. Finally, all the memories were shared, and it was time to hear the special singing. As she started the familiar melody of the bittersweet funeral hymn, the singer was singing not only for Miss Hester but for all under the sound of her voice:

"If when you give the best of your service,
Telling the world
That the Savior has come,
Be not dismayed
When men don't believe you.
He'll understand and say 'well done.'"

Richard Taylor

(1826–1879)

The son of Zachary Taylor, Mexican War hero and twelfth president of the United States, Richard Taylor was born at Springfield, the family plantation near Louisville, Kentucky. After attending an academy in Lancaster, Massachusetts, he spent a short time at Harvard before transferring to Yale, from which he graduated in 1845. When his father died, Taylor used his share of the inheritance to purchase Fashion, a vast sugar plantation in St. Charles Parish, Louisiana, where his profits were sufficient to enable him to stock a large library for his personal use. During the Civil War he served his state with distinction, rising to the rank of lieutenant general by the end of the fighting. His sugar plantation was confiscated and sold after the cessation of hostilities, and Taylor traveled in Europe extensively in the years leading up to his death.

The major portion of Taylor's Civil War memoirs, Destruction and Reconstruction: Personal Experiences of the Late War, published in 1879, is of primary interest to the military history buff. Recounting his battlefield experiences in Virginia during the early days of the conflict, then his exploits as a general in what was nearly a guerrilla operation in his home state of Louisiana during the remainder of the war, to his organization of the surrender of troops in Alabama, Taylor sprinkles his accounts with literary allusions and learned references to famous battles of antiquity. During the last quarter of the book, however, when Taylor describes his reaction to Reconstruction politics in Louisiana and the nation's capital, he seems to lower his defenses and speak with undisguised passion about the events that have transpired. It is here that modern readers are afforded a rare look into the psyche of the defeated southern aristocracy as it struggled to hold on to its failed vision of a harmonious social order built on the institution of slavery.

The following selection begins with Taylor's description of his efforts to secure permission to visit his sister's husband, Jefferson Davis, the former president of the Confederacy, who was imprisoned at the time in Fortress Monroe. By using the abolitionist politicians with whom he meets in Washington as character foils, Taylor sets up a contrasting portrait of white southern masculinity in which the virtues of restraint, loyalty, and integrity figure prominently. The second part of the selection comprises the narrative's conclusion where, in mournful tones that anticipate the combined bitterness and stoic resignation of Will Percy's Lanterns on the Levee, *Taylor notes the passing of an old order with which he clearly identifies.*

FROM *Destruction and Reconstruction: Personal Experiences of the Late War*

*T*HE PRESIDENT, between whom and the Congressional leaders the seeds of discord were already sown, dallied with me from day to day, and at length said that it would spare him embarrassment if I could induce Stevens, Davis, and others of the House, and Sumner of the Senate, to recommend the permission to visit Jefferson Davis; and I immediately addressed myself to this unpleasant task.

Thaddeus Stevens received me with as much civility as he was capable of. Deformed in body and temper like Caliban, this was the Lord Hategood of the fair; but he was frankness itself. He wanted no restoration of the Union under the Constitution, which he called a worthless bit of old parchment. The white people of the South ought never again to be trusted with power, for they would inevitably unite with the Northern "Copperheads" and control the Government. The only sound policy was to confiscate the lands and divide them among the negroes, to whom, sooner or later, suffrage must be given. Touching the matter in hand, Johnson was a fool to have captured Davis, whom it would have been wiser to assist in escaping. Nothing would be done with him, as the executive had only pluck enough to hang two poor devils such as Wirtz [Wirz] and Mrs. Surratt. Had the leading traitors been promptly strung up, well; but the time for that had passed. (Here, I thought, he looked lovingly at my neck, as Petit André was wont to do at those of his merry-go-rounds.) He concluded by saying that it was silly to refuse me permission to visit Jefferson Davis, but he would not say so publicly, as he had no desire to relieve Johnson of responsibility.

There was no excuse for longer sporting with this radical Amaryllis either in shade or in sunshine; so I sought Henry Winter Davis. Like the fallen angel, Davis preferred to rule in hell rather than serve in heaven or on earth. With the head of Medusa and the eye of the Basilisk, he might have represented Siva in a Hindoo temple, and was even more inaccessible to sentiment than Thaddeus Stevens. Others, too numerous and too insignificant to particularize, were seen. These were the cuttle-fish of the party, whose appointed duty it was to obscure popular vision by clouds of loyal declamation. As Sicilian banditti prepare for robberies and murders by pious offerings on shrines of favorite saints, these brought out the altar of the "nation," and devoted themselves afresh, whenever "Crédits Mobiliers" and kindred enormities were afoot, and sharpened every question of administration, finance, law, taxation, on the grindstone of sectional hate. So sputtering tugs tow from her moorings the stately ship, to send her forth to winds and waves of ocean, caring naught for the cargo with which she is freighted, but, grimy in zeal to earn fees, return to seek another.

Hopeless of obtaining assistance from such statesmen, I visited Mr. Charles Sumner, Senator from Massachusetts, who received me pleasantly. A rebel, a slave-driver, and, without the culture of Boston, ignorant, I was an admirable vessel into which he could pour the inexhaustible stream of his acquired eloquence. I was delighted to listen to beautiful passages from the classic as well as modern poets, dramatists, philosophers, and orators, and recalled the anecdote of the man sitting under a fluent divine, who could not refrain from muttering, "That is Jeremy Taylor; that, South; that, Barrow," etc. It was difficult to suppress the thought, while Mr. Sumner was talking, "That is Burke, or Howard, Wilberforce, Brougham, Macaulay, Harriet Beecher Stowe, Exeter Hall," etc.; but I failed to get down to the particular subject that interested me. The nearest approach to the practical was his disquisition on negro suffrage, which he thought should be accompanied by education. I ventured to suggest that negro education should precede suffrage, observing that some held the opinion that the capacity of the white race for government was limited, although accumulated and transmitted through many centuries. He replied that "the ignorance of the negro was due to the tyranny of the whites," which appeared in his view to dispose of the question of the former's incapacity. He seemed over-educated—had retained, not digested his learning; and beautiful flowers of literature were attached to him by filaments of memory, as lovely orchids to sapless sticks. Hence he failed to understand the force of language, and became the victim of his own metaphors, mistaking them for facts. He had the irritable vanity and weak nerves of a woman, and was bold to rashness in speculation, destitute as he was of the ordinary masculine sense of responsibility. Yet I hold him to have been the purest and most sincere man of his party. A lover, nay, a devotee of liberty, he thoroughly understood that it could only be preserved by upholding the supremacy of civil law, and would not sanction the garrison methods of President Grant. Without vindictiveness, he forgave his enemies as soon as they were overthrown, and one of the last efforts of his life was to remove from the flag of a common country all records of victories that perpetuated the memory of civil strife.

Foiled in this direction, I worried the President, as old Mustard would a stot, until he wrote the permission so long solicited. By steamer from Baltimore I went down Chesapeake Bay, and arrived at Fortress Monroe in the early morning. General Burton, the commander, whose civility was marked, and who bore himself like a gentleman and soldier, received me on the dock and took me to his quarters to breakfast, and to await the time to see Mr. Davis.

It was with some emotion that I reached the casemate in which Mr. Davis was confined. There were two rooms, in the outer of which, near the entrance, stood a sentinel, and in the inner was Jefferson Davis. We met in silence, with grasp of hands. After an interval he said, "This is kind, but no more than I expected of you." Pallid, worn, gray, bent, feeble, suffering from inflammation of the eyes, he was a painful sight to a friend. He uttered no plaint, and made no allusion to the irons (which had been removed); said the light kept all night in his room hurt his eyes a little, and, added to the noise made every two hours by relieving the sentry, prevented much sleep; but matters had changed for the better since the arrival of General Burton, who was all kindness, and strained his orders to the utmost in his behalf. I told him of my reception at Washington by the President, Mr. Seward, and others, of the attentions of Generals Grant and Humphreys, who promoted my wish to see him, and that with such aid I was confident of obtaining permission for his wife to stay with him. I could solicit favors for him, having declined any for myself. Indeed, the very accident of position, that enabled me to get access to the governing authorities, made indecent even the supposition of my acceptance of anything personal while a single man remained under the ban for serving the Southern cause; and therefore I had no fear of misconstruction. Hope of meeting his family cheered him much, and he asked questions about the condition and prospects of the South, which I answered as favorably as possible, passing over things that would have grieved him. In some way he had learned of attacks on his character and conduct, made by some Southern curs, thinking to ingratiate themselves with the ruling powers. I could not deny this, but remarked that the curse of unexpected defeat and suffering was to develop the basest passions of the human heart. Had he escaped out of the country, it was possible he might have been made a scapegoat by the Southern people, and, great as were the sufferings that he had endured, they were as nothing to coward stabs from beloved hands. The attacks mentioned were few, and too contemptible for notice; for now his calamities had served to endear him to all. I think that he derived consolation from this view.

The day passed with much talk of a less disturbing character, and in the evening I returned to Baltimore and Washington. After some delay Mr. Davis's family was permitted to join him, and he speedily recovered strength. Later I made a journey or two to Richmond, Virginia, on business connected with his trial, then supposed to be impending.

The slight service, if simple discharge of duty can be so called, I was enabled to render Mr. Davis, was repaid ten thousand fold. In the month of March, 1875, my devoted wife was released from suffering, long and patiently endured, originating in grief for the loss of her children and exposure during the war. Smitten by this calamity, to which all that had gone before seemed as blessings, I stood by her coffin, ere it was closed, to look for the last time upon features that death had respected and restored to their girlish beauty. Mr. Davis came to my side, and stooped reverently to touch the fair brow, when the tenderness of his heart overcame him and he burst into tears. His example completely unnerved me for the time, but was of service in the end. For many succeeding days he came to me, and was as gentle as a young mother with her suffering infant. Memory will ever recall Jefferson Davis as he stood with me by the coffin.

* * *

DISMISSING HOPE of making my small voice heard in mitigation of the woes of my State, in May, 1873, I went to Europe and remained many months. Returned to New York, I found that the characters on the wall, so long invisible, had blazed forth, and the vast factitious wealth, like the gold of the dervish, withered and faded in a night. The scenes depicted of Paris and London, after the collapse of Mississippi schemes and South Sea bubbles, were here repeated on a greater scale and in more aggravated form. To most, the loss of wealth was loss of ancestry, repute, respectability, decency, recognition of their fellows—all. Small wonder that their withers were fearfully wrung, and their wails piteous. Enterprise and prosperity were frozen as in a sea of everlasting ice, and guardians of trusts, like Ugolino, plunged their robber fangs into the scalps and entrails of the property confided to them.

A public journal has recently published a detailed list, showing that there has been plundered by fiduciaries since 1873 the amazing amount of thirty millions of money; and the work goes on. Scarce a newspaper is printed in whose columns may not be ' found some fresh instance of breach of trust. As poisoning in the time of Brinvilliers, stealing is epidemic, and the watch-dogs of the flocks are transformed into wolves.

Since the tocsin sounded we have gone from bad to worse. During the past summer (1877) laborers, striking for increased wages or to resist diminution thereof, seized and held for many days the railway lines between East and West, stopping all traffic. Aided by mobs, they took possession of great towns and destroyed vast property. At Pittsburgh, in Pennsylvania, State troops attempting to restore order were attacked and driven off. Police and State authorities in most cases proved impotent, and the arm of Federal power was invoked to stay the evil.

Thousands of the people are without employment, which they seek in vain; and from our cities issue heartrending appeals in behalf of the suffering poor. From the Atlantic as far to the west as the young State of Nebraska, there has fallen upon the land a calamity like that afflicting Germany after the Thirty Years' War. Hordes of idle, vicious tramps penetrate rural districts in all directions, rendering property and even life unsafe; and no remedy for this new disease has been discovered. Let us remember that these things are occurring in a country of millions upon millions of acres of vacant lands, to be had almost for the asking, and where, even in the parts first colonized, density of population bears but a small relation to that of western Europe. Yet we daily assure ourselves and the world that we have the best government under the canopy of heaven, and the happiest land, hope and refuge of humanity.

Purified by fire and sword, the South has escaped many of these evils; but her enemies have sown the seeds of a pestilence more deadly than that rising from Pontine marshes. Now that Federal bayonets have been turned from her bosom, this poison, the influence of three fourths of a million of negro voters, will speedily ascend and sap her vigor and intelligence. Greed of office, curse of democracies, will impel demagogues to grovel deeper and deeper in the mire in pursuit of ignorant votes. Her old breed of statesmen has largely passed away during and since the civil war, and the few survivors are naturally distrusted, as responsible for past errors. Numbers of her gentry fell in battle, and the men now on the stage were youths at the outbreak of strife, which arrested their education. This last is also measurably true of the North. Throughout the land the experience of the active portion of the present generation only comprises conditions of discord and violence. The story of the six centuries of sturdy effort by which our English forefathers wrought out their liberties is unknown, certainly unappreciated. Even the struggles of our grandfathers are forgotten, and the names of Washington, Adams, Hamilton, Jay, Marshall, Madison, and Story awaken no fresher memories in our minds, no deeper emotions in our hearts, than do those of Solon, Leonidas, and Pericles. But respect for the memories and deeds of our ancestors is security for the present, seed-corn for the future; and, in the language of Burke, "Those will not look forward to their posterity who never look backward to their ancestors."

Traditions are mighty influences in restraining peoples. The light that reaches us from above takes countless ages to traverse the awful chasm separating us from its parent star; yet it comes straight and true to our eyes, because each tender wavelet is linked to the other, receiving and transmitting the luminous ray. Once break the continuity of the stream, and men will deny its heavenly origin, and seek its source in the feeble glimmer of earthly corruption.

Mark Twain

(1835–1910)

Perhaps the most highly respected author of nineteenth-century America, Mark Twain's status as a "southern writer" is a complicated one. Like most communities in the southern part of the slaveholding state of Missouri, young Samuel Clemens's hometown of Hannibal was fiercely pro-southern, many of its families coming, like the Clemens's, from states to the south. (Twain's father was born in Virginia, his mother in Kentucky.) Although his pseudonym was taken from the riverboat jargon he learned as a pilot on the Mississippi, he began his career as a writer and fashioned his new literary identity while in the mining communities of California and Nevada (where he fled, at least in part, to avoid involvement in the sectional conflict back east) and never moved back to the South. It was not until the end of the Reconstruction period, when the national media began a push for sectional reconciliation, that Twain made much of his southern roots. In 1875 he contributed a series of autobiographical sketches called "Old Times on the Mississippi" to the Atlantic Monthly, *eventually expanding those sketches to book form as* Life on the Mississippi *(1883). In those writings and in* The Adventures of Huckleberry Finn *(1884) and a later novel,* Pudd'nhead Wilson *(1894), he addresses southern racism, invokes a number of popular stereotypes of southern whites, and displays a formidable knowledge of various southern regional dialects.*

While he is best known today as a novelist—primarily on the strength of Huck Finn—*Twain was a prolific writer of personal narratives, including his first two book-length works,* The Innocents Abroad *(1869) and* Roughing It *(1872), as well as* Life on the Mississippi *and the following selection, which was published in* Century Magazine *in 1885. At the time of his death, Twain was working on a sprawling autobiography that has been published in at least four very different forms. "The Private History of a Campaign that Failed" has an interesting history of its own. The publisher of Ulysses S. Grant's memoirs was none other than Mark Twain, and it was during the height of popularity of Grant's "public" memoirs that Twain decided to write his own "private" account of his efforts in the war. In the sketch, Twain manages to establish his "southern" credentials even as he disavows having had any strong ideological allegiance to the Confederacy. Not a bad move for an author who wanted to write about the South for a readership that was mostly concentrated in the urban North.*

FROM *Selected Shorter Writings of Mark Twain*

THE PRIVATE HISTORY OF A CAMPAIGN THAT FAILED

Y OU HAVE HEARD from a great many people who did something in the war; is it not fair and right that you listen a little moment to one who started out to do something in it, but didn't? Thousands entered the war, got just a taste of it, and then stepped out again, permanently. These, by their very numbers, are respectable, and are therefore entitled to a sort of voice,—not a loud one, but a modest one; not a boastful one, but an apologetic one. They ought not to be allowed much space among better people—people who did something—I grant that; but they ought at least to be allowed to state why they didn't do anything, and also to explain the process by which they didn't do anything. Surely this kind of light must have a sort of value.

Out West there was a good deal of confusion in men's minds during the first months of the great trouble—a good deal of unsettledness, of leaning first this way, then that, then the other way. It was hard for us to get our bearings. I call to mind an instance of this. I was piloting on the Mississippi when the news came that South Carolina had gone out of the Union on the 20th of December, 1860. My pilot-mate was a New Yorker. He was strong for the Union; so was I. But he would not listen to me with any patience; my loyalty was smirched, to his eye, because my father had owned slaves. I said, in palliation of this dark fact, that I had heard my father say, some years before he died, that slavery was a great wrong, and that he would free the solitary negro he then owned if he could think it right to give away the property of the family when he was so straitened in means. My mate retorted that a mere impulse was nothing—anybody could pretend to a good impulse; and went on decrying my Unionism and libeling my ancestry. A month later the secession atmosphere had considerably thickened on the Lower Mississippi, and I became a rebel; so did he. We were together in New Orleans, the 26th of January, when Louisiana went out of the Union. He did his full share of the rebel shouting, but was bitterly opposed to letting me do mine. He said that I came of bad stock—of a father who had been willing to set slaves free. In the following summer he was piloting a Federal gunboat and shouting for the Union again, and I was in the Confederate army. I held his note for some borrowed money. He was one of the most upright men I ever knew; but he repudiated that note without hesitation, because I was a rebel, and the son of a man who owned slaves.

In that summer—of 1861—the first wash of the wave of war broke upon the shores of Missouri. Our State was invaded by the Union forces. They took possession of St. Louis, Jefferson Barracks, and some other points. The Governor, Claib Jackson, issued his proclamation calling out fifty thousand militia to repel the invader.

I was visiting in the small town where my boyhood had been spent—Hannibal, Marion County. Several of us got together in a secret place by night and formed ourselves into a military company. One Tom Lyman, a young fellow of a good deal of spirit but of no military experience, was made captain; I was made second lieutenant. We had no first lieutenant; I do not know why; it was long ago. There were fifteen of us. By the advice of an innocent connected with the organization, we called ourselves the Marion Rangers. I do not remember that anyone found fault with the name. I did not; I thought it sounded quite well. The young fellow who proposed this title was perhaps a fair sample of the kind of stuff we were made of. He was young, ignorant, good-natured, well-meaning, trivial, full of romance, and given to reading chivalric novels and singing forlorn love-ditties. He had some pathetic little nickel-plated aristocratic instincts, and detested his name, which was Dunlap; detested it, partly because it was nearly as common in that region as Smith, but mainly because it had a plebian sound to his ear. So he tried to ennoble it by writing it in this way: *d'Unlap.* That contented his eye, but left his ear unsatisfied, for people gave the new name the same old pronunciation—emphasis on the front end of it. He then did the bravest thing that can be imagined,—a thing to make one shiver when one remembers how the world is given to resenting shams and affectations; he began to write his name so: *d'Un Lap.* And he waited patiently through the long storm of mud that was flung at his work of art, and he had his reward at last; for he lived to see that name accepted, and the emphasis put where he wanted it by people who had known him all his life, and to whom the tribe of Dunlaps had been as familiar as the rain and the sunshine for forty years. So sure of victory at last is the courage that can wait. He said he had found, by consulting some ancient French chronicles, that the name was rightly and originally written d'Un Lap; and said that if it were translated into English it would mean Peterson; *Lap,* Latin or Greek, he said, for stone or rock, same as the French *pierre,* that is to say, Peter; *d',* of or from; *un,* a or one; hence, d'Un Lap, of or from a stone or a Peter; that is to say, one who is the son of a stone, the son of a Peter—Peterson. Our militia company were not learned, and the explanation confused them; so they called him Peterson Dunlap. He proved useful to us in his way; he named our camps for us, and he generally struck a name that was "no slouch," as the boys said.

That is one sample of us. Another was Ed Stevens, son of the town jeweler,—trim-built, handsome, graceful, neat as a cat; bright, educated, but given over entirely to fun. There was nothing serious in life to him. As far as he was concerned, this military expedition of ours was simply a holiday. I should say that about half of us looked upon it in the same way; not consciously, perhaps, but unconsciously. We did not think; we were not capable of it. As for myself, I was full of unreasoning joy to be done with turning out of bed at midnight and four in the morning, for a while; grateful to have a change, new scenes, new occupations, a new interest. In my thoughts that was far as I went; I did not go into the details; as a rule, one doesn't at twenty-four.

Another sample was Smith, the blacksmith's apprentice. This vast donkey had some pluck, of a slow and sluggish nature, but a soft heart; at one time he would knock a horse down for some impropriety, and at another he would get homesick and cry. However, he had one ultimate credit to his account which some of us hadn't: he stuck to the war, and was killed in battle at last.

Jo Bowers, another sample, was a huge, good-natured, flax-headed lubber; lazy, sentimental, full of harmless brag, a grumbler by nature; an experienced, industrious, ambitious, and often quite picturesque liar, and yet not a successful one, for he had had no intelligent training, but was allowed to come up just any way. This life was serious enough to him, and seldom satisfactory. But he was a good fellow anyway, and the boys all liked him. He was made orderly sergeant; Stevens was made corporal.

These samples will answer—and they are quite fair ones. Well, this herd of cattle started for the war. What could you expect of them? They did as well as they knew how; but really what was justly to be expected of them? Nothing, I should say. That is what they did.

We waited for a dark night, for caution and secrecy were necessary; then, toward midnight, we stole in couples and from various directions to the Griffith place, beyond the town; from that point we set out together on foot. Hannibal lies at the extreme southeastern corner of Marion County, on the Mississippi River; our objective point was the hamlet of New London, ten miles away, in Ralls County.

The first hour was all fun, all idle nonsense and laughter. But that could not be kept up. The steady trudging came to be like work; the play had somehow oozed out of it; the stillness of the woods and the somberness of the night began to throw a depressing influence over the spirits of the boys, and presently the talking died out and each person shut himself up in his own thoughts. During the last half of the second hour nobody said a word.

Now we approached a log farm-house where, according to report, there was a guard of five Union soldiers. Lyman called a halt; and there, in the deep gloom of the overhanging branches, he began to whisper a plan of assault upon that house, which made the gloom more depressing than it was before. It was a crucial moment; we realized, with a cold suddenness, that here was no jest—we were standing face to face with actual war. We were equal to the occasion. In our response there was no hesitation, no indecision: we said that if Lyman wanted to meddle with those soldiers, he could go ahead and do it; but if he waited for us to follow him, he would wait a long time.

Lyman urged, pleaded, tried to shame us, but it had no effect. Our course was plain, our minds were made up: we would flank the farm-house—go out around. And that was what we did.

We struck into the woods and entered upon a rough time, stumbling over roots, getting tangled in vines, and torn by briers. At last we reached an open place in a safe region, and sat down, blown and hot, to cool off and nurse our scratches and bruises. Lyman was annoyed, but the rest of us were cheerful; we had flanked the farm-house, we had made our first military movement, and it was a success; we had nothing to fret about, we were feeling just the other way. Horse-play and laughing began again; the expedition was become a holiday frolic once more.

Then we had two more hours of dull trudging and ultimate silence and depression; then, about dawn, we straggled into New London, soiled, heel-blistered, fagged with our little march, and all of us except Stevens in a sour and raspy humor and privately down on the war. We stacked our shabby shotguns in Colonel Ralls's barn, and then went in a body and breakfasted with that veteran of the Mexican War. Afterwards he took us to a distant meadow, and there in the shade of a tree we listened to an old-fashioned speech from him, full of gunpowder and glory, full of that adjective-piling, mixed metaphor, and windy declamation which were regarded as eloquence in that ancient time and that remote region; and then he swore us on the Bible to be faithful to the State of Missouri and drive all invaders from her soil, no matter whence they might come or under what flag they might march. This mixed us considerably, and we could not make out just what service we were embarked in; but Colonel Ralls, the practiced politician and phrase-juggler, was not similarly in doubt; he knew quite clearly that he had invested us in the cause of the Southern Confederacy. He closed the solemnities by belting around me the sword which his neighbor, Colonel Brown, had worn at Buena Vista and Molino del Rey; and he accompanied this act with another impressive blast.

Then we formed in line of battle and marched four miles to a shady and pleasant piece of woods on the border of the far-reaching expanses of a flowery prairie. It was an enchanting region for war—our kind of war.

We pierced the forest about half a mile, and took up a strong position, with some low, rocky, and wooded hills behind us, and a purling, limpid creek in front. Straightway half the command were in swimming, and the other half fishing. The ass with the French name gave this position a romantic title, but it was too long, so the boys shortened and simplified it to Camp Ralls.

We occupied an old maple-sugar camp, whose half-rotted troughs were still propped against the trees. A long corn-crib served for sleeping quarters for the battalion. On our left, half a mile away, were Mason's farm and house; and he was a friend to the cause. Shortly after noon the farmers began to arrive from several directions, with mules and horses for our use, and these they lent us for as long as the war might last, which they judged would be about three months. The animals were of all sizes, all colors, and all breeds. They were mainly young and frisky, and nobody in the command could stay on them long at a time; for we were town boys, and ignorant of horsemanship. The creature that fell to my share was a very small mule, and yet so quick and active that it could throw me without difficulty; and it did this whenever I got on it. Then it would bray—stretching its neck out, laying its ears back, and spreading its jaws till you could see down to its works. It was a disagreeable animal, in every way. If I took it by the bridle and tried to lead it off the grounds, it would sit down and brace back, and no one could budge it. However, I was not entirely destitute of military resources, and I did presently manage to spoil this game; for I had seen many a steamboat aground in my time, and knew a trick or two which even a grounded mule would be obliged to respect. There was a well by the corn-crib; so I substituted thirty fathom of rope for the bridle, and fetched him home with the windlass.

I will anticipate here sufficiently to say that we did learn to ride, after some days' practice, but never well. We could not learn to like our animals; they were not choice ones, and most of them had annoying peculiarities of one kind or another. Stevens's horse would carry him, when he was not noticing, under the huge excrescences which form on the trunks of oak-trees, and wipe him out of the saddle; in this way Stevens got several bad hurts. Sergeant Bowers's horse was very large and tall, with slim, long legs, and looked like a railroad bridge. His size enabled him to reach all about, and as far as he wanted to, with his head; so he was always biting Bowers's legs. On the march, in the sun, Bowers slept a good deal; and as soon as the horse recognized that he was asleep he would reach around and bite him on the leg. His legs were black and blue with bites. This was the only thing that could ever make him swear, but this always did; whenever his horse bit him he always swore, and of course Stevens, who laughed at everything, laughed at this, and would even get into such convulsions over it as to lose his balance and fall off his horse; and then Bowers, already irritated by the pain of the horse-bite, would resent the laughter with hard language and there would be a quarrel; so that horse made no end of trouble and bad blood in the command.

However, I will get back to where I was—our first afternoon in the sugar-camp. The sugar-troughs came very handy as horse-troughs, and we had plenty of corn to fill them with. I ordered Sergeant Bowers to feed my mule; but he said that if I reckoned he went to war to be a dry-nurse to a mule, it wouldn't take me very long to find out my mistake. I believed that this was insubordination, but I was full of uncertainties about everything military, and so I let the thing pass, and went and ordered Smith, the blacksmith's apprentice, to feed the mule; but he merely gave me a large, cold, sarcastic grin, such as an ostensibly seven-year-old horse gives you when you lift his lips and find he is fourteen, and turned his back on me. I then went to the captain, and asked if it was not right and proper and military for me to have an orderly. He said it was, but as there was only one orderly in the corps, it was but right that he himself should have Bowers on his staff. Bowers said he wouldn't serve on anybody's staff; and if anybody thought he could make him, let him try it. So, of course, the thing had to be dropped; there was no other way.

Next, nobody would cook; it was considered a degradation; so we had no dinner. We lazied the rest of the pleasant afternoon away, some dozing under the trees, some smoking cob-pipes and talking sweethearts and war, some playing games. By late suppertime all hands were famished; and to meet the difficulty all hands turned to, on an equal footing, and gathered wood, built fires, and cooked the meal. Afterwards everything was smooth for a while; then trouble broke out between the corporal and

the sergeant, each claiming to rank the other. Nobody knew
which was the higher office; so Lyman had to settle the matter
by making the rank of both officers equal. The commander of
an ignorant crew like that has many troubles and vexations
which probably do not occur in the regular army at all. However, with the song-singing and yarn-spinning around the
camp-fire, everything presently became serene again; and by and
by we raked the corn down level in one end of the crib, and all
went to bed on it, tying a horse to the door, so that he would
neigh if anyone tried to get in.*

We had some horsemanship drill every forenoon; then, afternoons, we rode off here and there in squads a few miles, and visited the farmers' girls, and had a youthful good time, and got an
honest good dinner or supper, and then home again to camp,
happy and content.

For a time, life was idly delicious, it was perfect; there was
nothing to mar it. Then came some farmers with an alarm one
day. They said it was rumored that the enemy were advancing in
our direction, from over Hyde's prairie. The result was a sharp
stir among us, and general consternation. It was a rude awakening from our pleasant trance. The rumor was but a rumor—
nothing definite about it; so, in the confusion, we did not know
which way to retreat. Lyman was for not retreating at all in these
uncertain circumstances; but he found that if he tried to main-
tain that attitude he would fare badly, for the command were in
no humor to put up with insubordination. So he yielded the
point and called a council of war—to consist of himself and the
three other officers; but the privates made such a fuss about
being left out, that we had to allow them to remain, for they

---

*It was always my impression that that was what the horse was there for, and I know that
it was also the impression of at least one other of the command, for we talked about it at
the time, and admired the military ingenuity of the device; but when I was out West
three years ago I was told by Mr. A. G. Fuqua, a member of our company, that the horse
was his; that the leaving him tied at the door was a matter of mere forgetfulness, and that
to attribute it to intelligent invention was to give him quite too much credit. In support
of his position, he called my attention to the suggestive fact that the artifice was not
employed again. I had not thought of that before.

were already present, and doing most of the talking too. The question was, which way to retreat; but all were so flurried that nobody seemed to have even a guess to offer. Except Lyman. He explained in a few calm words, that inasmuch as the enemy were approaching them over Hyde's prairie, our course was simple: all we had to do was not to retreat *toward* him; any other direction would answer our needs perfectly. Everybody saw in a moment how true this was, and how wise; so Lyman got a great many compliments. It was now decided that we should fall back on Mason's farm.

It was after dark by this time, and as we could not know how soon the enemy might arrive, it did not seem best to try to take the horses and things with us; so we only took the guns and ammunition, and started at once. The route was very rough and hilly and rocky, and presently the night grew very black and rain began to fall; so we had a troublesome time of it, struggling and stumbling along in the dark; and soon some person slipped and fell, and then the next person behind stumbled over him and fell, and so did the rest, one after the other; and then Bowers came with the keg of powder in his arms, while the command were all mixed together, arms and legs, on the muddy slope; and so he fell, of course, with the keg, and this started the whole detachment down the hill in a body, and they landed in the brook at the bottom in a pile, and each that was undermost pulling the hair and scratching and biting those that were on top of him; and those that were being scratched and bitten scratching and biting the rest in their turn, and all saying they would die before they would ever go to war again if they ever got out of this brook this time, and the invaders might rot for all they cared, and the country along with him—and all such talk as that, which was dismal to hear and take part in, such smothered, low voices, and such a grisly dark place and so wet, and the enemy maybe coming any moment.

The keg of powder was lost, and the guns, too; so the growling and complaining continued straight along whilst the brigade pawed around the pasty hillside and slopped around in the brook hunting for these things; consequently we lost considerable time at this; and then we heard a sound, and held our breath and listened, and it seemed to be the enemy coming, though it could have been a cow, for it had a cough like a cow; but we did not wait, but left a couple of guns behind and struck out for Mason's again as briskly as we could scramble along in the dark. But we got lost presently among the rugged little ravines, and wasted a deal of time finding the way again, so it was after nine when we reached Mason's stile at last; and then before we could open our mouths to give the countersign, several dogs came bounding over the fence, with great riot and noise, and each of them took a soldier by the slack of the trousers and began to back away with him. We could not shoot the dogs without endangering the persons they were attached to; so we had to look on, helpless, at what was perhaps the most mortifying spectacle of the Civil War. There was light enough, and to spare, for the Masons had now run out on the porch with candles in their hands. The old man and his son came and undid the dogs without difficulty, all but Bowers's; but they couldn't undo his dog, they didn't know his combination; he was of the bull kind, and seemed to be set with a Yale time-lock; but they got him loose at last with some scalding water, of which Bowers got his share and returned thanks. Peterson Dunlap afterwards made up a fine name for this engagement, and also for the night march which preceded it, but both have long ago faded out of my memory.

We now went into the house, and they began to ask us a world of questions, whereby it presently came out that we did not know anything concerning who or what we were running from; so the old gentleman made himself very frank, and said we were a curious breed of soldiers, and guessed we could be depended on to end up the war in time, because no government could stand the expense of the shoe-leather we should cost it trying to follow us around. "Marion *Rangers!* good name, b'gosh!" said he. And wanted to know why we hadn't had a picket-guard at the place where the road entered the prairie, and why we hadn't sent out a scouting party to spy out the enemy and bring us an account of his strength, and so on, before jumping up and stampeding out of a strong position upon a mere vague rumor—and so forth, till he made us all feel shabbier than the dogs had done, not half so enthusiastically welcome. So we went to bed ashamed and low-spirited; except Stevens. Soon Stevens began to devise a garment for Bowers which could be made to automatically display his battle-scars to the grateful, or conceal them from the envious, according to his occasions; but Bowers was in no humor for this, so there was a fight, and when it was over Stevens had some battle-scars of his own to think about.

Then we got a little sleep. But after all we had gone through, our activities were not over for the night; for about two o'clock in the morning we heard a shout of warning from down the lane, accompanied by a chorus from all the dogs, and in a moment everybody was up and flying around to find out what the alarm was about. The alarmist was a horseman who gave notice that a detachment of Union soldiers was on its way from Hannibal with orders to capture and hang any bands like ours which it could find, and said we had no time to lose. Farmer Mason was in a flurry this time, himself. He hurried us out of the house with all haste, and sent one of his negroes with us to show us where to hide ourselves and our tell-tale guns among the ravines half a mile away. It was raining heavily.

We struck down the lane, then across some rocky pasture-land which offered good advantages for stumbling; consequently we were down in the mud most of the time, and every time a man went down he blackguarded the war, and the people that started it, and everybody connected with it, and gave himself the master dose of all for being so foolish as to go into it. At last we reached the wooded mouth of a ravine, and there we huddled ourselves under the streaming trees, and sent the negro back home. It was a dismal and heart-breaking time. We were like to be drowned with the rain, deafened with the howling wind and the booming thunder, and blinded by the lightning. It was indeed a wild night. The drenching we were getting was misery enough, but a deeper misery still was the reflection that the halter might end us before we were a day older. A death of this shameful sort had not occurred to us as being among the possibilities of war. It took the romance all out of the campaign, and turned our dreams of glory into a repulsive nightmare. As for doubting that so barbarous an order had been given, not one of us did that.

The long night wore itself out at last, and then the negro came to us with the news that the alarm had manifestly been a false one, and that breakfast would soon be ready. Straightway we were light-hearted again and the world was bright, and life as full of hope and promise as ever—for we were young then. How long ago that was! Twenty-four years.

The mongrel child of philology named the night's refuge Camp Devastation, and no soul objected. The Masons gave us a Missouri county breakfast, in Missourian abundance, and we needed it: hot biscuits; hot "wheat-bread," prettily criss-crossed in a lattice pattern on top; hot corn pone; fried chicken; bacon, coffee, eggs, milk, buttermilk, etc.;—and the world may be confidently challenged to furnish the equal of such a breakfast, as it is cooked in the South.

We stayed several days at Mason's; and after all these years the memory of the dullness, and stillness, and lifelessness of that slumberous farm-house still oppresses my spirit as with a sense of the presence of death and mourning. There was nothing to do, nothing to think about; there was no interest in life. The male part of the household were away in the fields all day, the women were busy and out of our sight; there was no sound but the plaintive wailing of a spinning-wheel, forever moaning out from some distant room,—the most lonesome sound in nature, a sound steeped and sodden with homesickness and the emptiness of life. The family went to bed about dark every night, and as we were not invited to intrude any new customs, we naturally followed theirs. Those nights were a hundred years long to youths accustomed to being up till twelve. We lay awake and miserable till that hour every time, and grew old and decrepit waiting through the still eternities for the clock-strikes. This was no place for town boys. So at last it was with something very like joy that we received news that the enemy were on our track again. With a new birth of the old warrior spirit, we sprang to our places in line of battle and fell back on Camp Ralls.

Captain Lyman had taken a hint from Mason's talk, and he now gave orders that our camp should be guarded against surprise by the posting of pickets. I was ordered to place a picket at the forks of the road in Hyde's prairie. Night shut down black and threatening. I told Sergeant Bowers to go out to that place and stay till midnight; and, just as I was expecting, he said he wouldn't do it. I tried to get others to go, but all refused. Some excused themselves on account of the weather; but the rest were frank enough to say they wouldn't go in any kind of weather. This kind of thing sounds odd now, and impossible, but there was no surprise in it at the time. On the contrary, it seemed a perfectly natural thing to do. There were scores of little camps scattered over Missouri where the same thing was happening. These camps were composed of young men who had been born and reared to a sturdy independence, and who did not know what it meant to be ordered around by Tom, Dick, and Harry, whom they had known familiarly all their lives, in the village or on the farm. It is quite within the probabilities that this same thing was happening all over the South. James Redpath recognized the justice of this assumption, and furnished the following instance in support of it. During a short stay in East Tennessee he was in a citizen colonel's tent one day talking, when a big private appeared at the door, and, without salute or other circumlocution, said to the colonel,—

"Say, Jim, I'm a-goin' home for a few days."

"What for?"

"Well, I hain't b'en there for a right smart while, and I'd like to see how things is comin' on."

"How long are you going to be gone?"

" 'Bout two weeks."

"Well, don't be gone longer than that; and get back sooner if you can."

That was all, and the citizen officer resumed his conversation where the private had broken it off. This was in the first months of the war, of course. The camps in our part of Missouri were under Brigadier-General Thomas H. Harris. He was a townsman of ours, a first-rate fellow, and well liked; but we had all familiarly known him as the sole and modest-salaried operator in our telegraph office, where he had to send about one dispatch a week in ordinary times, and two when there was a rush of business; consequently, when he appeared in our midst one day, on the wing, and delivered a military command of some sort, in a large military fashion, nobody was surprised at the response which he got from the assembled soldiery,—

"Oh, now, what'll you take to *don't,* Tom Harris!"

It was quite the natural thing. One might justly imagine that we were hopeless material for war. And so we seemed, in our ignorant state; but there were those among us who afterwards learned the grim trade; learned to obey like machines; became valuable soldiers; fought all through the war, and came out at the end with excellent records. One of the very boys who refused to go out on picket duty that night, and called me an ass for thinking he would expose himself to danger in such a foolhardy way, had become distinguished for intrepidity before he was a year older.

I did secure my picket that night—not by authority, but by diplomacy. I got Bowers to go by agreeing to exchange ranks with him for the time being, and go along and stand the watch with him as his subordinate. We stayed out there a couple of dreary hours in the pitchy darkness and the rain, with nothing to modify the dreariness but Bowers's monotonous growlings at the war and the weather; then we began to nod, and presently found it next to impossible to stay in the saddle; so we gave up the tedious job, and went back to the camp without waiting for the relief guard. We rode into camp without interruption or objection from anybody, and the enemy could have done the same, for there were no sentries. Everybody was asleep; at midnight there was nobody to send out another picket, so none was sent. We never tried to establish a watch at night again, as far as I remember, but we generally kept a picket out in the daytime.

In that camp the whole command slept on the corn in the big corn-crib; and there was usually a general row before morning, for the place was full of rats, and they would scramble over the boys' bodies and faces, annoying and irritating everybody; and now and then they would bite some one's toe, and the person who owned the toe would start up and magnify his English and begin to throw corn in the dark. The ears were half as heavy as bricks, and when they struck they hurt. The persons struck would respond, and inside of five minutes every man would be locked in a death-grip with his neighbor. There was a grievous deal of blood shed in the corn-crib, but this was all that was spilt while I was in the war. No, that is not quite true. But for one circumstance it would have been all. I will come to that now.

Our scares were frequent. Every few days rumors would come that the enemy were approaching. In these cases we always fell back on some other camp of ours; we never staid where we were. But the rumors always turned out to be false; so at last even we began to grow indifferent to them. One night a negro was sent to our corn-crib with the same old warning: the enemy was hovering in our neighborhood. We all said let him hover. We resolved to stay still and be comfortable. It was a fine warlike resolution, and no doubt we all felt the stir of it in our veins— for a moment. We had been having a very jolly time, that was full of horse-play and school-boy hilarity; but that cooled down now, and presently the fast-waning fire of forced jokes and forced laughs died out altogether, and the company became silent. Silent and nervous. And soon uneasy—worried—apprehensive. We had said we would stay, and we were committed. We could have been persuaded to go, but there was nobody brave enough to suggest it. An almost noiseless movement presently began in the dark, by a general but unvoiced impulse.

When the movement was completed, each man knew that he was not the only person who had crept to the front wall and had his eye at a crack between the logs. No, we were all there; all there with our hearts in our throats, and staring out toward the sugar-troughs where the forest footpath came through. It was late, and there was a deep woodsy stillness everywhere. There was a veiled moonlight, which was only just strong enough to enable us to mark the general shape of objects. Presently a muffled sound caught our ears, and we recognized it as the hoof-beats of a horse or horses. And right away a figure appeared in the forest path; it could have been made of smoke, its mass had so little sharpness of outline. It was a man on horseback, and it seemed to me that there were others behind him. I got hold of a gun in the dark, and pushed it through a crack between the logs, hardly knowing what I was doing, I was so dazed with fright. Somebody said, "Fire!" I pulled the trigger. I seemed to see a hundred flashes and hear a hundred reports; then I saw the man fall down out of the saddle. My first feeling was of surprised gratification; my first impulse was an apprentice-sportsman's impulse to run and pick up his game. Somebody said, hardly audibly, "Good—we've got him!—wait for the rest." But the rest did not come. We waited—listened—still no more came. There was not a sound, not the whisper of a leaf; just perfect stillness; an uncanny kind of stillness, which was all the more uncanny on account of the damp, earthy, late-night smells now rising and pervading it. Then, wondering, we crept stealthily out, and approached the man. When we got to him the moon revealed him distinctly. He was lying on his back with his arms abroad; his mouth was open and his chest heaving with long gasps, and his white shirt-front was all splashed with blood. The thought shot through me that I was a murderer; that I had killed a man—a man who had never done me any harm. That was the coldest sensation that ever went through my marrow. I was down by him in a moment, helplessly stroking his forehead; and I would have given anything then—my own life freely—to make him again what he had been five minutes before. And all the boys seemed to be feeling in the same way; they hung over him, full of pitying interest, and tried all they could to help him, and said all sorts of regretful things. They had forgotten all about the enemy; they thought only of this one forlorn unit of the foe. Once my imagination persuaded me that the dying man gave me a reproachful look out of his shadowy eyes, and it seemed to me that I could rather he had stabbed me than done that. He muttered and mumbled like a dreamer in his sleep, about his wife and his child; and I thought with a new despair, "This thing that I have done does not end with him; it falls upon *them* too, and they never did me any harm, any more than he."

In a little while the man was dead. He was killed in war; killed in fair and legitimate war; killed in battle, as you may say; and yet he was as sincerely mourned by the opposing force as if he had been their brother. The boys stood there a half hour sorrowing over him, and recalling the details of the tragedy, and wondering who he might be, and if he were a spy, and saying that if it were to do over again they would not hurt him unless he attacked them first. It soon came out that mine was not the only shot fired; there were five others,—a division of guilt which was a great relief to me, since it in some degree lightened and diminished the burden I was carrying. There were six shots fired at once; but I was not in my right mind at the time, and my heated imagination had magnified my one shot into a volley.

The man was not in uniform, and was not armed. He was a stranger in the country; that was all we ever found out about him. The thought of him got to preying upon me every night; I could not get rid of it. I could not drive it away, the taking of that unoffending life seemed such a wanton thing. And it seemed an epitome of war; that all war must be just that—the killing of strangers against whom you feel no personal animosity; strangers whom, in other circumstances, you would help if you found them in trouble, and who would help you if you needed it. My campaign was spoiled. It seemed to me that I was not rightly equipped for this awful business; that war was intended for men, and I for a child's nurse. I resolved to retire from this avocation of sham soldiership while I could save some remnant of my self-respect. These morbid thoughts clung to me against reason; for at bottom I did not believe I had touched that man. The law of probabilities decreed me guiltless of his blood; for in all my small experience with guns I had never hit anything I had tried to hit, and I knew I had done my best to hit him. Yet there was no solace in the thought. Against a diseased imagination demonstration goes for nothing.

The rest of my war experience was a piece with what I have already told of it. We kept monotonously falling back upon one camp or another, and eating up the country. I marvel now at the patience of the farmers and their families. They ought to have shot us; on the contrary, they were as hospitably kind and courteous to us as if we had deserved it. In one of these camps we found Ab Grimes, an Upper Mississippi pilot, who afterwards became famous as a dare-devil rebel spy, whose career bristled with desperate adventures. The look and style of his comrades suggested that they had not come into war to play, and their deeds made good the conjecture later. They were fine horsemen and good revolver-shots; but their favorite arm was the lasso. Each had one at his pommel, and could snatch a man out of the saddle with it every time, on a full gallop, at any reasonable distance.

In another camp the chief was a fierce and profane old blacksmith of sixty, and he had furnished his twenty recruits with gigantic home-made bowie-knives, to be swung with two hands, like the *machetes* of the Isthmus. It was a grisly spectacle to see that earnest band practicing their murderous cuts and slashes under the eye of that remorseless old fanatic.

The last camp which we fell back upon was in a hollow near the village of Florida, where I was born—in Monroe County. Here we were warned, one day, that a Union colonel was sweeping down on us with a whole regiment at his heels. This looked decidedly serious. Our boys went apart and consulted; then we went back and told the other companies present that the war was a disappointment to us, and we were going to dis-band. They were getting ready, themselves, to fall back on some place or other, and were only waiting for General Tom Harris, who was expected to arrive at any moment; so they tried to persuade us to wait a little while, but the majority of us said no, we were accustomed to falling back, and didn't need any of Tom Harris's help; we could get along perfectly well without him—and save time too. So about half of our fifteen, including myself, mounted and left on the instant; the others yielded to persuasion and staid—staid through the war.

An hour later we met General Harris on the road, with two or three people in his company—his staff, probably, but we could not tell; none of them were in uniform; uniforms had not come into vogue among us yet. Harris ordered us back; but we told him there was a Union colonel coming with a whole regiment in his wake, and it looked as if there was going to be a disturbance; so we had concluded to go home. He raged a little, but it was of no use; our minds were made up. We had done our share; had killed one man, exterminated one army, such as it was; let him go and kill the rest, and that would end the war. I did not see that brisk young general again until last year; then he was wearing white hair and whiskers.

In time I came to know that Union colonel whose coming frightened me out of the war and crippled the Southern cause to that extent—General Grant. I came within a few hours of seeing him when he was as unknown as I was myself; at a time when anybody could have said, "Grant?—Ulysses S. Grant? I do not remember hearing the name before." It seems difficult to realize that there was once a time when such a remark could be rationally made; but there *was,* and I was within a few miles of the place and the occasion too, though proceeding in the other direction.

The thoughtful will not throw this war-paper of mine lightly aside as being valueless. It has this value: it is a not unfair picture of what went on in many and many a militia camp in the first month of the rebellion, when the green recruits were without discipline, without the steadying and heartening influence of trained leaders; when all their circumstances were new and strange, and charged with exaggerated terrors, and before the invaluable experience of actual collision in the field had turned them from rabbits into soldiers. If this side of the picture of that early day has not before been put into history, then history has been to that degree incomplete, for it had and has its rightful place there. There was more Bull Run material scattered through the early camps of this country than exhibited itself at Bull Run. And yet it learned its trade presently, and helped to fight the great battles later. I could have become a soldier myself, if I had waited. I had got part of it learned; I knew more about retreating than the man that invented retreating.

Century Magazine, December, 1885; 1892

Robert Penn Warren

(1905–1989)

The only writer to win the Pulitzer Prize for both poetry and fiction, Robert Penn Warren stands as one of the luminaries of twentieth-century American literature. He was born and raised in Guthrie, Kentucky, not far from Clarksville, Tennessee, where Allen Tate and Evelyn Scott grew up. While a young boy in Guthrie, Warren witnessed a populist revolt by tobacco farmers that was quelled by the National Guard, a bit of local history that he later used as the setting for his novel Night Rider *(1939). At age sixteen he entered Vanderbilt University in Nashville, where his freshman writing professor, John Crowe Ransom, brought him into the circle of poets that would come to be called the Fugitives (after the title of their short-lived journal,* The Fugitive*). In 1930, he and three other members of that group—Ransom, Allen Tate, and Donald Davidson—contributed to the Agrarian manifesto* I'll Take My Stand, *though Warren publicly distanced himself from that project before the book appeared in print. With Cleanth Brooks he coauthored two highly influential textbooks,* Understanding Poetry *(1938) and* Understanding Fiction *(1943), that helped usher in the New Criticism as the dominant mode of literary analysis in the United States for decades. Warren's writings reflect a keen interest in the history of the South. In addition to the Tobacco War setting of* Night Rider, *his Pulitzer Prize–winning novel* All the King's Men *(1946) is based loosely on the life of Louisiana politician Huey Long;* Band of Angels *(1955),* Wilderness *(1961), and a large section in the middle of* All the King's Men *are set in the Civil War; one long verse narrative,* Brother to Dragons *(1953), is an imaginative speculation on the life of Thomas Jefferson's nephew, Lilburn Lewis, who murdered a slave for breaking a dish; and the collection of poems* Audubon: A

Vision *(1969) takes as its subject the famed naturalist's travels along the Natchez Trace. Though he first gained critical attention as part of the Fugitive poetry group and continued to write verse afterward, Warren focused his energies on fiction for the first half of his literary career, then turned increasingly to poetry to express his ideas in the second half. Ranging from the colloquial in poems like "The Ballad of Billie Potts" (1944) to lyric meditation in much of his later work, Warren's poetry balances the concrete image with philosophical speculation on the meaning of memory, time, love, and death.*

Portrait of a Father first appeared in The Southern Review *(spring 1987) and was edited by the author to appear in book form the following year. In this memoir, Warren tries to reach beyond his memories of the father he knew in order to investigate the "mystery" of the man's past. As is the case with so many other writers in this anthology, the act of remembering others becomes an intimate form of self-disclosure. In the following excerpt, taken from the end of the memoir, Warren searches for the secrets that lay behind his father's reticence as he neared his time of death.*

FROM *Portrait of a Father*

SUCH ECHOES of the past were very rare. For my mother as well as my father, a characteristic image, I must repeat, is that of the two walking somewhere—perhaps an image from those early picnics when they would wander off into the woods. The heads would be slightly bowed as though they were trapped in an interminable conversation never finished, and always there waiting to be resumed.

What were they talking about? I have no idea. Our mother was very affectionate to the children and to our father. He was not a demonstrative man, not even to his children. He did not have to be. His whole life was a kind of demonstration clearly understood. But I vividly remember his face when, thinking himself unobserved, he once leaned over the bed where my little brother lay ill. He was not seriously ill.

Self-control is a single quality that for my father seemed to underlie everything. Self-control was to survive even the death of his wife and, a little later, his bankruptcy. That quality was the mark of his life especially in the years when he lived in a rather drab rented room in walking distance of the house of my much younger brother, Thomas, and in decent weather in walking distance of the grave of his wife.

When little more than a boy, Thomas, who had dropped out of college after the death of our mother, had created a very thriving business, and badly needed somebody to manage the "inside" while he exploited his talent for the "outside." He persuaded his father to take over. In all ways it was a perfect arrangement, but our father insisted on a minimum salary. His pride had already blocked a project that my brother and I had had of building a little house with quarters—inside or out—for some couple to take care of housekeeping and meals and chores.

But our father, in that crazy pride, had stayed in his room, walked into town for his picked-up and lonely meals, and, except when Thomas might come by, read at night. For he had begun again to accumulate some books. Thus he waited for the ritual dinner on Sunday, when he could see his three little granddaughters. I remember one Sunday when I was on a visit. Amid the scattered sheets of the big Sunday newspaper, he was sitting on a couch with a little girl some eight or nine years old, to whom he was teaching the first conjugation in Latin. She would keep repeating "*amo, amas, amat, amamus. . . .* " Then she would burst into gales of laughter.

It was so crazy she said. Then she would scream for more. Years later that little girl, at the university, was mad for French literature, and was to live in France for many years until her untimely death.

About the time of that visit, well after I had truly discovered my father, he was visiting me in Louisiana. Before coming to my house, he wanted to explore New Orleans for himself. When he arrived I met him briefly there. I asked him why he hadn't put up in a hotel nearer to Frenchtown. He said that the place where he had put up was very good and comfortable, and added that it was more reasonable because of the distance. Anyway, he liked to walk.

He examined me in what for the moment seemed a cool and detached way, and then said: "The first thing a man should do is to learn to deny himself."

There was a shock to that remark, perhaps because I was suddenly aware of all past self-indulgence.

He had not, of course, spoken to me. How the silence was broken, I cannot remember, but the conviction solidly grew that he was speaking of his whole life.

Some days later my father came to visit me in Baton Rouge. There an old friend of mine gave us a little dinner, some eight or nine people at the table. This was the day after news of Pearl Harbor had interrupted the Sunday dinner at my house. Now all conversation was the new war.

At last the hostess turned to my father and asked his opinion.

He thanked her, somewhat humorously, then said: "When one reaches my age he realizes how little his opinions mean. The world goes driving on its own way."

I left Baton Rouge for good in June, 1942. My father was never to come to my house again. It was not merely distance or war, and I often visited him. He was to survive the war a long time, and after the war he and I took various trips together, short and long.

The first was to Smithland, a village where the Tennessee River joins the Ohio. Toward two hundred years ago it had been a little river port with a promising future, but in the late 1940s was a forgotten spot. Near here the sister of Thomas Jefferson and her husband had once settled, and their two sons had been involved in the hideous butchery of a slave boy. I thought this was a natural symbol, and wanted to know the very spot where lay the ruins of their house.

My father and I drove there, northwestward from our town, skirting the land of his childhood. While driving to Smithland, he was extraordinarily attentive to the country, but said nothing of relevance. Near Smithland I found the track, not even a path, up the bluff to the site of the terrible house. My father drowsed in the car until I came back.

Later as we drove homeward, again through the land of his childhood, he was stirred to say that his father had, in the spring, always lined up the boys. "We were a house of boys," he said. This was to get a dose of an old remedy, crushed "percoon" steeped for months in whiskey, supposedly a medicine to "unthicken the blood of boys," and "keep them from mean-ness." My father could not remember what plant "percoon" was. For years I had never remembered at a convenient time to ask a botanist. But lately several have written to me.

This triviality seemed very important to me, something about a past that was a mystery. The trivial matter finally had to enter a book, a long narrative-dramatic poem, *Brother to Dragons*.

Another trip with my father, the last one, was to Mexico. Even in childhood, though without reflection, I had sensed his appetite to see the world. I had sensed it long back from the way he would talk of places which he had visited, or from the stories read to me, or to the other children. It could be sensed, too, from the way he spoke of certain novels he had read in the period of Clarksville, or from accounts of trips then taken.

For instance, he had been in New York and in Chicago at the time of the World's Fair. He must have been in St. Louis at the time of the Louisiana Purchase Exposition, for he had seen, unless my memory is totally at fault, the famous Indian warrior, Geronimo, who had caused the United States army great trou-ble, and whose name reenters history in the cry of American paratroopers as they peel off. (Or so it is sometimes reported.) Geronimo, according to a ghosted autobiography, was indeed at the Exposition, where he sold photographs and autographs to crowds, and averaged a take of some two dollars a day. But the Exposition was in 1904, the year of the marriage of our parents.

Could St. Louis have been on a wedding trip? There is no way
of knowing. But one thing I do know. After I, the eldest child,
had become a big boy, our father never even mentioned, in any
way, his trips.

When he and I took our last trip together, in 1952, to Mexico
City, he became as vigorous as a boy, and as full of all kinds of
curiosity. His big brother, Sam, had been there, and that fact
seemed to have made all the difference.

At Mexico City we put up at a pleasant hotel where I had
once stayed for a time. His energy was appalling. We saw bull
fights, frescoes, jai alai games, bars, restaurants, markets, muse-
ums, the mountains. He loved jai alai and wanted to see a game
every night. I had assumed that he would want to visit mines
where Sam had once been, and Guadalajara, where Sam had
once lived and where I had often been during a long stay at
Chapala. It would have been easy to go. Get a car in Mexico
City and take the spectacular route west. But somehow my
father kept postponing the idea. Until it was too late. I never
guessed why. So we flew to Cuba.

Now, however, the most persistent recollection I have of our
last trip is a moment when I woke up in our hotel room in
Mexico City, about two or three in the morning. Somehow a
very faint light, not more than a dimness, penetrated through
the blinds. Only with effort could I make out the figure in the
other bed, some six or seven feet away. The figure never moved.
I was still lying awake when I heard a very faint sound, so faint
that it could scarcely be called a sound. But it was. And was, I
suddenly realized, words.

Then I realized that the words were the tail end of a poem. It
was a poem which I now cannot identify. Then after a long
silence, came another poem in that same hushed susurrus. I recognized this one, a poem I had not seen or thought of since
boyhood, but a great favorite which I had often made him read
to me. It was about the burial of Sir John Moore, a hero killed
during the Peninsular War against Napoleon, when the English
troops were about to evacuate their coastal toehold. The poem

was "The Burial of Sir John Moore." Even then I could recognize the first two lines, and the last of that favorite of my boyhood. The first two lines are:

> Not a drum was heard, not a funeral note,
> As his corse to the rampart we hurried

I remembered that "hurried" rhymes with "buried." I recognized the rest of the poem, but later could remember only the last line, which comes after the hero has been left as the English sail away:

> And left him alone in his glory.

Later, after a long search, I found a text. This, of course, would be in a forgotten and dilapidated copy of *The Home Book of Verse,* edition of 1912—a book that had never belonged to my father, God knows to whom. The author of the poem is a certain Charles Wolfe, a poet of no fame who died around 1820. It was one of the poems, I remember, which I had made my father read to me over and over, but not from that book.

Some time after the Mexican trip Eleanor went with me on a visit to meet my father and brother. On a Sunday afternoon, at my brother's house, I stood with a group of his friends, ice tinkling in glasses. I could see into another room where Eleanor and my father sat with chairs drawn almost together, heads leaning a little forward in a close and uninterrupted conversation.

By that time my father had announced to my brother that he himself had already made arrangements to go to a "retirement home" in Clarksville, where he would have a little apartment with a sitting room. The home was in a quiet section, where he could take walks.

On a later visit which Eleanor and I made to Kentucky my father was to come from Clarksville to my brother's house to see, and hold, our new baby daughter: a baby who so many years later would be thumbing over and over his old lexicon of

Liddell and Scott. Of that afternoon of her babyhood I remember little beyond the fact that he held her, his face leaning
slightly over her.

That was all I seemed to remember for some years except one
fact of great clarity: a day or two later, as I backed our car out of
the driveway of the retirement home I saw his face looking out
at us. He had drawn the curtains apart at the window of his sitting room and was watching us go.

We went off through the streets of Clarksville. The town had
long since become a booming little city. We went off through
streets largely unfamiliar to me so long after the time when I had
spent a year at school there. We drove on past factories and other
signs of progress, down the buzzing and humming concrete slab
to the point we joined the great highway northward.

That visit to Clarksville, then the face at a window, was the
last time I was to see my father. Alive and conscious.

One night a year or so later I woke to the telephone by my
bed. My father was dying. I managed to get a flight, and next
morning at my arrival, he was still alive. He had collapsed the
evening before while writing a letter and had fallen from his
chair, unconscious. Later, when he became conscious, injections
had relieved obviously intense pain. Now, unconscious, he occasionally moved. Once, as though by remarkable effort, his right
arm slowly rose in the air, and the hand moved as though trying
to grasp something.

My sister drove her fingernails into the biceps of my right
arm until the tips seemed to be touching in the muscle. She said:
"The medicine just drives the pain deeper."

After death had been certified, I went into his sitting room.
The unfinished letter was still on the desk. Across the sheet, to
the edge, was a long pen-stroke from the last word written,
downward—apparently made as he fainted and fell. The pen was
on the floor. I picked it up. I looked at the scarcely begun letter.
It began: "Dear Son."

He was approaching his eighty-sixth birthday. He had willed
to die alone, and without any medical intervention. The doctor

discovered that it was cancer of the prostate. My father, as I have earlier said, had never in his life seen a doctor or spent a day in bed except during a long illness when he was forty-two years old. This was simply independence of spirit.

Katherine Anne Porter, my dear old friend, wrote me a letter from Liège, Belgium, dated February 4, 1955. I quote a passage with some indicated deletions:

> The thought of your father suffering by himself because he didn't want to be trouble to any one is very painful; and must be to you. It was very heroic and characteristic, maybe he did what he wished to do, it takes very pure courage, surely above all at that age, to know death is near, and not ask any one to know what is happening. . . . I love his toughness of spirit, but he shouldn't have expected *you* to be tough about him! . . . I am sure everything was clear and right in his mind, but I understand the nature of loneliness.

He was not lonely. He was himself.

Once, when he was already very old, he and I were taking one of our walks together. Suddenly, out of silence, he said: "I don't think anybody could ever say that I didn't have guts." At the moment I was struck by his use of that lingo, a phrase so oddly uncharacteristic of him. More recently, however, I have been struck by another fact—the fact that he did not seem to be talking to me, simply to empty air. As to the world in a lingo which it would understand.

Later, on another such occasion, without context, as though looking into distance, he was to say: "I have lived a very happy life."

Booker T. Washington

(1856–1915)

The most widely recognized spokesman for African America in the decades following the death of Frederick Douglass, Booker T. Washington's most lasting legacy is the Tuskeegee Institute, which he founded on July 4, 1881, near the town of Tuskeegee, Alabama. Washington was born a slave in Franklin County, Virginia, located in an area of the state that soon became part of the newly formed state of West Virginia. After receiving an education at the Hampton Institute in Virginia, he taught there for a number of years before leaving to solicit funding for, then assist in the construction of, Tuskeegee Institute. The most outspoken advocate of the "accommodationist" view toward African-American racial uplift, Washington preached the necessity of acquiescence to white segregationist policies and the importance of basic agricultural and industrial education that would move former slaves further toward economic self-reliance. The highlight of his public speaking career occurred during the 1895 Atlanta Cotton States Exposition, organized by the prototypical New South booster Henry Grady. There he addressed a predominantly white southern audience and implored his fellow African Americans to "Drop your buckets where you are," for the white South stood ready to assist in the progress of the black race, if only blacks would accede to Jim Crow segregation laws. "In all things that are purely social," he told the crowd, "we can be as separate as the fingers, yet one as the hand in all things essential to mutual progress." The following year, the Supreme Court would codify this "separate but equal" doctrine in its decision on the Plessy v. Ferguson *case, essentially sanctioning the white South's solution to what was referred to at the time as "the Negro Problem."*

Originally published in serial form in Outlook, *a popular maga-*

zine of the day, Up from Slavery *(1901) represents a marked departure from earlier representations of slavery by Douglass, Jacobs, and others. Instead of emphasizing the outrages, abuses, and dehumanizing effects of human bondage, Washington attempts to portray it as an unfortunate but ultimately beneficial institution that lifted the African from ignorance and paganism to a state approaching civilization. All that was necessary to complete the civilizing process, he urged, was a solid education in the industrial or agricultural arts and the opportunity for useful work. Perhaps because he realized that the survival of Tuskeegee hinged upon the good graces of his white benefactors, Washington also takes the opportunity in his autobiography to downplay the racial violence that had been steadily increasing in the South since the end of Reconstruction, claiming—incredibly—that "in all my contact with the white people of the South I have never received a single personal insult." An easy target for intellectuals like W. E. B. DuBois, who decried the accommodationist position, Washington's views represented a pragmatic, if ultimately inadequate, response to southern racism. If Douglass was adept in writing his life within the conventions of the American success story, then Washington was even more conscious of invoking Benjamin Franklin's rags-to-riches motif, as is evident in the following excerpt from his autobiography, where he recounts the travails he experienced in order to gain admission to Hampton Institute.*

FROM *Up from Slavery*

ONE DAY, while at work in the coal-mine, I happened to overhear two miners talking about a great school for coloured people somewhere in Virginia. This was the first time that I had ever heard anything about any kind of school or college that was more pretentious than the little coloured school in our town.

In the darkness of the mine I noiselessly crept as close as I could to the two men who were talking. I heard one tell the other that not only was the school established for the members of my race, but that opportunities were provided by which poor but worthy students could work out all or part of the cost of board, and at the same time be taught some trade or industry.

As they went on describing the school, it seemed to me that it must be the greatest place on earth, and not even Heaven presented more attractions for me at that time than did the Hampton Normal and Agricultural Institute in Virginia, about which these men were talking. I resolved at once to go to that school, although I had no idea where it was, or how many miles away, or how I was going to reach it; I remembered only that I was on fire constantly with one ambition, and that was to go to Hampton. This thought was with me day and night.

After hearing of the Hampton Institute, I continued to work for a few months longer in the coal-mine. While at work there, I heard of a vacant position in the household of General Lewis Ruffner, the owner of the salt-furnace and coal-mine. Mrs. Viola Ruffner, the wife of General Ruffner, was a "Yankee" woman from Vermont. Mrs. Ruffner had a reputation all through the vicinity for being very strict with her servants, and especially with the boys who tried to serve her. Few of them had remained with her more than two or three weeks. They all left with the same excuse: she was too strict. I decided, however, that I would rather try Mrs. Ruffner's house than remain in the coal-mine, and so my mother applied to her for the vacant position. I was hired at a salary of $5 per month.

I had heard so much about Mrs. Ruffner's severity that I was almost afraid to see her, and trembled when I went into her presence. I had not lived with her many weeks, however, before I began to understand her. I soon began to learn that, first of all, she wanted everything kept clean about her, that she wanted things done promptly and systematically, and that at the bottom of everything she wanted absolute honesty and frankness. Nothing must be sloven or slipshod; every door, every fence, must be kept in repair.

I cannot now recall how long I lived with Mrs. Ruffner before going to Hampton, but I think it must have been a year and a half. At any rate, I here repeat what I have said more than once before, that the lessons that I learned in the home of Mrs. Ruffner were as valuable to me as any education I have ever gotten anywhere since. Even to this day I never see bits of paper scattered around a house or in the street that I do not want to pick them up at once. I never see a filthy yard that I do not want to clean it, a paling off of a fence that I do not want to put it on, an unpainted or unwhitewashed house that I do want to paint or whitewash it, or a button off one's clothes, or a grease-spot on them or on a floor, that I do not want to call attention to it.

From fearing Mrs. Ruffner I soon learned to look upon her as one of my best friends. When she found that she could trust me she did so implicitly. During the one or two winters that I was with her she gave me an opportunity to go to school for an hour in the day during a portion of the winter months, but most of my studying was done at night, sometimes alone, sometimes under some one whom I could hire to teach me. Mrs. Ruffner always encouraged and sympathized with me in all my efforts to get an education. It was while living with her that I began to get together my first library. I secured a dry-goods box, knocked out one side of it, put some shelves in it, and began putting into it every kind of book that I could get my hands upon, and called it my "library."

Notwithstanding my success at Mrs. Ruffner's I did not give up the idea of going to Hampton Institute. In the fall of 1872 I determined to make an effort to get there, although, as I have stated, I had no idea of the direction in which Hampton was, or what it would cost to go there. I do not think that anyone thoroughly sympathized with me in my ambition to go to Hampton unless it was my mother, and she was troubled with a grave fear that I was starting out on a "wild-goose chase." At any rate, I got only a half-hearted consent from her that I might start. The small amount of money that I had earned had been consumed by my stepfather and the remainder of the family, with the exception of a very few dollars, and so I had very little with which to buy clothes and pay travelling expenses. My brother

John helped me all that he could, but of course that was not a great deal, for his work was in the coal-mine, where he did not earn much, and most of what he did earn went in the direction of paying the household expenses.

Perhaps the thing that touched and pleased me most in connection with my starting for Hampton was the interest that many of the older coloured people took in the matter. They had spent the best days of their lives in slavery, and hardly expected to live to see the time when they would see a member of their race leave home to attend a boardingschool. Some of these older people would give me a nickel, others a quarter, or a handkerchief.

Finally the great day came, and I started for Hampton. I had only a small, cheap satchel that contained what few articles of clothing I could get. My mother at the time was rather weak and broken in health. I hardly expected to see her again, and thus our parting was all the more sad. She, however, was very brave through it all. At that time there were no through trains connecting that part of West Virginia with eastern Virginia. Trains ran only a portion of the way, and the remainder of the distance was travelled by stagecoaches.

The distance from Malden to Hampton is about five hundred miles. I had not been away from home many hours before it began to grow painfully evident that I did not have enough money to pay my fare to Hampton. One experience I shall long remember. I had been travelling over the mountains most of the afternoon in an old-fashioned stage-coach, when, late in the evening, the coach stopped for the night at a common unpainted house called a hotel. All the other passengers except myself were whites. In my ignorance I supposed that the little hotel existed for the purpose of accommodating the passengers who travelled on the stagecoach. The difference that the colour of one's skin would make I had not thought anything about. After all the other passengers had been shown rooms and were getting ready for supper, I shyly presented myself before the man at the desk. It is true I had practically no money in my pocket with which to pay for bed or food, but I had hoped in some way to beg my way into the good graces of the landlord, for at that season in the mountains of Virginia the weather was cold, and I wanted to get indoors for the night. Without asking as to whether I had any money, the man at the desk firmly refused to even consider the matter of providing me with food or lodging. This was my first experience in finding out what the colour of my skin meant. In some way I managed to keep warm by walking about, and so got through the night. My whole soul was so bent upon reaching Hampton that I did not have time to cherish any bitterness toward the hotel-keeper.

By walking, begging rides both in wagons and in the cars, in some way, after a number of days, I reached the city of Richmond, Virginia, about eighty-two miles from Hampton. When I reached there, tired, hungry, and dirty, it was late in the night. I had never been in a large city, and this rather added to my misery. When I reached Richmond, I was completely out of money. I had not a single acquaintance in the place, and, being unused to city ways, I did not know where to go. I applied at several places for lodging, but they all wanted money, and that was what I did not have. Knowing nothing else better to do, I walked the streets. In doing this I passed by many foodstands where fried chicken and half-moon apple pies were piled high and made to present a most tempting appearance. At that time it seemed to me that I would have promised all that I expected to possess in the future to have gotten hold of one of those chicken legs or one of those pies. But I could not get either of these, nor anything else to eat.

I must have walked the streets till after midnight. At last I became so exhausted that I could walk no longer. I was tired, I was hungry, I was everything but discouraged. Just about the time when I reached extreme physical exhaustion, I came upon a portion of a street where the board sidewalk was considerably elevated. I waited for a few minutes, till I was sure that no passers-by could see me, and then crept under the sidewalk and lay for the night upon the ground, with my satchel of clothing for a pillow. Nearly all night I could hear the tramp of feet over my head. The next morning I found myself refreshed, but I was extremely hungry, because it had been a long time since I had had sufficient food. As soon as it became light enough for me to see my surroundings I noticed that I was near a large ship, and that this ship seemed to be unloading a cargo of pig iron. I went at once to the vessel and asked the captain to permit me to help unload the vessel in order to get money for food. The captain, a white man, who seemed to be kind-hearted, consented. I worked long enough to earn money for my breakfast, and it seems to me, as I remember it now, to have been about the best breakfast that I have ever eaten.

My work pleased the captain so well that he told me if I desired I could continue working for a small amount per day. This I was very glad to do. I continued working on this vessel for a number of days. After buying food with the small wages I received there was not much left to add to the amount I must get to pay my way to Hampton. In order to economize in every way possible, so as to be sure to reach Hampton in a reasonable time, I continued to sleep under the same sidewalk that gave me shelter the first night I was in Richmond. Many years after that the coloured citizens of Richmond very kindly tendered me a reception at which there must have been two thousand people present. This reception was held not far from the spot where I slept the first night I spent in that city, and I must confess that my mind was more upon the sidewalk that first gave me shelter than upon the reception, agreeable and cordial as it was.

When I had saved what I considered enough money with which to reach Hampton, I thanked the captain of the vessel for his kindness, and started again. Without any unusual occurrence I reached Hampton, with a surplus of exactly fifty cents with which to begin my education. To me it had been a long, eventful journey; but the first sight of the large, three-story, brick school building seemed to have rewarded me for all that I had undergone in order to reach the place. If the people who gave the money to provide that building could appreciate the influence the sight of it had upon me, as well as upon thousands of other youths, they would feel all the more encouraged to make such gifts. It seemed to me to be the largest and most beautiful building I had ever seen. The sight of it seemed to give me new life. I felt that a new kind of existence had now begun—that life would now have a new meaning. I felt that I had reached the promised land, and I resolved to let no obstacle prevent me from putting forth the highest effort to fit myself to accomplish the most good in the world.

As soon as possible after reaching the grounds of the Hampton Institute, I presented myself before the head teacher for assignment to a class. Having been so long without proper food, a bath and change of clothing, I did not, of course, make a very favourable impression upon her, and I could see at once that there were doubts in her mind about the wisdom of admitting me as a student. I felt that I could hardly blame her if she got the idea that I was a worthless loafer or tramp. For some time she did not refuse to admit me, neither did she decide in my favour, and I continued to linger about her, and to impress her in all the ways I could with my worthiness. In the meantime I saw her admitting other students, and that added greatly to my discomfort, for I felt, deep down in my heart, that I could do as well as they, if I could only get a chance to show what was in me.

After some hours had passed, the head teacher said to me: "The adjoining recitation-room needs sweeping. Take the broom and sweep it."

It occurred to me at once that here was my chance. Never did I receive an order with more delight. I knew that I could sweep, for Mrs. Ruffner had thoroughly taught me how to do that when I lived with her.

I swept the recitation-room three times. Then I got a dusting-cloth and I dusted it four times. All the woodwork around the walls, every bench, table, and desk, I went over four times with my dusting-cloth. Besides, every piece of furniture had been moved and every closet and corner in the room had been thoroughly cleaned. I had the feeling that in a large measure my future depended upon the impression I made upon the teacher in the cleaning of that room. When I was through, I reported to the head teacher. She was a "Yankee" woman who knew just where to look for dirt. She went into the room and inspected the floor and closets; then she took her handkerchief and rubbed it on the woodwork about the walls, and over the table and benches. When she was unable to find one bit of dirt on the floor, or a particle of dust on any of the furniture, she quietly remarked, "I guess you will do to enter this institution."

I was one of the happiest souls on earth. The sweeping of that room was my college examination, and never did any youth pass an examination for entrance into Harvard or Yale that gave him more genuine satisfaction. I have passed several examinations since then, but I have always felt that this was the best one I ever passed.

Sam R. Watkins

(1839–1901)

Born in the middle Tennessee town of Columbia, Sam Watkins fought with the Army of the Tennessee in most of the major engagements of the Civil War. His regiment saw so many battles that, out of 120 men who enlisted in his company at the beginning of the war in 1861, only seven survived to return to their homes at the conclusion of the conflict. Watkins returned to civilian life upon the defeat of the Confederacy, writing his memoirs twenty years later with "a house full of rebels clustering around my knees and bumping my elbows."

"Co. Aytch": A Side Show of the Big Show was first published in Watkins's hometown newspaper, the Columbia Herald, *in 1881– 82, then appeared as a book shortly thereafter. Because he saw firsthand so much of the war and described the events in which he participated with such frankness, his account is an invaluable resource, not only for military historians but for readers interested in understanding how enlisted men viewed the cause of the Confederacy. His caustic remarks about his commanding officers and descriptions of lax discipline in the ranks are a strong corrective to the largely mythologized tales of the common soldier's unquestioning loyalty to the Confederacy; however, his accounts of the rebels' heroism and deadly aim suggest that their reputation as fierce fighters was well earned. Quotes from "Co. Aytch" are a prominent feature of Ken Burns's award-winning 1991 television documentary* The Civil War. *In the first half of the excerpt that follows, Watkins describes the retreat after the southern defeat at Shiloh, where the enlisted men react to news of the so-called twenty slave law and ridicule their officers; conversely, the second portion recounts the tremendous sacrifices made at the Battle of Franklin, fought in Novem-*

ber of 1864. Half a century later, "Fugitive" poet Allen Tate would be inspired to write his "Ode to the Confederate Dead" after visiting the Confederate cemetery at Franklin and meditating on the fallen soldiers' willingness to die for a cause that was, by that late point in the war, clearly lost.

FROM *"Co. Aytch":*
A Side Show of the Big Show

CORINTH

WELL, here we were, again "reorganizing," and after our lax discipline on the road to and from Virginia, and after a big battle, which always disorganizes an army, what wonder is it that some men had to be shot, merely for discipline's sake? And what wonder that General Bragg's name became a terror to deserters and evil doers? Men were shot by scores, and no wonder the army had to be reorganized. Soldiers had enlisted for twelve months only, and had faithfully complied with their volunteer obligations; the terms for which they had enlisted had expired, and they naturally looked upon it that they had a right to go home. They had done their duty faithfully and well. They wanted to see their families; in fact, wanted to go home anyhow. War had become a reality; they were tired of it. A law had been passed by the Confederate States Congress called the conscript act. A soldier had no right to volunteer and to choose the branch of service he preferred.* He was conscripted.

From this time on till the end of the war, a soldier was simply a machine, a conscript. It was mighty rough on rebels. We cursed the war, we cursed Bragg, we cursed the Southern Con-

---

* Watkins was in error on this point. The conscription act allowed soldiers held to service by its terms thirty days to enter units of their own choice.

federacy. All our pride and valor had gone, and we were sick of war and the Southern Confederacy.

A law was made by the Confedcrate States Congress about this time allowing every person who owned twenty negroes to go home. It gave us the blues; we wanted twenty negroes. Negro property suddenly became very valuable, and there was raised the howl of "rich man's war, poor man's fight." The glory of the war, the glory of the South, the glory and the pride of our volunteers had no charms for the conscript.

We were directed to re-elect our officers, and the country was surprised to see thc sample of a conscript's choice. The conscript had no choice. He was callous, and indifferent whether he had a captain or not. Those who were at first officers had resigned and gone home, because they were officers. The poor private, a contemptible conscript, was left to howl and gnash his teeth. The war might as well have ended then and there. The boys were "hacked," nay, whipped. They were shorn of the locks of their glory. They had but one ambition now, and that was to get out of the army in some way or other. They wanted to join the cavalry or artillery or home guards or pioneer corps or to be "yaller dogs," or anything.

[The average staff officer and courier were always called "yaller dogs," and were regarded as non-combatants and a nuisance, and the average private never let one pass without whistling and calling dogs. In fact, the general had to issue an army order threatening punishment for the ridicule hurled at staff officers and couriers. They were looked upon as simply "hangers on," or in other words, as yellow sheep-killing dogs, that if you would say "booh" at, would yelp and get under their master's heels. Mike Snyder was General George Maney's "yaller dog," and I believe here is where Joe Jefferson, in Rip Van Winkle, got the name of Rip's dog Snyder. At all times of day or night you could hear, "wheer, hyat, hyat, haer, haer, hugh, Snyder, whoopee, hyat, whoopee, Snyder, here, here," when a staff officer or courier happened to pass. The reason of this was that the private knew and felt that there was just that much more loading, shooting and fighting for him; and there are the fewest number of instances on record where a staff officer or courier ever fired a gun in their country's cause; and even at this late day, when I hear an old soldier telling of being on some general's staff, I always think of the letter "E." In fact, later in the war I was detailed as special courier and staff officer for General Hood, which office I held three days. But while I held the office in passing a guard I always told them I was on Hood's staff, and ever afterwards I made those three days' staff business last me the balance of the war. I could pass any guard in the army by using the magic words, "staff officer." It beat all the countersigns ever invented. It was the "open sesame" of war and discipline.]

Their last hope had set. They hated war. To their minds the South was a great tyrant, and the Confederacy a fraud. They were deserting by thousands. They had no love or respect for General Bragg. When men were to be shot or whipped, the whole army was marched to the horrid scene to see a poor trembling wretch tied to a post and a platoon of twelve men drawn up in line to put him to death, and the hushed command of "Ready, aim, fire!" would make the soldier, or conscript, I should say, loathe the very name of Southern Confederacy. And when some miserable wretch was to be whipped and branded for being absent ten days without leave, we had to see him kneel down and have his head shaved smooth and slick as a peeled onion, and then stripped to the naked skin. Then a strapping fellow with a big rawhide would make the blood flow and spurt at every lick, the wretch begging and howling like a hound, and then he was branded with a red hot iron with the letter D on both hips, when he was marched through the army to the music of the "Rogue's March." It was enough. None of General Bragg's soldiers ever loved him. They had no faith in his ability as a general. He was looked upon as a merciless tyrant. The soldiers were very scantily fed. Bragg never was a good feeder or commissary-general. Rations with us were always scarce. No extra rations were ever allowed to the negroes who were with us as servants. No coffee or whisky or tobacco were ever allowed to be issued to the troops. If they obtained these luxuries, they were not from the government. These luxuries were withheld in order to crush the very heart and spirit of his troops. We were crushed. Bragg was the great autocrat. In the mind of the soldier, his word was law. He loved to crush the spirit of his men. The more of a hang-dog look they had about them the better was General Bragg pleased. Not a single soldier in the whole army ever loved or respected him. But he is dead now.

Peace to his ashes!

We became starved skeletons; naked and ragged rebels. The chronic diarrhea became the scourge of the army. Corinth became one vast hospital. Almost the whole army attended the sick call every morning. All the water courses went dry, and we used water out of filthy pools.

Halleck was advancing; we had to fortify Corinth. A vast army, Grant, Buell, Halleck, Sherman, all were advancing on Corinth. Our troops were in no condition to fight. In fact, they had seen enough of this miserable yet tragic farce. They were ready to ring down the curtain, put out the footlights and go home. They loved the Union anyhow, and were always opposed to this war. But breathe softly the name of Bragg. It had more terror than the advancing hosts of Halleck's army. The shot and shell would come tearing through our ranks. Every now and then a soldier was killed or wounded, and we thought what "magnificent" folly. Death was welcome. Halleck's whole army of blue coats had no terror now. When we were drawn up in line of battle, a detail of one-tenth of the army was placed in our rear to shoot us down if we ran. No pack of hounds under the master's lash, or body of penitentiary convicts were ever under greater surveillance. We were tenfold worse than slaves; our morale was a thing of the past; the glory of war and the pride of manhood had been sacrificed upon Bragg's tyrannical holocaust. But enough of this.

*   *   *

Franklin

"The death-angel gathers its last harvest."

Kind reader, right here my pen, and courage, and ability fail me. I shrink from butchery. Would to God I could tear the page from these memoirs and from my own memory. It is the blackest page in the history of the war of the Lost Cause. It was the bloodiest battle of modern times in any war. It was the finishing stroke to the independence of the Southern Confederacy. I was there. I saw it. My flesh trembles, and creeps, and crawls when I think of it today. My heart almost ceases to beat at the horrid recollection. Would to God that I had never witnessed such a scene!

I cannot describe it. It beggars description. I will not attempt to describe it. I could not. The death-angel was there to gather its last harvest. It was the grand coronation of death. Would that I could turn the page. But I feel, though I did so, that page would still be there, teeming with its scenes of horror and blood. I can only tell of what I saw.

Our regiment was resting in the gap of a range of hills in plain view of the city of Franklin. We could see the battleflags of the enemy waving in the breeze. Our army had been depleted of its strength by a forced march from Spring Hill, and stragglers lined the road. Our artillery had not yet come up, and could not be brought into action. Our cavalry was across Harpeth river, and our army was but in poor condition to make an assault. While resting on this hill-side, I saw a courier dash up to our commanding general, B. F. Cheatham, and the word, "Attention!" was given. I knew then that we would soon be in action. Forward, march. We passed over the hill and through a little skirt of woods.

The enemy were fortified right across the Franklin pike, in the suburbs of the town. Right here in these woods a detail of skirmishers was called for. Our regiment was detailed. We deployed as skirmishers, firing as we advanced on the left of the turnpike road. If I had not been a skirmisher on that day, I would not have been writing this today, in the year of our Lord 1882.

It was four o'clock on that dark and dismal December day when the line of battle was formed, and those devoted heroes were ordered forward, to

> "Strike for their altars and their fires,
> For the green graves of their sires,
> For God and their native land."

As they marched on down through an open field toward the rampart of blood and death, the Federal batteries began to open and mow down and gather into the garner of death, as brave, and good, and pure spirits as the world ever saw. The twilight of evening had begun to gather as a precursor of the coming blackness of midnight darkness that was to envelop a scene so sickening and horrible that it is impossible for me to describe it. "Forward, men," is repeated all along the line. A sheet of fire was poured into our very faces, and for a moment we halted as if in despair, as the terrible avalanche of shot and shell laid low those brave and gallant heroes, whose bleeding wounds attested that the struggle would be desperate. Forward, men! The air loaded with death-dealing missiles. Never on this earth did men fight against such terrible odds. It seemed that the very elements of heaven and earth were in one mighty uproar. Forward, men! And the blood spurts in a perfect jet from the dead and wounded. The earth is red with blood. It runs in streams, making little rivulets as it flows. Occasionally there was a little lull in the storm of battle, as the men were loading their guns, and for a few moments it seemed as if night tried to cover the scene with her mantle. The death-angel shrieks and laughs and old Father Time is busy with his sickle, as he gathers in the last harvest of death, crying, More, more, more! while his rapacious maw is glutted with the slain.

But the skirmish line being deployed out, extending a little

wider than the battle did—passing through a thicket of small
locusts, where Brown, orderly sergeant of Company B, was
killed—we advanced on toward the breastworks, on and on. I
had made up my mind to die—felt glorious. We pressed forward
until I heard the terrific roar of battle open on our right. Cleburne's division was charging their works. I passed on until I got
to their works, and got over on their (the Yankees') side. But in
fifty yards of where I was the scene was lit up by fires that
seemed like hell itself. It appeared to be but one line of streaming fire. Our troops were upon one side of the breastworks, and
the Federals on the other. I ran up on the line of works, where
our men were engaged. Dead soldiers filled the entrenchments.
The firing was kept up until after midnight, and gradually died
out. We passed the night where we were. But when the morrow's sun began to light up the eastern sky with its rosy hues,
and we looked over the battlefield, O, my God! what did we see!
It was a grand holocaust of death. Death had held high carnival
there that night. The dead were piled the one on the other all
over the ground. I never was so horrified and appalled in my life.
Horses, like men, had died game on the gory breastworks. General Adams' horse had his fore feet on one side of the works and
his hind feet on the other, dead. The general seems to have been
caught so that he was held to the horse's back, sitting almost as if
living, riddled, and mangled, and torn with balls. General Cleburne's mare had her fore feet on top of the works, dead in that
position. General Cleburne's body was pierced with forty-nine
bullets, through and through. General Strahl's horse lay by the
roadside and the general by his side, both dead, and all his staff.
General Gist, a noble and brave cavalier from South Carolina,
was lying with his sword reaching across the breastworks still
grasped in his hand. He was lying there dead. All dead! They
sleep in the graveyard yonder at Ashwood, almost in sight of my
home, where I am writing today. They sleep the sleep of the
brave. We love and cherish their memory. They sleep beneath
the ivy-mantled walls of St. John's church, where they expressed
a wish to be buried. The private soldier sleeps where he fell,

piled in one mighty heap. Four thousand five hundred privates! all lying side by side in death! Thirteen generals were killed and wounded. Four thousand five hundred men slain, all piled and heaped together at one place. I cannot tell the number of others killed and wounded. God alone knows that. We'll all find out on the morning of the final resurrection.

Kind friends, I have attempted in my poor and feeble way to tell you of this (I can hardly call it) battle. It should be called by some other name. But, like all other battles, it, too, has gone into history. I leave it with you. I do not know who was to blame. It lives in the memory of the poor old Rebel soldier who went through that trying and terrible ordeal. We shed a tear for the dead. They are buried and forgotten. We meet no more on earth. But up yonder, beyond the sunset and the night, away beyond the clouds and tempest, away beyond the stars that ever twinkle and shine in the blue vault above us, away yonder by the great white throne, and by the river of life, where the Almighty and Eternal God sits, surrounded by the angels and archangels and the redeemed of earth, we will meet again and see those noble and brave spirits who gave up their lives for their country's cause that night at Franklin, Tennessee. A life given for one's country is never lost. It blooms again beyond the grave in a land of beauty and of love. Hanging around the throne of sapphire and gold, a rich garland awaits the coming of him who died for his country, and when the horologe of time has struck its last note upon his dying brow, Justice hands the record of life to Mercy, and Mercy pleads with Jesus, and God, for his sake, receives him in his eternal home beyond the skies at last and forever.

Eudora Welty

(1909–   )

Regarded by many as the most respected living southern writer today, Eudora Welty's fiction has graced the world with its humor, its eye for suggestive detail, and its attention to the nuances of the spoken word. Though her roots in the interior South do not run especially deep—her mother and father, who came from West Virginia and Ohio, respectively, moved to Jackson shortly before the birth of their daughter—Welty evokes a sense of place in her writing that only a handful of other southern authors have matched. She attended Mississippi State College for Women for two years but finished her bachelor's degree at the University of Wisconsin, where she majored in English. After a year at the Columbia University School of Business she returned to Mississippi, working as a reporter for the Memphis Commercial Appeal *and as a photographer for the Works Progress Administration before settling into her vocation as a fiction writer. Her first story, "Death of a Traveling Salesman," published in 1936, signaled the entrance of a skilled storyteller. In the early years of her career she produced numerous undisputed masterpieces of short fiction, including "Why I Live at the P. O.," "A Worn Path," "Petrified Man," and "The Wide Net." Though her first novel,* The Robber Bridegroom *(1942), received favorable reviews, it was her second effort at long fiction,* Delta Wedding *(1954), that provided conclusive proof of Welty's mastery of that genre. Her other books include four collections of short stories, now combined in* The Collected Stories of Eudora Welty *(1980), and three other novels,* The Ponder Heart *(1954),* Losing Battles *(1970), and* The Optimist's Daughter *(1972), for which she won the Pulitzer Prize. The photographs that Welty took of depression-era Mississippi while working for the WPA have been published in* One Time, One Place *(1971) and an expanded collection,* Photographs *(1989).*

One Writer's Beginnings, *published in 1984, began as a series of three lectures delivered at Harvard in 1983. Like other southern writers' reminiscences, it traces the sources of the author's art to the region's rich storytelling tradition. Titled "Listening," "Learning to See," and "Finding a Voice," the three sections recount in stages the gradual process by which Welty came to take possession of her own sense of place and transform it into literature of lasting quality. The following excerpt, taken from the "Learning to See" chapter, explores the manner in which the remembered particular can provide a key to unlocking the mystery of our parents' personalities.*

FROM *One Writer's Beginnings*

WHEN WE SET OUT in our five-passenger Oakland touring car on our summer trip to Ohio and West Virginia to visit the two families, my mother was the navigator. She sat at the alert all the way at Daddy's side as he drove, correlating the AAA Blue Book and the speedometer, often with the baby on her lap. She'd call out, "All right, Daddy: '86-point-2, crossroads. Jog right, past white church. Gravel ends.'—and there's the church!" she'd say, as though we had scored. Our road always became her adversary. "This doesn't surprise me at all," she'd say as Daddy backed up a mile or so into our own dust on a road that had petered out. "I could've told you a road that looked like that had little intention of going anywhere."

"It was the first one we'd seen all day going in the right direction," he'd say. His sense of direction was unassailable, and every mile of our distance was familiar to my father by rail. But the way we set out to go was popularly known as "through the country."

My mother's hat rode in the back with the children, suspended over our heads in a pillowcase. It rose and fell with us
when we hit the bumps, thumped our heads and batted our ears
in an authoritative manner when sometimes we bounced as high
as the ceiling. This was 1917 or 1918; a lady couldn't expect to
travel without a hat.

Edward and I rode with our legs straight out in front of us
over some suitcases. The rest of the suitcases rode just outside
the doors, strapped on the running boards. Cars weren't made
with trunks. The tools were kept under the back seat and were
heard from in syncopation with the bumps; we'd jump out of
the car so Daddy could get them out and jack up the car to
patch and vulcanize a tire, or haul out the tow rope or the tire
chains. If it rained so hard we couldn't see the road in front of
us, we waited it out, snapped in behind the rain curtains and
playing "Twenty Questions."

My mother was not naturally observant, but she could scrutinize; when she gave the surroundings her attention, it was to
verify something—the truth or a mistake, hers or another's. My
father kept his eyes on the road, with glances toward the horizon
and overhead. My brother Edward periodically stood up in the
back seat with his eyelids fluttering while he played the harmon-
ica, "Old Macdonald had a farm" and "Abdul the Bulbul Amir,"
and the baby slept in Mother's lap and only woke up when we
crossed some rattling old bridge. "*There's* a river!" he'd crow to
us all. "Why, it certainly *is*," my mother would reassure him,
patting him back to sleep. I rode as a hypnotic, with my set gaze
on the landscape that vibrated past at twenty-five miles an hour.
We were all wrapped by the long ride into some cocoon of our
own.

The journey took about a week each way, and each day had
my parents both in its grip. Riding behind my father I could see
that the road had him by the shoulders, by the hair under his
driving cap. It took my mother to make him stop. I inherited his
nervous energy in the way I can't stop writing on a story. It
makes me understand how Ohio had him around the heart, as

West Virginia had my mother. Writers and travelers are mesmerized alike by knowing of their destinations.

And all the time that we think we're getting there so fast, how slowly we do move. In the days of our first car trip, Mother proudly entered in her log, "Mileage today: 161!" with an exclamation mark.

"A Detroit car passed us yesterday." She always kept those logs, with times, miles, routes of the day's progress, and expenses totaled up.

That kind of travel made you conscious of borders; you rode ready for them. Crossing a river, crossing a county line, crossing a state line—especially crossing the line you couldn't see but knew was there, between the South and the North—you could draw a breath and feel the difference.

The Blue Book warned you of the times for the ferries to run; sometimes there were waits of an hour between. With rivers and roads alike winding, you had to cross some rivers three times to be done with them. Lying on the water at the foot of a river bank would be a ferry no bigger than somebody's back porch. When our car had been driven on board—often it was down a roadless bank, through sliding stones and runaway gravel, with Daddy simply aiming at the two-plank gangway— father and older children got out of the car to enjoy the trip. My brother and I got barefooted to stand on wet, sun-warm boards that, weighted with your car, seemed exactly on the level with the water; our feet were the same as in the river. Some of those ferries were operated by a single man pulling hand over hand on a rope bleached and frazzled as if made from cornshucks.

I watched the frayed rope running through his hands. I thought it would break before we could reach the other side.

"No, it's not going to break," said my father. "It's never broken before, has it?" he asked the ferry man.

"No sirree."

"You see? If it never broke before, it's not going to break this time."

His general belief in life's well-being worked either way. If you had a pain, it was "Have you ever had it before? You have? It's not going to kill you, then. If you've had the same thing before, you'll be all right in the morning."

My mother couldn't have more profoundly disagreed with that.

"You're such an optimist, dear," she often said with a sigh, as she did now on the ferry.

"You're a good deal of a pessimist, sweetheart."

"I certainly *am*."

And yet I was well aware as I stood between them with the water running over my toes, he the optimist was the one who was prepared for the worst, and she the pessimist was the dare-devil: he the one who on our trip carried chains and a coil of rope and an ax all upstairs to our hotel bedroom every night in case of fire, and she the one—before I was born—when there *was* a fire, had broken loose from all hands and run back—on crutches, too—into the burning house to rescue her set of Dickens which she flung, all twenty-four volumes, from the window before she jumped out after them, all for Daddy to catch.

"I make no secret of my lifelong fear of the water," said my mother, who on ferry boats remained inside the car, clasping the baby to her—my brother Walter, who was destined to prowl the waters of the Pacific Ocean in a minesweeper.

As soon as the sun was beginning to go down, we went more slowly. My father would drive sizing up the towns, inspecting the hotel in each, deciding where we could safely spend the night. Towns little or big had beginnings and ends, they reached to an edge and stopped, where the country began again as though they hadn't happened. They were intact and to themselves. You could see a town lying ahead in its whole, as definitely formed as a plate on a table. And your road entered and ran straight through the heart of it; you could see it all, laid out for your passage through. Towns, like people, had clear identities and your imagination could go out to meet them. You saw houses, yards, fields, and people busy in them, the people that had a life where they were. You could hear their bank clocks striking, you could smell their bakeries. You would know those towns again, recognize the salient detail, seen so close up. Nothing was blurred, and in passing along Main Street, slowed down from twenty-five to twenty miles an hour, you didn't miss anything on either side. Going somewhere "through the country" acquainted you with the whole way there and back.

My mother never fully gave in to her pleasure in our trip—for pleasure every bit of it was to us all—because she knew we were traveling with a loaded pistol in the pocket on the door of the car on Daddy's side. I doubt if my father fired off any kind of gun in his life, but he could not have carried his family from Jackson, Mississippi, to West Virginia and Ohio through the country, unprotected.

THIS WAS NOT the first time I'd been brought here to visit Grandma in West Virginia, but the first visit I barely remembered. Where I stood now was inside the house where my mother had been born and where she grew up. It was a low, gray-weathered wooden house with a broad hall through the middle of it with the light of day at each end, the house that Ned Andrews, her father, had built to stand on the very top of the highest mountain he could find.

"And here's where I first began to read my Dickens," Mother said, pointing. "Under that very bed. Hiding my candle. To keep them from knowing what I was up to all night."

"But where did it all *come* from?" I asked her at last. "All that Dickens?"

"Why, Papa gave me that set of Dickens for agreeing to let them cut off my hair," she said, as if surprised that a reason like that wouldn't have occurred to me. "In those days, they thought very long, thick hair like mine would sap a child's strength. I said *No!* I wanted my hair left the very way it was. They offered me gold earrings first—in those days little girls often developed a wish to have their ears pierced and fitted with little gold rings. I said *No!* I'd rather keep my hair. Then Papa said, 'What about books? I'll have them send a whole set of Charles Dickens to you, right up the river from Baltimore, in a barrel.' I agreed."

Ned Andrews had been the county's youngest member of the bar. He quickly made a name for himself on the side as an orator. When he gave the dedicatory address for the opening of a new courthouse in Nicholas County, West Virginia, my mother put away a copy. He is praising the architecture of the building: "The student turns with the sigh of relief from the crumbling pillars and columns of Athens and Alexandria to the symmetrical and colossal temples of the New World. As time eats from the tombstones of the past the epitaphs of primeval greatness, and covers the pyramids with the moss of forgetfulness, she directs the eye to the new temples of art and progress that make America the monumental beacon-light of the world."

People may have expected the highfalutin in oratory in those days, but they might not have expected Ned's courtroom flair. There was a murder trial of a woman given to fortunetelling. She had been overheard reading in an old man's cards that his days were numbered. When, the very next day, this old man had been found in his bed dead from a gunshot wound, it appeared to the public that the fortuneteller might have known too much about it. She was put on trial for murder. Ned Andrews' defense centered on the well-known fact that the old man kept his loaded gun mounted at all times over the head of his bed. This was the gun that had shot him. The old man could have discharged it perfectly easily himself, Ned argued, by carelessly bouncing on the bed a little bit. He proposed to prove it, and invited the jury of dubious mountaineers to watch him do it. Leading them all the way up the mountain to the old man's cabin, he mounted the gun in place on its rests, having first loaded it with blank shells, and while they watched he mimicked the old man and made a running jump onto the bed. The gun jarred loose, tumbled down, and fired at him. He rested his case. The fortuneteller was without any more ado declared not guilty.

He was brim full of talents. He'd attended Trinity College (later, Duke University) where he organized a literary society; he'd been a journalist and a photographer in Norfolk, Virginia, and in West Virginia where he'd run away to, to seek adventure, he'd turned into a lawyer. He seems to have been a legendary fisherman in those mountain streams, is still now and then referred to in local sportsmen's tales. Ned was impervious to the sting of bees and could always be summoned to capture a wild swarm. Ned was the one they sent for when someone fell down an empty well, because he was not afraid to harness himself and be lowered into the deathly gasses at the bottom and bring the unconscious victim up again.

Yet the human failings Mother could least forgive in other people, she regarded with only tenderness in him. I gathered—slowly and over the years I gathered—that sometimes he drank. He told tall tales to his wife, Eudora Carden. He told one to begin with, in order to marry her, saying he was of age to do so, when he was nineteen and four years younger than she. She was superstitious; he loved to tease her with tricks, to stage elaborate charades with the connivance of one of his little boys, that preyed on her fear of ghosts. He shocked her with a tale—Mother said there was nothing to prove it wasn't a fact—that one of the Andrews ancestors had been hanged in Ireland. Eudora Carden came from the home of a strongly dedicated Baptist preacher, and about all preachers he was irreverent and irrepressible. I have seen photographs he took of her—tintypes; it's clear that he took them with great care to show how beautiful he found her. In one she is standing up behind a chair, with her long hands crossed at the wrist over the back of it; she is dressed in her best, with her dark hair drawn high above her oval face and tucked with a flower that looks like a wild rose. She is very young. She has long gray eyes over high cheekbones; she is gazing to the front, looking straight at him. Her mouth is sensitive, her lips youthfully full. She told her daughter Chessie years later that she was objecting to his taking this picture because she was pregnant at the time, and the pose—the crossed hands on the back of a chair—had been to hide that. (With my mother herself, I wondered, her first child?) When she came back from the well on cold mornings, her hands would be bleeding from breaking the ice on it: this is what my mother would remember when she looked at those soft hands in the tintypes.

I don't know from whom it came or to whom it was passed, but at one time an old, home-made drawing of the Andrews family tree came into my mother's hands. It was rolled up; if unrolled it was capable of rattling shut the next instant. The tree was drawn as a living tree, spreading from a rooted trunk, every branch, twig, and leaf in clear outline, all with names and dates on them in a copperplate handwriting. The most riveting feature was the thick branch stemming from near the base of the main trunk: it was broken off short to a jagged end, branchless and leafless, and labeled "Joseph, Killed by lightning."

It had been executed with the finest possible pen in ink grown very pale, as if it had been drawn in watered maple syrup. The leaves weren't stiffly drawn or conventional ellipses, all alike, but each one daintily fashioned with a pointed tip and turned on its stem this way or that, as if this family tree were tossed by a slight breeze. The massed whole had the look, at that time to me, of a children's puzzle in which you were supposed to find your mother. I found mine—only a tiny leaf on a twig of a branch near the top, hardly big enough to hold her tiny name.

The Andrews branch my mother came from represents the mix most usual in the Southeast—English, Scottish, Irish, with a dash of French Huguenot. The first American one, Isham, who fought in the Revolutionary War, was born in Virginia and moved to Georgia, where succeeding generations lived. The Andrewses were not a rural clan, like the Weltys; they lived in towns, were educators and preachers, with some Methodist circuit riders; one cousin of Ned's (Walter Hines Page) was an ambassador to England. Trinity College educated some of them, including, for an impatient time, young Ned. By the time my mother's father, Edward Raboteau Andrews (Ned) was born in

1862, the family had returned to Virginia. He broke from the mold and at eighteen ran away from a home of parents, grand-parents, sisters, brothers, and aunts in Norfolk to become the first West Virginian.

Here in the center of the Andrews kitchen, at the same long table where the family always ate, not too far from where Grandma seemed to be always busy at the warm stove, Ned had sat and worked up his cases for the defense in Clay Courthouse, far below and out of sight straight down the mountain. Mother remembered him transposing band music there, too; he had sent off for the instruments, got together a band, and proceeded to teach them to play in concert, lined up on the courthouse lawn: he had a strong need of music. His children had an instrument to learn to play too: he assigned my mother the cornet. (When I think back to how she sang "Blessed Assurance" while washing the dishes, I realize she flatted her high notes just where a child's cornet might.)

It was in the quilted bed in the front room of this house where he lay in so much pain (probably from the affliction that brought on his death, an infected appendix) that he once told Mother, a little girl, to bring the kitchen knife and plunge it into his side; she, hypnotized, almost believed she must obey. It was from that door that later she went with him on the frozen winter night when it was clear he had to get, somehow, to a hospital. The mountain roads were impassable, there was ice in the Elk River: but a neighbor vowed he could make way by raft. She was fifteen. Leaving her mother and the five little brothers at home, Chessie went with him. Her father lay on the raft, on which a fire had been lit to warm him, Chessie beside him. The neighbor managed to pole the raft through the icy river and eventually across it to a railroad. They flagged the train. (It seems likely that the place they flagged it was the same as where my mother and I were let off that train when I was three, arriving on that nearly forgotten visit. It was an early summer dawn; everything was a cloud of mist—we were standing on the bank of a river and I didn't know it. When my mother pulled the rope of an iron bell, we watched a boat come out of the mist to meet us, with her five brothers all inside.)

Mother had to return by herself from Baltimore, her father's body in a coffin on the same train. He had died on the operating table in John Hopkins, of a ruptured appendix, at thirty-seven years of age. The last lucid remark he'd made to my mother was "If you let them tie me down, I'll die." (The surgeon had come out where she stood waiting in the hall. "Little girl," he'd said, "you'd better get in touch now with somebody in Baltimore." "Sir, I don't know anybody in Baltimore," she said, and what she never forgot was his astounded reply: "You don't know anybody in *Baltimore*?")

It was from this house that my mother very soon after that piled up her hair and went out to teach in a one-room school, mountain children little and big alike. The first day, some fathers came along to see if she could whip their children, some who were older than she. She told the children that she did intend to whip them if they became unruly and refused to learn, and invited the fathers to stay if they liked and she'd be able to whip them too. Having been thus tried out, she was a great success with them after that. She left home every day on her horse; since she had the river to cross, a little brother rode on her horse behind her, to ride him home, while she rowed across the river in a boat. And he would be there to meet her with her horse again at evening. All this way, to pass the time, she told me, she recited the poems in McGuffey's Readers out loud.

She could still recite them in full when she was lying helpless and nearly blind, in her bed, an old lady. Reciting, her voice took on resonance and firmness, it rang with the old fervor, with ferocity even. She was teaching me one more, almost her last, lesson: emotions do not grow old. I knew that I would feel as she did, and I do.

———

AT THE END of the day at Grandpa's house, there wasn't much talking and no tales were told, even for the first time. Sometimes we all sat listening to a music box play.

There was a rack pulled out from inside the music box; we could see it holding shining metal discs as large as silver waiters, with teeth around the edges, and pierced with tiny holes in the shape of triangles or stars, like the tissue-paper patterns by which my mother cut out cloth for my dresses. When the discs began to turn, taking hold by their little teeth, a strange, chime-like music came about.

Its sounds had no kinship with those of "His Master's Voice" that we could listen to at home. They were thin and metallic, not exactly keeping to time—rather as if the spoons in the spoonholder had started a quiet fretting among themselves. Whatever song it was was slow and halting and remote, as if the music box were playing something I knew as well as "Believe Me If All Those Endearing Young Charms" but did not intend me to recognize. It seemed to be reaching the parlor from far away. It might even have been the sound going through the rooms and up and down the stairs of our house in Jackson at night while all of us were here in Ohio, too far from home even to hear the clock striking from the downstairs hall. While we listened, there at the open window, the moonflowers opened little by little, and the song continued like a wire spring allowing itself slowly, slowly to uncoil, then just stopped trying. Music and moonflower might have been geared to move together.

Then, in my father's grown-up presence, I could not imagine him as a child in this house, the sober way he looked in the little daguerreotype, motherless in his fair bangs and heavy little shoes, sitting on one foot. Now I look back, or listen back, in the same desire to imagine, and it seems possible that the sound of that sparse music, so faint and unearthly to my childhood ears, was the sound he'd had to speak to him in all that country silence among so many elders where he was the only child. To me it was a sound of unspeakable loneliness that I did not know how to run away from. I was there in its company, watching the moonflower open.

I NEVER SAW until after he was dead a small keepsake book given to my father in his early childhood. On one page was a message of one sentence written to him by his mother on April 15, 1886. The date is the day of her death. "My dearest Webbie: I want you to be a good boy and to meet me in heaven. Your loving Mother." Webb was his middle name—her maiden name. She always called him by it. He was seven years old, her only child.

He had other messages in his little book to keep and read over to himself. "May your life, though short, be pleasant / As a warm and melting day" is from "Dr. Armstrong," and as it follows his mother's message may have been entered on the same day. Another entry reads: "Dear Webbie, if God send thee a cross, take it up willingly and follow Him. If it be light, slight it not. If it be heavy, murmur not. After the cross is the crown. Your aunt, Nina Welty." This is dated earlier—he was then three years old. The cover of the little book is red and embossed with baby ducklings falling out of a basket entwined with morning glories. It is very rubbed and worn. It had been given him to keep and he had kept it; he had brought it among his possessions to Mississippi when he married; my mother had put it away.

In the farmhouse, the staircase was not in sight until evening prayers were over—it was time to go to bed then, and a door in the kitchen wall was opened and there were the stairs, as if kept put away in a closet. They went up like a ladder, steep and narrow, that we climbed on the way to bed. Step by step became visible as I reached it, by the climbing yellow light of the oil lamp that Grandpa himself carried behind me.

BACK ON Congress Street, when my father unlocked the door of our closed-up, waiting house, I rushed ahead into the airless hall and stormed up the stairs, pounding the carpet of each step with both hands ahead of me, and putting my face right down into the cloud of the dear dust of our long absence. I was welcoming ourselves back. Doing likewise, more methodically, my father was going from room to room re-starting all the clocks.

I think now, in looking back on these summer trips—this one and a number later, made in the car and on the train—that another element in them must have been influencing my mind. The trips were wholes unto themselves. They were stories. Not only in form, but in their taking on direction, movement, development, change. They changed something in my life: each trip made its particular revelation, though I could not have found words for it. But with the passage of time, I could look back on them and see them bringing me news, discoveries, premonitions, promises—I still can; they still do. When I did begin to write, the short story was a shape that had already formed itself and stood waiting in the back of my mind. Nor is it surprising to me that when I made my first attempt at a novel, I entered its world—that of the mysterious Yazoo–Mississippi Delta—as a child riding there on a train: "From the warm window sill the endless fields glowed like a hearth in firelight, and Laura, looking out, leaning on her elbows with her head between her hands, felt what an arriver in a land feels—that slow hard pounding in the breast."

The events in our lives happen in a sequence in time, but in their significance to ourselves they find their own order, a timetable not necessarily—perhaps not possibly—chronological. The time as we know it subjectively is often the chronology that stories and novels follow: it is the continuous thread of revelation.

Richard Wright

(1908–1960)

The first African-American author to write a best-selling novel, Richard Wright was born on a plantation near Natchez, Mississippi, the son of a sharecropper and a schoolteacher. After moving his wife and two sons to Memphis, Wright's father abandoned the family when Richard was five, initiating a series of disruptions in the boy's life that would continue throughout his youth and early adulthood. In 1917, when Wright and his mother and younger brother were living in Elaine, Arkansas, with his maternal aunt and her husband, Maggie and Silas Hopkins, his uncle Silas was murdered by whites who wanted to take over his prosperous saloon. The family fled with the aunt, never to return to Elaine; the killers were never punished. Despite the instability of his home life, Wright excelled in school and graduated valedictorian of his junior high class in Jackson, Mississippi. After spending two years in Memphis, he followed the example of thousands of other African-American southerners by journeying to Chicago, where he eventually found work as a postal clerk. While in Chicago he joined the ranks of the Communist Party, which at the time was actively recruiting in the African-American communities of the urban North. In 1938 he published Uncle Tom's Children, *a collection of short fiction, and then in 1940 the critically acclaimed novel* Native Son, *which tells the harrowing story of Bigger Thomas, a ghetto youth who responds with violence to the dehumanizing effects of racial inequities. Wright broke from the Communist Party in 1942, and in 1947 moved permanently to Paris with his wife and daughter, continuing to write but never again achieving the positive reception he had enjoyed in the forties.*

The popular success of Wright's autobiography, published in 1945 as Black Boy: A Record of Childhood and Youth *but originally* titled American Hunger, *was virtually ensured when it was chosen as a Book-of-the-Month Club selection. Before his publishers would accept the book, however, Wright had to agree to change the title and expurgate the entire second half of the narrative, ending the story on a falsely positive note with his decision to flee the South. The second section, chronicling his continuing "hunger" in the North for equality and his exploitation by the Communists, was published as* American Hunger *in 1977, and the fully restored text, now titled* Black Boy (American Hunger), *was published for the first time in 1991. Wright has been faulted for taking extreme liberties with the facts of his life in* Black Boy (American Hunger: A Record of Childhood and Youth); *nevertheless, it stands as one of the most compelling autobiographies ever written in this country and may well be the most powerful autobiographical indictment of racism in America. In the following excerpt, Wright recounts his growing sense of fear and desperation over his inability to don the smiling mask of subservience to whites and their representatives in the African-American community.*

FROM *Black Boy*
(American Hunger)

S UMMER. Bright hot days. Hunger still a vital part of my consciousness. Passing relatives in the hallways of the crowded home and not speaking. Eating in silence at a table where prayers are said. My mother recovering slowly, but now definitely crippled for life. Will I be able to enter school in September? Loneliness. Reading. Job hunting. Vague hopes of going north. But what would become of my mother if I left her in this queer house? And how would I fare in a strange city? Doubt. Fear. My friends are buying long-pants suits that cost from seventeen to twenty dollars, a sum as huge to me as the Alps! This was my reality in 1924.

Word came that a near-by brickyard was hiring and I went to investigate. I was frail, not weighing a hundred pounds. At noon I sneaked into the yard and walked among the aisles of damp, clean-smelling clay and came to a barrow full of wet bricks just taken from the machine that shaped them. I caught hold of the handles of the barrow and was barely able to lift it; it weighed perhaps four times as much as I did. If I were only stronger and heavier!

Later I asked questions and found that the water boy was missing; I ran to the office and was hired. I walked in the hot sun lugging a big zinc pail from one laboring gang of black men to another for a dollar a day; a man would lift the tin dipper to his lips, take a swallow, rinse out his mouth, spit, and then drink in long, slow gulps as sweat dripped into the dipper. And off again I would go, chanting:

"Water!"

And somebody would yell:

"Here, boy!"

Deep into wet pits of clay, into sticky ditches, up slippery slopes I would struggle with the pail. I stuck it out, reeling at times from hunger, pausing to get my breath before clambering up a hill. At the end of the week the money sank into the endless expenses at home. Later I got a job in the yard that paid a dollar and a half a day, that of bat boy. I went between the walls of clay and picked up bricks that had cracked open; when my barrow was full, I would wheel it out onto a wooden scaffold and dump it into a pond.

I had but one fear here: a dog. He was owned by the boss of the brickyard and he haunted the day aisles, snapping, growling. The dog had been wounded many times, for the black workers were always hurling bricks at it. Whenever I saw the animal, I would take a brick from my load and toss it at him; he would slink away, only to appear again, showing his teeth. Several of the Negroes had been bitten and had been ill; the boss had been asked to leash the dog, but he had refused. One afternoon I was wheeling my barrow toward the pond when something sharp sank into my thigh. I whirled; the dog crouched a few feet away, snarling. I had been bitten. I drove the dog away and opened my trousers; teeth marks showed deep and red.

I did not mind the stinging hurt, but I was afraid of an infection. When I went to the office to report that the boss's dog had bitten me, I was met by a tall blonde white girl.

"What do you want?" she asked.

"I want to see the boss, ma'am."

"For what?"

"His dog bit me, ma'am, and I'm afraid I might get an infection."

"Where did he bite you?"

"On my leg," I lied, shying from telling her where the bite was.

"Let's see," she said.

"No, ma'am. Can't I see the boss?"

"He isn't here now," she said, and went back to her typing.

I returned to work, stopping occasionally to examine the teeth marks; they were swelling. Later in the afternoon a tall white man wearing a cool white suit, a Panama hat, and white shoes came toward me.

"Is this the nigger?" he asked a black boy as he pointed at me.

"Yes, sir," the black boy answered.

"Come here, nigger," he called me.

I went to him.

"They tell me my dog bit you," he said.

"Yes, sir."

I pulled down my trousers and he looked.

"Humnnn," he grunted, then laughed. "A dog bite can't hurt a nigger."

"It's swelling and it hurts," I said.

"If it bothers you, let me know," he said. "But I never saw a dog yet that could really hurt a nigger."

He turned and walked away and the black boys gathered to watch his tall form disappear down the aisles of wet bricks.

"Sonofabitch!"

"He'll get his someday!"

"Boy, their hearts are hard!"

"Laws, a white man'll do anything!"

"Break up that prayer meeting!" the white straw boss yelled. The wheelbarrows rolled again. A boy came close to me.

"You better see a doctor," he whispered.

"I ain't got no money," I said.

Two days passed and luckily the redness and swelling went away.

Summer wore on and the brickyard closed; again I was out of work. I heard that caddies were wanted and I tramped five miles to the golf links. I was hired by a florid-faced white man at the rate of fifty cents for nine holes. I did not know the game and I lost three balls in as many minutes; it seemed that my eyes could not trace the flight of the balls. The man dismissed me. I watched the other boys do their jobs and within half an hour I had another golf bag and was following a ball. I made a dollar. I returned home, disgusted, tired, hungry, hating the sight of a golf course.

School opened and, though I had not prepared myself, I enrolled. The school was far across town and the walking distance alone consumed my breakfast of mush and lard gravy. I attended classes without books for a month, then got a job working mornings and evenings for three dollars a week.

I grew silent and reserved as the nature of the world in which I lived became plain and undeniable; the bleakness of the future affected my will to study. Granny had already thrown out hints that it was time for me to be on my own. But what had I learned so far that would help me to make a living? Nothing. I could be a porter like my father before me, but what else? And the problem of living as a Negro was cold and hard. What was it that made the hate of whites for blacks so steady, seemingly so woven into the texture of things? What kind of life was possible under that hate? How had this hate come to be? Nothing about the problems of Negroes was ever taught in the classrooms at school; and whenever I would raise these questions with the boys, they would either remain silent or turn the subject into a joke. They were vocal about the petty individual wrongs they suffered, but they possessed no desire for a knowledge of the picture as a whole. Then why was I worried about it?

Was I really as bad as my uncles and aunts and Granny repeatedly said? Why was it considered wrong to ask questions? Was I right when I resisted punishment? It was inconceivable to me that one should surrender to what seemed wrong, and most of the people I had met seemed wrong. Ought one to surrender to authority even if one believed that that authority was wrong? If the answer was yes, then I knew that I would always be wrong, because I could never do it. Then how could one live in a world in which one's mind and perceptions meant nothing and authority and tradition meant everything? There were no answers.

THE EIGHTH GRADE days flowed in their hungry path and I grew more conscious of myself; I sat in classes, bored, wondering, dreaming. One long dry afternoon I took out my composition book and told myself that I would write a story; it was sheer idleness that led me to it. What would the story be about? It resolved itself into a plot about a villain who wanted a widow's home and I called it *The Voodoo of Hell's Half-Acre*. It was crudely atmospheric, emotional, intuitively psychological, and stemmed from pure feeling. I finished it in three days and then wondered what to do with it.

The local Negro newspaper! That's it . . . I sailed into the office and shoved my ragged composition book under the nose of the man who called himself the editor.

"What is that?" he asked.

"A story," I said.

"A news story?"

"No, fiction."

"All right. I'll read it," he said.

He pushed my composition book back on his desk and looked at me curiously, sucking at his pipe.

"But I want you to read it *now*," I said.

He blinked. I had no idea how newspapers were run. I thought that one took a story to an editor and he sat down then and there and read it and said yes or no.

"I'll read this and let you know about it tomorrow," he said.

I was disappointed; I had taken time to write it and he seemed distant and uninterested.

"Give me the story," I said, reaching for it.

He turned from me, took up the book and read ten pages or more.

"Won't you come in tomorrow?" he asked. "I'll have it finished then."

I honestly relented.

"All right," I said. "I'll stop in tomorrow."

I left with the conviction that he would not read it. Now, where else could I take it after he had turned it down? The next afternoon, en route to my job, I stepped into the newspaper office.

"Where's my story?" I asked.

"It's in galleys," he said.

"What's that?" I asked; I did not know what galleys were.

"It's set up in type," he said. "We're publishing it."

"How much money will I get?" I asked, excited.

"We can't pay for manuscript," he said.

"But you sell your papers for money," I said with logic.

"Yes, but we're young in business," he explained.

"But you're asking me to *give* you my story, but you don't *give* your papers away," I said.

He laughed.

"Look, you're just starting. This story will put your name before our readers. Now, that's something," he said.

"But if the story is good enough to sell to your readers, then you ought to give me some of the money you get from it," I insisted.

He laughed again and I sensed that I was amusing him.

"I'm going to offer you something more valuable than money," he said. "I'll give you a chance to learn to write."

I was pleased, but I still thought he was taking advantage of me.

"When will you publish my story?"

"I'm dividing it into three installments," he said. "The first installment appears this week. But the main thing is this: Will you get news for me on a space rate basis?"

"I work mornings and evenings for three dollars a week," I said.

"Oh," he said. "Then you better keep that. But what are you doing this summer?"

"Nothing."

"Then come to see me before you take another job," he said. "And write some more stories."

A few days later my classmates came to me with baffled eyes, holding copies of the *Southern Register* in their hands.

"Did you really write that story?" they asked me.

"Yes."

"Why?"

"Because I wanted to."

"Where did you get it from?"

"I made it up."

"You didn't. You copied it out of a book."

"If I had, no one would publish it."

"But what are they publishing it for?"

"So people can read it."

"Who told you to do that?"

"Nobody."

"Then why did you do it?"

"Because I wanted to," I said again.

They were convinced that I had not told them the truth. We had never had any instruction in literary matters at school; the literature of the nation or the Negro had never been mentioned. My schoolmates could not understand why anyone would want to write a story; and, above all, they could not understand why I had called it *The Voodoo of Hell's Half-Acre*. The mood out of which a story was written was the most alien thing conceivable to them. They looked at me with new eyes, and a distance, a suspiciousness came between us. If I had thought anything in writing the story, I had thought that perhaps it would make me more acceptable to them, and now it was cutting me off from them more completely than ever.

At home the effects were no less disturbing. Granny came into my room early one morning and sat on the edge of my bed.

"Richard, what is this you're putting in the papers?" she asked.

"A story," I said.

"About what?"

"It's just a story, granny."

"But they tell me it's been in three times."

"It's the same story. It's in three parts."

"But what is it about?" she insisted.

I hedged, fearful of getting into a religious argument.

"It's just a story I made up," I said.

"Then it's a lie," she said.

"Oh, Christ," I said.

"You must get out of this house if you take the name of the Lord in vain," she said.

"Granny, please . . . I'm sorry," I pleaded. "But it's hard to tell you about the story. You see, granny, everybody knows that the story isn't true, but . . . "

"Then why write it?" she asked.

"Because people might want to read it."

"That's the Devil's work," she said and left.

My mother also was worried.

"Son, you ought to be more serious," she said. "You're growing up now and you won't be able to get jobs if you let people think that you're weak-minded. Suppose the superintendent of schools would ask you to teach here in Jackson, and he found out that you had been writing stories?"

I could not answer her.

"I'll be all right, mama," I said.

Uncle Tom, though surprised, was highly critical and con-
temptuous. The story had no point, he said. And whoever heard
of a story by the title of *The Voodoo of Hell's Half-Acre?* Aunt
Addie said that it was a sin for anyone to use the word "hell" and
that what was wrong with me was that I had nobody to guide
me. She blamed the whole thing upon my upbringing.

In the end I was so angry that I refused to talk about the story.
From no quarter, with the exception of the Negro newspaper
editor, had there come a single encouraging word. It was
rumored that the principal wanted to know why I had used the
word "hell." I felt that I had committed a crime. Had I been
conscious of the full extent to which I was pushing against the
current of my environment, I would have been frightened altogether out of my attempts at writing. But my reactions were
limited to the attitude of the people about me, and I did not
speculate or generalize.

I dreamed of going north and writing books, novels. The
North symbolized to me all that I had not felt and seen; it had
no relation whatever to what actually existed. Yet, by imagining
a place where everything was possible, I kept hope alive in me.
But where had I got this notion of doing something in the
future, of going away from home and accomplishing something
that would be recognized by others? I had, of course, read my
Horatio Alger stories, my pulp stories, and I knew my Get-
Rich-Quick Wallingford series from cover to cover, though I
had sense enough not to hope to get rich; even to my naïve
imagination that possibility was too remote. I knew that I lived
in a country in which the aspirations of black people were limited, marked-off. Yet I felt that I had to go somewhere and do
something to redeem my being alive.

I was building up in me a dream which the entire educational
system of the South had been rigged to stifle. I was feeling the
very thing that the state of Mississippi had spent millions of dollars to make sure that I would never feel; I was becoming aware

of the thing that the Jim Crow laws had been drafted and passed to keep out of my consciousness; I was acting on impulses that southern senators in the nation's capital had striven to keep out of Negro life; I was beginning to dream the dreams that the state had said were wrong, that the schools had said were taboo.

Had I been articulate about my ultimate aspirations, no doubt someone would have told me what I was bargaining for; but nobody seemed to know, and least of all did I. My classmates felt that I was doing something that was vaguely wrong, but they did not know how to express it. As the outside world grew more meaningful, I became more concerned, tense; and my classmates and my teachers would say: "Why do you ask so many questions?" Or: "Keep quiet."

I was in my fifteenth year; in terms of schooling I was far behind the average youth of the nation, but I did not know that. In me was shaping a yearning for a kind of consciousness, a mode of being that the way of life about me had said could not be, must not be, and upon which the penalty of death had been placed. Somewhere in the dead of the southern night my life had switched onto the wrong track and, without my knowing it, the locomotive of my heart was rushing down a dangerously steep slope, heading for a collision, heedless of the warning red lights that blinked all about me, the sirens and the bells and the screams that filled the air.

Grateful acknowledgment is made to the following for permission to reprint previously published material:

Algonquin Books of Chapel Hill and Darhansoff and Verrill Literary Agency: Excerpt from *On Fire* by Larry Brown, copyright © 1994 by Larry Brown. Reprinted by permission of Algonquin Books of Chapel Hill, a division of Workman Publishing, and Darhansoff and Verrill Literary Agency.

Frances Collin, Literary Agent: Excerpt from *Proud Shoes* by Pauli Murray (Harper & Row Publishers, 1956, 1978), copyright © 1978 by Pauli Murray. Reprinted by permission of Frances Collin, Literary Agent.

The Continuum Publishing Group: Excerpt from *Brother to a Dragonfly* by Will D. Campbell, copyright © 1977 by Will D. Campbell. Reprinted by permission of The Continuum Publishing Group.

Council Oak Publishing: Excerpt from *Once Upon a Time When We Were Colored* by Clifton Taulbert, copyright © 1989 by Clifton Taulbert. Reprinted by permission of Council Oak Publishing.

Darhansoff and Verrill Literary Agency: "The First Grade, Jesus, and the Hollyberry Family" by Kaye Gibbons, copyright © 1988 by Kaye Gibbons. Reprinted by permission of Darhansoff and Verrill Literary Agency.

Doubleday: Excerpt from *Coming of Age in Mississippi* by Anne Moody, copyright © 1968 by Anne Moody. Reprinted by permission of Doubleday, a division of Bantam Doubleday Dell Publishing Group, Inc.

Firebrand Books: "Gun Crazy" from *Skin: Talking About Sex, Class & Literature* by Dorothy Allison, copyright © 1994 by Dorothy Allison. Reprinted by permission of Firebrand Books, Ithaca, NY.

JAMES WATKINS was born in Memphis, Tennessee, and moved with his family to Nashville at age thirteen. After obtaining a bachelor's degree at the University of Tennessee in Knoxville, he attended graduate school at the University of Florida, where he earned his doctorate in 1995. He and his wife and two sons currently live on the campus of Berry College in Rome, Georgia, where he teaches southern and nineteenth-century American literature.